Social Geographies in England

(1200-1640)

Social Geographies in England

(1200-1640)

David A. Postles

New Academia Publishing
Washington, DC

Library of Congress Control Number: 2007934325
ISBN 978-0-9794488-5-0 paperback (alk. paper)

NEW ACADEMIA
PUBLISHING

New Academia Publishing, LLC
P.O. Box 27420
Washington, DC 20038-7420
www.newacademia.com - info@newacademia.com

Contents

Technical Note   vii

Abbreviations   ix

List of Illustrations   xi

Acknowledgments   xiv

Introduction   1

Part I The Formation of Locality

1. Migration and Mobility in a Less Mature Economy: 33
   English Internal Migration, ca.1200-1350

2. The Pattern of Rural Migration in a Midlands County: 55
   Leicestershire, ca.1270-1350

3. Movers and Prayers: Penance, Penitence, Pilgrimage   77
   and "Involuntary" Movement in Medieval England

4. "Localism" in Late-medieval England   97

5. Young People's Space: Contours of Courtship,
   1580-1700   123

Part II "Sacred" Space?

6. Penitential Spaces   145

7. Church Space and Contingency   175

8. Micro-spaces: Church Porches   199

Part III: In and Out of Place

9. The Politics of Urban Habitation, 1550-1640:
   Immigration, Poverty and Urban Space   225

10. Marginal Geographies:
     Poor Single Mothers, 1560-1640   243

11. "Community": Reflections on *The Established
     and the Outsiders*   269

12. "Community": Ins and Outs of the Medieval Village   281

13. What Was Core about "Core" Families?   299

Conclusion

Space Considered: The Public Space of the Market Place
in Early-modern England   315

Works cited   339
Index   365

Technical Note

Chapter 1 was originally published under the same title in *Social History* 25 (2000): 285-99 and is reprinted here with some changes and additions, with permission from Taylor and Francis.

Chapter 2 was originally published under the same title in *Continuity and Change* 7 (1992): 139-61 and is reprinted here with some changes and additions, with permission from Cambridge University Press.

Chapter 3 was originally presented at the Harlaxton Medieval Symposium and benefited from suggestions by the audience.

Chapter 4 is a new paper. I am grateful to Charles Phythian-Adams and Henry French for kindly reading it in an early form and making valuable suggestions.

Chapter 5 is a new paper.

Chapter 6 is a combination of two articles: "Penance and the Market Place: A Reformation Dialogue with the Medieval Church, *c.*1250-*c.*1600," *Journal of Ecclesiastical History* 54 (2003): 441-68, and "What Happened to Penance in the Sixteenth Century?" in *Mender of Disorders. Court and Community in the Archdeaconry of Nottingham, 1560-1756*, ed. Kate Holland (Nottingham: University of Nottingham, 2004), 51-61, and is reprinted here with some changes and additions, with permission from Cambridge University Press.

Chapter 7 is an expanded version of a paper given at the Social History Society in Rouen in January 2003.

Chapter 8 was published in the *Journal of Historical Geography* in 2007 in an amended form, with permission from Elsevier.

Chapter 9 is an expanded version of a paper given at a symposium "Thinking Space in Early Modern England" at the University of Warwick in 2005 and has benefited from the audience's comments.

Chapter 10 was originally published as "Surviving Lone Motherhood in Early-modern England," *The Seventeenth Century* 21 (2006): 160-83 and is reprinted here with some changes and additions, with permission from Manchester University Press.

Chapter 11 was originally read as a paper ("'Winston Parva': What Lessons for 'Community'?") to an international conference on Norbert Elias, University of Leicester, April 10-11, 2006. I am grateful to Eric Dunning and the audience for suggestions.

Chapter 12 was originally published as "Personal Pledging: Medieval 'Reciprocity' or 'Symbolic Capital'?" *Journal of Interdisciplinary History* 26 (1996): 419-35, and is revised for this volume.

Chapter 13 was originally published as Suella and Dave Postles, "Surnames and Stability: A Detailed Case Study," in *Names, Time and Place. Essays in Memory of Richard McKinley* ed. Della Hooke and Dave Postles (Oxford: Leopard's Head Press, 2003), 193-207, and is revised here for this volume.

The *Conclusion* was originally published as "The Market Place as Space in Early-modern England," *Social History* 29 (2004): 41-58 and is reprinted here with some changes and additions, with permission from Taylor and Francis.

Abbreviations

Claval, *Regional Geography*	Paul Claval, *An Introduction to Regional Geography.* Trans. Ian Thompson. Oxford: Blackwell, 1998.
Coster and Spicer, *Sacred Space*	Will Coster and Andrew Spicer, eds., *Sacred Space in Early Modern Europe.* Cambridge: Cambridge University Press, 2005.
CUL	Cambridge University Library
CYS	Canterbury and York Society
Dodgshon, *Society in Time and Space*	Robert A. Dodgshon, *Society in Time and Space. A Geographical Perspective on Change.* Cambridge: Cambridge University Press, 1998.
Douglas, *Purity and Danger*	Mary Douglas, *Purity and Danger: An Analysis of the Concept of Pollution and Taboo.* London: Routledge and Kegan Paul, 1966.
EDR	Ely Diocesan Records (in CUL)
ERO	Essex Record Office
HRO	Hampshire Record Office
LeFebvre, *Production of Space*	Henri Lefebvre, *The Production of Space.* Trans. D. Nicholson-Smith Oxford: Blackwell, 1998.
LRS	Lincoln Record Society (Horncastle and Lincoln)
NARO	Nottinghamshire Archives and Record Office
NNRO	Norwich and Norfolk Record Office.
NRO	Northamptonshire Record Office

n.s.	new series
Peet, *Modern Geographical Thought*	Richard Peet, *Modern Geographical Thought*. Oxford: Blackwell, 1998.
ROLLR	Record Office for Leicestershire, Leicester and Rutland.
ser.	series
Sibley, *Geographies of Exclusion*	David Sibley, *Geographies of Exclusion: Society and Difference in the West*. London: Routledge,1995.
Soja, *Postmodern Geographies*	Edward W. Soja, *Postmodern Geographies: The Reassertion of Space in Critical Social Theory*. London: Verso, 1989.
SS	Surtees Society (Durham)
TRHS	*Transactions of the Royal Historical Society*
UoN	University of Nottingham
WSRO	Wiltshire and Swindon Record Office

Illustrations

Tables

2.1 Rank Distribution of Inferred Distances of Migration, 1327   71

2.2 Relationship of Distance and Tax Assessment, 1327   72

2.3 Inferred Migration Between Pays, 1327   72

4.1 Rank Distribution of Bequests to Multiple Parishes (Excluding Leicestershire)   111

5.1 Sample of Parishes with Extended Information   133

5.1 Sample of Parishes with Extended Information (continued)   134

5.1 Sample of Parishes with Extended Information (continued)   135

5.2 Sample of Parishes with Basic Information   136

5.2 Sample of Parishes with Basic Information (continued)   137

5.2 Sample of Parishes with Basic Information (continued)   138

5.2 Sample of Parishes with Basic Information (continued)   139

6.1 Frequency of Penance in Market Places, Essex Archdeaconry   164

6.2 Frequency of Penance in Market Places, Colchester Archdeaconry   165

12.1 Summary of the Kibworth Data   291

12.2 Descriptive Statistics of Pledging per Pledge   291

12.3 Statistics of Density and Overall Centralization   292

12.4 Descriptive Statistics of Local Centrality   292

12.5 Freeman's Degree Centrality for Significant Actors   293

12.6 Prosopography of Principal Actors   294

13.1 Vital Events: by Ten-year Periods   307

13.2 Child Mortality by Ten-year Periods   308

13.3 Population Estimates from Listings   309

13.4 Persistence and Loss of Surnames   310

Figures

3.1 Origins of Pleas for Entry to Durham Sanctuary, 1464-
1524   88

3.2 Origins of Pleas for Entry to Beverley Sanctuary, 1505-
1540   89

3.3 Origins of Claimants to Benefit of Clergy, Worcester
Diocese, 1502-1544 (Mainly Before 1527)   90

4.1 Diocese of Norwich: Testamentary Bequests to Several
Parishes   112

4.2 Buckinghamshire and Bedfordshire: Testamentary
Bequests to Several Parishes   113

4.3 Lincolnshire: Testamentary Bequests to Several   114
Parishes

4.4 Somerset: Testamentary Bequests to Several Parishes   115

4.5 Archdeaconry of Leicester: Testamentary Bequests to   116
Several Parishes

7.1 Reconciliation of Churches and Churchyards by
Commission, Diocese of Lincoln, 1290-1297   193

8.1 Payment of Legacies in Parish Church Porches in the
Archdeaconries of Suffolk, Early Seventeenth Century   217

13.1 The Longevity of Bynames and Surnames   311

Conc. 1 Penance in Market Places, Archdeaconry of Colchester   324

Conc. 2 Penance in Market Places, Archdeaconry of Leicester   325

Conc. 3 Penance in Market Places, Archdeaconry of Not-   326
tingham

Conc. 4 Penance in Market Places, Archdeaconry of Essex   327

Conc. 5 Punishment in Market Places, Devizes and Marl-
     borough   328
Conc. 6 Punishment in Market Places, Salisbury   329
Conc. 7 Punishment in Market Places, Somerset   330
Conc. 8 Ritual Route of Penance in Nottingham   331

Sources: All figures and tables were produced by the author,
except where otherwise stated.

Acknowledgments

My interest in locality, region and *pays* extends back to the very early 1970s under the influence of my wife, Suella, when she was undertaking the Museum Studies course at the University of Leicester. It is a shared interest which has remained with us; but it is one of the minor debts of the many which I owe her. For almost two decades, this adventure with topography was a laconic affair, as I struggled with the day-to-day demands of being an archivist. More urgency was instilled when I moved to the then Department of English Local History in 1988 and my amateur understanding had necessarily to be placed into a more compelling framework. Although I reserved the right to disagree on some points, I have always valued the ideas of Charles Phythian-Adams; working within his proximity was ever stimulating and certainly gave more depth to my fallible ruminations. The same expression of debt is due to Richard Smith whose seminal work was equally inspiring, and who, like Charles Phythian-Adams, also gave personal encouragement. My early attempts to work through questions of migration and mobility were unfailingly helped by Larry Poos. By the mid 1990s, spatial questions had come to the forefront of my thinking, through browsing through the section of geographical literature in the University of Leicester Bookshop. As it slowly dawned on me, those were important times in the wider context of the epistemology of space and place. That awareness was also stimulated by encounters with Paul Griffiths when he was at the UoL. Three further associations influenced my comprehension and thinking: the Post-Colonial Seminar at the UoL, organized by Clare Anderson, the North American Conference on British Studies, and the Social History Society. I left their seminars and conferences feeling that my thought about space and place was still immature and jejune, but also with rich rewards. In one of my early ventures at the NACBS in Toronto in 2001, Bob Tittler, Paul Griffiths and Joe Ward revived my flagging confidence. The article which forms part of Chapter 6 benefited from readings by Professors Diarmaid MacCulloch and Margo Todd.

Recently, some interesting e-mail exchanges with Shannon McSheffrey have all been to my benefit. Along the way, other help has been gratefully received on particular issues and those people are, I hope, acknowledged in the individual chapters. Even when not reflecting directly on space and place, some colleagues and friends have been especially good for me, in particular Greg Walker, Elaine Treharne, Audrey Larrivé, and Eric Dunning at the UoL and Jennie Jordan at Nottingham Trent University. With real sincerity, I also wish to acknowledge the space for reflection that has been provided so admirably and willingly by the staff of the Senior Common Room and the Piazza: Catherine; Charlotte; Gaz; Jackie; Jean; Liz; Odette; Peter; Rose; and Sue; and I extend the appreciation to those less visible, the "other" Catherine, Jan, Jo, and Nick. I thank them all for making each day at the UoL an enjoyable time.

Why have I written this book now in this form? I had hoped and intended to compose a more lucid new text, but I have to admit that I feel spaced out. The best that I can offer is to revise some previously published material in the light of recent advances, to introduce some new ideas with a new introduction which (I hope) gives some overall coherence and direction, and to hope that there is still something valuable in the mix.

David A. Postles
East Leake
2007

Introduction

Space is at a premium. Not only have geographers re-taken the spatial turn, but some historians have too.[1] In the case of historians, the predominant direction has been towards the representation of space, cultural and symbolic geography and topographies.[2] Those approaches have not, however, only been constituted around post-structural epistemology. Although discursive representations have been predicated, the debt to Foucauldian influence has not always been acknowledged.[3] Some will be disappointed that what follows in this book does not adopt one consistent approach to space and place. It attempts to adopt from the various discussions what resonates in particular situations. Its only consistency is to regard space and place as situational–perhaps even contingent. The intention is not to assert some sort of Derridean *différence*–some deferral of meaning–but to contend that no single position will explain what happens in space and place at all times.

An attempt is made in this introduction to separate out various categories, although this is an artificial and entirely heuristic exercise: representation and reality/practice; structure, "structuration", and agency; gender; "sacred" and "profane"; public and private; emotions and space; and (em)placed and displaced.[4] The purpose is to give some guidance to readers who wish to have some indication of recent research into spatial matters. Those who are already well-versed in the literature and contentions might more profitably move on quickly to the following chapters.

Although what follows concentrates on the matter of space, the attempt is made not to fall into "spatial fetishism", or reifying space and investing it with its own agency, a point to which we will return at the end of this introduction.[5]

The second aspect of this book is place. Although they are different categories of analysis, space and place are not totally divorced from each other. Place has also been increasingly of interest to historians and sociologists. From one angle, that renewal of investigation has been generated through post-structural critique of globalization, particularly inspired by Lyotard, but place has always had an intrinsic interest as the *locus* of events and social relations.[6] The current preoccupation with "belonging" and "identity" accounts for the investigation of place. Place is one aspect (although only one) of belonging and identity, and for some (but not all), relatedly, of sites of memory (*lieux de mémoire*).[7] In this epistemology of belonging, a sense of place is of paramount importance. It is the special features of a place– the *genius loci*–which engender part (but only part) of the sense of belonging and place-identity. The concealed genealogy then is to phenomenology, the existence and movement of the body in space and place.[8] Here, however, the concern is as much with being out of place, placeless, and not integrated into place as being (em)placed. The contention–not new, but sometimes ignored–is that for the *longue durée* under consideration here most people were in motion, or, to adopt Patricia Fumerton's felicitous phrase, "unsettled".[9] Wider verification of this concern with the "rootless" may be elicited: "that the emphasis they gave to the rooted over the unrooted or the uprooted, to the in-place over the out-of-place, was at best problematical and perhaps 'inauthentic'".[10]

Some of these categories might look binary oppositions, but that differentiation is not privileged here, for a few reasons. Attitudes towards and involvement in place and space are not so consistent; fuzziness is another category; and all the categories enumerated above interact and react upon each other. Separating them out as is done below, is an artificial, heuristic process, removed from the complexity of real life. In examining in this way the various categories below, there are two objectives. The first is simply to recapitulate and rehearse the different approaches that have been taken in previous literature. Doing so acquits the obligation of an introduction by establishing contexts and a state of play. On the other hand, the exposition is merely that: a brief survey. It does not have particular depth and is no substitute for the works cited. Within the space available, it cannot respect the complexity of the original theses and, in any case, it would be beyond the simple capability of this author.[11] The second intention is to indicate how the individual chapters below can be located within these frameworks.

Since the chapters together do not address all the categories evenly or equally, some themes receive more attention in the introduction, and others are explicated more cursorily. It will be self-evident that recent geographical literature has elucidated expansively the different approaches. It would be impossible for this author to revisit in the same depth or with the same erudition the way in which geographers have recently visited the questions surrounding place and space. References to this literature will be found in the chapters below.[12]

There now follows brief discussions of the salient aspects of space. It must be reiterated again that the categories are separated out for heuristic purposes only. Life as it is lived is much more complex than this categorization allows.

"Structured space" and "representation"

Historians' perceptions of how spaces were represented owe as much to structuralism, to, for example, Mary Douglas's binaries of purity and danger, inside and outside. That conceptualization has, moreover, influenced the cultural geography depicted by some geographers, such as David Sibley.[13] The result is the formulation of notions about spaces being homologous and in binary divisions, with an intermediate and external "liminality", and ideas that incursions from one space to another are impure, that is, transgressive. These penetrations are thus analogous with Douglas's conclusion that orifices in the body allow the intrusion of impurities and danger. The principal problem of the representation of space is that it privileges one perception of that space, which is mostly the perspective of the elite. For representations of space are normally imposed by elites, those with "power" to pronounce the "closed" (that is, unitary) nature of the space.[14] So representation of space in fact involves a politics of space, in which the symbolism is hegemonic.[15] Another general problem is that not all penetrations elicit the disgust associated with pollution.[16]

Critical geographers (and, indeed, critical social theorists), particularly David Harvey, on the other hand, taking into account hegemony and materialism, have been more reluctant to accept representations *qua* representations only.[17] This cultural materialism still respects the structures of space. Another approach has emphasized the enduring features of space through time: persistence of spatial structures.[18] This structuralist argument owes something to the *Annales* School with its privileging of deep structures. Some, like Lefebvre, have endeavored to emphasize how spaces are socially produced, and this epistemology is not necessarily antithetical to structural geography.[19]

"Agency" and space

Yet a further strand of geographers has addressed the "structuration" theories of Bourdieu and Giddens, to understand how structure and agency interact. In Allan Pred's case, the emphasis is on the inter-action between individual and structure, that is, the agenda established by

Giddens. illustrating how recursive and repetitive actions by individuals establish and confirm structures. Bourdieu, by contrast, began with the influence of "class" and how that relates to structure, producing ideas of the *habitus*. The relationship between structure, agency, and structuration is deliberated in many chapters below, but especially 1, 6-8, and the CONCLUSION.

Two other writers have, in contrast, associated space with contingency, de Certeau and Benjamin, but with different contexts in mind. Walter Benjamin conceived of the middle-class *flâneur* who distractedly meandered the streets and spaces of the city. Such a deliberate itinerary belonged to the privileged, whose loitering would not arouse suspicion.[20] Although owing some debt to Benjamin, de Certeau considered meandering in a different context, if in the same space. Unconscious random weaving about the urban space could be engaged in by all and sundry, and in so doing these urban ramblers inadvertently subverted the meanings associated with spaces. There is much that is attractive in de Certeau's idea. Whilst it is an action, the meandering is purposeless, unconscious and unselfconscious, but in its process traduces spatial proprieties. The spatial is then also psychoanalytical. What it neglects, however, is the surveillance of space, especially urban space, whether formal or informal, official or unofficial, publicly-exerted or personally-imposed and self-disciplined. Conscious and unconscious monitoring of people moving in spaces elicits suspicion and marginalization.[21]

What is left? We have a plethora of conceptualizations of what constitutes and forms space. We have equally, then, a plurality of social and cultural geographies of space. Indeed, we have not reverted to a Cartesian or a Kantian notion of space as merely metrical or a container. We can perceive that space is never neutral, but we do not agree on what informs the rhetoric of spaces. Perhaps we can move forward by recognizing that space is where humans act and have their being and existence, so that not everyone in the same space will entertain the same perceptions of the space. Space, as a particular entity, therefore becomes fragmented and it may not, indeed, be appropriate to refer to space in the singular since every "space" consists of multiple "spacialities". The CONCLUSION explores these possibilities in the context of interactions within the space of the market place in early-modern England. So space may be contingent on the actor. It may, moreover, be that the nature of the space is transient as the actor('s body) moves through and out of it. It is with this residual concept that spaces are complex, heterogeneous, fragmented, even contingent, that the rest of this small book follows: a "collective" phenomenology of spaces.[22]

Before moving on, nonetheless, it may be productive to rehearse how contemporaries in the past represented their spaces, in this restricted sense: What rhetoric did they use and what adjectives did they propose about their spaces?[23] What complicates this issue is that the persuasive voices that we hear are only those of authority, those with the power to represent spaces as unitary in meaning and purpose. We shall see later how their representations were contradicted by actions in those spaces by non-elite people who had no authority but had the capacity to subvert the representation of the space.

"Sacred space"

On Sunday morning, December 6, 1601, Mr. Arthur Greene read the first lesson in the chancel of his parish church. Greene interrupted divine service that morning and in the chancel "did thear pluck out violently" Robert Lightfoote because Greene had admonished all the congregation not to sit in the chancel because he had reserved it for his own male and female servants "because they could not be permitted to sitt in the body of the Church ...", by which we must assume that he would not allow them so to do.[24]

This episode brings into relief a number of issues: the representation of the social hierarchy in church through the segregation of the congregation; the potential for zoning of space; observation of "sacred" space; and whether, if the notion of "sacred" space obtained, it had been subverted by the religious transformations of sixteenth-century England.[25]

Whilst the concept of "sacred" and "profane" spaces is examined in more detail below in chapters 6-8, the opportunity is taken here to address the issues, since they have become once again integral to much historical thinking.[26] We shall also return to the notion below (EMOTIONS AND SPACE) with reference to Rudolf Otto. The conceptualization has, of course, a long genealogy in sociological epistemology. From Durkheim onwards, there has been a tendency to proclaim the difference between "sacred" and "profane" space, although at the core of Durkheim's thought was that society (as "community") was sacred rather than its religion and its religious spaces, which were merely manifestations of the divine nature of society and community. Notwithstanding that, Mircea Eliade proclaimed the primeval distinction of sacred and profane space. Let me immediately indicate the position taken here: any differentiation into "sacred" and "profane" inherently makes ontological assumptions–that people *always* and *without exception* map the world into binary distinctions. That belief is not uncontested.[27]

Most frequently, we are privileged with the *dicta* of ecclesiastical authorities, quite often referring to their "spiritual" space. In 1420 and several times again shortly thereafter, Edmund Lacy, bishop of Exeter, could refer to spiritual space as "honest place". In authorizing the celebration of divine service (the mass) in a private oratory or chapel for William Monke, esquire, the bishop ordained a chapel, oratory or any other honest place appropriate for divine service ("aut alio loco honesto cultui divino disposito"). He repeated this phrase ("locis honestis cultui divino dispositis") when making allowances for the mass within the city of Exeter.[28] Here, the intention behind "honest" seems to have been suitable or appropriate to the dignity of the occasion. Notions of the distinction between the "holy" and "sacred" as against the "profane" and "secular" are continued below in the section on EMOTIONS AND SPACE since the division depends on an *a priori* ontology which is influenced by a sentient and emotional response. In chapters 6-8, ideas of this binary differentiation of space are confronted.[29]

In fact, the question of "sacred" space has been examined in some detail in recent studies of church space. Chapter 8 below addresses the issue in the context of the church porch: a microspace. In this introduction, then, there is no great need to re-examine the problem in great detail.

We can, however, place these issues into a comparative context: punishment and penance invoked by the unitary courts in British colonial North America. Instead of a plurality of courts, the colonists instituted single courts with comprehensive competence, so there was no division between cases in secular courts and causes in ecclesiastical courts. These unitary courts imposed sentences which involved action in both secular and ecclesiastical spaces. When in 1638 Deborah Glasscocke wife of Robert, of New Norfolk, carpenter, scandalized Captain Sibsey that his maid had a child by him, Deborah was condemned to receive a hundred stripes on her shoulders and to solicit Sibsey's forgiveness now in court and on the next Sabbath in the parish church at the time of divine service.[30]

So two years later, the same court decided that Saville Gaskin and his wife Anne, having uttered allegations of childbirth against Anne, wife of Richard Foster, should receive respectively twenty and ten lashes on their bare backs; but after their supplication, the sentence was converted to their begging forgiveness in open court and next Sabbath before the congregation when the minister preached after the first lesson in the morning, reciting after the minister such words as he required them.[31] From these examples we can perceive how the court, technically a local administrative and "criminal" jurisdiction, employed different types of space provided those spaces involved the most public (open) example and humiliation. The court met monthly in one of the houses, entertaining all types of offense: commercial, civil, moral and some criminal. Sometimes, the punishments were regarded hierarchically; when a person defaulted, a higher correction was substituted. Anne Gaskine, condemned for defamation and slanderous speeches against Richard Forster's wife, escaped rather lightly with the sentence to perform penance in the parish church of Linhaven; on her refusal, she was arrested by the sheriff and delivered to the house of Captain Thomas Willoughby to receive twenty lashes on bare back, followed by her performing penance at the parish church on Sunday. If she refused again, she would be subjected to increments of whipping (thirty/forty/fifty) for each delict on each successive Monday.[32] The resistance by Eady Tolker for fornication resulted in the same escalation on her failure to enjoin her penance in the chapel of ease more demonstratively by ignoring the minister, cutting up her sheet and defacing it; for this outrage she was condemned to twenty lashes on her back, and penance was enjoined again (1641).[33] In cases of defamation ("scandalizing"), the court often demanded that the guilty party ask forgiveness in the face of the court, but as often in the parish church, or in both fora. In 1638 Richard Low, planter, "scandalized" Anne Batkings, wife of Wm, to the great "impeaching" of her name and credit; Low was informed that he must ask her forgiveness on the next Sabbath at the parish church of Lower Norfolk County.[34] Like Deborah Glasscocke above, Anne Fowler, wife of William, of Linhaven, planter, in 1637 engaged in insubordinate and abusive language against officialdom, for which she was sentenced to twenty stripes upon her bare shoulders, but also to ask forgiveness of Captain Thorowgood now in court and on the ensuing Sunday at Linhaven (parish church).[35]

In the instances of fornication, the unitary court resorted to ecclesiastical space for penance. When the churchwardens of Linhaven parish presented a couple for fornication, they were enjoined to do penance in the parish church on the following Sunday when the minister preached, standing in the middle aisle on a stool in a white sheet and a white wand in their hands all the time of divine service and to recite such words before the congregation as the minister asks them.[36] No doubt this stipulation in the British new world was designed to follow the practice familiar in the old country. On the other hand, these judicial punishments also demonstrate adjustment in the use of space in different circumstances, by a unitary court not a divided judicial organization.

The court of assistants of New Hampshire operated in a similar fashion, opting for the use of both spaces. George Burdet, minister of Agamenticus, indicted for ill fame and incontinence, which was constituted by dangerous talk and seduction of women (one got with child), received two fines twenty pounds; but the pregnant woman was condemned to stand, six weeks after delivery of her child, in a white sheet publicly in the congregation at Agamenticus on two Sundays and one day in General Court in 1640.[37]

What we also notice in Virginia is the absence of punishment in the market place–another adaptation to the use of space for judicial purposes. The different settlement topography of the Bay area, by contrast, allowed the perpetuation of the market place for judicial punishment. The Quarterly Courts of the Bay Company retained this option. For his drunkenness then (a frequently adjudicated offense here) James Brown was sentenced to stand publicly in 1637 for two hours in the bilbows on the market day at Boston.[38] The husband of Eleanor Pierce, for his wife's light behavior, in 1639 was bound over in ten pounds to bring her to stand in the market place on market day with a paper explaining her offense.[39] To recite one more example, Thomas Scott and his wife, because of their pre-marital sexual relationship, had to stand one hour in the market place with a paper with great letters in their hats.[40] The market place at Boston thus permitted the continuation of the humiliation of offenders in that public space.

Even in this colonial society, there was an adjustment in the (time) and space for performance of punishment.[41] The unitary court employed the market place, but also resorted to ecclesiastical (time and) space. For her offense, Francis Weston's wife was enjoined to stand for two hours in the bilbows in Cambridge and two hours at Salem, not on a market day, but on a lecture day.[42] For indulging in pre-marital fornication, Henry Leake and his wife were to appear at the next lecture day at Dorchester and acknowledge their fault after the lecture (1643).[43] Drunkenness in one case in 1639 was admonished by the male standing at the meeting house door on the next lecture day with a cleft stick on his tongue and paper on his hat for gross lying, additional to a fine of 40s.[44] Commission of a burglary in the following year resulted in whipping on a lecture day and to be set an hour before the lecture with a paper on the culprit's head.[45] Numerous transgressions in these years engendered punishment on lecture days: for abduction of a servant, whipping on a lecture day or before the town meeting; for scurrilous speeches and tippling, standing in the meeting house with a paper on the head for a false accuser; for reproachful and unseemly speeches against the rule of the church, sitting in the stocks for an hour and severe whipping on the next lecture day; for cursing his master, severe whipping at the lecture day or town meeting; a pregnant woman for pilfering, sitting in the stocks on next lecture day for one hour; Eunice Cole for slanderous speeches in breach of her binding over, sitting half an hour on the next lecture day and (there?) making public acknowledgment of her slanderous speeches (1645).[46]

We can then agree with William Offutt, that a certain amount of "legal capital" was imported, an accumulated legal knowledge from the old country, and that such capital was employed, nonetheless, only in conjunction with a "legal imagination" which involved an intellectual ability to produce new forms, unitary courts, and further, as we have illustrated here (but which is not suggested by Offutt) to make similar accommodation in the deployment of judicial space.[47]

One of the problems of church space, finally, was a difficulty of all open space: any open space was likely to be appropriated for secular purposes. So, no doubt because of their constant experience, the assembly of Yarmouth had to introduce a fine of 5s. for anyone shooting a bow and arrows in the church or churchyard.[48]

Gender and space

It was within churches that a division of space by gender conventionally occurred. Historians have remarked upon this frequent distinction, which was no doubt facilitated by the introduction of seating.[49] In some instances, the separation by gender also had hierarchical motivation. In Yarmouth in 1582, the wives of the twenty-four were placed in the chapel where the bailiffs' wives sat, enabled by the removal of all other women who customarily sat there. The husband of any woman who refused to leave was subject to a fine of 5s. Henceforth it became the chapel exclusively for the wives of the twenty-four.[50]

Attempts to decipher separate spaces inhabited by men and women on a quotidian basis in medieval England are not free from ambiguity.[51] Women might have refrained from frequenting inns except for the publicity afforded there to betrothal arrangements.[52] In some urban places, women's markets might have been provided at which women traded in those commodities symbolically associated with their gender: dairy produce and small livestock, especially fowl.[53] Rigid delineation of space by gender was not, however, sustainable.[54] There were, nonetheless, particular spaces and places that women habitually frequented or spaces which on special occasions were reserved to women.[55]

C. CUSTANCE Good wenches would not so rampe abrode ydelly,
But keepe within doores, and plie their worke earnestly;[56]

Chapter 10, however, is concerned with some women who were displaced and were, in some senses, place-less. Poor, single, pregnant women were compelled to uproot precipitately. Some locations provided temporary refuge, such as West Ham for women from the metropolitan area and Lenton for poor women from Nottingham, but always illicitly and with the prospect of detection.[57]

"Public" and "private" space

In the ecclesiastical courts, a notion of "public space" was enunciated. In, for example, an office cause of April 4, 1579, in the consistory court of Ely, the sentence demanded that the man and woman–accused of evil conversation–do not encounter each other "except in foro publico mercates [sic] Ecclesia, et aliis locis publicis", thus defining market place and church as the principal public places.[58] The understanding of "public space" therefore depended on social visibility, as opposed to hidden from social view. Further definition is found in the consistory court of Canterbury in 1562, in which the couple were admonished in future only to meet in the church or market place; if the woman and man should both happen to be in the same house, the woman must leave.[59] We find the same expressions employed in the consistory court of Durham, where, in 1453 and 1455, men and women were ordered to refrain [from meeting] in "suspicious" places.[60] In 1535, the court ordered that another couple meet only in "public places".[61] Bishop Barnes followed his predecessors' example in 1579 in prohibiting fornicating couples to come into contact except in the church and market place.[62]

In contrast to "loca publica" were opposed "loca suspecta": that is, places which lacked social visibility were categorized as "suspicious" places, hidden from view, where nefarious activities might secretly occur. In the consistory court of bishop Arundel in 1377, then, Joan Seustere renounced her sin ("abiurauit peccam") and "suspicious places" ("loca suspecta") on pain of flogging on six days round the market and church.[63] Denouncing an adulterous liaison in the early seventeenth century, the archdeaconry court of Nottingham located the sin as having taken place "in loco secreto", even though it was committed in the village of North Wheatley, a far from substantial place.[64] What is intended by the adjective "public", then, is "open" and visible, where people's actions were automatically under general surveillance and monitored, where people were prevented, by the openness, from engaging in prohibited relationships and illicit communication. By allowing people to meet only in "public" places and spaces, it was ensured that their relationships and communications were overseen in the natural course. Any location which was not so perceptible, constituted a suspicious place or was secret in the sense of occluded. Public, suspect and secret were thus associated with the capacity to monitor social relationships between people whose communication with each other should be limited to what was acceptable.

In quotidian affairs, the distinction between public and private spaces was ambiguous and ill-formed. It is generally accepted that, especially in urban places, the distinction and boundary between public and private could not be consistently maintained amongst most social groups.[65] The "offense" of eavesdropping persisted. The report of common fame quickly dispersed more widely communications made immediately between individuals.[66] So in Linaker *c*. Jacksone in defamation in 1582 the complaint was expressed: "Fie upon the thou blacke mouthed Jade, comest thou into my owne house to call me hore."[67] Words exchanged inside the home extended outside to affect honor and reputation–or so it was feared. We might summarize the situation that some places were more overtly public and open–and regarded and represented as such (as above)–whilst other places, whilst superficially more intimate, secret and concealed, might not be so easily demarcated and separated.[68]

Contention brings into relief notions of privacy, property and propriety and emotional eruptions were seminal to this process. In 1621, Catherine Wrighte, maid to the wife of Thomas Greaves of Coddington, impleaded Robert Otterbie in a cause of defamation in the archdeaconry court of Nottingham.[69] At issue was Otterbie's reaction to Catherine using his backyard as a shortcut, he reportedly exclaimed:

> I can keepe nothing in my yarde for her ... shee comes like an amblinge whore and your fence is downe, you thincke to do as you did the laste yeere, you keepe a trippinge whore I can never keepe her out of my yarde as well as you keepe a trippinge whore to your maide the fence is broken downe, I can have no profit of my yard for you

Ignoring the proprieties of public view, it was alleged that one Beever "hath had bodily dealing with Elizabeth Wade of Missen in the towne streete, and occupied her against the wall..." The words led to a defamation cause in the ecclesiastical court, so it is uncertain whether the deed was actually perpetrated, but it was not unimaginable.[70]

Binary divisions into sacred and profane, public and private, and so on, require some effort in the maintenance of boundaries. Historians, concerned with the diachronic and temporal, can elucidate how boundaries change and fluctuate over time. Especially is that the case with any distinction between public and private. Some might indeed argue that the perception of such a boundary is an aspect of modernity. Others might contend that even now the boundaries are not firmly established. Boundaries might not only *not* be fixed then, but might be matters of perception, visible only to the eye of the beholder or differently observed.

Emotions and space

Division of the life-world into spaces is influenced to a greater or lesser extent by our emotions. Some predications about space have accordingly recognized that perception. We might commence with Rudolf Otto's (1869-1937) notion of the holy (*das Heilige*), the *numen*, which explicitly depends on sentiment aroused by proximity to the numinous: *Ahndung*. The encounter with the numinous is a personal experience of the *mysterium tremendum et fascinans*, an overwhelming complex of awe, dread, foreboding, apprehension, a *sense* of the ineffable Other. The space is thus defined by personal experience–a sensing–of the individual, but a sentience with which all individuals are acquainted to a greater or lesser extent according to their receptivity and induction. By the latter is meant that some individuals, through their special position (office) will have a higher sense of the numinous.[71] The numinous is thus defined as in space, but not necessarily precisely situated. The encounter might take place anywhere it is experienced.[72]

The location of the sacred was more exactly situated by Mircea Eliade (1907-86), extrapolating from Otto's suggestion. Durkheim had already predicated the separation of the sacred and the profane, but with an emphasis on the maintenance of community and the social. Eliade's direction placed the sacred completely within the realm of the religious. In Eliade's exegesis of the geography of the sacred, emotion is less explicit–less fundamental perhaps–than in Otto's enunciation, but it still implicitly exists. Being in Eliade's religious life-world is an emotional economy in which specific points in space have heightened significance as "centers" of the world and as "openings" or portals between the visible and invisible worlds, ruptures in an otherwise profane, uniform space.

In the equally binary arrangement of the life-world in terms of purity and danger, Mary Douglas was informed by structuralism and the phenomenology of the body. The former emphasized the mental division into binary and opposing categories from the triad of structural linguistics which Lévi-Strauss accepted from Roman Jakobson. Although structuralism's intention was to explain the life-world (cosmology) by the (different) rationalism or rationale–logic–of those experiencing it, leading to the *Annaliste* conception of *mentalité*, it is not possible–despite the exponents' protestations, perhaps–to exclude emotion, and that particularly applies to Douglas. For, by taking as its primary analogy and, indeed, phenomenology, of the body, Douglas inevitably engages with the emotions. Concepts of purity and danger cannot be conceived purely in terms of a different rationalism. By introducing the body, we immediately confront the emotions. No more clearly has that been demonstrated than by Bill Miller in his anatomy of disgust. The concatenation of purity, danger and penetration of the impure through orifices necessarily engages with the senses, with perception, and with emotional reactions like disgust.

Indeed, in this context, we might well consider very closely how sociologists have recently re-engaged with the Kantian rejection of pure reason. Reason does not operate without the influence and injection of emotions. The two "faculties" are not separable.[73]

Since in some measure spaces were constituted emotionally, failure to control emotions might be perceived as transgressive of spaces. Correspondingly, any trespass of space might well incur an emotional response (Chapters 7-8). What matters also, nonetheless, is whether emotions erupt or whether, in some circumstances, displays of emotion are strategic and purposeful.[74]

Critique of binary divisions of spaces

Subsequent chapters will illustrate the issues surrounding the binary allocations of space. They can be briefly enumerated here. Although prescriptive, these binary representations may not be consistently normative, and certainly not descriptive. Subversion–deliberate or inadvertent–is a constant threat, whether by groups or individuals. We can never assume a homology of culture and attitude. Particular difficulties pertain to the separation of sacred and profane, especially in the context of the religious life-world. In the past there have been proprietary claims on sacred places–secular claims to "ownership". Moreover, sacred places tend to attract "profane" activities around them, especially places of pilgrimage, but also any sacred place which encourages the intermittent congregation of people. Within sacred places, the social cannot be excluded, so that the social order or hierarchy is and has been reproduced inside the sacred place or space. Finally, as has been suggested many times, not everyone thinks in binary terms some or all of the time. Mental mapping is often personal and idiosyncratic.[75] More importantly, some reflection on the life-world contains more fuzziness and complexity than clarity and simplicity. Interactions between and within "sacred" and "secular" spaces are examined in particular in chapters 6-8.

"Liminality"

Liminal space is particularly associated with Van Gennep and with Victor Turner's structural-functionalism. We might consider "liminality" as "between-space". In that sense, it is neither one major space nor another major space, but a connecting, but different, removed space, between two principal spaces. Put another way, it correlates, it seems, with the structuralism of Lévi-Strauss in the notion of binary oppositions, but a triad of possibilities, following the structural linguistics of Roman Jakobson, ultimately derived from Fernand de Saussure. According to this rationalization of space, one is removed from one space into between-space (liminality) and then reintegrated into a new space. The characteristic of this between-space for Turner was the dissolution of social structure and hierarchy, the (temporary) permission for *communitas*. Even allowing for this rigid division of space, why should between-space be so different? If it is transitional space, why shouldn't it be ambiguous in the sense of not quite being just one space or the other, but a *mélange* of the characteristics of the two primary spaces: confusing, ambiguous, an in-betweenness which is shifting and volatile? This possibility is explored in chapter 8.

(Em)placed and displaced; "belonging" and "unsettled"

Two of the inter-related preoccupations of some recent research have been identity and belonging. The converse of those phenomena are equally characteristic: displacement and mobility. It is quite likely that the preponderance of the population was in motion, constantly in movement. Lee Beier referred to these perpetual migrants as "masterless men", without intending to exclude migratory women.[76] It is now acknowledged that not all this movement was associated with the "vagrancy" problem in the sense of indigent people. The larger cohort comprised people in search of work: the able-bodied poor looking for employment. As Keith Wrightson has indicated, household strategies involved dispersal as well as stability: encouraging some of the young members of the household to leave the family home. In that sense, movement was a life-course stage associated with servant-hood.[77] A proportion of these people would pass through this life-course, transient stage, to a stable life in terms of livelihood and locality.

We have, for example, the rather self-fulfilling depositions of witnesses in ecclesiastical courts: self-fulfilling since these witnesses were selected for their credibility in court and were likely to be constituted from those who had attained stability. Tithe causes in particular were likely to be resolved through the depositions of those who had achieved stability, since these causes depended on long memory. When witnesses were interrogated about tithes in East Stoke in 1621, the first witness, Richard Johnson, yeoman, had lived in the parish from birth to his current age of at least fifty-four; the second, Henry Heptinstall, now about fifty-eight; there for the last three decades; the next, William Bromhead, husband-man, now about forty-five, from birth; William Good, tailor, aged about fifty, also all his life; George Ellison, yeoman, for the last thirty-eight of his about seventy years; Ralph Watkinson, laborer, still working at age about seventy-six, there for about thirty-six years; Richard Humbie, of Newark, basket maker, aged over sixty, in the area for fifty years.[78] Some of these men had never had to leave their parish of birth then. Note, however, that some had established their permanent residence only in maturity.

When we direct our attention to other causes, however, such as defa-mation, we discover that many of the deponents had experienced con-siderable mobility, especially (but not exclusively) women. Anne Hoo-ton of Wilford, now a widow aged at least sixty, had been resident there for seven years or more, but had been at one of the Burtons for six years previously, before that at Shelford a year, before that at Bingham for six years, and before then at Shelford for twenty years.[79] Now consider the younger Frances Hooton of Lenton, aged about thirty-four at the time of her deposition for the same cause. She had inhabited Lenton for the last six years or more, but before that she had been resident in Sneinton three years, Glapton one year, Wilford six years, and earlier than then had been domiciled in Clifton where she was born. Both women had experienced some periods of stability, but had mostly been peripatetic within a small locality, moving locally from parish to parish. These life-course details are, of course, highly selective, but they fall into a known paradigm of high mobility.

Many, therefore, remained in a state of perpetual motion and move-ment, to whom Patricia Fumerton has recently applied the epithet "unset-tled" in the sense of a "culture of mobility" rather than simply lacking an acknowledged place of legal settlement and entitlement. Those engaged in this continuous cycle of migration comprised the mobile "working poor", itinerant workers.[80] The compulsion to migrate was the necessity to find work–usually of a temporary nature. Yet others were compelled to migrate because of mischance: in the case of young, single women, to avoid the consequences of pregnancy. What these itinerant people inhab-ited then was not place but a "space of unsettledness".[81] Belonging, in the sense of to a particular place, was thus a privileged sentiment reserved to a minority who were able to remain in their natal parish or later in life ac-quired some longer-term residence. Overwhelming numbers, particularly (but not exclusively) through earlier stages of the life-course, must have had an attenuated sense of belonging, perhaps some sense of the cluster of parishes through which they moved–moved being the operative term.

These marginal geographies are explored in Chapters 9-12. Chapter 10 is concerned with the "displaced", single pregnant women compelled to move away from their "place". Although that "place" of residence may have been a temporary one, it was one conceded to the single woman, and what is important here is the necessity and compulsion to move on. Some found "place" but were not accepted as being "in place". Immigrants into early-modern urban places were considered out of place and at risk of being expelled from "place" (Chapter 9). Others were received as being legitimately "in place" (and so, perhaps, "emplaced"), but were not, in fact, insiders, but remained outsiders, not integrated and perhaps never integrated into their local society (Chapters 11-12).

"Locality"

At the most, then, these highly mobile people were conscious of a locality through which they might be moving. In their case, their sense was pragmatically formed through their movement through places: a local phenomenology. For those kin groups which have been designated "core", "focal" or "stable" families–those privileged to remain in one parish or have permanent residence over a group of contiguous parishes–their sense of belonging might well have been focused on the parish, but they too might well have had a concept of their "locality". In Chapters 4 and 13, this consciousness of locality is explored in the context of recent literature about locality and "localism" in early-modern England. Since that literature is cited fully in Chapter 4, it is not rehearsed here. The intention here is simply to signpost some of the ways in which we can understand how late-medieval and early-modern English women and men might construct their local worlds.

The usual term of reference for locality in pre-modern England was the "country" or, in its Latin equivalent, *patria*. Some examples of its usage are given in Chapter 4. In one sense the "country" was not a static concept, for it was confirmed by movement–the migration of people within the "country". How localized movement contributed to the definition of the "country" is described in Chapters 1 and 2, particularly in the latter. Chapter 2 also relates to the concept of *pays* and the inter-relationship between some types of *pays*. The purpose of those two chapters is to illustrate how migration and mobility, because they were so localized and circumscribed, rather than dissolving locality and eroding local customs, actually tended towards their reinforcement–in some contexts (with *caveats* explained in Chapter 13).

Another way of understanding what contemporaries considered to be their locality is through defamation causes in ecclesiastical courts in the early seventeenth century. After the introduction of a doctrine of *mitior sensus* by these courts in an attempt to mitigate litigation, complainants were required to show how their reputation had been damaged. Some litigants referred to the effect on their integrity within their locality, where their good fame had previously been acknowledged and how now the words of defamation were taken to be understood.

> ... ex communi usu loquendi in Estradford predicta aliisque locis vicinis et circumvicinis per spatium decennij ultra ante hanc causam inceptam
> [... in common use of speech in East Retford aforesaid and other adjacent and neighboring places for a decade before this cause [was] initiated][82]

The concern then was how one's reputation ("common fame", *fama*) was tarnished within the locality, a locality which comprised not only one's parish but the adjacent parishes too.[83]

Urban space

One of the continuing debates amongst historians is whether the urban differs qualitatively as well as quantitatively from the rural. Their deliberations have been influenced by approaches from other directions: from early cultural studies by Raymond Williams in his *The City and the Country*; and by Philip Abrams who maintained that there were only differences of scale in social relations–reflecting density rather than character.[84] To remain with these themes, the question of difference between urban and rural has recently been revisited in a collection of essays inspired by Williams, and an examination of the material culture of urban and rural in and around Bristol has attempted to give empirical depth to the question.[85]

The concentration within the urban must certainly have brought about different perceptions of space. Here, attempts to demarcate space took on a particular resonance. It was here that the representation of space had repercussions. Karen Newman has illustrated how the impact of the changing Cityscape captured the poetic imagination of John Donne.[86] The political dimensions of attempts to redefine the urban landscape in the City–in Cheapside–in the early seventeenth century have been addressed by Paul Griffiths.[87] The City was extraordinary in English urban terms, but these concerns with the character of the townscape were replicated in other places.

In the early sixteenth century, environmental concerns of borough authorities were directed towards the decay (physical loss) of housing and building, resulting, somewhat rhetorically, in the statute for the re-edification of towns.[88] Concern about the condition of English urban places was not confined to local urban authorities, however, but reached much further. That decay was, indeed, something which exercised contemporary opinion quite markedly. According to Thomas Starkey, Reginald Pole was much concerned by the contrast between the condition of continental cities which he had observed, and the condition of English cities.

> ... as gudly cytes and townys, with magnyfycal and gudly housys, fayr tempullys and churchys, wyth other commyn places; concerning the wych I wold haue men to conferre euery yere a certayn summe, accordyng to theyr abylyte, to the byldyng and reformyng of al such commyn placys in euery grete cyte and towne'

> [plan to] ... restore our cytes to such bewty as we see in other cuntreys ... beutyfyl and fayre, formyd wyth much cyuylyte ...[89]

Pole's proposals belonged perhaps to the end of the 1530s, perhaps 1538. They were then slightly in advance of the statute for the re-edification of towns, but at a time when the perception of a decline of English urban places was evident. Pole's observations firstly contrasted the contemporary built environment with the superior continental urban fabric. He associated, moreover, the improvement of the urban environment with the progress of civility. In his context of an English Renaissance, urban civility was a positive objective not to be contrasted negatively with rural hospitality.[90] Moreover, at the heart of his plan was to reintroduce the aristocracy into urban places to re-create higher status buildings in urban locations. What, in essence, Pole was suggesting then was the promulgation of civil society through enhancement of the urban environment through high-status buildings.

The representation of city space thus mattered on two levels: for the projection of the urban place itself–its own self-presentation; and at a higher, national level for the inculcation of Renaissance civility. So, in the early sixteenth century, there was a discourse about enhancing the urban environment. Now, it might also be concluded that this discourse was essentially new in England. In the middle ages, the self-presentation or projection of urban places had been propagated through borough constitutions: the number and types of offices and borough privileges. The status of boroughs was still associated with the extent of their self-government, immunity and constitutions. In the early sixteenth century, attention turned to urban space. This transformation was stimulated in part by a perceived decay of urban space, but also by wider comparisons with European cities and the concerns of Renaissance civility.

The response of urban authorities involved two strategies: first, the protection of the symbolic spaces of the urban *enceinte*; and secondly, preventing the collapse of the wider environment. Although the first strategy had long antecedents in English medieval boroughs, there was both a qualitative and quantitative transformation in the early-modern borough, before, but not as emphatic as, the suggested "English urban renaissance".[91] The effort before 1660 was concentrated on enhancing the existing central area, particularly the public space of the market place, developing actions of the medieval urban corporation. At various points in the sixteenth and early seventeenth century, urban corporations adopted measures to improve the central precinct. In 1555-6, the small borough of Banbury expended 12s. 4d. on paving ninety-six yards of the market place.[92] The resolution of the corporation of St Albans in 1586 to construct a new market house was supported by cash assistance given by the mayor and aldermen.[93] The purpose behind these improvements was to assert urban dignity through the symbolism of the market space, projected to outsiders, but also expressed to the burgesses themselves. Urban status was signaled comparatively to other towns; urban was differentiated from rural by the different configuration of the market place; and urban authority was confirmed.

Some of this improvement was, of course, reserved for the privileged and urban amelioration was not always intended to benefit all the urban inhabitants. In 1607, there was a proposal to the mayor and corporation of Southampton to improve the two walking places with benches for the benefit of the mayor, aldermen and burgesses "or other men of qualitie". The pleasant promenade was thus another aspect of that civility reserved to the elite.

Demographic increase and the revival of trade during the sixteenth century also made some improvement imperative. The council of Southampton reached a decision to build a new market house because of the inadequacy of the old, open market around St. Laurence Cross. The new covered market at the south end of the Audit House would furnish "a convenient and comly place".[95] A new market house was constructed at about the same time in Yarmouth and subsequently leased to Mr. Custumer Smith for a term of ten years.[96] The borough authority in Devizes embarked upon a sequence of rebuilding in the early seventeenth century, commencing with the new shambles in 1600, the almshouses in 1615, the measuring house in the same year, and the restoration and improvement of the gildhall in 1632 in preparation for the next quarter sessions, to render it "convenient for the purpose aforesaid and for the beautifieing or adorninge thereof."[97] Whilst this effort was concentrated on the central precinct of the borough, the officials also maintained periodic surveys of their own houses and the housing stock of the borough.[98]

The countervailing tendency was immigration into urban places, a constant feature of patterns of migration (rural-urban in direction), which, however, escalated to new levels in the late sixteenth century.[99] Three inter-related consequences ensued: the peopling of urban spaces with beggars; demands on urban residents to maintain the poor; and degradation of some of the building and housing stock of urban places. Undoubtedly, the greatest fear of permanent residents of urban places was that immigrants would become chargeable to their urban parishes. We should not, however, discount the other, spatial, impact. Although expulsion of beggars no doubt had a primary aim of removing any financial costs, there was probably also an element of disgust at the encounter with beggars in the urban streets and precinct. Yarmouth was not the only borough to appoint beadles of the beggars to clear the streets.[100]

Behind the attempts to regulate "inmates" (incomers taking up residence usually in poorer accommodation) lay then an intention to avoid becoming chargeable for the poor. There is no doubt, however, that the degradation of urban housing and building also concerned the authorities, even if it was predominantly not located in the central precinct. Chapter 9 explores this aspect of the effect of the immigrant poor on urban space.

Urban space was, of course, already residentially segregated, with the wealthiest inhabiting the central location, and the poorest consigned to the outer parts of wards and suburbs. Unlike beggars, then, the accommodation of "inmates" was not in the immediate view of the urban elite. The presence of the immigrant poor was, nonetheless, sufficient for corporations to adopt several strategies, as explored in Chapter 9. One obvious mechanism, as in Yarmouth, was the constant repetition of orders to the urban constables to be vigilant in enforcing the ordinances against "incomers" "according to its true tenour".[101] Allied to that, the Assembly, like other borough corporations, intended to prevent the letting of houses or parts of houses to "inmates" without the consent of the bailiffs or justices subject to heavy fines on the landlords, in the case of Yarmouth 10s. or 20s. for every week the infraction persisted. The constables were directed to give warning in their wards.[102] The third instrument was the regular survey, as instructed by the assembly of Norwich in 1600:

Inprimis you shall inquire & make diligent serche what Inmates or borders you haue or shall herafter come lately come out of any other place or Countie into the Cytie likely to be Chardgable to your parish which shall not haue dwelt here by the space of One whole yeare togither[103]

The remit of the surveys was to investigate every nook and cranny of the urban space. Those appointed in 1653 to inspect for and dispose of inmates, foreigners and strangers in Preston, had distinct parts of the borough assigned to them. More than that, they were reminded that they should diligently check all wends (back lanes) and backsides of their streets. The first itinerary consisted of a route along Friargate; the second was composed of the market place and Fishergate; and the third Churchgate.[104]

Returning to representations/practice or reality

"The framed space of representation" is in the eye of the beholder and of a beholder usually with the power to make the representation and induce others to see it too.[105] Representation has an ideological purpose and those who accede to the representation against their own interests may be supposed to be under some form of false consciousness. The purpose of representation is often to portray and thus propagate or fix: stability. By contrast, the reality beneath may be instability and uncertainty.

Representation and reality are not always to be assumed to be in opposition, however, for they interconnect. The representation of space for some people will be their real experience of space rather than illusion. Matters might be even more confused, in the sense of not differentiated. Barbara Rosenwein has advanced a complex argument about the formation of space through "negotiation" from a position of power which both produces and represents space.[106] "Negotiation" , which is very much a current notion in historical writing, does not imply equality of position, merely contact over the terms of resolution, agreement or settlement. Accordingly, then, re-negotiation could ensue, whether formally or informally. The criteria and characteristics of space were never fixed for all time–or even for a long time. This attention to the contingencies of relationships of power perhaps contrasts quite strongly with Dodgshon's attachment to structure (above).

The text which follows is divided into three parts, intended to provide some coherence. The first part explores how migration and mobility paradoxically contributed to the definition of "country" and locality. In the second section, the category of "sacred" space is considered through three examinations of particular places and spaces. With the third part we move to an examination of people's experience of being in and out of place and what that might mean for notions of solidarity, "community" and "belonging".

We conclude this brief investigation of the themes and theories approached in the following papers by noting that the CONCLUSION appropriately recapitulates many of the ideas implicitly or explicitly considered in the earlier papers within a particular space: the market place. Space is a contentious issue; the epistemology of its discussants clash. To some extent, the divergent approaches to space epitomize the fragmentation of academic society. This small book will not appeal to all. Some might see it as the worst of *différence*, the Derridean notion of deferral of meaning, even whilst they despise the very idea of "deconstruction". The spirit of the book is, however, merely one of *bricolage*, to try to put together something workable by taking bits and pieces from the resources made available by others. It attempts to avoid over-determined categories.

There remains a lacuna in this book: the widening world. Although there is some discussion about the adjustment in society and space in the British North American colonies in the early seventeenth century, no further attempt is made to engage with the processes of transatlantic migration: the deracination involved; how far the "countries" of the new world replicated those in the old; the impact of longer-distance migration on society and customs; merely as examples. Those issues are simply beyond the scope of this book.

Finally, some justification must be offered why this discussion of space, place and movement ends in ca.1640. It is not merely an artificial cut-off. Douglas Chambers has made an eloquent case for a reconsideration of spatial exegesis from ca.1650–although it was not uncontested. Although not totalizing in its spatial or scientific fetishism, a transition was made from a chorographical, imaginative world, to a geographical, measured world.[108] That perception allows a *caesura*. More importantly, 1641 heralded a period of immense disruption which eradicated the normative. Finally, the Settlement Acts of 1662–though preceded by the Poor Laws of 1597-1601–complicated movement and mobility.

Notes

[1]It must be admitted from the outset that this book does not really address geographers' metrological models of space and place. In some of the chapters, some models are identified, but this introduction will not dwell on them. A fine introduction is Masahisa Fujita, Paul Krugman, and Anthony J. Venables, *The Spatial Economy. Cities, Regions, and International Trade* (Cambridge, MA: MIT Press, 1999). The spatial turn by geographers is illustrated by the journal *Society and Space*. In this introduction, the literature about space and place will be recited sparingly. More substantial references will be found in each of the following chapters.

[2]The geographical literature is reviewed in detail throughout and in the CONCLUSION below. For a succinct examination of the various positions, Peet, *Modern Geographical Thought*, 98-108, 119-29, 158-60, 170-2, 274. See also the formative David Gregory and John Urry, eds., *Social Relations and Spatial Structures* (London: Macmillan, 1985). For more detailed considerations, Nigel Thrift, *Spatial Formations* (London: Sage, 1996). The representational (cultural) strand is perhaps epitomized by Denis Cosgrove and Steven Daniels, eds., *The Iconography of Landscape. Essays on the Symbolic Representation, Design and Use of Past Environments* (Cambridge: Cambridge University Press, 1988). For an historical geographer's examination of the representation of medieval urban space, Keith D. Lilley, "Mapping Cosmopolis: Moral Topographies of the Medieval City," *Society and Space* 22 (2004): 681-98.

[3]Barbara A. Hanawalt and Michael Kobialka, eds., *Medieval Practices of Space*, Medieval Cultures vol. 23 (Minneapolis: University of Minnesota Press, 2000) shows how representation and the reality of space are irreducibly interconnected. A helpful reflection on the interconnectedness is Rob Shields, *Places on the Margin. Alternative Geographies of Modernity* (London: Routledge, 1991).

[4]For the background to structuration theories, John Parker, *Structuration* (Buckingham: Open University Press, 2000), which explains the divergent structuration ideas of Giddens and Bourdieu, predicated through their different emphases on individual agency and class as formative of structuration.

[5]Chris Collinge, "The *Différence* Between Society and Space: Nested Scales and the Return of Spatial Fetishism," *Society and Space* 23 (2005): 189-206.

[6]Jean-François Lyotard, *The Postmodern Condition* (Manchester: Manchester University Press, 1984).

[7]Even, more diffusely, in the everyday sites of activity: Michael Hebbert, "The Street as a Locus of Collective Memory," *Society and Space* 23 (2005): 581-96.

[8]For these hidden genealogies, Peet, *Modern Geographical Thought*, passim, but also succinctly Steven Field and Keith H. Basso, eds., *Senses of Place* (Santa Fe: School of American Research Press, 1996), 3-4.

[9]Patricia Fumerton, *Unsettled. The Culture of Mobility and the Working Poor in Early Modern England* (Chicago: Chicago University Press, 2006). The point is elaborated below.

[10]Cited by Field and Basso, *Senses of Place*, 4.

[11]The introduction to Field and Basso, *Senses of Place*, although succinct, has wonderful nuance.

[12]Special mention is made here of Peet, *Modern Geographical Thought*, as a lucid

introduction to all these issues, including the resurgence of phenomenology–the experience of the lived body in space; Claval, *Regional Geography*; Mike Crang, *Cultural Geography* (London: Routledge, 1998) (e.g. p. 2: "cultures are spread over space ... cultures make sense of space").

[13]Sibley, *Geographies of Exclusion*: so his constant reference, even in titles of chapters, to "border crossings", "mapping the pure and defiled", "bounding space: purification and control".

[14]For a complication of this argument, Lorraine Young, "The 'Place' of Street Children in Kampala, Uganda: Marginalisation, Resistance, and Acceptance of the Urban Environment," *Society and Space* 21 (2003): 607-27.

[15]This proposition is beautifully encapsulated in Rhonda L. Sanford, *Maps and Memory in Modern England. A Sense of Place* (Basingstoke: Palgrave, 2002).

[16]This point is well made by Bill Miller: "Douglas needs more than just the notion of not fitting, because only certain kinds of not fitting are upsetting": William Ian Miller, *The Anatomy of Disgust* (Cambridge, MA: Harvard University Press, 1997), 267, n. 12. See also his critique of Douglas's "cold structure" at 271, n. 4.

[17]David Harvey, *Social Justice and the City* (London: Edward Arnold, 1973) and *Consciousness and the Urban Experience* (Oxford: Blackwell, 1985): cultural materialism.

[18]Dodgshon, *Society in Time and Space*.

[19]Lefebvre, *Production of Space*.

[20]For Benjamin's life and thought, Esther Leslie, *Walter Benjamin. Overpowering Conformism* (London: Pluto Press, 2000) (for this present context, 183-92); Michel de Certeau, *The Practice of Everyday Life* trans. Steven Rendall (Berkeley: University of California Press, 1988), 91-110, 115-30; for commentary, Ian Buchanan, *Michel de Certeau. Cultural Theorist* (London: Sage, 2000), 108-25; Jeremy Ahearne, *Michel de Certeau. Interpretation and its Other* (Stanford: Stanford University Press, 1995), 177-8.

[21]De Certeau thus inherits, but questions, the Foucauldian legacy of surveillance and self-disciplinary techniques. Foucault's symbolic order is also, of course, significant for the representation of space, although not realized in some historical writing about the representation of space.

[22]That term is awkward, of course; for one way of reconciling individual phenomenology and collective experience, Paul Harrison, "Making Sense: Embodiment and Sensibilities of the Everyday," *Society and Space* 18 (2000): 497-517, which adapts Williams's "structures of feeling" as the "sensate" which enables the transformation to collective experience and defining personal experience as emergent and "elusory", unperfected process which contributes to wider sentiment.

[23]See in general Lawrence J. Prelli, ed., *Rhetorics of Display* (Columbia SC: University of South Carolina Press, 2006).

[24]ROLLR 1D41/13/24, fol. 26r..

[25]C. John Sommerville, *The Secularization of Early Modern England. From Religious Culture to Religious Faith* (Oxford: Oxford University Press, 1992), 18-32: yet Sommerville himself asks whether this was not more a sacralization of church space than a secularization (p. 30). See now, Christian Grosse, "Places of Sanctification: The Liturgical Sacrality of Genevan Reformed Churches, 1535-1566," and John Craig, "Psalms, Groans and Dogwhippers: The Soundscape of Worship in the English Parish Church, 1547-1642," both in *Sacred Space* ed. Coster and Spicer, 60-

80, 104-23; Andrew Pettegree, *Reformation and the Culture of Persuasion* (Cambridge: Cambridge University Press, 2005), 10-75.

[26]It pervades most medieval historical writing, although often without reference to its genealogy. More substantively, it has recently been re-examined in early-modern contexts. Coster and Spicer, *Sacred Space*. See also Christopher Marsh, "Sacred Space in England, 1560-1640: The View from the Pew," *Journal of Ecclesiastical History* 53 (2002): 286-311.

[27]For brevity, see Michael Pickering, *Stereotyping. The Politics of Representation* (Basingstoke: Palgrave, 2001), 29; Eviatar Zerubavel, *Social Mindscapes. An Invitation to Cognitive Sociology* (Cambridge, MA: Harvard University Press, 1997), 30-31, 59-63.

[28]Gordon R. Dunstan, ed., *The Register of Edmund Lacy Bishop of Exeter, 1420-1455. Registrum Commune*, vol. 1, Devon and Cornwall Record Society n.s. 7 (Exeter, 1963), 8, 73, 87, 176.

[29]A structurational (rather than structuralist) consideration, derived from both Bourdieu and Giddens, is contained in C. P. Graves, "Social Space in the English Medieval Parish Church," *Economy and Society* 18 (1989): 297-322. Parker, *Structuration* for a sociological discussion; for the geographical perspective, Peet, *Modern Geographical Thought*, 153-62.

[30]Alice Granbery Walter, ed., *Lower Norfolk County, Virginia, Court Records. Book "A" 1637-1646 & Book "B' 1646-1651/2* (Baltimore: Cleanfield Company Inc., 1994), 8.

[31]Walter, ed., *Lower Norfolk County, Virginia, Court Records*, 57.

[32]Walter, ed., *Lower Norfolk County, Virginia, Court Records*, 82.

[33]Walter, ed., *Lower Norfolk County, Virginia, Court Records*, 71.

[34]Walter, ed., *Lower Norfolk County, Virginia, Court Records*, 8.

[35]Walter, ed., *Lower Norfolk County, Virginia, Court Records*, 1-2.

[36]Walter, ed., *Lower Norfolk County, Virginia, Court Records*, 58, 65.

[37]Nathaniel Bouton, ed., *Provincial Papers: Documents and Records Relating to the Province of New Hampshire* (Concord: State Printer, 1867), 121.

[38]Massachusetts State Archives Massachusetts Quarterly Courts microfilm, p. 68 (paginated not foliated). For the problem of drunkenness, Sharon V. Salinger, *Taverns and Drinking in Early America* (Baltimore and London: Johns Hopkins University Press, 2004), 83-120

[39]Ibid., p. 89 (paginated not foliated). (See also the two other contemporary cases: pp. 89-90).

[40]Ibid., p. 124 (paginated not foliated).

[41]For the background, David T. Konig, *Law and Society in Puritan Massachusetts: Essex County, 1629-1692* (Chapel Hill, NC: University of North Carolina Press, 1979)

[42]As n. 38 above, p. 75 (paginated not foliated).

[43]Ibid., p. 131 (paginated not foliated).

[44]*Record and Files of the Quarterly Courts of Essex County Massachusetts vol. I, 1636-1656* (Salem Mass.: Essex Institute, 1911), 15.

[45]*Record and Files of the Quarterly Courts of Essex*, 18.

[46]*Record and Files of the Quarterly Courts of Essex*,33,34,36,49,51.

[47]William M. Offutt, "The Atlantic Rules. The Legalistic Turn in Colonial Brit-

ish America," in *The Creation of the British Atlantic World* ed. Elizabeth Mancke and Carole Shammas (Baltimore and London: Johns Hopkins University, 2005), 160-81

[48]NNRO Y/C19/4, fol. 48v.

[49]We await Amanda Flather, *Gender and Space in Early Modern England* (Woodbridge: Boydell for the Royal Historical Society, 2007).

[50]NNRO Y/C19/4, fols. 57v, 189v, 201v.

[51]P. Jeremy P. Goldberg, "The Public and the Private: Women in the Pre-Plague Economy," in *Thirteenth Century England III* ed. Peter R. Coss and Simon D. Lloyd (Woodbridge: Boydell, 1991), 75-89.

[52]Shannon McSheffrey, *Marriage, Sex, and Civic Culture in Late Medieval London* (Philadelphia: University of Pennsylvania Press, 2006), 128-34.

[53]Michael Roberts, "Women and Work in Sixteenth-century English Towns," in *Work in Towns 850-1850*, ed. Penelope Corfield and Derek Keene (Leicester: Leicester University Press, 1990), 94, 101 (n. 67); Marjorie K. McIntosh, *Working Women in English Society 1300-1620* (Cambridge: Cambridge University Press, 2005), 129; P. Jeremy P. Goldberg, *Women, Work, and Life Cycle in a Medieval Economy. Women in York and Yorkshire c.1300-1520* (Oxford: Oxford University Press, 1992), 104; for the women's market at High Wycombe in 1652, Robert W. Greaves, ed., *The First Ledger Book of High Wycombe*, Buckinghamshire Record Society vol. 11 (1956), 145 (no. 208).

[54]Excellently illustrated by Laura Gowing, '"The Freedom of the Streets': Women and Social Space, 1560-1640," in *Londinopolis. Essays in the Cultural and Social History of Early Modern London,* ed. Paul Griffiths and Mark Jenner (Manchester: Manchester University Press, 2000), 130-51, with important bibliographical references at 148.

[55]Gowing, *Common Bodies. Women, Touch and Power in Seventeenth-century England* (New Haven: Yale University Press, 2003), 149-76 (before the intrusion of male midwives); Bernard Capp, *When Gossips Meet. Women, Family, and Neighbourhood in Early Modern England* (Oxford: Oxford University Press, 2003), 49-55. See also Sarah Mendelson and Patricia Crawford, *Women in Early Modern England* (Oxford: Oxford University Press, 1998), 205-12; Corinne S. Abate, ed., *Privacy, Domesticity, and Women in Early Modern England* (Aldershot: Ashgate, 2003). CUL D2/10, fol. 239v: office *c*. Agnes Haseldon (adultery): "& ys deliuered of a childe by John Dale as she saythe before all the wemen at the tyme of hir travell."

[56]Nicholas Udall, *Roister Doister* [*c*.1552-66], Act II, scene iv, lines 775-6.

[57]I owe the information about Lenton to Dr. Linda Lees.

[58]CUL EDR D2/10, fol. 134v.

[59]Arthur J. Willis, ed., *Church Life in Kent being Church Court Records of the Canterbury Diocese 1559-1565* (London and Chichester: Phillimore, 1975), 49 (410). Further examples: only to meet in public places (49 (413); 51 (425); 53 (435); 59 (471)).

[60]James Raine, ed., *Depositions and Other Ecclesiastical Proceedings from the Courts of Durham*, SS vol. 21 (1845), 34, 36 ("quod obstineant a loco suspecto/locis suspectis").

[61]Raine, *Depositions and Other Ecclesiastical Proceedings*, 51 ("nisi solum modo in publicis locis").

[62]Raine, ed., *The Injunctions and Other Ecclesiastical Proceedings of Richard Barnes,*

Bishop of Durham, from 1575 to 1587, SS vol. 22 (1850), 123.

[63]CUL EDR D/2/1, fol. lxxxvijr. The phrase was reiterated in another office cause in 1378: "abiurauit peccam et loca suspecta": D/2/1, fol. lxxxvijr-v [sic].

[64]UoN Dept. of MSS. AN/LB 222/5/2/1-2.

[65]Shannon McSheffrey, "Place, Space, and Situation: Public and Private in the Making of Marriage in Late-Medieval London," *Speculum* 79 (2004): 960-90, and now her *Marriage, Sex, and Civic Culture*, 121-63.

[66]A fascinating discussion of the effects of common fame in medieval society is Thelma Fenster and Daniel Lord Smail, eds., *Fama: The Politics of Talk and Reputation in Medieval Europe* (Ithaca, NY: Cornell University Press, 2003); UoN Dept. of MSS. AN/LB 218/2/7/4 *communis vox et fama*; *publica vox et fama*; "common voice and fame".

[67]UoN Dept. of MSS. AN/LB 216/2/2/1.

[68]Capp, *When Gossips Meet*, 49-68; the implications of Mark Jenner, "From Conduit Community to Commercial Network? Water in London, 1500-1725," in *Londinopolis*, ed. Griffiths and Jenner, 250-72; Marjorie K. McIntosh, *Controlling Misbehavior in England, 1370-1600* (Cambridge: Cambridge University Press, 1998), 65-9; McSheffrey, *Marriage, Sex, and Civic Culture*, 121-34

[69]UoN Dept. of MSS. AN/LB 224/1/50/1-6.

[70]UoN Dept. of MSS. AN/LB 224/1/8 Beever *c*. Ridley Libel in defamation, 1621 (Misson).

[71]Rudolf Otto, *The Idea of the Holy. An Inquiry into the Non-rational Factor in the Idea of the Divine and its Relation to the Rational* trans. John W. Harvey (London: Oxford University Press, 1969) [original German publication 1917].

[72]For the dismissal of such religious ontology as "hauntology" (Derrida) and obscurantism, Willi Braun, "Religion," in *Guide to the Study of Religion* ed. Braun and Russell T. McCutcheon (London and New York: Cassell, 2000), 5.

[73]For example, Jack Barbalet, ed., *Emotions and Sociology* (Oxford: Blackwell Publishing for *The Sociological Review* Monographs, 2002). In this genealogy, we should include Norbert Elias as an important intermediary, for, although his primary concern was how (con)figurations of people advanced changes in quotidian habits and the *habitus*, much of the transformation depended on the operation of sensitivity and emotional responses.

[74]Barbara H. Rosenwein, ed., *Anger's Past. The Social Uses of an Emotion in the Middle Ages* (Ithaca: Cornell University Press, 1998), is a good starting point.

[75]For the original formulation, Peter Gould and Rodney White, *Mental Maps* (Harmondsworth: Penguin, 1974), but see Cosgrove's brief critique: Denis Cosgrove, *Mappings* (London: Reaktion Books Ltd., 1999), 7.

[76]A. Lee Beier, *Masterless Men. The Vagrancy Problem in England 1560-1640* (London: Methuen, 1985); see now, Steve Hindle, *On the Parish? The Micro-politics of Poor Relief in Rural England, c.1550-1750* (Oxford: Oxford University Press, 2004).

[77]Keith Wrightson, *Economic Necessities. Economic Lives in Early Modern Britain* (New Haven and London: Yale University Press, 2000), 56-64, recapitulating the conclusions of Ann Kussmaul and others on the process of servant-hood.

[78]UoN Dept. of MSS. AN/LB224/1/35/2.

[79]UoN Dept. of MSS. AN/LB 220/4/2/1 (1603).

[80]Fumerton, *Unsettled*.

[81]Fumerton, *Unsettled*, 6.

[82]UoN Dept. of MSS. AN/LB 224/1/6/1 Libel in Brighte *c*. Goodale in defamation, 1621.

[83]For notions of *fama* in the middle ages, Fenster and Smail, *Fama*.

[84]Raymond Williams, *The Country and the City* (London: Chatto & Windus Ltd., 1973); Philip Abrams, "Towns and Economic Growth: Some Theories and Problems," in *Towns in Societies: Essays in Economic History and Historical Sociology* ed. Abrams and E. A. (Tony) Wrigley (Cambridge: Cambridge University Press, 1978), 9-33.

[85]Carl B. Estabrook, *Urbane and Rustic England. Cultural Ties and Social Spheres in the Provinces, 1660-1780* (Stanford: Stanford University Press, 1998); Gerald MacLean, Donna Landry, and Joseph P. Ward, eds., *The Country and the City Revisited: England and the Politics of Culture 1550-1850* (Cambridge: Cambridge University Press, 1999).

[86]Karen Newman, "Walking Capitals. Donne's First Satyre," in *The Culture of Capital. Property, Cities, and Knowledge in Early Modern England,* ed. Henry S. Turner (London: Routledge, 2002), 203-21. It might then be construed as Donne's mental mapping of the City and that mental mapping–that individual understanding of the complex landscape–again has particular (if not exclusive) relevance to the townscape.

[87]Paul Griffiths, "Politics Made Visible: Order, Residence and Uniformity in Cheapside, 1600-45," in *Londinopolis*, ed. Griffiths and Jenner, 176-96.

[88]Tittler, "'For the re-edification of townes': The Rebuilding Statutes of Henry VIII," *Albion* 22 (1990):591-605; as an illustration, the assembly of Boston fretted about the re-edification of houses in 1544 and as late as 1561: Peter and Jenny Clark, eds., *The Boston Assembly Minutes 1545*-1575, LRS vol. 77 (1987), 14-15, 35.

[89]Thomas Starkey, "A Dialogue between Cardinal Pole and Thomas Lupset, Lecturer in Rhetoric at Oxford," in *England in the Reign of King Henry the Eighth,* ed. Sidney J. Heritage, Early English Text Society Extra Series vol. 32 (1878), Part 2, 177-8, lines 1184-1219.

[90]Felicity Heal, *Hospitality in Early-modern England* (Oxford: Oxford University Press, 1990).

[91]Peter Borsay, *The English Urban Renaissance. Culture and Society in the Provincial Town, 1660-1770* (Oxford: Oxford University Press, 1989).

[92]Jeremy S. W. Gibson & Edwin R. C. Brinkworth, eds., *Banbury Corporation Records: Tudor and Stuart*, Banbury Historical Society vol. 15 (Banbury, 1977).

[93]Arthur E. Gibbs , ed., *The Corporation Records of St Albans* (St Albans, 1890), 24, 27, 47.

[94]William J. Conner, ed., *The Southampton Mayor's Book of 1606-1608*, Southampton Record Series vol. 21 (Southampton, 1978), 85.

[95]Allan L. Merson, ed., *The Third Book of Remembrance of Southampton 1514-1602 volume II (1540-1573)*, Southampton Record Series vol. 3 (Southampton, 1955), 110-12 (284), 122 (295).

[96]NNRO Y/C19/4, fol. 30r.

[97]Frederick H. Goldney, ed., *Records of Chippenham* (London, 1889), 52-53, 63, 64.

[98]Goldney, *Records of Chippenham*, 13-14, 36-37.

[99]For the demographic process in urban places, see now Chris Galley, *The Demography of Early Modern Towns: York in the Sixteenth and Seventeenth Centuries* (Liverpool: Liverpool University Press, 1998). Still important, however, is A. Lee Beier, "The Social Problems of an Elizabethan Country Town: Warwick, 1580-90," in *Country Towns in Pre-Industrial England,* ed. Peter Clark (Leicester: Leicester University Press, 1981), 45-85. A valuable synthesis is Paul Griffiths, John Landers, Margaret Pelling, and R. Tyson, "Population and Disease, Estrangement and Belonging," in *The Cambridge Urban History of Britain Volume II 1540-1840,* ed. Peter Clark (Cambridge: Cambridge University Press, 2000), 195-233.

[100]NNRO Y/C19/4, fol. 89r.

[101]NNRO Y/C19/4, fol. 5r.

[102]NNRO Y/C19/4, fol. 16v.

[103]NNRO NCR case 16c/5, fol. 244r.

[104]Anthony Hewitson, ed., *Preston Court Leet Records. Extracts and Notes* (Preston, 1905), 17. The appointment of "houselookers" extended back to at least 1622: ibid., 49, n.1.

[105]For "framed space of representation", Denis Cosgrove in his "Introduction: Mapping Meaning" in Cosgrove, *Mappings,* 7.

[106]Barbara Rosenwein, *Negotiating Space. Power, Restraint, and Privileges of Immunity in Early Medieval Europe* (Chicago: University of Chicago Press, 1999).

[107]The issues have been recently admirably contemplated in David Armitage and Michael J. Braddick, eds., *The British Atlantic World, 1500-1800* (Basingstoke: Palgrave, 2002) esp. the contribution by Alison Games, "Migration," 31-50, which has interesting points to make about social and cultural convergence in the earlier life of the colonies; and see also here Colin Kidd, *British Identities Before Nationalism: Ethnicity and Nationhood in the Atlantic World, 1600-1800* (Cambridge: Cambridge University Press, 1999). For the term "country", see chap. 4. For its use in the colonies: Nathaniel B. Shurtleff, ed., *Records of the Colony of New Plymouth in New England. Court Orders. vol 1 1633-1640 vol II 1641-1651* (2 vols., Boston: William White, Printer to Commonwealth, 1855), vol. 1, 162 (1640: William Chase censured for disturbance of the proceedings of the church, court and "countrey"), vol. 2, 85 (fine of £5 for causing trouble and charge to "the countrey").

[108]Douglas Chambers, *The Reinvention of the World. English Writing 1650-1750* (London: Arnold, 1996), 20-47. The literature about these changes in world-view are summarized by Karen Raber, "Recent Ecocritical Studies of English Renaissance Literature," *English Literary Renaissance* 37 (2007): 151-71

Part I
The Formation of Locality

1
Migration and Mobility in a Less Mature Economy[1]: English Internal Migration, ca. 1200-1350

Migration is an important social, economic and cultural historical phenomenon for a range of reasons and meanings, which can be elicited with varying levels of success for different times, dependent on the nature of the sources available.[2] Recent research into migration and mobility in the high middle ages has concentrated on the character of migration fields and the turnover of population, since these issues can be more satisfactorily addressed through the available sources.[3] The importance of migration in the high middle ages has been principally related to: issues of urbanisation; of regional restructuring and development; and of the formation and persistence, paradoxically, of local norms and customs.[4] The last question is predicated on the conclusions that, although population mobility and migration reached considerable levels in the high middle ages, the localised nature of movement yet confirmed local customs rather than prejudiced them. That sort of recursive aspect of mobility is considered further below.[5] Quantitative studies of migration in the high middle ages have thus largely been directed towards migration fields and their character, with an emphasis on rural-urban migration, and the elucidation of "betterment" migration, with the emphasis on patterns rather than processes, because the evidence available reveals more about the former.[6] Other questions are more difficult to answer from the sources available and certainly not possible to examine in a quantitative manner. That problem applies, however, to migration in England at all historical times.[7] The *experience* of migration and, in particular, longitudinal life-histories of migration, thus remain concealed to us especially in the high middle ages.

Some aspects of the personal experience of migration can be elicited, if imperfectly and by inference, from sources before 1350, so that one objective here is to re-establish those intimate aspects of migration–decisions, movement, and reception. On the other hand, such personal experiences were contingent and were located within an overall context of control over persons (lordship and villeinage), but also control, organisation and representation of space, again seigniorial, but also religious. Some attempt is therefore also made to elucidate the nature of those spaces and their impact on migration.

The principal result of research into migration in high medieval England has been the production of a distance-decay model for rural to urban migration. Although that model was intuitively perceived by Reaney, it was fundamentally established by McClure. As a result of McClure's and later studies of immigration into towns, a correlation was established between the rank-size and status of English urban places and distances of migration to them. Thus York, Bristol, Norwich, Winchester and Exeter have been established as "regional capitals" with about fifty percent of immigrants deriving from distances of up to twenty to twenty-five miles, whilst Leicester and Nottingham, as county boroughs, had predominantly smaller migration fields, of ten to fifteen miles, and places such as Grimsby, because of its status as a port and important small town within its *pays*, had a catchment area as extensive as that of Nottingham (that is, up to half its immigrants arrived from fourteen to fifteen miles distant).[8] In current research into rural-urban migration in the East Midlands, however, Bischoff has demonstrated how there is interference from small towns, such as Grantham, in the pattern of migration to larger urban centres, such as Lincoln, Leicester and Nottingham.[9] In effect, smaller urban places might, at some times, provide "intervening opportunities".[10] A still unexplored aspect of rural-urban movement, however, is migration into suburban vills around urban centres, which might have provided opportunities in the suburban economy without the restrictions and regulations imposed within the borough (but see further below).[11]

The overall context of this urban-rural migration before 1350 has been explored through three principal sources: lay subsidies and, in boroughs, internal subsidies (taxation lists); admissions to the freedom for immigration into urban centres; and, for rural mobility, manorial court rolls.[12] Like all sources for migration, none of these materials is immune from criticism. Lay subsidies and admissions to the freedom are a particularly problematic source, for both are selective and exclusive. Lay subsidies, as tax records, comprehended only a proportion of the population. Levied by central authority, they were assessed on personal estate (chattels) not required for subsistence, thus on disposable income above a tax threshold, which varied from subsidy to subsidy. A substantial element of the population was thus exempt or omitted, regardless of levels of evasion. Thus Dyer suggests that on average only forty percent of the *tenants* of the Bishop of Worcester contributed to the lay subsidy of 1327, whilst Barbara Harvey maintained that in the densely-populated Fenland of south Lincolnshire only twenty-six to thirty-five percent of the tenantry contributed.[13] The migrants visible in lay subsidies through their toponymic (place-name) bynames are thus self-evidently those who have been sufficiently successful to be captured by the taxation.

In the urban context, internal lay subsidies and admissions to the freedom exhibit the same exclusive characteristics, both possibly encompassing the same limited population. The burgess social group– those admitted to the freedom and thus enjoying the franchise–was a restricted and privileged section of the total urban population. It has been estimated that those in the freedom in Exeter in 1377 comprised at the most thirty-four percent of householders, in York perhaps fifty-four percent, and in Wells about fifty-one percent of all male adults.[14] The rate of participation at an earlier time is not likely to have been higher. It is probable that internal subsidies were levied by the burghal authorities on the same limited sector of the urban population.

In contrast, the total urban population was much wider and it might be expected of somewhat different composition. It might equally be expected that the margins of urban societies were also reinforced by immigration as much as natural increase and consequently that urban centres were an attraction for subsistence migrants as well as betterment migrants. That expectation is illustrated, for example, by William de Kynardeby, a tailor, who took sanctuary in St. John's church in Coventry in 1262, acknowledged many larcenies, and abjured the realm. It was established that he had no chattels (which would have been forfeit) and that he was out of tithing (collective security) because he was a vagrant.[15] Also a migrant to Coventry was Margery daughter of Henry Koc, who married there, but without the license of her lord, the Abbot of Halesowen, so that she was consequently fined 2s. 6d. "pro pace habenda."[16] At Wakefield in 1296, a stranger known only as Frode was indicted at the tourn for larceny; as he was under age, he abjured the town, but afterwards returned, so it was ordered that he be brought before the steward.[17] William *filius Bernardi* preferred to remain in London than return to six acres of land which he inherited in Hinderclay in Suffolk, but there is little prosopographical evidence about migrants to towns.[18] In two cases, the migrants to Coventry and Wakefield remained on the margin of subsistence, in another case a woman probably of slender means, and the migrant to London from Hinderclay decided to relinquish an opportunity of rural landholding. Immigration into urban centres was thus not simply an issue of "betterment" migration. Rarely, however, are such unsuccessful migrations and the motives behind and consequences of rural-urban migration so visible.

Something resembling migration into a suburban village is presented in Clarke's examination of Chesterton between 1277 and 1325, but with some caution. Chesterton is now within Cambridge, but was a village a few miles outside the borough.[19] Some circumspection must be exercised because Chesterton was ancient demesne and so perhaps an attraction as a protective space for migrant peasants (for which, see below).[20] Whilst Clarke characterised the village as "an atypical agrarian economy", its distinctive nature might have been its suburban position.[21] Of 322 different peasant kinship bynames identified, thirty-one percent were toponymic, from which Clarke deduced that twenty-seven bynames represented immigration from within a distance of seven miles to Chesterton, but thirty-nine from further than seven or eight miles but from within the county, and a further thirty-four from outside the county. In fact, seventy-three percent of these bynames thus constituted immigration from outside the customary marketing distance of seven miles.[22] Additional caution is necessary, however, because of the nature of the source of these bynames: a register of peasant land transactions. What is represented here then is peasant immigrants who have successfully entered the peasant land market in Chesterton. Nevertheless, migration into Chesterton might be indicative of the potential of migration into villages close to, but outside the walls of, boroughs.

Naturally, the further problem of these sources is their gender-specific content, for lay subsidies encompassed predominantly male taxpayers, with a sprinkling of females, whilst admissions to the freedom were exclusively male. Geographical modeling has constantly considered females to be more at risk of migrating, although over shorter distances.[23] To some extent, the significance of female migration in the late middle ages has been elucidated, from evidence not extensively available before then, but female migration before 1350 remains largely invisible.[24]

One of these sources, lay subsidies, was employed by McClure to aggregate quantitative data about migration in a rural context and into small towns. The same methodological difficulties result: *ipso facto* evidence of "betterment" migration and gender-bias. By contrast, a number of other studies of rural migration have concentrated on the two types of evidence in manorial court rolls: licensed movement (by payment of chevage where its context was mobility) and the recovery of villeins who have taken flight from the manor (*fugitivi*).[25] Much of this research, however, has related to villein mobility after 1350, which might raise a methodological dilemma: were lords more interested before 1350 in immigrants, whether from the perspective of control of social behaviour or the status of land and landholding?

The most suggestive of the studies of mobility before 1350, using court roll studies, is probably Smith's analysis of the movement of the villeins of Spalding Priory in 1268-69, for he tentatively proposes that the tightly circumscribed pattern of their movement was analogous to the pattern of recursive migration of servants in husbandry in the eighteenth century.[26] Superficially, therefore, there is a similarity of peasant movement in this *pays*, but as a result of different variables, it must be suggested. For the pattern of migration in the thirteenth century was occasioned at least in part by lordship, whilst that in the eighteenth century resulted from the formation of a "country" around a statute or hiring fair and the definition of a *pays*.[27]

The experience of lordship by the peasantry thus differentiates and marks out medieval migration. Thus, although Anne DeWindt represents a "regional perspective" of peasant kinship networks and connections in northern Huntingdonshire, what might well have been the informing influence was less the formation of a *pays* or "region" or "country", but rather the influence of lordship on the dispersal of kin relations over constituent manors of the estate of the Benedictine Abbey of Ramsey.[28] Returning to the Spalding manors, whilst some movement was contained with the estate in the thirteenth century, producing a localised pattern of migration, Jones has revealed how in the fifteenth century lordship acted in a contrary fashion (as a "push" variable), compelling longer distance migrations to prevent recovery by lords, which is thus disruptive of the localised pattern of the thirteenth and eighteenth centuries. Perhaps fifty to sixty percent of fugitive unfree males from the Priory's estates travelled twenty miles or more in the later middle ages, inconsistent with the more localised migration pattern of the middle of the thirteenth century, and probably affected by the different experience of lordship at the two dates.[29]

Whilst payments of chevage to leave the manor in manorial court rolls provide the most unambiguous data of peasant movement, they too are limited in their nature and in quantity. Usually the record does not provide details of destinations of peasants. Moreover, it is difficult to aggregate large datasets which might be regarded as significant in size. It is perhaps for this last reason that lay subsidy data have been used as a substitute, because they do allow large aggregate datasets, flawed as the data are.

What characterises medieval peasant migration from later migration is the formative influence of lordship as it was variously experienced. Sometimes lordship simply generated an information field–what opportunities were available within an estate–but it was also a productive force for movement. In particular, movement within an estate might have been dictated by the labour requirements of lords. Thus in the late thirteenth century three tenants were elected by the homage (effectively the male suitors of the manorial court) of Gussage in Dorset, the largest manor of the hospital of God's House, Southampton, to take up tenements, probably small holdings, on the house's smallest property at Hickley, just east of Southampton (a distance of just under 30 miles), no doubt to provide labour since Hickley had only insubstantial numbers of tenants.[30] In the twelfth century, William, earl Ferrers, made a benefaction to Tutbury Priory, of which he was the patron, of Henry *filius Galfridi*, no doubt a villein tenant, whom the Priory could move where it wished around the land which he had given to the house in alms.[31] Although the Ferrers' estate in south Derbyshire and Staffordshire was territorially compact by baronial standards, the distances involved might have still been large.[32]

Evidence of how villeins moved around an estate is reflected in the rental of Leicester Abbey in 1341. In the rental, twenty-three unfree tenants (nineteen percent) bore toponymic bynames whilst twenty-one cottars (eighteen percent) also had such a form of byname. Ten of the twenty-three villeins' toponymic bynames derived from other manors of the Abbey and six of the cottars'.[33] Whether through the labour requirements of lordship or from the influence of an information field, unfree tenants of the Abbey were moving around its estate, from one manor to another. Perhaps forced movement also lies behind an event in the manorial court of Barnet, a manor of the Abbey of St Albans, when three tenants objected in 1249 that they were not villeins because they had been born at St Albans, despite the fact that all three were of low status, one a lad or servant and another a manorial carter.[34]

It was not only in the rural context, however, that lordship influenced the movement of the Abbey's tenantry. In the rental of 1341 is a listing of the urban tenants of the Abbey in Leicester, clustered in a few parishes. Several of these tenants in Leicester were distinguished by toponymic bynames from the rural properties of the Abbey: de Stoucton (Stoughton), de Ansty (Anstey), de Burstalle (Birstall) and de Schepeshed (Shepshed), all properties in the same county. More intriguingly, the Abbey's urban tenantry included three householders described as Alice de Kokerham, Adam de Cokerham and William de Cokerham, toponymic bynames derived from the Abbey's remote property at Cockerham in the N.W. of England.[35] The Abbey's lordship thus influenced very long-distance migration as well as localised movement.

This movement choreographed by the influence of lordship can be discerned also on the estate of the bishop of Ely in the survey of 1222, but a further interesting aspect is introduced, some limited perception of step-wise migration as part of a longitudinal, life-history of the migrant.[36] Importantly, perhaps, the movements reflected in the toponymic bynames of the tenants of the Bishop allow some limited vista in step-wise migration. Excluding Wisbech because of its urban character, the Bishop had about 3,760 tenants, about 3,340 of whom were male. About ten percent of all tenants bore toponymic bynames, that is, forty-nine percent of all free tenants, forty-three percent of the unfree or "semi-free", but only eight percent of the cottars.[37] Amongst the unfree and semi-free, seventy-three tenants were identified by toponymic bynames from identifiable and unambiguous place-names, seventeen of which derived from other manors or vills within the episcopal estate. It seems, however, that movement of other peasants might have been influenced by lordship in a more complex way. For example, William de Croxton at Gransden might have moved to that place (Gransden) by step migration, for Croxton is situated next to Brandon (Suffolk), one of the episcopal manors, so that William might have moved from Croxton (not an episcopal manor) first to Brandon (an episcopal manor adjacent to Croxton) and then to another episcopal manor, Gransden. Amongst the free tenantry of the Bishop, 109 bore bynames from specific place-names, twenty-six of which were eponymous with episcopal manors, such as Henry de Walpol (Walpole, an episcopal manor) at Emneth (an episcopal manor). Another five, however, bore bynames from vills adjacent to episcopal manors, such as Bartholomew de Tiuetshale living in Ely, who might have moved first from Tivetshall (not an episcopal manor) to adjacent Pulham (an episcopal manor) and then on to Ely. Similarly, seventeen cottars bore toponymic bynames, four deriving from episcopal manors and two which might represent step-wise migration. Since the survey is assigned to 1222, it is possible that some of this movement occurred at the end of the twelfth century.

Extending migration back into the twelfth century is problematic because so few of the unfree tenantry in surveys of the twelfth century have toponymic bynames.[38] In the second decade of the twelfth century, eight *censarii* in survey B of Burton Abbey bore toponymic bynames, half of which derived from other manors of the estate. About the same time, in survey A, three tenants *ad malam*, molmen, equivalent to *censarii*, bore such names, all of which related to other conventual manors. Since the labour services of these tenants had been commuted, it is perhaps more probable that they had moved to accept opportunities for landholding on other manors rather than been distributed for the lord's labour supply.

In some ways, then, lordship facilitated and provided opportunities for movement, but it was also, of course, a repulsive force. In 1200, two sisters denied villein status against their lord, Roger de Graft, and further pleaded that Roger had so aggrieved and harmed their father that he could remain no longer on the manor, making an agreement with Roger that he might leave. Roger complained that their father had left his land with its chattels such that its buildings were dilapidated, tantamount to waste to the sum of twenty marks. Their father made his way into the lordship of William de St John.[39] It might be suspected too that the depredation of lordship was an influence in the flight of Matilda *Carpentar'* from Barkby (Leicestershire), a manor of Merton College, in the late thirteenth century. About the time of her flight, and shortly after the College had acquired the manor, the unfree tenants and the College became embroiled in dispute over various matters of seigniorial exaction, one of which taxes was *merchet*, around which the unfree tenants claimed free status. In contrast, the College expected *merchet* levied *pro rata* on the chattels of the unfree. In the event, Matilda fled northwards, was married at *Warrum*, and eventually relocated to St Andrews in Scotland.[40] Her personal estate of cash of 2s. 6d. and chattels of 4s. were confiscated. It seems likely that such extreme long-distance migration, perhaps unusual not only for a female migrant, was in part a response to the experience of lordship.

The exertion of lordship might also render some spaces less attractive. The importance of the representation of space is considered further below, but lordship as a part of that process is discussed here. Some lords, for example, because they had a predilection in favour of the inheritance of land, discriminated against both those whom they accepted as tenants on the failure of inheritance and against those who were accepted into lands but had not been born inside the lordship. An example of this process also derives from Barkby, for the lord of one of the manors there, Merton College, invoked such a discrimination in entry fines for admission to lands, revealed in a "Memoracio de ingressibus eorum [of the tenants] Tempore scolarium de Merton Oxon'" [Memorandum of their entry fines in the time of the scholars of Merton Oxford].[41] Ralph *bercarius*, for example, was required to discharge an entry fine of four marks for a messuage and six acres "et non erat natus super terram dominorum" [and–implying perhaps because–he was not born on the lords' lands], whilst William Savage contributed 2s. for his entry fine to a cottage, Geoffrey de Roteby 20s. for half a virgate and four acres, for the same reason in the same words, and John Wysman 13s. 4d. for a *quart'* of land and four acres "et non natus erat ibi." The Warden and Scholars demanded of both Richard and John Arnold 20s. both of whom received half a virgate and four acres, in the case of Richard "et non erat hereditas sua" [and it was not his inheritance], but more strongly in John's case "quia non herat hereditas sua" [because it was not his inheritance]. Compare now the cases of William son of Hugh de Tilton and Henry Bonde who each rendered only 6s. 8d. each to have admission to half a virgate and four acres "et est hereditas sua." Although there were some exceptions, and although such fines are not enormous in the general framework of entry fines at this time, the College discriminated against outsiders in the level of entry fines because of its predisposition or favour of inheritance of peasant tenements.[42] It is by no means clear that Merton College extended this regime to all its manors and it is thus possible that the arrangement at Barkby had some element of agreement between tenants and lord. How far the same policy was followed by other lords in the vill–for example, Leicester Abbey–is uncertain, but Merton was at this time the principal lord of customary holdings and so in a position to control entry into the vill to some degree.

A similar attitude towards entry fines was exhibited by Westminster Abbey, on whose estates entry fines for admission to customary land by those not inheriting was likely to be double those of inheriting tenants.[43] How widespread across the estate this propensity extended remains again unclear, but it certainly operated at Launton (Oxfordshire). Although entry fines were not heavy on the Abbey's estates, discrimination against new tenants was evident. The possibility thus exists that some spaces were represented as unattractive to immigrants.[44]

Small town space might also be restricted–or at least the attempt made to restrict it. When Abbot Samson allowed the parishioners of Southwold their chapel in 1206, he exacted from them a concession that they would not receive outsiders into the township ("Concessum quoque est quod predicti homines nunquam recipient aliquem extraneum ad inhabitandum in eadem uilla").[45]

Restrictions on the sort of person entering lordships might have also had a gender bias, for there might have been more reluctance to accept singlewomen into rural manors. The attitude is best perceived for lords, but perhaps other peasants too had some distrust. Merton College thus exacted hens as annual recognition from two women who entered the lordship of Kibworth Harcourt. During their sojourn on the manor, Emma de Langton and Matilda Leche made this symbolic payment–symbolic not merely for its purpose, but also because of the association of small livestock as women's concern–each "pro aduocacione domini dum manet in villa", Emma from 1296 to 1320 and Matilda in 1309-10.[46] Such a payment might be construed as specially related to female entrants into the lordship, for they were otherwise "out of hand" or out of male as well as seigniorial authority. Whereas young males entering the lordship would ultimately, if not immediately, belong to such authority in the tithing or frankpledge system, singlewomen would not. For that reason also, perhaps, the peasants finding pledges on the manor of Hales "pro bona gestione" (for good behaviour) were predominantly (but not exclusively) female, seemingly of independent status, and probably amongst whom some at least were newcomers.[47] The context is also the possibility that singlewomen, with slender resources, might be responsible for some forms of misbehaviour, such as hedge breaking for firewood; that indeed was the circumstance for the finding of pledges for good behaviour by Lucy ate Wele in Hales in 1294.[48] It was often, moreover, (single)women who harboured outsiders.[49] Consequently, prejudice against singlewomen might have made their settlement in some rural vills difficult.[50]

Hales, however, also contained an urban centre, which was an attractive venue for female immigrants. Hilton has suggested that fully three-quarters of immigrants to small town Hales were female between 1272 and 1350. It was precisely these females who were suspected of disorder and it was often female hucksters who extended hospitality to the immigrants, establishing quasi-lodging houses.[51] In this small-town context, then, immigration was female-led and it is only through the survival of the court rolls that this phenomenon can be detected.

Early evidence of flight from lordship is provided by the evolution of the writ *de nativo habendo*. Although by the early thirteenth century, its deployment had become a means to initiate a trial in the royal courts about status, yet its origins must have been in actual flights. The existence of royal demesne operated alongside flight from lordship, at least for some time, for the writ, before 1238, could not be executed on royal demesne, and after 1238 could not be executed there if the villein had been resident for more than a year and a day.[52] It is possible, nevertheless, that in the thirteenth century, the fugitive villeins were not seriously pursued as unfree labour was abundant.[53] On the other hand, reception of villeins remained a problem, because of the possible confusion of status and land, perhaps exemplified in Robert *de Gloucestria*, who was unfree ("qui non est liber nacione [sic]") who held a virgate of free land on the Bishop of Hereford's manor of Sevenhampton, but was emphatically defined as holding it at the lord's will ("ad voluntatem domini").[54]

The intermittent manner in which villeins were pursued by some lords is demonstrated on the immense, composite manor of Wakefield. In 1275, the earl's officials instigated an effort to recover villein *fugitivi*, locating where the fugitives were staying and ordering their arrest and return. Nine villeins were thus identified in 1275 as residing in six places in Yorkshire, four of them at Pontefract, but others at Snaith, Rowcliffe, Birley, Haldworth and Heaton.[55] The policy, however, did not, it seems, persist. Conversely, the earl's officials made some attempts to regulate the entry of immigrants, occasionally to a considerable effort. Thus when Marmeduke de Nottingham was found on the manor in 1297, the earl's officials sought written testimonials from the mayor and officials of Nottingham as to Marmeduke's character.[56]

The earlier development of the writ might have been informed or complicated by another aspect of mobility, however, in the provisions for the itinerant (*homo uagans*) who has a lord and the one who has no lord.[57] The *dictum* of the *Leges Henrici Primi* of 1114x1118 on this point of the itinerant, allows a perception of mobility in the early twelfth century, but it is impossible to consider its extent. The importance of the problem exercised the mind of the author of the *Leges*, for he further recounted that no one should harbour a stranger (*ignotus*) or itinerant (*vagrans*) for more than three days without a pledge of good conduct.[58] The *Leges* indeed provide more information about mobility, for it was already customary that persons who were landless might find work elsewhere, even in another county.[59] Such movement might best be considered subsistence.

Rural mobility was already experienced by the peasantry by the early twelfth century, despite the restrictions of mobility on the unfree. Indeed, the definition of carrying services in the twelfth and thirteenth centuries might assist further in elucidating the formation of migration fields in the twelfth century, although a considerable amount of the movement would have been to urban centres.[60] Again, sufficient is understood about the normal distances (in the statistical sense and sense of customary) of migration fields in the rural context. McClure considered the normative migration pattern in rural Nottinghamshire as up to ten miles, for, from an analysis of toponymic bynames in lay subsidies, fifty-eight to sixty-one percent of migrations were between one and ten miles.[61] Similar distances were experienced in rural Leicestershire.[62] In this context allusion has been made to Bracton's notion of distance to market in the context of tortious nuisance, assumed to be six and two thirds miles, so that implicitly one influence on migration fields was peasant marketing arrangements and periodic markets .[63] It might, equally, however, be as important to define movement in terms of the number of parishes traversed as distances measured in miles, especially in woodland regions with large parishes and dispersed settlement. What is apparent, however, is that rural movement was much more circumscribed than rural-urban migration, that male migrants moved shorter distances in the countryside than males who moved from countryside into larger urban centres, although movement into small towns involved no greater movements than migration within the countryside.

Whilst some of this migration within a rural context was undoubtedly to acquire landholding opportunities, some no doubt was less ambitious. In the late thirteenth century, William son of Roger de Syston' quit the lordship of Merton College at Barkby illicitly to take up service, but later acknowledged the lordship of the College and was permitted licence to take up service outside the lordship.[64] Movement for servanthood was thus already a customary phenomenon in the rural milieu of the late thirteenth century.

There are, nevertheless, other patterns which might be worth investigating, which concern the directions of migration rather than simply distances. The importance of this approach was perhaps implicit in an early study by Raftis of peasant movements in Huntingdonshire from an analysis of the toponymic bynames of peasants in the lay subsidies.[65] Whilst, however, Raftis mapped the directions of movements, patterns were not really elicited, other than the localised nature of migration.

One of the issues of late medieval economic transition is the relative balance between *pays*–the contrasting fortunes of, for example, woodland and champion regions.[66] It is an interesting point how far migration reflected and contributed to any changes between different *pays*. Moreover, there were persistent inter-relationships between some *pays* which were complementary, such as river and wold, and the extent of migration between such inter-locking *pays* might be explored.[67]

Interestingly, Kristensson also investigated the direction of movement, from an analysis of toponymic bynames in the lay subsidies for Lindsey, the northern "Part" of Lincolnshire, from which he deduced that Lindsey exhibited a closer association with southern Yorkshire than with the rest of Lincolnshire, the southern "Parts" of Kesteven and Holland.[68] Such a suggestion alluringly introduces the question of "cultural provinces" which has been expounded by Phythian-Adams, although Kristensson's conclusion is inconsistent with those "provinces".[69] Such socio-spatial configurations–bounded in physical but also cultural terms–were defined by drainage basins and associated watersheds and consisted of a combination of counties with complementary features, culturally and socially, which were significantly inward-looking.[70] Analysis of the direction of migration might thus allow some sort of representation of those cultural and social spaces of an intermediate size. In this context, there is a larger framework for migration reinforcing localised customs and practices, for at the lower level there remains the intensely localised pattern and process, confirming the *espace vécu*, whilst the "province" represents a higher and intermediate level (intermediate between local society and nation).[71] An investigation into the meaning of these provinces might be elicited by analysis of the general direction of movement within the province or an examination of migration at their edges or margins. What investigation of some aspects of the edges of some of these provinces has revealed to date is short-distance migration across the edges, but no deep penetration across cultural provinces. Nevertheless, the lack of deep penetration might simply be a function of intensely localised migration rather than an indicator of the resilience of "cultural provinces".[72]

Sometimes, however, long-distance migration was dictated by personal circumstance, a tactic of evasion and avoidance. Adultery or separation were, for example, just such circumstances. Thus Robert Huthe of Grantham (Lincolnshire) had moved about seventy miles to Babraham (Cambridgeshire.) to live in adultery with Agnes la Rus, whilst his wife, Mariota Carter of Grantham and his six children were deserted.[73] Perhaps a similar distance was moved by Ralph son of William son of Thomas de Torkeseye who was intending to commit adultery in Peterborough, but was to be compelled by ecclesiastical authority to return to his wife, Beatrice de Walcote.[74] Gilbert de Humberstone had migrated to Lincoln, perhaps thirty-eight miles away, when Agnes *dicta Maydended'* claimed to be his deserted wife, although Gilbert denied the union, so perhaps at issue was the ambiguity of the formation of marriage.[75] In 1274, Alice, the wife of Elias Baugecler broke into another tenant's grange and stole four sheaves of grain; her chattels, consequently, were confiscated for this theft and, as a result, she was compelled to sell her land to Robert, the very neighbour from whom she had stolen.[76] Her destitution, it transpired, resulted because Elias had fled the manor. Migration in these cases was not by singletons, but by those with commitments, but as a consequence of their ties had perhaps moved longer distances.

Short-distance mobility, rather than migration, was motivated by a variety of personal reasons, sometimes associated with kinship as when his nephew from Dorset was the first finder of the body of Thomas Anderbode who had drowned in the River Yarty on the Devon side. In Colyton Hundred, also in Devon, Nicholas Pain was mortally wounded as he returned from an *alefest* in Dorset. Further into Devon, Gerald de Tottwurthe fell from his horse on Widecumbe Moor, the value of the horse as a deodand being discounted as Gerald hailed from Somerset.[77]

The representation and status of some spaces was another important influence on the movement of some particular groups of migrants. The flight of "criminals" is perhaps atypical, but the existence of "sacred" spaces was an attraction. Discounting parish churches as minor sanctuaries, providing forty days of refuge for the outlawed or waived before abjuration of the realm, the greater sanctuaries functioned as an important attraction if the felony was committed in their vicinity. When, in the mid thirteenth century, John de Elaund killed William *filius Petri*, he fled to the sanctuary (*ad pacem*) of Tynemouth; he was followed there by another perpetrator, Alan *filius Laurencii* who had beaten Richard Arkill in the liberty of Hexham. Another accused of homicide, Lyolf *Braciator*, also took refuge there, as did Agnes, who had killed Susan, been imprisoned at Newcastle, but escaped, and fled to the sanctuary.[78] The liberty of Ripon was the sanctuary to which Elias son of Thomas Spynk fled from the manor of Wakefield after killing Roger de Wyrunth' in 1275.[79] Within these privileged spaces, there was always the possibility of penance and then survival as a *grithman*.[80]

In a different vein, "the geography of pilgrimage", "sacred" spaces invited others, not as permanent migrants, perhaps, but encouraged movement. Movement to some shrines, like that of St. Godric at Finchale, was intensely localised, predominantly from within a radius of forty miles. Even more localised were the visits to the shrine of St. William of Norwich, overwhelmingly from within a radius of ten miles. The greater cults attracted longer distances of movement, so there is a sort of distance-decay of the geography of saints' cults.[81] Pentecostal processions to the mother church of the diocese or an appointed closer alternative were another influence of spiritual space upon secular movement, as noted above.

In the later middle ages, after 1350 and especially in the fifteenth century, the survival of depositions in litigation, especially spousal causes, in the ecclesiastical forum allows a detailed perception of migration. Although that source represents largely a particular life-course servanthood—and a particular circumstance—bethrothal—it provides a more elaborate understanding of migration and mobility of *both* gender than is available for an earlier time.[82] Before the fourteenth century, our comprehension of the processes as well as the patterns of migration and mobility is restricted by the evidence available. Lordship was a formative, but variable, influence in the process of migration, both in controlling people and defining spaces. Fundamental to the movement of people in the middle ages, especially before 1348, its impact was variable, as it might not only inform patterns of migration, but also the decision to migrate and the choice of where to migrate, inside or outside the lordship, depending on contingent circumstances. Lordship was thus a quintessential variable in medieval migration. Migration was, however, not only a social, legal and economic process, but was also embedded in cultural activity. Even in terms of the geographical aspects of migration, cultural expectations were inherent, for the decision had to be made whether to move within what was familiar and thus to reinforce the known, or whether to move outside the certain. It is possible that such considerations structured migration over the *longue durée*, but within that structuration, agency and contingency still intervened. The decision to migrate was still personal and movement was a personal experience. Accordingly, an attempt has been made to reinsert here what we know of personal experience of migration before 1348, within the context of the control of people and space.

Whilst this chapter has endeavoured to provide an overview of migration during the "high" middle ages, it is still desirable to investigate at the local level in more detail exactly how the mechanism of migration worked and contributed towards the formation of localities. The following chapter therefore attempts to elucidate those processes, but more particularly the patterns, of migration, through an examination of quantifiable data from the late thirteenth and early fourteenth centuries.

Notes

[1]With apologies to Dudley Baines, *Migration in a Mature Economy. Emigration and Internal Migration in England and Wales 1861-1900* (Cambridge: Cambridge University Press, 1985). The status of the English economy contemporary with the migration described here is probably most succinctly elucidated by Richard H. Britnell, *The Commercialisation of English Society 1000-1500* (Cambridge: Cambridge University Press, 1993); an argument for a more integrated economy, connecting peasant productivity and urban commercialism has been advanced by James Masschaele, *Peasants, Merchants and Markets. Inland Trade in Medieval England, 1150-1350* (London: Macmillan, 1997).

[2]These theoretical issues have recently been diagrammatically represented by Colin Pooley and Jean Turnbull, *Migration and Mobility in Britain since the 18th Century* (London: UCL Press,1999), 5.

[3]Laurence R. Poos, "Population Turnover in Medieval Essex: The Evidence of Some Early-fourteenth century Tithing Lists," in *The World We Have Gained. Histories of Population and Social Structure* ed. Lloyd Bonfield, Richard Smith and Keith Wrightson (Oxford: Blackwell, 1986), 1-22, is an innovative approach to an intractable problem using a less usual source. The paradigmatic study remains Peter McClure, "Patterns of Migration in the Late Middle Ages: The Evidence of English Place-name Surnames," *Economic History Review* 2nd ser. 32 (1979): 167-82, a methodology considered by Maryanne Kowaleski, *Local Markets and Regional Trade in Medieval Exeter* (Cambridge: Cambridge University Press, 1995), 84-86; Simon Penn, "The Origins of Bristol Migrants in the Early Fourteenth Century: The Surname Evidence," *Transactions of the Bristol and Gloucestershire Archaeological Society* 101 (1983): 123-30; and Gervase Rosser, *Medieval Westminster 1200-1540* (Oxford: Oxford University Press, 1989), 349-61. Research using evidence from court rolls is reviewed below. Since all these studies have confirmed that migration was localised, the methodology adopted here is to accept the nearest place-name.

[4]The nature of this intensely localised social organisation is perhaps best established in the description by French geographers of *l'espace vécu*: Claval, *Regional Geography*, 22, 45-46. For how migration confirmed rather than weakened local cultural space, see also Pooley and Turnbull, *Migration and Mobility*, 308.

[5]For the full implications of recursion in migration, Allan Pred, *Making Histories and Constructing Human Geographies: The Local Transformation of Practice, Power Relations and Consciousness* (Boulder, CO: Westview Press, 1990), a concept partly adapted from the structuration theory of Anthony Giddens; the localised, repetitive and circular aspects of personal patterns of migration (longitudinal

migration paths) have been revealed by Göran Hoppe and Jack Langton around Vadstena.

[6]This characterisation of migration fields is thus somewhat in accord with Peter Clark and David Souden, eds., *Migration and Society in Early Modern England* (London: Hutchinson, 1987), "Introduction", 11-48.

[7]This point is emphatically treated by Pooley and Turnbull, *Migration and Mobility.*

[8]Kowaleski, *Local Markets and Regional Trade*, 84-86; McClure, "Patterns of Migration in the Late Middle Ages," which established a paradigm which is now twenty years old; Penn, "The Origins of Bristol Migrants," 123-30; Steven H. Rigby, *Medieval Grimsby. Growth and Decline* (Hull: Hull University Press, 1993), 20-22; Derek Keene, *Survey of Medieval Winchester*, Winchester Studies vol. 2 (Oxford: Oxford University Press, 1985), 376. For an earlier study of a small town, Eleanor M. Carus-Wilson, "The First Half-century of the Borough of Stratford-upon-Avon," repr. in *The Medieval Town. A Reader in English Urban History 1200-1540* ed. Richard Holt and Gervase Rosser (London: Longman, 1990), 49-70. For the metropolis, Eilert Ekwall, *Studies on the Population of Medieval London* (Stockholm: Vitterhets Historie och Antikvitets Handlingar. Filologisk-filosofiska Serien 2, 1956).

[9]Paper presented at the Anglo-American Symposium on the Medieval Economy and Society at Witham, Essex, July 1998.

[10]For the concept of "intervening opportunities", developed by Stouffer, Huw Jones, *Population Geography* (London: Chapman, 1990), 178-255; for the original proposition, Samuel Stouffer, "Intervening Opportunities: A Theory Relating Mobility and Distance," *American Sociological Review* 5 (1940): 845-67, and "Intervening Opportunities and Competing Migrants," *Journal of Regional Science* 2 (1960): 1-26.

[11]For these suburban opportunities, Christopher C. Dyer, "Towns and Cottages in Eleventh-century England," in his *Everyday Life in Medieval England* (London: Hambledon. 1994), 241-56; Derek J. Keene, "Suburban Growth," in *The Medieval Town*, ed. Holt and Rosser, 97-119. Whilst McClure refined the methodology relating to the problem of ambiguous place-names, there remains the issue of heritability of surnames in the urban context, which might have been more precocious than in the rural; this issue is addressed by Kowaleski, *Local Markets and Regional Trade*, 84, n. 23.

[12]Mention should again be made, however, to Poos, "Population Turnover," for an innovative approach to mobility; Barbara Hanawalt, *Crime and Conflict in English Communities 1300-1348* (Cambridge, Mass.: Harvard University Press,1979), 133-4, raises the prospect of using Crown Pleas and "criminal" proceedings for the life-histories of a specific type of migrant.

[13]Christopher Dyer, *Lords and Peasants in a Changing Society. The Estates of the Bishopric of Worcester 680-1540* (Cambridge: Cambridge University Press,1980), 109; Barbara F. Harvey, "The Population Trend in England Between 1300 and 1348," *Transactions of the Royal Historical Society* 5th ser. 16 (1966), 28; for an extreme example of low numbers assessed Alexander T. Gaydon, ed., *The Taxation of 1297*, Bedfordshire Historical Record Society vol. 39 (1959 for 1958), xxxiii, and compare Andrew Jones, "Caddington, Kensworth, and Dunstable in 1297," *Economic History Review* 2nd ser. 32 (1979), 324; for the reasons, the basis for the assessments, James

F. Willard, *Parliamentary Taxes on Personal Property 1290-1334: A Study in Medieval English Financial Administration* (Cambridge, Mass.: Medieval Academy of America, 1934), 81-85; John R. Maddicott, "The English Peasantry and the Demands of the Crown 1294-1341," repr. in *Landlords, Peasants and Politics in England* ed. Trevor H. Aston (Cambridge: Cambridge University Press,1987), 302.

[14]Kowaleski, *Local Markets and Regional Trade*, 96; David G. Shaw, *The Creation of a Community. The City of Wells in the Middle Ages* (Oxford: Oxford University Press, 1993), 142.

[15]Peter R. Coss, ed., *The Early Records of Medieval Coventry*, British Academy Records of Social and Economic History n.s. 11 (Oxford, 1986), 55 (37.13).

[16]John Amphlett, Sidney G. Hamilton, and R. A. Wilson, eds., *Court Rolls of the Manor of Hales, 1272-1307*, 3 vols., Worcestershire Historical Society (Worcester, 1910-33), vol. 1, 122.

[17]William P. Baildon, ed., *Court Rolls of the Manor of Wakefield*, vol. 1, Yorkshire Archaeological Society Record Series vol. 29 (1901), 248.

[18]Chicago Bacon MS 114: "Matilda filia Ber[n]ardi dat .vij.s. pro habendo partem que fuit Willelmi filii Ber[n]ardi et post mortem matris habebit partem matris sue quia Willelmus filius Ber[n]ardi rectus heres manet apud London' et weyuauit dictam terram et Dominus cepit in manum suam partem suam et tradidit illam dicte Matilde ... Willelmus filius Ber[n]ardi manet apud London' [et] tenet .vj. acras terre de Conuentu et est fugitiuus" (1259).

[19]C. A. Clarke, "Peasant Society and Land Transactions in Chesterton, Cambridgeshire, 1277-1325," unpublished D.Phil. (University of Oxford, 1985), 3.

[20]Clarke, "Peasant society," 4.

[21]Clarke, "Peasant society," 161.

[22]Clarke, "Peasant society," 160-1.

[23]D. B. Grigg, "E. G. Ravenstein and the 'Laws of Migration'," in *Time, Family and Community. Perspectives on Family and Community History*, ed. Michael Drake (Oxford, 1994), 154, but for a contrary perception, Pooley and Turnbull, *Migration and Mobility*, 308.

[24]P. Jeremy P. Goldberg, "Marriage, Migration, Servanthood and Life-cycle in Yorkshire Towns in the Later Middle Ages," *Continuity and Change* 1 (1986): 141-69; Goldberg, "Urban Identity and the Poll Taxes of 1377, 1379, and 1380-1," *Economic History Review* 2nd ser. 43 (1990): 194-216; Goldberg, *Women, Work, and Life Cycle in a Medieval Economy*, esp. 280-304; for a critique of the use of ecclesiastical cause papers relating to marriage litigation, *idem*, "Marriage, Migration, and Servanthood: The York Cause Paper Evidence," in *Women in Medieval English Society* ed. Goldberg (Gloucester: Sutton,1997), 1-15.

[25]J. Ambrose Raftis, *Tenure and Mobility. Studies in the Social History of the Mediaeval English Village* (Toronto: University of Toronto Press, 1964); Frances Davenport, "The Decay of Villeinage in East Anglia," in *Essays in Economic History* vol. 2, ed. Eleanor M. Carus-Wilson (London: Edward Arnold, repr. 1966), 112-24; Ernie Jones, "Villein Mobility in the Later Middle Ages: The Case of Spalding Priory," *Nottingham Medieval Studies* 36 (1992): 151-66; R. K. Field, "Migration in the Later Middle Ages: The Case of the Hampton Lovett Villeins," *Midland History* 8 (1983): 29-48; Cecily (Sally) Howell, *Land, Kinship and Inheritance in Transition: Kibworth Harcourt 1280-1700* (Cambridge: Cambridge University Press, 1983). For

circumstances in which chevage did not necessarily represent migration, Harold S. A. Fox, "Exploitation of the Landless by Lords and Tenants in Early Medieval England," in *Medieval Society and the Manor Court* ed. Zvi Razi and Richard Smith (Oxford: Oxford University Press, 1996), 518-68. The problem of data about *fugitivi* is that the new location of the escaped villeins is not always specified: "Johannes filius Walteri de Wyllynghbear' Petrus de Wyllynghbear' Henricus de eadem et Ricardus atte Pytte proximores parentes Henrici Sherlouk' et Roberti Sherloc' natiuorum dominorum et fugitiuorum in misericordia quia ipsos non habuerunt": Devon Record Office CR 1435 (Yarcombe, 1338).

[26]Richard M. Smith, "Some Issues Concerning Families and Their Property in Rural England, 1250-1800," in *Land, Kinship and Life-cycle* ed. Smith (Cambridge: Cambridge University Press,1984), 35; Ann Kussmaul, "The Ambiguous Mobility of Farm Servants," *Economic History Review* 2nd ser. 34 (1981): 222-35; Herbert E. Hallam, "Some Thirteenth-century Censuses," *Economic History Review* 2nd ser. 10 (1957-8): 340-61, indicated the level of movement between the Priory's manors in the middle of the thirteenth century.

[27]For the later period, Michael Roberts, "'Waiting upon chance': English Hiring Fairs and Their Meaning from the 14th to the 20th Century," *Journal of Historical Sociology* 1 (1988): 119-60; Alan Everitt, "Country, County and Town: Patterns of Regional Evolution in England," *Transactions of the Royal Historical Society*, 5th ser. 29 (1979): 79-108.

[28]Anne DeWindt, "Redefining the Peasant Community in Medieval England: The Regional Perspective," *Journal of British Studies* 26 (1987): 163-207.

[29]Jones, "Villein mobility," 164.

[30]"Homagium elegit ad terram apud Hekkele tenendam Willelmum Russel Johannem le Rede et Johannem Seward": Bodleian Library Oxford Queen's College MS 99. I am grateful to the College for permission to examine and cite this document.

[31]Avrom Saltman, ed., *The Cartulary of Tutbury Priory*, Historical Manuscripts Commission JP2 (1962), 72 (no. 63).

[32]Robin Fleming, *Kings and Lords in Conquest England* (Cambridge: Cambridge University Press, 1991), 149–perhaps a territorial lordship constituted on a hundredal basis.

[33]Bodleian Library Oxford MS Laud Misc. 625, fols. 191r-211r.

[34]A. Elizabeth Levett, *Studies in Manorial History* ed. Helen M. Cam, M. Coate and Lucy S. Sutherland (Oxford: Clarendon Press, 1938), 327.

[35]Bodleian Library Oxford MS Laud Misc. 625, fols. 187-189; Rodney H. Hilton, *The Economic Development of Some Leicestershire Estates in the XIVth and XVth Centuries* (Oxford: Oxford University Press, 1947). For more details, see Chapter 2.

[36]For the potential importance of longitudinal studies, difficult as they are to acquire, Pooley and Turnbull, *Migration and Mobility*.

[37]British Library Cotton MS. Tib. BII; *Censuarii* and *consuetudinarii* have been defined as semi-free, although their status was more towards unfreedom. For the background, Edward Miller, *The Abbey and Bishopric of Ely* (Cambridge: Cambridge University Press, 1951).

[38]This statement is based on an examination of G. C. Bridgman, ed., "The Burton Abbey Twelfth-century Surveys", *Collections for a History of Staffordshire*

edited by the William Salt Archaeological Society (1918 for 1916), 212-47; William H. Hart and Ponsonby A. Lyons, eds., *Cartularium Monasterii de Rameseia* vol. 3, Rolls Series (London, 1894), 241-315; Marjorie Chibnall, ed., *Charters and Custumals of the Abbey of Holy Trinity, Caen,* British Academy Records of Social and Economic History, n.s. 5 (1982), 39-74; Beatrice A. Lees, ed., *Records of the Templars in England in the Twelfth Century,* BARSEH 9 (1935), 1-135; William H. Hale, ed., *The Domesday of St Paul's in the Year* M.CC.XXII, Camden Society vol. 69 (London, 1858), 1-106.

[39]*Curia Regis Rolls* vol. 1 (London, 1922), 126 (Surrey).

[40]Merton College, Oxford, MM 6565: William *Carpentar'* found pledges to satisfy the lords "pro Matillda sorore sua desponsata apud Warrum sine licencia... Inquisicio facta de Catallis et bonis que Matill' Carpentar' habuit die quo perexit apud sanctum andream in scocia quia maritatur dudum extra libertatem dominorum sine licencia."

[41]Merton College, Oxford, MM 6568: perhaps ca.1300.

[42]Jan Z. Titow, 'Some Differences Between Manors and Their Effects on the Condition of the Peasantry in the Thirteenth Century," *Agricultural History Review* 10 (1962): 113-28; but compare Barbara F. Harvey, "The Population Trend in England Between 1300 and 1348"; for the present purposes, fines to marry widows with their land are not considered.

[43]Barbara F. Harvey, *Westminster Abbey and its Estates in the Middle Ages* (Oxford: Oxford University Press, 1977), 225.

[44]Such a convoluted phrase is perhaps even so more felicitous than notions of "open" and "closed" villages, which may be an anachronism for this time, and are, even for a much later period, somewhat contested: Sarah Banks, "Nineteenth-century Scandal or Twentieth-century Model? A New Look at 'open' and 'closed' parishes," *Economic History Review* 2nd ser. 41 (1988): 51-73.

[45]Ralph H. C. Davis, ed., *The Kalendar of Abbot Samson of Bury St Edmunds and Related Documents,* Camden Society, 3rd ser. 84 (London, 1954), 151 (no. 130).

[46]Merton College, Oxford, MM 6206-6222 (account rolls).

[47]*Court Rolls of the Manor of Hales,* for example, vol. 1, 234 for a female, but 8 for a male; for other reasons for males taking out such bindings over, 247 (William le Turner "de verbis contumeliosis").

[48]*Court Rolls of the Manor of Hales,* vol. 1, 270. Note that all the (six) peasants accused of this misbehaviour in 1293 were (single)women: ibid., 261. For the general context, McIntosh, *Controlling Misbehavior,* esp. 82-88.

[49]*Court Rolls of the Manor of Hales,* vol. 1, 193.

[50]For the whole issue, Judith Bennett and Amy Froide, eds., *Singlewomen in the European Past 1200-1800* (Chicago: University of Chicago Press, 1999).

[51]Rodney H. Hilton, "Lords, Burgesses and Hucksters," in his *Class Conflict and the Crisis of Feudalism* (London: Hambledon, 1985), 200; Heather Swanson, *Medieval British Towns* (Basingstoke: Palgrave, 1999), 70.

[52]Paul R. Hyams, *King, Lords and Peasants in Medieval England. The Common Law of Villeinage in the Twelfth and Thirteenth Centuries* (Oxford: Oxford University Press, 1980), 162-3 and 168-9.

[53]Swanson, *Medieval British Towns,* 70.

[54]Arthur T. Bannister, ed., "A Transcript of 'The Red Book' of the Bishopric of

Hereford (*c.*1290)," *Camden Miscellany XV,* Camden Society, 3rd ser. 41 (London, 1929), 27.

[55]*Court Rolls of Wakefield,* vol. 1, 35 and 50-51.

[56]*Court Rolls of Wakefield,* vol. 1, 272.

[57]Leslie J. Downer, ed., *Leges Henrici Primi* (Oxford: Oxford University Press, 1972), 180-1 (c. 58,1).

[58]*Leges Henrici Primi,* 102-3 (c. 8,5).

[59]*Leges Henrici Primi,* 102-3 (c. 8,4). Perhaps this recognition is similar to that under the Statute of Labourers of 1351 which allowed customary migration for summer work from Staffordshire, Lancashire, Derbyshire, Craven, and the Welsh Marches: Robert Palmer, *English Law in the Age of the Black Death 1348-1381. A Transformation of Government and Law* (Chapel Hill, NC: University of North Carolina Press, 1993), 20. Information fields, migration and itinerancy might have been informed in the twelfth century by other processes: Pentecostal processions and monastic distributions of alms: Martin Brett, *The English Church under Henry I* (Oxford: Oxford University Press, 1975), 162-4; Barbara F. Harvey, *Living and Dying in England 1100-1540. The Monastic Experience* (Oxford: Oxford University Press, 1993), 30; Reginald R. Darlington, ed., *The Cartulary of Worcester Cathedral Priory (Register 1),* Pipe Roll Society n.s. 38 (1968 for 1962-63) (the itinerant poor might be prepared as the day was fixed, St. Wulfstan's day). For a later example, the distribution of alms at East Monkton by the rector, Glastonbury Abbey, in 1393-4: "In quadam distribucione facta pauperibus apud Est Monketon' die sancti Basilii .viij.s. cuilibet venienti .j.d.": Longleat MS 10699. In a large diocese, like Lincoln, the Pentecostal processions might be redirected to more local centres, such as Eynsham or St Albans, either to encourage participation or to benefit the religious house: David M. Smith, *English Episcopal Acta I Lincoln 1067-1185* (London: British Academy, 1980), 75-76 (nos 116-17); Charles W. Foster, ed., *Registrum Antiquissimum of the Cathedral Church of Lincoln,* LRS 13 (no. 322); in York diocese to Southwell minster, cited by Brett; in Chichester diocese to Lewes or Hastings: Frederick M. Powicke and Christopher R. Cheney, eds., *Councils & Synods with Other Documents Relating to the English Church* II *A.D. 1205-1313* Part 1 *1205-1265* (Oxford: Oxford University Press, 1964), 416-18. See also chapter 3.

[60]The Queen's College, Oxford, MS 366, fol. 17r (Kilsby, manor of the Bishop of Lincoln, 1225x1257): *Operarii* holding one virgate: "et qualibet septimana dum bladum episcopi fuerit ad uendendum cariare per j diem dimidium quarterium bladi apud Kouentre uel Northhamton' et habere j quadrantem de quolibet dimidio quarterio." See, in general, Masschaele, *Peasants, Merchants and Markets,* 204-7.

[61]McClure, "Patterns of Migration,"175-6.

[62]Below, chapter 2.

[63]Samuel E. Thorne, ed. and trans., *Bracton on the Laws and Customs of England* vol. 3 (Cambridge, Mass., 1977), 198-9. The most recent statement about periodic markets and the integration of peasant marketing with urban trade is Masschaele, *Peasants, Merchants and Markets,* esp. 165-88.

[64]Merton College, Oxford, MM 6565: "Quia Willelmus filius Roggeri de Syston' non venit in libertatem dominorum quorum custumarius ipse est set se subtraxit de dominis suis et est in seruicio extra libertatem ideo preceptum est facere ipsum

venire cognossendi dominos suos et capiendi ab eis licenciam seruiendi ubi voluerit."

[65]J. Ambrose Raftis, "Geographical Mobility in Lay Subsidy Rolls," *Mediaeval Studies* 38 (1976):385-403.

[66]For the late middle ages, the comparisons are explored extensively in Edward Miller, ed., *The Agrarian History of England and Wales* vol. III *1348-1500* (Cambridge: Cambridge University Press, 1991).

[67]Harold S. A. Fox, "The People of the Wolds in English Settlement History," in *The Rural Settlement of Medieval England* ed. Michael Aston, David Austin and Christopher Dyer (Oxford: Blackwell, 1989), 77-101.

[68]Gillis Kristensson, *Studies on the Early Fourteenth Century Population of Lindsey* (Lund: Lund University, 1976-77).

[69]Charles Phythian-Adams, "Introduction: An Agenda for English Local History,' in *Societies, Cultures and Kinship, 1580-1850. Cultural Provinces and English Local History* ed. Phythian-Adams (Leicester and London: Scholar Press,1993), 1-23.

[70]The construction of space, however, is both representational and socially practised or produced, part of that practice being, it might be supposed, migration: Lefebvre, *Production of Space.*

[71]For the *espace vécu*, Claval, *Regional Geography*, 138-60.

[72]Dave Postles, "Surnames and the Composition of Local Populations: Rutland, 13th to 17th Centuries," *East Midland Geographer* 16 (1993): 27-38; projects for the University of Leicester M.A. course in English Local History: Societies, Cultures and Nation by Beryl Tracey (1998) and Matt Badcock (1999), which examined respectively south Lincolnshire (Witham "province") and the edges of three "provinces" in the South-West.

[73]Rosalind M. T. Hill, ed., *The Rolls and Register of Bishop Oliver Sutton 1280-1299* vol. 6, LRS vol. 64 (1969), 84.

[74]*The Rolls and Register of Bishop Oliver Sutton*, vol. 6, 195.

[75]*The Rolls and Register of Bishop Oliver Sutton*, vol. 6, 202.

[76]*Court Rolls of the Manor of Wakefield*, vol. 1, 4 and 6.

[77]Henry Summerson, ed., *Crown Pleas of the Devon Eyre*, Devon and Cornwall Record Society n.s. vol. 28 (1985), 12, 18, 22. These examples illustrate the potential of Crown Pleas for the mobility of medieval populations, for the movements of persons other than "criminals".

[78]William Page, ed., *Three Early Assize Rolls for the County of Northumberland Saec. XIII*, SS vol. 88 (1891), 87-88, 93, 98 and see also 338.

[79]*Court Rolls of the Manor of Wakefield*, vol. 1, 50.

[80]Perhaps the best exposition of the formation of these privileged places is now Rosenwein, *Negotiating Space.*, esp. for England, 192-202.

[81]Ronald C. Finucane, *Miracles and Pilgrims. Popular Beliefs in Medieval England* (Basingstoke: Macmillan, repr. 1995), 152-72; the term "the geography of pilgrimage" is his.

[82]Questions are asked of the York evidence also by Frederick Pedersen, "Demography in the Archives: Social and Geographical Factors in the Fourteenth-century Cause Paper Marriage Litigation," *Continuity and Change* 10 (1995): 405-36.

2
The Pattern of Rural Migration in a Midlands County: Leicestershire, ca. 1270-1350

Levels and patterns of migration are better documented for early-modern than for medieval England.[1] Despite earlier and more recent research by J. Ambrose Raftis and members of the "Toronto School", Larry Poos and Richard Smith, there is still room for additional information.[2] To some extent, all these studies are local or regional, so that evidence from other localities and regions may add towards perceiving the general pattern. Medieval populations, unlike those of early-modern England, were divided into two legal statuses: free and unfree. The unfree were subjected to seigniorial restraints and restrictions on their mobility, but, as recent research has shown, not immobilization.[3] Investigations of the patterns of medieval migration are primarily concerned with three aspects: geographical patterns and distances involved; the life-course stages of migration; and the proportion of the population which was mobile. All these aspects relate to wider sociological issues of household formation, persistence of local populations, and localized customs.

Evidence of rural migration in the middle ages is sparse. The best source for the unfree peasantry is undoubtedly payments of chevage, where this fine was paid to the lord by unfree tenants specifically for license to leave the manor, and the presentment of *fugitivi* (villeins who had fled the manor without the lord's license) in manorial court rolls.[4] For some manors, information of this type can be acquired, but only when the court rolls are both informative and survive in a sufficiently complete series. Bynames have been used as an alternative indicator of rural migration by, for example, Raftis.[5] They have been used more frequently, however, for inferred patterns of migration into towns, as in earlier studies by Ekwall (London), Carus-Wilson (Stratford), and Reaney (Norwich).[6] More recently, Peter McClure has established a clearer methodology, which has subsequently been followed by others who have examined what can be derived from bynames about migration into towns, such as Penn and Kowaleski.[7] Fewer investigations, using bynames, have been made into rural migration than into immigration into boroughs.[8] Further research into patterns of rural migration through the use of bynames may therefore be helpful, since this sort of evidence allows a quantitative approach to the question.

Bynames are second qualifying names (as opposed to forenames) which have not become hereditary, family surnames. Hereditary surnames are defined here as those which are transmitted over three generations of a kinship group. Bynames were still unstable; they might be attached to an individual rather than inherited. Moreover, an individual might be known by different bynames in different contexts and records produced for different purposes. Toponymic bynames are those derived from places of origin, such as John de Craft (John of Croft, Croft being a parish and vill in Leicestershire). Such bynames may thus serve as evidence of migration by individuals or, where they were becoming incipiently hereditary, as *recent* migration by a previous generation.

The only aspect which can be approached through analysis of bynames, however, is that of geographical patterns of migration. This source of data does not illuminate life-course stages of migration, since the evidence is not inherently biographical or prosopographical. Nor do levels of toponymic bynames illuminate population turnover through migration. Firstly, it cannot be assumed that all migrants were allocated a toponymic form of byname in their receiving communities. Secondly, in some sources, such as lists for taxation (lay subsidies), the poorest sections of local societies were probably omitted.[9] These lists do not therefore embrace the whole of village society. Consequently, proportions of toponymic bynames in these lists do not represent the percentage of the population which had moved. Such bynames are therefore best used as quantitative evidence of geographical patterns of migration.

The sources used here are of several different types. The first is that of the lay subsidy of 1327 for Leicestershire, although the analysis has to be ever-mindful of the *caveats* of this type of evidence, which are discussed further above.[10] The subsidy embraces the whole of the county. In an attempt to resolve the difficulties of the lay subsidy, other sources, such as court rolls, rentals, and custumals, have been examined. These other sources provide more prosopographical material than the subsidy and so they illustrate better the process and timing of change from unstable bynames to hereditary surnames, which affects the interpretation of nominal evidence quite critically.

The problem with these other sources, on the other hand, is that they have only a limited geographical coverage, being specific to certain manors. The widest geographical coverage is provided by the custumal of Rothley, produced in the mid-thirteenth century (probably ca.1245).[11] The soke of Rothley comprised dependent manors in about a dozen vills in east and north-east Leicestershire. The rental compiled in 1341 for the estate of Leicester Abbey (called Geryn's rental) enumerated lands in about twenty vills in the county, but there are substantial lists of tenants for only a small number of these vills (for example, the principal manors of Stoughton and Lockington).[12] The great problem with this rental is that hereditary surnames may have become more commonplace by the time of its compilation. The court rolls and rentals of the manors of Merton College in the county, Kibworth Harcourt and Barkby, allow more detailed reconstruction of migration.[13] These manorial sources are examined later on in this chapter. Finally, the evidence of the fragmentary *Rotuli Hundredorum* of 1279-1280 for the county has been considered.[14] After this examination of rural-rural migration, some consideration is given to migration into a small town, Melton Mowbray, for which the evidence is probably better than for other small towns in the county.[15]

The use of bynames is complicated by several variables. Bynames developed into hereditary surnames at different times amongst different social groups and in different regions.[16] For example, bynames remained flexible and unstable in the north of England until much later than in other regions. Whereas unfree peasants in Durham or Lancashire might still have unstable bynames in the late fourteenth and even fifteenth century, those in Oxfordshire, for example, had become stable, hereditary surnames by the end of the thirteenth century.[17] In Devon, it seems that stable surnames developed amongst the free peasantry during the thirteenth century, and amongst the unfree peasantry during the early fourteenth century.[18] In any region, the peasantry acquired stable, hereditary surnames later than other, higher, social groups.

In Leicestershire, both unfree and free peasantry were assuming stable, hereditary surnames during the late thirteenth century and early fourteenth century. The evidence of their acquisition of surnames can only be intimated here. In many vills in the lay subsidy of 1327, several of the taxpayers had the same *cognomen* (roughly , "byname"); in a fair proportion of these cases, the common byname was a toponymic one. These taxpayers probably represented generations of the same kinship group, since many toponymic *cognomina* would seem to be monophyletic (having a single source of origin) rather than polyphyletic (having several sources of origin) *within that settlement*; it seems unlikely that several taxpayers in the same community would have been known coincidentally by the same less common, toponymic byname.[19]

(See Table 2.1, page 71, Recurrent Toponymic Bynames in Single Vills in 1327, showing numbers of instances in one vill)

Where two or three taxpayers in one vill held the same topnymic byname, they may all have been unrelated migrants from the same place of origin to that vill, but they more likely belonged to the same kinship group, one member of which was a recent migrant and whose byname was becoming hereditary. More concrete evidence occurs in manorial court rolls. In those of Barkby and Kibworth Harcourt, for example, it is quite clear that surnames were developing amongst a core of customary tenants of Merton College during the late thirteenth century and had become established more widely before the third decade of the fourteenth. The absolute reliability of the data in the lay subsidy of 1327 is therefore compounded by this transition from flexible bynames to hereditary surnames. Some toponymic bynames were held by more than a single taxpayer in one village, but usually by no more than two, or, at most, three. For example, at Diseworth, three taxpayers were included with the byname *de Wolueye* and in Frisby-on-the-Wreake three with *de Sixteneby*. Overall, two taxpayers with the same byname occurred in forty vills and three with the same byname in three vills. In these cases, it seems likely that the byname was becoming hereditary, so that the incidence of this toponymic byname is not firm evidence of the migration of all its bearers. In the large boroughs of England, hereditary surnames were being assumed by at least the most prominent burgess families. It is quite evident that this was also the case in Leicester. Whether the same situation obtained in the lesser towns of the county is not clear. At best, these complicated data suggest only that one of the several bearers or their recent ancestors may have migrated.

In an earlier study, Raftis suggested that the syndetic form of bynames (that is, when the byname was prefixed by a preposition, usually *de*) is a reliable indicator of recent movement. This contention was based on the belief that, in Huntingdonshire, asyndetic forms (without the prefix) developed only during the later fourteenth century.[20] Syndetic forms are not necessarily a reliable indicator, however, since hereditary surnames did develop initially in syndetic form. Considerable caution must therefore be exercised in using even syndetic forms of toponymic bynames as indicators of recent migration. This problem is considered further below, particularly through prosopographical evidence of the inheritance of syndetic forms found in some manorial court rolls. Where there seems to be evidence that syndetic forms were becoming hereditary, the byname should be counted only once as a recent migration.

Nor can it be assumed that toponymic bynames necessarily reflect migration by a single person. McClure has intimated that, by the time hereditary surnames developed, toponymic surnames reflect no more in concrete terms than the migration of a surname, not necessarily the actual migration of its *current* bearer.[21] Even at an earlier time, when bynames were still flexible, the meaning and derivation of toponymic bynames was not necessarily related to movement of population. The formation of such bynames varied by region. In regions of dispersed settlement, such as parts of the South-West or the North, this form of byname was formed predominantly as a reflection of the pattern of dispersed settlement. Since some people inhabited dispersed hamlets or tenements appurtenant to a manorial center, they became known by the place-name of that dispersed settlement. In this sense, they were truly habitation bynames, and no movement or migration was involved in the process of attributing their byname. This tendency is emphatic in the lay subsidy rolls for these regions, since the tax collectors would have tended to assign place-name bynames in this way to taxpayers living in dispersed settlements (although, in Devon, the evidence of contemporary court rolls suggests that locals may also have known those taxpayers by the same bynames, at least in formal and semi-formal records).[22] Nevertheless, it can be assumed that in the Midlands, by and large, toponymic bynames were formed predominantly through the process of movement and migration, although a small percentage still derived from habitation rather than movement (see below).

Lay subsidies may, furthermore, exaggerate the extent of toponymic bynames. Another problem is the inclusion of the nobility in the taxation. In the following analysis, this social group has, as far as possible, been segregated and excluded from the data. In some regions, toponymic bynames tended to be specifically associated with the legal status of the peasantry. In parts of Oxfordshire, for example, toponymic bynames were held predominantly by the free peasantry rather than the unfree, possibly because there was less seigniorial restriction on the mobility of the free peasantry.[23] It may be also that wealthier social groups tended to have a higher proportion of toponymic bynames. If these bynames thus had a social cachet, then the wealthier peasantry may have had a preference for this form of byname. Since lay subsidies tended to be wealth-specific, the problem of over-representation is thus compounded. The taxation was levied only on those with net disposable personal estate (over and above that needed for subsistence) above a tax threshold. Consequently, it has been established that large numbers of the poorer sections of the peasantry were exempted.[24] These poorer levels of society may have borne other forms of byname (such as patronymic bynames or bynames derived from personal names, which may have been in some cases, elisions of patronymic bynames). The result is that the occurrence of toponymic bynames in lay subsidies is likely to be an over-representation of their actual level within the entire local society.

Conversely, toponymic bynames in the lay subsidy represent only those implicit migrants who had (presumably) successfully constructed a new life, in their new place of residence. There may have been others, migrants also with toponymic bynames, who had not accumulated sufficient wealth after migration to be encompassed by the taxation. The evidence of the subsidy may thus relate perhaps to established rather than more recent migrants, although this suggestion is entirely supposition.

One other caveat is that the subsidy is skewed by gender. It represents basically the assessment of males, with only a small percentage of females, usually widows. The subsidy does not therefore provide an indicator of female migration, which was certainly important throughout the middle ages, but may have been even more localized than migration by males.[25] Toponymic bynames in the lay subsidy therefore pertain really only to fairly successful, male migrants.

With these caveats in mind, it is possible to analyze the toponymic bynames in the lay subsidy for Leicestershire in 1327 as an indicator of rural migration. This chapter concentrates on several aspects of this migration: mean distances migrated; migration between different types of *pays* within the county; the mean levels of taxation of the bearers of toponymic bynames vis-a-vis taxpayers with other forms of byname; and, with some circumspection, the correlation of distances moved and taxation. The relationship between distance moved and level of taxation may have been affected by the nature of the migration: whether for subsistence or betterment. It is not possible to do more than speculate on this point. It is demonstrated that, in Leicestershire (but not necessarily elsewhere), the highest mean level of taxation was associated with those who acquired their toponymic byname from the place at which they were assessed in 1327–that is, those whose byname was eponymous with their permanent place of residence. Not all of these eponymous or homonymous taxpayers were of seigniorial status. Their eponymous toponymic bynames may thus have been a reflection of their affluence within the community, since, in Leicestershire, only a small proportion of these bynames was eponymous in this way.

Leicestershire comprised a number of different *pays* and can also be divided into equivocal dialectal regions. The north and east of the county were dominated by the Wolds, the north and west by woodland, and the south and south-west by a pastoral economy. The river valleys, of the Soar and Wreake, formed another distinctive *pays*. These differences are reflected in the distribution of wealth and population in Domesday Book.[26] The county was also located at the confluence of several dialectal regions, so that dialectal accommodation would be expected within the county. Although within the area of East Midlands Middle English (ME), the county was located at the southern tip of Northern ME dialect, but the south and south-west of the county were influenced also by Southern ME and, particularly, West Midlands ME.[27] Patterns of migration can therefore be related to migration within and between *pays:* but also between dialectal regions, across those bundles of isoglosses which composed dialect boundaries. The whole county formed part of that area of the Five Boroughs (surrounding Derby, Leicester, Nottingham, Lincoln, and Stamford) which came under Scandinavian influence. The need, however, is principally to assess the extent of movement over the isoglosses which ran along the course of Watling Street (the present A5 road). Analysis of ME dialect has already illustrated that there was no clear division here, but that West Midlands dialect spilled over into south-west Leicestershire. Migration between north-east Warwickshire and south-west Leicestershire may have reinforced West Midlands ME in the south-west of the county. Data are thus presented here in several different ways: for the whole county as a comparative measure; for the different *pays;* and for the north and north-east of the county by comparison with the south and south-west. The latter division roughly reflects the two dialectal influences in the county. These two dialectal regions are basically coincidental with the Hundreds and Wapentakes of Gartree, Goscote, and Framland (north and north-east) and Guthhaxton and Sparkenhoe (south and south-west).

In the lay subsidy of 1327 for Leicestershire, just about a quarter of the taxpayers bore toponymic by names. In terms of the total population, this proportion may be too high, for the reasons suggested above. Moreover, these figures include seigniorial bearers of Anglo-Norman toponymic bynames and taxpayers who held toponymic bynames such as le *Northerne.* In subsequent tables, these specific types of byname are excluded. Some imperfections still occur in the figures in the tables here. In some cases, the assessment is illegible; in others, the byname is only partially legible; other *noms d' origine* are ambiguous or unidentifiable.

We can summarize the data for the county's taxpayers in 1327 as follows. In the north and north-east of the county, 741 of 2,834 contributors to the subsidy bore toponymic bynames (twenty-six percent), whilst in the south and south-west 324 of 1,382 did (twenty-three percent).

By and large, the taxpayers with toponymic bynames were assessed at a slightly higher level than taxpayers with all forms of byname in Leicestershire (although not necessarily elsewhere). In the north and north-east of the county, they were assessed at a mean level of 37.78d., compared with 34.18d. for taxpayers with all types of byname; in the south, the differential was between 34.48d. (toponymic) and 29.49d. (all forms of byname). By comparison, taxpayers with patronymic bynames were assessed at considerably lower rates: a mean assessment of 27.51d. in the south and 29.74d. in the north and north-east. Overall, therefore, taxpayers with toponymic bynames may have comprised the wealthiest social group, although there was a wide diversity in individual wealth and some toponymic bynames were associated with very low levels of taxation.

The mean differences of migration implied by the bynames was 13.6 miles in the north and north-east and 10.4 in the south and south-west (with medians of seven miles and five miles respectively). The pattern was thus very localized, confirming what is known of patterns of migration from other sources. The mean figure conceals some longer-distance movement, but the preponderance of movement was within twenty-five miles (See Table 2.1, page 71, Rank Distribution of Inferred Migration in 1327). The taxpayers who had implicitly migrated between one and twenty-five miles had tax assessments broadly in line with the mean figure for all toponymic bynames. The highest taxation fell on those taxpayers who bore toponymic bynames eponymous with the place where they were assessed (See Table 2.2, page 72, Relationship Between Inferred Distances of Migration and Tax Assessment in 1327: Taxpayers at zero miles). Not all of these higher-rate taxpayers were of seigniorial status by any means. In many cases, high taxpayers with eponymous toponymic bynames seem to have been attributed those eponymous bynames precisely because they were the wealthiest and most influential in the community, without necessarily being of seigniorial status.

One important feature of migration into the county was immigration from the West and South Midlands, penetrating into south-west Leicestershire. Some seventeen percent of the toponymic bynames in this part of the county had their origins in the West Midlands (predominantly adjacent Warwickshire) or Northamptonshire. This inward movement may have maintained some aspects of West Midlands dialect across Watling Street in south-west Leicestershire.

The circumscribed distances of migration meant that most moved within a single *pays* (See Table 2.3, page 73, Inferred Migration Within and Between Pays in 1327). Thus most migrants in the Wolds tended to move to another village within the Wolds, and similarly in the pastoral regions, river valleys, and woodlands. To some extent, this pattern may have been influenced by distinctive types of husbandry and occupations within those regions, as specialization may have developed between *pays* during the later middle ages. Where migration occurred between *pays,* the highest movement was between river and Wold, an established interrelationship, and, to a lesser degree, between the Wolds and the pastoral region. There was a basic equilibrium between the *pays*, although the Wolds may have been a net loser of migrants and the river valleys a net gainer.

The numbers involved in net loss and gain are, however, very small and can support only tentative interpretation. On the other hand, it might be expected that the Wolds would be a region susceptible to a net loss of population. The Wolds were a region of late settlement and consequently sparser population. During the later middle ages, the region underwent substantial depopulation. By contrast, the river valleys constituted the most valuable land of the county. The migration from the river valleys to the Wolds, which accounted for a considerable proportion of toponymic bynames in the river valleys, can be explained in the context of the established symbiosis of these two adjacent regions.[28]

The sources of manorial provenance allow a more detailed appraisal of both the nature of bynames and rural migration in the county. The custumal of Rothley was compiled in the mid-thirteenth century (ca.1245), and includes dependent manors in about a dozen vills in east and north-east Leicestershire. The principal problem in using this source derives from the nature of the soke. Since Rothley was, as it were, the central place, there was a tendency to know some of the tenants in dependent manors in other vills by the place of their residence. Consequently, there is a higher proportion of eponymous toponymic bynames caused by the nature of territorial organization. These eponymous toponymic bynames do not represent migration, and are recorded as zero miles in the tables. On the other hand, the custumal has a wide geographical coverage and was also compiled before the general transition from bynames to surnames. There is, therefore, little doubt that most of the bynames represent actual migration by individuals bearing the toponymic byname in the custumal.

The mean distance of inferred migration in the custumal is as low as 9.04 miles, the median being even lower at four miles. Although the maximum distance was ninety miles, the range of distances was fairly compact, indicated by a standard deviation of only 14.09 and a third quartile of only fourteen miles. Of fifty-six toponymic bynames, fourteen were eponymous and another fourteen represented migration of from one to five miles. Over half the bynames indicated migration of under ten miles.[29]

The court rolls and rentals of Barkby provide an even smaller database of toponymic bynames, some twenty-two in all. The documents relate only to the manor of Merton College in the parish of Barkby, which was situated some five miles north-east of the borough of Leicester (and, indeed, included some appurtenant holdings in the borough). The landholding population of the manor comprised twenty-eight customary tenancies in the early fourteenth century. On the other hand, much more prosopographical evidence is available from this source. In particular, more meaningful statements can be advanced about the nature and timing of the change from bynames to hereditary surnames. Some of the toponymic bynames were becoming hereditary surnames by the late thirteenth century and had stabilized in the early fourteenth.

In fact, the development of some other forms of byname illustrates this process more clearly. For example, one of the principal customary tenants of the manor in the late thirteenth century (ca.1279-1296) was known simply as Sampson, with no byname. In the rental of ca.1300, Sampson held nineteen acres of land, the maximum size of holding here. He was reeve in 1286 and possibly in other years. On one occasion, he was known as Sampson de Bark' (1289). In 1287 Henry *filius Sampsonis* occurred, bearing a patronymic byname. This Henry was subsequently known as Henry Sam(p)son, the patronymic form having been elided (1294-1312). His wife, Agnes, held nineteen acres in the rental of 1315. Robert Sam(p)son occurred in the court rolls between 1340 and 1352, and he was succeeded by one or more tenants called Richard Sam(p)son from 1356 through to 1418. When Richard died in 1418, his widow, Matilda, was allowed her free bench in one and a half bovates. Without considering the prosopography of the family in more detail, the evidence illustrates very well the transition to hereditary surnames.

Despite the general change to hereditary surnames in the early fourteenth century, some flexibility could still obtain in a few instances. The most notable example is Pellesone, a metronymic byname. Petronilla de Thorpe appeared in court between 1340 and 1348, twice with the hypocoristic (short- or pet-) form of her forename, Pelle (1348). Her son, Richard, was known as Richard Pellesone de Thorpe, and held a half bovate in 1348. Richard Pellesone occurred in the court rolls between 1348 and 1353. Despite these instances of continued flexibility, however, there was a general transition from bynames to hereditary surnames.

The data for Barkby reveal a pattern of inferred migration even more circumscribed than that of the soke of Rothley. The mean distance was only 5.45 miles, the median four miles. The range of distances, despite a high of forty miles, was fairly compact, reflected in the standard deviation of only 8.59 and the third quartile of seven miles. Nineteen of the twenty-two toponymic bynames indicated migration of less than ten miles. As in Rothley, the proportion of eponymous bynames was high. This level was similarly caused by the pattern of settlement. Although the township of Barkby was a nucleated vill, the parish and manor contained also a few dispersed hamlets: at Barkby Thorpe, Hamilton (later a deserted medieval village), and North Thurmaston. Tenants at these places tended to be known by a byname eponymous with the hamlet, represented as zero miles in the tables.

The College's manor at Kibworth Harcourt comprised a much larger population. The payments of tithing (or hundredpenny) sporadically recorded in the rolls of the view of frankpledge, allow some notion of total resident population. This payment was made by all males over the age of twelve. It is clear from a dispute over obligations that the rate was a penny per male in tithing.[30] From a list of names of those in tithing (ca.1280-1290), Cecily Howell believed that there were about 146 males over twelve in the village.[31] It seems likely, however, that this is an over-estimate, not taking sufficient account of cancellations of some names. Another count of those in the four tithings, undated, but of similar date, noted that there were 112-115 males over twelve (the difference caused by the uncertainty as to whether there were thirty-one or twenty-eight in one of the tithings). The tithings, nonetheless, comprehended the whole village, but the College's manorial tenants only part as there were other lordships. The payments of hundredpenny (*de capitalibus denariis*) can be abstracted from the court rolls and account rolls between 1281 and 1348. For thirty-nine years, we have these data, which suggest a mean population of eighty on the College's manor. In 1349 the receipt from hundred penny fell to 3s. 9d., representing only forty-five males over twelve.[32]

Only a very small proportion of these males bore toponymic bynames. In the listing of those males in tithing in ca.1280-1290, only eight per cent bore such bynames. It seems clear, moreover, that many of these bynames were becoming hereditary surnames. The most prolific byname in this listing was (de) Harcurt. This byname seems to be a toponymic byname received by some of the customary (unfree) tenants as a nickname derived from the (previous) lords of the manor, the Harcourt family. In the tithing list were enumerated Hugh *filius Harcurt*, Hugh Harcurt, and Nicholas and John Harcurt. A rental of the time of Edward III included Robert, Juliana, Nicholas, and Thomas Harcurt, as customary tenants. Numerous Harcurts occurred in the court rolls (dates are those of first appearance): William, Nicholas, and Hugh (1277); Simon (1280); Robert (1320); Matilda (1326); Thomas (1327); Sarah (1343); Juliana (1344); John (1344); Robert and Sarah (1346). The byname (de) Pe(e)k (*de Pecco*) similarly became hereditary. William Pek occurred first in 1277, but was described as William *de Pek scilicet filius Stephani de Rolland* in 1289. He was succeeded by Agnes (1327) and Roger Pek (1329). Emmota de Mar(n)ham appeared in the rolls in 1279, followed by Thomas (1289), Robert (1324), John and Emma (1326), Joan (1330), and Henry (1348). Many of these bynames were thus rapidly becoming hereditary surnames of unfree and free families towards the end of the thirteenth century. In these cases, the place of origin of the byname has been counted once only.

During the same period, however, new migrants were arriving in the village and manor. In 1292, for example, William de Hyngwardesby paid a fine to be allowed to enter the lordship, as did John de Wellesby de Welden in 1320. Other unnamed persons were entering the fee, although perhaps from other manors in Kibworth. The hue was raised by or against many *extranei*, including one known only by his forename, Luke (simply *Lucas*, but once *Lucas extraneus*). Several tenants of the manor were fined for harboring outsiders (*hospitauit extraneum* or, in the case of Nicholas Wilimot in 1343, *extraneos*).[33] Some of the tenants of the manor had contacts with neighboring villages. For example, in 1337, John and William le Chapman became embroiled in pleas of debt ensuing from their activities on behalf of other villagers in Yaxley(?) and Medbourne, the latter seven miles from Kibworth. (Incidentally this implies that in this case, their byname reflected their occupation, and that there was still some residual flexibility of bynames). John *filius prepositi*, as a result of buying wool from John *Faber* of neighboring Newton Harcourt, became involved in a case of debt with Bartholomew de Rolliston.[34]

Taking into consideration the movement to heritability of bynames, it is possible to infer distances of migration. Between 1277 and 1348, only thirty-five different toponymic bynames were borne by tenants of the College's manor, as listed in the rentals, court rolls, and tithing lists. Of these, two have been eliminated, as they are generic toponyms (le Walche and Fleming) and three are of unidentified provenance, leaving thirty which can be used for more precise distances moved. The data for Kibworth thus confirm the mean and median distances of rural migration suggested from other information. From these bynames, the inferred distances of migration present a slightly different pattern, with a mean of 13.06 miles, but a similar median of four and a half miles, the mean affected by a maximum distance of ninety miles, reflected in the standard deviation of 20.00.

If we aggregate the data for Rothley, Barkby and Kibworth, we have 108 toponymic bynames. Almost a fifth (twenty) were eponymous with the location where the taxpayer was assessed. Thirty-nine suggested migration within five miles–equivalent, perhaps, to the adjacent parish. Another eighteen imply movement over a distance of six to ten miles, perhaps a depth of two parishes. The soke of Rothley differs, however, in that twenty toponymic bynames indicate distances of more than ten miles. We might attribute that pattern to the dispersed nature of the soke, which produced a different information field and movement.

The data in Geryn's rental, listing tenants on the estates of Leicester Abbey in 1341, are perilously late for considering the names as being still bynames reflecting the actual migration of individuals.[35] The data are considered here, however, because they illuminate a further point about the pattern of migration of the peasantry: the potential influence of lordship. Of the unfree tenants of the abbey in the county, twenty-three (nineteen percent) bore toponymic bynames or surnames; twenty-one (eighteen percent) of the cottagers also held such bynames or surnames. Ten of the twenty-three villeins had names derived from other manors of the abbey. Thus at Thurmaston was listed Ivetta de Stocton (Stoughton: one of the larger manors of the abbey), and at Stoughton, Roger de Barkeby and William de Ansty (the Abbey holding manors in Barkby and Anstey), whilst William de Humburston held land in Lockington (Humberstone being another of the abbey's manors). Almost half the unfree tenants with toponymic bynames may thus have migrated from one manor of the Abbey to another. The same pattern obtained for the cottagers. Six of the twenty-one with toponymic bynames had names derived from another manor of the abbey. If generic toponyms are discounted, of which there were five, then a third of the cottagers with toponymic bynames may have moved from one manor of the abbey to another. Unfortunately, little more can be construed from this evidence about the processes of migration under the influence of lordship. The inferred distances of migration for villein migrants are similar for both those migrating within and from outside the estate, in the former case a mean of 9.2 miles (standard deviation 5.79) and median of six and a half miles, and in the case of the latter a mean of 10.22 miles (standard deviation 7.41) and median of six. Cottagers who migrated within the estate, however, seem likely to have moved longer distances than those who migrated to one of the abbey's manors from outside the estate. Cottagers who had their origins outside the estate migrated only a mean (and median) of four and a half miles (standard deviation 1.29). Cottagers moving within the estate, however, had an inferred distance of migration of 12.6 miles (standard deviation 7.16) (median sixteen miles). It might be speculated that the cottagers moving longer distances inside the estate did so at the abbey's behest as part of its labor requirements, but this is no more than speculative and the figures are small.

The *Rotuli Hundredorum* of 1279-80 provide a further source for analysis of inferred distances of migration through toponymic bynames. Unfortunately, the data survive only in a later transcription made by William Burton in the early seventeenth century, and for parts of the county only. The transcription mainly relates to the south and west of the shire. Moreover, Burton's transcription presents many problems. The accuracy of his transcription of some of the toponymic bynames seems unreliable.

Burton could not decipher the whole of some bynames, and the full byname cannot be interpolated from what he wrote. The bynames of individual tenants are often not provided by the rolls; there are very few bynames given for customary or unfree tenants, unlike, for example, the rolls for Oxfordshire.[36] An attempt has therefore been made to capture the bynames of all those tenants holding less than two and a half virgates. Most of these tenants were of free status, but a small number were unfree. Of these 261 tenants, sixty-six bore toponymic bynames (twenty-six percent). Of these sixty-six, one byname was illegible (except for the syndetic element *de*), nine were generic toponyms ((le) Franc(e)is, le Waleis, Breton), and ten were unreliable in Burton's transcription, since they do not seem to make sense. The remaining forty-six toponymic bynames provide an inferred mean distance of migration of 4.5 miles (standard deviation 3.631), with a similar median at three miles.[37] Four taxpayers' bynames were eponymous with their place of settlement, whilst eighteen toponymic bynames implied distances of migration below five miles. Another nine suggested movement of between six and ten miles.

According to McClure's analysis of toponymic bynames, the "primary catchment area" of the borough of Leicester fell within a radius of ten miles. The hinterland of Nottingham, defined on the same basis, was slightly wider, at ten to fifteen miles. By contrast, he suggested much wider hinterlands for regional capitals, such as York and Norwich, a feature confirmed for other regional capitals such as Bristol and Exeter, where the influence of the borough extended about twenty-five miles.[38] Patterns of migration to rural places in the county of Leicestershire are not dissimilar from those to the borough of Leicester, which had a rather narrow hinterland. The distance moved by the large proportion of migrants in the county was between one and ten miles. The pattern of migration in rural Leicestershire is also similar to that in rural Nottinghamshire in 1327-1332, also detected by McClure. In Nottinghamshire, fifty-eight to sixty-one percent of migrations were between one and ten miles.[39] In Leicestershire, the proportion was about fifty-six percent.

Unfortunately, little can be detected about the pattern of migration into small towns in Leicestershire. The best documented of these towns (which did not receive royal charters) is Melton Mowbray. Melton was included in the custumal of Rothley of the thirteenth century; its taxpayers are listed in the lay subsidy of 1327; and several hundred charters of ca.1272-1350 occur in the Brokesby cartulary.[40] The custumal comprehends very few toponymic bynames in Melton; there are only four identifiable ones, from which distances can be inferred of migration of three, five, eighteen, and nineteen miles. The lay subsidy of 1327 contains eight such bynames, which imply migrational patterns which are very localized: a mean distance of 6.12 miles (with a low standard deviation of 5.33); median of five; minimum of two and maximum of nineteen miles; and first and third quartiles in the range which are extremely low at 3.5 and five miles.

The most comprehensive source of these bynames for Melton is perhaps paradoxically, given the selective nature of this kind of source, the Brokesby cartulary. This source yields a total of twenty-six *different* toponymic bynames. Such bynames (and other forms) were already becoming hereditary in this small town in the late thirteenth century. As above, toponymic bynames relating to the same place of origin have only been accepted as one migration. The count is therefore not of persons, but of places of origin. The data have been abstracted from the names of parties to charters (donors and beneficiaries) and witness lists. The byname has only been accepted as evidence of migration if it has the qualifying affix *de Melton*: thus, John de Grantham de Melton' senior.[41] Without this qualification, there is no real proof of actual residence in Melton.

Occasionally migrants were designated in a more specific manner in charters: either by the qualifying phrase *manens in Melton'*; or by a shorter phrase (probably an elision of *manens in Melton'*), simply *in Melton'*. Thus charters related to Walter de Dalby *tannator manens in Melton'*; John de Hiclynge *faber manens in Melton'*; Thomas de Belton *manens in Melton'*; and Adam de Rameseye *in Melton'*.[42] In many cases these forms (*de Melton* and *[manens] in Melton'*) are alternative descriptions of the same person. There are only five persons described as *manens in Melton'* who do not also appear as *de Melton*. These five hailed from Hickling, Croxton, Sileby, Burrough, and Scalford, all from within a radius of ten miles. The analysis presented below relates to data other than these five.

The twenty-six toponymic bynames derived from different places of origin impute a mean distance of migration of 12.62 miles (with a relatively low standard deviation of 13.67). The median distance was seven miles. The figures from all twenty-six are skewed by two long-distance migrants, from Norfolk and Ramsey (Huntingdonshire). Adam *de Rameseye* had relocated to Melton by 1272. He married Margery Orger, the daughter of a prominent family in Melton. By her, he had two sons, the homonymous Adam, and Ralph. Adam senior had died by 1301.[43] William *de Northfolke* had arrived in the town by 1324. John *de Northfolk* occurred in a charter some twenty years later.[44] If these two bynames are excluded from the analysis, the mean distance of migration diminishes to 9.25 miles (standard deviation at 6.99) and the median is reduced to six miles.[45] The field of migration to this small market town in Leicestershire was thus extremely localized, corresponding almost exactly to those distances to market cited by Bracton which would presumably have borne on social and economic relations which induced migration.[46]

Faute de mieux, toponymic bynames in the lay subsidies can provide a quantitative assessment of geographical patterns of migration. Since the subsidies are arranged, like many administrative records, by county, the easiest exploitation is at the level of the county. Within that framework, it is also possible to consider migration within and between *pays*. More attention has been directed to rural-urban migration, but there was also a considerable level of rural-rural migration. The evidence of lay subsidies is heavily weighted towards the wealthiest sector of local society. How far that population represented all migrants is a moot question. It is quite probable that large numbers of poorer migrants, not yet benefiting from "betterment migration", might have been excluded from the tax assessment. With these *caveats* in mind, the implicit migration reflected in toponymic bynames does confirm on a large scale in some regions a high level of intensely localized movement, even between villages. In rural Leicestershire, migration was on average over distances not exceeding 10-14 miles, often within a single *pays*, and was usually associated with those who ultimately became slightly higher-rate taxpayers, above the mean level of taxation of all taxpayers. Such a pattern is what might be expected; but the toponymic bynames are a gross indicator based on a large database. Evidence from more detailed study of small communities in Leicestershire confirms this pattern. Movement within the county was circumscribed geographically, with the exception of a very few migrations over longer distances. This localized migration might have helped to perpetuate local customs, dialects and societies, rather than eroding them.

| | Hundreds | | | |
| | North/north-east | | South/south-west | |
Distance (miles)	No.	%	No.	%
0	46	8	26	11
1–5	179	31	84	36
6–10	135	23	46	20
11–15	71	12	28	12
16–20	43	7	9	4
21–25	27	5	13	5
26+	81	14	29	12
From the South and West Midlands (for distances from all places outside Leics.)			39	17

Table 2.1 Rank Distribution of Inferred Distances of Migration, 1327

Distance (miles)	No. of taxpayers	Tax in pennies						
		Mean	Median	Min.	Max.	1st quartile	3rd quartile	st. dev.
0	44	51.3	42	8	168	24	60	36.94
1–5	179	33.8	30	4	144	18	42	22.18
6–10	135	37.4	25	6	612	20	42	54.67
11–15	70	34.2	24	6	168	18	48	26.25
16–20	42	38.5	31	6	168	18	42	34.45
21–25	26	30.9	23	6	71	15	48	19.01
26+	80	33.8	27	4	160	18	42	24.49

Table 2.2   Relationship of Distance and Tax Assessment, 1327

Inferred migration within and between pays *in 1327*[a]

Gainers	Losers				
	Wolds	Pastures	Woodlands	River valleys	Total
Wolds	[123][b]	24	8	27	182
Pastures	28	[113]	13	3	157
Woodlands	13	13	[54]	2	82
River valleys	38	7	4	[27]	76
Total	202	157	79	59	497

[a] Total N = 497.
[b] Figures in [] indicate movement within a *pays*. Net change: Wolds −20; woodland +3; river valleys +17; pastures 0.

Table 2.3   Inferred Migration Between Pays, 1327

Notes

[1]For a recent overview of early-modern migration, Clark and Souden eds., *Migration and Society*. For the full details of references, see the notes to Chapter 1. See also Ian D. Whyte, *Migration and Society in Britain 1550-1830* (London: Macmillan, 2000).

[2]Raftis, "Geographical Mobility"; Poos, "Population Turnover in Medieval Essex"; Richard M. Smith, "Hypothèses sur la nuptialité en Angleterre au XIIIe-XIVe siècles," *Annales: Economies, Sociétés, Civilisations* 38 (1983): 128-9. An older, but still valuable, study is Davenport, "The Decay of Villeinage in East Anglia."

[3]Field, "Migration in the Later Middle Ages."

[4]Raftis, *Tenure and Mobility*. Chevage could also be collected from those unfree peasants remaining on the manor, but not holding land, in recognition of lordship, who were often called *garciones*: Fox, "Exploitation of the Landless."

[5]Raftis, "Geographical Mobility".

[6]Ekwall, *Studies on the Population of Medieval London*; Carus-Wilson, "The First Half-century of the Borough of Stratford-upon-Avon"; Percy H. Reaney, *The Origin of English Surnames* (London: Routledge and Kegan Paul, 1967, repr. 1987), 331-49.

[7]McClure, "Patterns of Migration in the Late Middle Ages," esp. 177-82; Penn, "The Origins of Bristol Migrants"; Kowaleski, *Local Markets and Regional Trade*, 84-86; Rosser, *Medieval Westminster*, 349-61; Rigby, *Medieval Grimsby*, 20-2; Keene, *Survey of Medieval Winchester* vol. 2, 376.

[8]McClure, "Patterns of Migration."

[9]Chapter 1, n. 13.

[10]William G. D. Fletcher, "The Earliest Leicestershire Lay Subsidy Roll 1327," *Associated Architectural Societies Reports* vol. 19 (Lincoln, 1888-1889), 130-78, 209-312, 447-8. See the critique of taxation lists in Chapter 1.

[11]G. T. Clark, "The Customary of the Manor and Soke of Rothley in the County of Leicester," *Archaeologia* 47 (1882): 89-130. Clark assigned the custumal to the mid thirteenth century (p. 90). A dispute between the lord (the Templars) and tenants of the soke in 1245 seems contemporary with the custumal: see The National Archives, London, C260/86.

[12]Bodleian Library, Oxford, MS. Laud Misc. 625 fols.. 191r-211r.

[13]Merton College Oxford MM 6376--6406 and 6556-6573

[14]Bodleian Library Rawl. MS. 350, pp. 1-51.

[15]Bodleian Library MS. Wood, empt. 7, fols. 4v-91r. All those listed were probably of free status.

[16]James C. Holt, *What's in a Name: Family Nomenclature and the Norman Conquest* (University of Reading, Stenton Lecture, 1981).

[17]Richard A. McKinley, *The Surnames of Lancashire*, English Surnames Series (hereafter ESS) vol. 4 (London: Leopard's Head Press, 1981), 30-49; Tim Lomas, "South-east Durham: Late Fourteenth and Fifteenth Centuries," in *The Peasant*

Land Market in *Medieval England* ed. Paul D. A. Harvey (Oxford: Oxford University Press, 1984), 291-3; McKinley, *The Surnames of Oxfordshire*, ESS vol. 3 (London: Leopard's Head Press, 1977) 109-29.

[18]Dave Postles, *The Surnames of Devon*, ESS vol. 7 (Oxford: Leopard's Head Press, 1995)..

[19]For the terms polyphyletic and monophyletic, see Gabriel Lasker, *Surnames and Genetic Structure* (Cambridge: Cambridge University Press, 1985).

[20]Raftis, "Geographical Mobility," 386.

[21]McClure, "Patterns of Migration."

[22]Postles, *Surnames of Devon;* Oliver Padel, "Cornish Surnames in 1327," *Nomina* 9 (1985): 81-88.

[23]McKinley, *Surnames of Oxfordshire*, 109-29.

[24]Chapter 1.

[25]Smith, "Hypothèses sur la Nuptialité"; P. Jeremy P. Goldberg, "Female Labour, Service and Marriage in the Late Medieval Urban North," *Northern History* 22 (1986): 18-38, "Marriage, Migration, Servanthood and Life-cycle," and "Urban Identity and the Poll Taxes," 208.

[26]D. Holly, "Leicestershire," in *The Domesday Geography of Midland England* ed. Henry C. Darby and Ian. B. Terrett (Cambridge: Cambridge University Press, 1954), 315-53; Fox, "The People of the Wolds."

[27]Based on the phonemic analysis in Angus McIntosh, M. L. Samuels, and Michael Benskin, *A Linguistic Atlas of Late Mediaeval English*, 4 vols. (Aberdeen: Aberdeen University Press, 1986); see also Ingrid Hjertstedt, *Middle English Nicknames in the Lay Subsidy Rolls for Warwickshire*, Acta Universitatis Upsaliensis, Studia Anglistica Upsaliensia vol. 63 (Uppsala, 1987), 26-27, which does not, however, take into account phonemic evidence east of the A5 road; nor does Gillis Kristensson, *A Survey of Middle English Dialects 1290-1350: The West Midland Counties*, Publications of the New Society of Letters at Lund, vol. 78 (Lund, 1987); see also Charles V. Phythian-Adams, *Re-thinking English Local History*, University of Leicester, Occasional Papers in English Local History, 4th ser. vol. 1 (1988), 38, based on Martyn Wakelin, *English Dialects: An Introduction* (London: Athlone, 1972), 10. Phonemes are simply sounds; lexis consists of words; isoglosses are lines on maps dividing areas where these different patterns are observed. For migration in the other direction, from Leicestershire to Warwickshire, across Watling Street, see, for example, John de Hinkelay, William de Hinkelay, and Ralph de Hinkelay, all in Atherstone in the early to mid-thirteenth century: Marjorie Chibnall ed., *Select Documents of the English Lands of the Abbey of Bec*, Camden 3rd ser. vol. 73 (London, 1951), 104-5. The fact that all three were cottagers emphasizes the problems of using lay subsidies since all three would probably have been exempted from that sort of taxation.

[28]Fox, "People of the Wolds."

[29]Merton College, Oxford, MM 6556-6671 [Barkby: court rolls and rentals]; MM

6367-6405 [Kibworth Harcourt: court rolls and rentals]; Clarke, "The Customary of the Manor and Soke of Rothley."

[30]See chapter 12 below. MM 6382: "Unde Inquisicio dicit quod nichil dedit nec aliquid exigunt [sic] nisi j.d. pro capite suo." Later entries relating to the payment of *capitales denarii* (or an equivalent term) have the qualification: "et non plus quia non sunt pluria capita". Other entries confirm the nature of the payment as being on males aged over twelve in tithing at the rate of 1d. per head.

[31]Howell, *Land, Family and Inheritance in Transition*, 29-30 and 209-10.

[32]The complexities of these data are explored further in Chap. 12 below.

[33]MM 6399.

[34]MM 6398 and 6404.

[35]Bodleian Library MS. Laud Misc. 625, fols. 191r-211r.

[36]William Illingworth and John Caley eds., *Rotuli Hundredorum temp Hen III & Edw I in Turr' Lond' et in Curia Scaccarij asservati*, vol. ii (London: Record Commission, 1818); Eric Stone ed., *Oxfordshire Hundred Rolls of 1279* vol. I: *The Hundred of Bampton*, Oxfordshire Record Society, 46 (Oxford, 1968).

[37]Bodleian Library MS. Rawl. 350, pp. 1-51.

[38]McClure, "Patterns of Migration," 176-82

[39]McClure, "Patterns of Migration," 175-6. Compare also statistics for the viII of Gaddesby, derived from charters in the Brokesby cartulary: Bodleian Library MS. Wood, empt. 7, fols. 105r-140r: seven toponymic bynames from different places; mean distance 7.29 miles (standard deviation 10.26); median three miles; minimum one mile; maximum thirty miles; first quartile two miles; third quartile eight miles. Since they were involved in charters, all these subjects must have been of free status.

[40]Bodleian Library MS Wood, empt. 7, fols. 4v-91r.

[41]*Ibid.*, fol. 20v.

[42]*Ibid.*, fols. 12r, l3r-v, 14r-v, 17r-v, 29v-30r.

[43]*Ibid.*, fols. 29v-30r, 80v-84r, 83v-84r (charter of Margery Orger referring to lands *quondam Ade de Rameseye viri mei;* charter of Ralph *de Rameseye* referring to Margery Orger as *uxor quondam Ade patris mei;* charters describing Adam and Ralph as sons of Adam senior and as brothers).

[44]*Ibid.*, fols. 9v, 73r-v.

[45]Bodleian Library MS. Wood, empt.7, fols. 4v-9lr.

[46]Thorne, *Bracton on the Laws and Customs of England*, 198-9.

3
Movers and Prayers: Penance, Penitence, Pilgrimage and "Involuntary" Movement in Medieval England[1]

Perhaps the influence of the church on the movement of people in medieval England has been associated more with freedom of movement and encouragement to move. Recently, Robert Swanson has, for example, examined episcopal indulgences for visits to specified places and tombs.[2] In the wider context, pilgrimage to officially-constituted shrines and crusading confirm the impetus provided by the church to freedom of movement, if not permanent migration.[3] There was, however, a converse influence of the Church: ecclesiastical coercion and compulsion to journey which will be explored in this chapter.[4] The church choreographed movement as part of a penitential disciplinary regime, which will be examined here through four aspects: Pentecostal processions; penitential pilgrimage by individuals; entreating the protection of the greater sanctuaries *in extremis*; and referral to the Ordinary of those claiming benefit of clergy.

Penance imposed by the sentence of ecclesiastical courts in office causes comprised a wide variety of forms, including metonymic penance which symbolised the offence.[5] Indeed, it is worth recollecting that attendance at the ecclesiastical court when summoned in an office cause or correction might involve arduous and unwelcome travel and by the early fourteenth century at least was a cause of complaint.[6]

Ant seththe y go coure at constory,
Ant falle to fote uch a fayly,
Heore is this worldes wynne,
Sehthen y pleide at bisshopes plee.[7]

The discomfort might have been aggravated too in some cases by a strict timetable determined by the court.[8] Itineraries imposed as penance in office cases required even further movement. In extreme cases, violence against clerks in holy orders, the penitent was directed to travel to the Roman curia for absolution.[9] Movement at the behest of the courts was usually less arduous, but most penance imposed by the courts spiritual did insist on some travelling. In the vast majority of causes, the sentence involved whippings or beatings–the *fustigatio* of the act books–both round the parish church and in a specified market place. Rural offenders thus confronted the prospect of journeying to the market place for their ritual humiliation. That aspect of the imposition of penance has recently been well rehearsed.[10] Although less frequent than these beatings, the obligation to undertake local–as opposed to long-distance–pilgrimage deserves attention, refracting an aspect of peregrination not fully represented in the literature on pilgrimage.[11]

Whilst the enforced local pilgrimage appears more clearly in the records of the later middle ages than earlier, the converse applies to another form of directed movement by the church, Pentecostal processions. Actual movement at Pentecost probably declined after the end of the thirteenth century, commuted to smoke-penny. From the "high" and late middle ages, however, it is apparent that some movement of people was stimulated by the Church, without resulting in permanent migration, but consolidating information fields.

Pentecostal processions:
inducement to collective movement

Certainly in the twelfth and thirteenth centuries, movement of people accompanied the processions to diocesan centres at Pentecost. It is assumed that these processions were introduced by Norman bishops.[12] If their introduction was the responsibility of a new Norman higher clergy, then it may have constituted a demand for allegiance by an uncertain episcopacy.[13] Another motive might have been a celebration of and stimulus towards the unity of the Church.[14] At least as important might have been the necessity to prepare for one of the three main liturgical occasions of the year.[15]

The imputation exists that the processions continued into the late thirteenth century. A mandate of that time from the official of the Bishop of Norwich to the chaplains of the deaneries of Sudbury, Clare, Stow et al. exhorted the performance of the customary processions at

Bury St Edmunds at Pentecost, the abbey delegated as an alternative to the diocesan centre at Norwich.[16] It does, nevertheless, appear that Pentecostal processions became less observed by personal movement in the thirteenth century, perhaps the beginnings of formal commutation to a money payment. Some reluctance to process might be inferred from the mandate in 1247 to all archdeacons, rural deans and rectors to compel their parishioners to make pilgrimages to Chichester cathedral at Pentecost in return for which they would receive an indulgence of forty days.[17] In particular, the proclamation of the indulgence has something of an air of desperation. Confirmation of the lapse into desuetude is implicit also in a further mandate in April 1248 exhorting the clergy to lead their parishioners in procession at Pentecost to the cathedral, Lewes or Hastings. In addition, this order commanded the clergy to compile lists of the houses and families in their parishes for submission to the proctors of rural deans so that those who did not participate should lose the benefit of the indulgence–lose their remission–and suffer canonical distraint.[18] Such exhortations might have constituted no more than rhetoric, for they were promulgated in the late twelfth century. In 1198x1206, Henry, bishop of Exeter, instructed his archdeacons throughout the entire diocese (and therefore presumably including Cornwall) to enforce the custom of Pentecostal processions and oblations to the cathedral church.[19] Every *capellanus* was enjoined to produce a roll of the names of parishioners by manor who had a hearth or the ability to contribute a halfpenny *per* head. Defaulters should be excluded from communion.[20] The bishop of Lincoln advised his archdeacons to ensure the more regular observance of processions at some time between 1186 and 1200, a direction reiterated in 1203x1206.[21] In the diocese of Lichfield, the ordinary at some time between 1160 and 1176 encouraged his archdeacons and rural deans in Staffordshire to give the same attention to Pentecostal processions as in the previous year, requiring the clergy to be convened and enjoined to instruct their parishioners to attend on the appointed day at Lichfield. He too permitted a remission of one third of penance, allowing an indulgence for a regular obligation.[22]

The extent of movement implicit in the bishop of Lichfield's injunction was more focused and circumscribed–referring only to parishioners in the archdeaconry of Stafford, omitting the more distant archdeaconry of Chester. That sensitivity to distance of movement applied in other dioceses too, not least the immense diocese of Lincoln. Noted above too is how the bishop of Chichester allowed parishioners to process to Lewes or Hastings as well as the cathedral. From at least 1138x1139, parishioners from the archdeaconry of Oxford were permitted to make the more circumscribed journey to Eynsham Abbey at Pentecost, explicitly because of the distance involved to the episcopal see.[23] By another *actum* of 1148x1166, the bishop, because of poverty and remoteness, authorised parishioners from some archdeaconries to process to specific places ordained by their archdeacons. For two years, in 1154-56, the processions of the parishioners from the deaneries of Fritwell, Hanwell and Chipping Norton in Oxfordshire, were diverted to Banbury to promote the bishop's new fair there–an interesting counterpoise to the prohibition of Sunday markets detracting from devotional priorities as secular impinging on the sacred was here confounded by the spiritual assisting the secular.

Undoubtedly, the diversion of some of the processions to alternative venues was influenced not only by the convenience of the parishioners but also by the promotion of the venues. That motive was suggested in the nomination of Southwell minster in 1109x1114 as the location for the parishioners of Nottinghamshire, explicitly for the assistance of the building work at Southwell.[24] Quite obviously convening at Southwell rather than York also eased the obligation of the parishioners of the archdeaconry of Nottingham, as well as promoting Southwell's status amongst the *secunde sedes*.[25] The other possibility for permitting processions and oblations to these other centers is that the chrism was collected from them on Maundy Thursday, for which the oblations had been payment.[26]

Such attention to the fabric and furnishing of alternative venues was appropriate, for the oblations or pence offered the cathedral at Pentecostal processions were increasingly directed towards the lights of the cathedral church or the chapter–to the sacristan.[27] At Winchester, the Pentecostal oblations were assigned by the ordinary from the 1120s to the priory for lights and necessities, specifically to the sacristan from the late twelfth century.[28] At Bath, the bishop of Bath and Wells donated the pence to the priory church by 1174x1191.[29] At Exeter too the bishop confirmed the Pentecostal receipts to the cathedral church.[30]

The spiritual requirement of the whole body of parishioners in the diocese to process at Pentecost either to congregate at the cathedral or some other designated place thus engendered a wholesale movement of people, partly by their free will if religion was voluntary, but perhaps also through latent coercion and perhaps sometimes encouraged by the granting of indulgences. It seems likely that this mass movement declined somewhat from the late thirteenth century as an entire movement of a local population. During its most extensive observance in the twelfth and thirteenth century, it constituted a grand occasion for the convergence of popular masses into tumultuous congregations in high naves, parish banners waving, identifying parochial allegiances with those of the ecclesiastical and perhaps spiritual centers.[31] In the case of some alternatively designated venues, the obligation confirmed the affective importance of these more localised spiritual centres to their local societies.[32]

Penitential pilgrimage: instructions for individual movement

In one sense, the journeying of penitents to the cathedral church on Ash Wednesday perpetuated a penitential tradition.[33] For example, the absolution of those three men who intruded into the church of Kirkby in Kendal in 1293/4 depended on two *fustigationes*, one locally in the church at Kirkby, but the other on Ash Wednesday (*dies Cinerum*)–the 3rd March–at the metropolitan cathedral in York with the dignity and reflection required of penitents (*solempniter ... humiliter et devote*).[34]

In the process of local pilgrimage, official local saints' cults were affirmed and sponsored. The Ely consistory court of the late fourteenth century regularly demanded pilgrimage to the shrine of St. Ethelreda at the cathedral as penance. John Grebby *capellanus* was summarily directed in 1375 that for his penance he would visit the shrine of Ethelreda, without further elaboration.[35]   Evidently having offended again in 1376 by solemnising an uncanonical marriage, Grebby was ordered again to journey from Wichford to Ely on foot to offer 4d. at the shrine and to make the pilgrimage before the middle of Lent.[36] In the previous year, the vicar of Littleport, Simon de Lakyngheth', having indulged in fornication, was also assigned pilgrimage to the shrine to deliver a groat.[37] In addition to penance expressed in his own parish church, Sir Robert Mustel, *capellanus* of Wilburton, was commanded in 1378 to walk barefoot–the truly penitential fashion–from Wilburton to the shrine to offer a candle of two pounds of wax.[38] This sanction might have been applied more readily to clerks in holy orders, but it did also extend to the laity of the diocese.

Now such punishments–the satisfaction required of penance, but also intended to engender contrition–were extended to the laity. Eight men who violated the parish church of Foxton in 1376 conducted local penance in their parish church with tapers in their hands, but, in view of the serious nature of their offence, their restitution also involved walking to the shrine, each to make an oblation of 1d.[39] Another layman, Richard Fysshere of Chatteris, denounced for excessive violence against his wife, received a sentence of restitution to her, local penance in the parish church, and that bare-bodied he would process round the cathedral church on the feast of St. Ethelreda in the formal procession bearing a candle in his hand–symbolising his penance.[40] In this manner, Arundel, whilst bishop of Ely, enforced a penitential regime partially based on local pilgrimage and also promoted the shrine of the cathedral's and the region's patronal saint.[41]

Sometimes penitents received sentences of visiting not a single penitential venue, but several. For their infraction of the liberty of St. Wilfred at Ripon in 1452, Gilbert Lye, esquire, and his ten accomplices, were sentenced to *fustigaciones* before the processions with bare feet and a lit candle of 1 lb. weight in their hands to be offered at the high altar first at Ripon itself, but then at York, and then at Beverley. In the event, after the first procession at Ripon, they were absolved from the other two.[42] The same punishment at the three venues was imposed in 1453 on others who disturbed penitents to St. Wilfred.[43]

Not only the celebrated shrines benefited from penitential pilgrimage, however, for some penitents, particularly in the later middle ages, were assigned routes to intimately local images or churches. To publicise locally her infamy, Agnes Badeley was ordered in 1528/9 to perform penance on three Sundays in respectively the parish churches of Stanton, Melbourne and Ticknall.[44] In a similar manner, for producing bastard children, Joan Reedes of Newton performed penance not only in her own parish church at Newton, but also in those of Rolston and Melbourne.[45] Melbourne may have been perceived here as the principal church in the vicinity. Places associated with the Virgin were promoted through penance in the south of the diocese of Winchester about this time. In 1522, William Flecher of Littleton was denounced in the consistory court for carnal knowledge of his former servant, Agnes Hussey, for which he was consigned to make a pilgrimage before Easter to the image of the Blessed Virgin of Southwick (presumably in Southwick Priory), here to hear mass in the Lady Chapel and to make an oblation to the image, and then to make a further journey on foot to the image of the Blessed Mary of Grace of Southampton and to hear mass in that chapel.[46] After his confession in court of carnal relations with his servant, Richard Pers of Haddenham was sentenced in 1520 to make the journey on foot to the Blessed Virgin Mary at Northampton.[47]

The register of Hamo Hethe as bishop of Rochester, since it incorporates extracts from the office act book of his consistory court, allows a glimpse of penitential pilgrimages in the early fourteenth century. Amongst the fullest examples of journeying imposed, Simon Heyroun, convicted of adultery, received the sentence of annual pilgrimages for seven years to St. Thomas of Canterbury, and within those seven years to make three pilgrimages to each of St. Thomas of Hereford, St. Edmund of Bury, and St. Mary of Walsingham.[48] For defaming Joan, a wife, alleging her adultery with a monk of Rochester, Sybil, also a married woman, was obliged in 1327 to make three pilgrimages to Canterbury, one each to Chichester and Bury St Edmunds, and to offer a candle at Rochester cathedral. Both inhabited Rochester.[49] Convicted of fornication, Thomas Mellhale of Aylesford consented in 1332 to make the pilgrimage on foot to St. Thomas at Canterbury within a fortnight of Michaelmas and to the shrine of St. William at Rochester on the following Saturday or Monday. His co-respondent, Godleva, of the same place, was ordered, however, to journey barefoot to St. Mary at Chatham within the next fortnight.[50] Primarily, Hethe ordered penitents to visit Canterbury and/or Rochester (about sixty percent), but he also directed them to Gloucester (Edward II's tomb), Bury St Edmunds, Greenwich (Holy Cross), Walsingham and, in extreme cases, Compostella and Rome.[51] To Walsingham, he despatched two females and two clerks in holy orders (although one commuted the penance) and only one male.[52] St. Andrew's day–the feast of the patronal saint–occasioned some of the penitential visits to Rochester.[53] Journeys to Compostella were prescribed for the worst adulteries: the beatings decided for one woman for adultery were commuted to pilgrimage to Compostella at Candlemas in 1325 whilst in the same year John Mayde was ordered to make the same journey for congress with his godmother.[54]

The emphasis on penitential congregation at Rochester Cathedral is illustrated by Hethe's commissions for the expulsion of penitents from the cathedral (i.e. from the Church) on Ash Wednesday and their reconciliation on Maundy Thursday (re-admission into the "community" of the Church symbolically through their entry into the cathedral). In 1322, Hethe authorised the prior of the regular cathedral chapter to absolve penitents, whilst in 1345 the sub-prior was commissioned in the prior's absence to cast out penitents assembled in the cathedral and to receive them back the following day.[55] What those commissions might indicate is that the number of penitents was not insubstantial and that commutation did not release all, or indeed, most, from their obligation to travel.

About the same time as Hethe's instructions, such penitential journeys were being imposed in the diocese of Lichfield, although the surviving evidence is sporadic. In 1317, upon a visitation of Tarvin (Cheshire), pilgrimages were prescribed twice to Canterbury and once to the diocesan see, Lichfield.[56] In the early fourteenth century also, the bishops of Hereford imposed similar penance to those of Hethe. In particular, on the authority of the Papal penitentiary in 1326, Richard de Staunton, a layman, enjoined to perform penance in the greater churches in the diocese, was directed by the bishop to the churches of Leominster, Almeley, Preston-on-Wye, Eardisland, Shobdon, Staunton-on-Arrow, Pembridge and Kington.[57] Peregrination of the greater churches of the diocese as penance was also received in 1320 by Hugh de Kaerdif, a layman originating in the diocese of Coventry and Lichfield, who had killed a priest. Although excommunicated and despite the protestations to the bishop of Hereford by his counterpart at Lichfield, Hugh was absolved by the Papal penitentiary and provided with a penitential route by the Ordinary in Hereford diocese since Hugh feared to return to his native diocese.[58] Those laymen who had violated the bishop's woods in Ross in 1307 were ordered by the bishop to make a progress on foot to the Cathedral, there to make oblations before the images of the Blessed Virgin in the choir and of the blessed Ethelbert, the patronal saints.[59] Four parishioners of Old Radnor were cited to appear at the cathedral for correction in a cause of office promoted in 1346.[60] In other instances, however, the distance travelled was mitigated. In 1346, the commission to the Friar, John de Hoggeschawe, permitted him to conduct the office for penitents on Ash Wednesday in Ludlow church, reconciling and absolving in the same church on the following Thursday.[61] Offenders presented at the visitation of the deanery of the Forest in 1346 were cited to appear for correction by the bishop in the church of Newent.[62] During Swinfield's episcopacy, the consistory court was also convened in the parish church of Wellington.[63] In particular causes, however, uncertainty was restored, as in Bishop Trillek's mandate in 1346 to Isabel Barry, living in Tidenham, to appear for correction before the bishop or his commissary wherever they might be in the diocese on Monday before the feast of St. Ethelbert (the patronal saint of the diocese).[64]

As with the referral to Melbourne church above, penitents were directed sometimes to local parish churches which had local significance. For example, Anne Martynmasse, was convicted in 1514 of carnal relationships with the curate of Uppingham, the liaison having been perpetrated in the rectory of Uppingham. Now, although she resided in Sharnford, her penance involved perambulating in the market place at Uppingham and processing on two Sundays in the parish church of Uppingham. No doubt the intention here was not only to humiliate her but also the curate and to signify where the offence occurred. Furthermore, her penance extended on the third Sunday to perform penance in Lyddington. That parish comprised an episcopal manor and residence and was indeed where the court which sentenced her had been convened, in the chapel there. Anne was thus demonstrably compelled to travel from Sharnford to Lyddington on the third Sunday to a place of symbolic importance to atone for her offense against the spiritual authority of the bishop.[65] Similarly, Giles Mawyer of Chalfont St Giles, convicted of getting Joan Clarke pregnant, offered to make five pilgrimages to Missenden on five feasts days of the Virgin as penance. Significantly, he received his correction in the episcopal court held in the chamber on the manor of Missenden.[66] When Agnes Lee of Chesham was pronounced guilty of adultery in 1511, she swore on the gospels to perform the penance imposed on her, to process as a penitent not only in her own church at Chesham but also in the parish church of the larger, but adjacent Amersham.[67]

Much further north, the chapel of St. Michael in the castle of Clitheroe was used as a venue for numerous penitential journeys in the locality. The court of the peculiar of Whalley in the early sixteenth century regularly conferred sentences of penance in the castle chapel.[68] Illustrative of this imposition is the dispute within the Cronkshay kinship which resulted in a sentence to visit first the chapel of Padham, then the castle chapel, then the parish church of Burnley, and finally on the feast of the Conception of the Blessed Virgin Mary to process from the castle of Clitheroe across the market place to the parish church there.[69]

In the early sixteenth century, the consistory court of Worcester very occasionally demanded penance to be conducted in local churches additional to the offender's own church. An intimation of a specific rationale for this more considerable atonement was furnished in the office cause against Joan in 1542. Although she belonged in the parish of St. Peter in Worcester, Joan had become pregnant in St. Michael's parish. Her action, it was recounted, had resulted in her infamy throughout several parishes of the city.[70] Accordingly, at a time when the regular penance comprised three Sundays in the offender's own parish church, Joan had to certify her performance of penance first in St. Michael's, then on the following Sunday in St. Peter's and finally, on the third Sunday, in St. Stephen's.[71]

A decade previously, the same consistory court had taken the same opinion of the immorality of Agnes Carter in Bristol in 1533, extending her penance to first St. Andrew's, secondly to St. Werburgh's and on the final Sunday to All Saints.[72] Although the penance of Agnes was confined to the city, the incontinence of William Rosar' and Joan Moyle, both of Shrawley, three years later, incurred a penitential progress on successive Sundays in three rural parish churches–Shrawley, Witley and Astley.[73]

The great sanctuaries: movement *in extremis*

The protection afforded by the greater sanctuaries might be conceived as a "pull" for freedom of movement, but that movement was inherently compulsory in the evasive action necessarily taken by the "criminal".[74] The context for movement can be illustrated by Figs 3.1 and 3.2 which represent the origins of those requesting the *grith* of the great sanctuaries of Durham and Beverley in the later middle ages.[75] Whilst the movement of suspected criminals has been demonstrated from Crown Pleas, often involving localized movement to sanctuary in parish churches where protection obtained for forty days, the journeys to the greater sanctuaries reveal more extensive patterns of movement which presumably reflect on wider information fields and widespread knowledge of these special ecclesiastical spaces.[76]

Furthermore, in contrast to the recourse to local sanctuaries which occurred mainly to evade capture for felonies, travel to the some of the greater sanctuaries, particularly Beverley, was also designed to avoid debt. Debtors are as significant as felons at the gates of this sanctuary. Probably for that reason and because of its commercial connections in the late middle ages, Beverley received a much greater concentration of migrants but also migrants from a greater expanse of the entire country.[77] In this context too, the term migrant is accurate for, if admitted, the movers became permanent sworn inhabitants of the liberty.

Benefit of clergy

Perhaps benefit of clergy had similar implications for movement as sanctuary in the great liberties, for in both cases ecclesiastical privilege promoted the movement of lay persons. The debasement of benefit of clergy by the early sixteenth century is, of course, well known.[78] Interestingly, the act book of Silvester, bishop of Worcester, includes details of those referred from the criminal courts to the bishop on a claim of benefit of clergy.[79] Some of the initial absolutions in the act book provide the flavour of the business. At the hearing of August 8, 1504, three laymen were absolved and restored to their original good fame (*pristina bona fama*): Thomas Broune, late of Castle Combe, yeoman, John Sklatter, late of Evesham, labourer, and John Vaughan, late of 'Worsworth' in Derbyshire (presumably Wirksworth), yeoman. Amongst their offenses, Broune had broken into the house of John Carter at Oxenton in Gloucestershire and had also stolen from Carter a sorrel horse valued at 26s., whilst Sklatter had illegally entered the close of Thomas Wilmer at Hinton in the same county and removed three black cows assessed at 20s. Finally, but not least, Vaughan had purloined five oxen valued at 50s. from Thomas Hunt of Bordesley and two horses assessed at 26s. 8d. from John George. All had therefore committed grand larceny, a capital offence.[80] All successfully purged themselves through compurgation on their own oath.[81]

Recorded in the act book is the status of just under fifty laymen who established benefit of clergy, eleven of whom were labourers, nine yeomen, three bakers, two each of saddlers, shearmen, tailors, smiths, weavers, and chapmen, complemented by a panelmaker, fishmonger, organ player, bowyer, walker, corveser, peddler, capper, butcher, cook, painter and husbandman.[82] Their places of origin are represented in Fig. 3.3, including eleven from Bristol. To escape the inevitable sentence of the secular courts, these peasants and artisans, probably already itinerant, were compelled to visit diocesan centers to receive absolution from the ordinary.

Perhaps we might conclude with some events in the diocese of Salisbury in 1411. Five local men broke into the parish church of Grittleton to extract Robert Jordan from the sanctuary that he had sought there. The bishop commissioned the dean of Salisbury to oversee their penance when they appeared at the west door of Salisbury cathedral before high mass on January 1. There, with linen shirts as their only apparel, they should prostrate themselves in the sight of the people whilst the dean recited a specified psalm. If they exhibited contrition, they could proceed into the cathedral with a candle, genuflect at the font, and offer the candle into the hands of the celebrant of the mass at the high altar after the reading of the gospel.[83] The sequence of these events encapsulates how spiritual spaces influenced the movement of people in medieval England.

Whilst in the case of the great sanctuaries migration involved a complex mix of "push" and "pull" variables, movement collectively in Pentecostal processions and individually in those penitential journeys which were imposed by the courts spiritual, derived from the compulsion of spiritual direction. Combined with the pretensions to benefit of clergy, these three influences demonstrate how the organization of spiritual space promoted movement of people. In like manner, the impulsion illustrates how the continuing recognition of spiritual and ecclesiastical authority elicited mobility. If religious observance and affiliation were voluntary, it should not be assumed that the movement it inspired was entirely without coercion. Latent and overt compulsion interfered in the process, influencing the information fields of peasants and burgesses, and promoting and confirming both the authority of place and the organization of space through the social practice of movement.[84]

Figure 3.1   Origins of Pleas for Entry to Durham Sanctuary, 1464-1524

Figure 3.2   Origins of Pleas for Entry to Beverley Sanctuary, 1505-1540

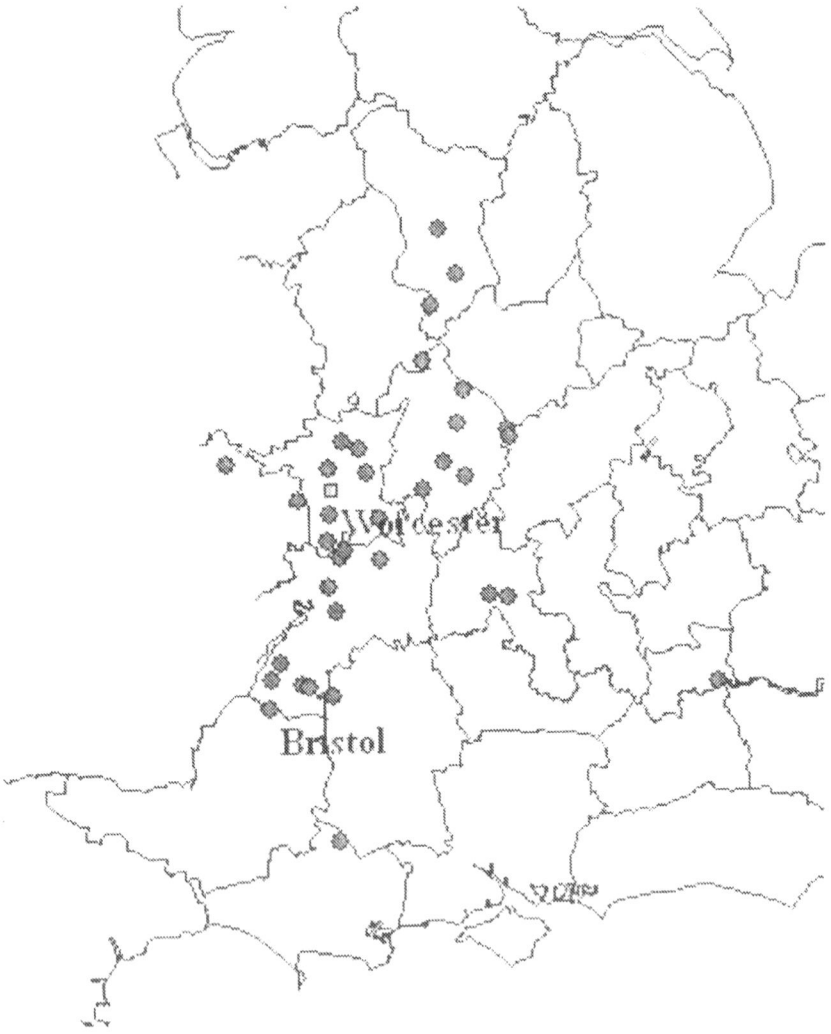

Figure 3.3   Origins of Claimants to Benefit of Clergy, Worcester Diocese, 1502-1544 (Mainly Before 1527)

Notes

[1] The pun on the early-modern notion of "movers and stayers" is intentional!

[2] Robert N. Swanson, "Indulgences for Prayers for the Dead in the Diocese of Lincoln in the Early Fourteenth Century," *Journal of Ecclesiastical History* 52 (2001): 197-217; Swanson, "Fund-raising for a Medieval Monastery: Indulgences and Great Brickett Priory," *Proceedings of the Suffolk Institute of Archaeology & History* 40 (2001): 1-7.

[3] Diana Webb, *Medieval European Pilgrimage c.700-c.1500* (Basingstoke: Palgrave, 2002); Ben Nilson, *Cathedral Shrines of Medieval England* (Woodbridge: Boydell, 1998); Finucane, *Miracles and Pilgrims.*; E. R. Labande, "De Saint Edouard à Saint Thomas Becket: Pèlerinages Anglais au XIIe Siècle," in *Medievalia Christiana XIe-XIIe Siècles. Hommage à Raymond Foreville*, ed. C. E. Viola (Tournai, 1989), 307-19; and for the later middle ages, George W. Bernard, "Vitality and Vulnerability in the Late Medieval Church: Pilgrimage on the Eve of the Break with Rome," in *The End of the Middle Ages. England in the Fifteenth and Sixteenth Centuries*, ed. John L. Watts (Stroud: Sutton, 1998), 199-237, Eamon Duffy, "The Dynamics of English Pilgrimage," in *Pilgrimage. The English Medieval Experience from Becket to Bunyan*, ed. Colin Morris and Peter Roberts (Cambridge: Cambridge University Press, 2002), 164-77 (esp. pp. 173-4 where Duffy briefly considers imposed penance and pp. 175-6 where he notes the inducement of indulgences as Swanson, n. 2 above) and also Duffy, *The Stripping of the Altars.Traditional Religion in England 1400-1580* (New Haven: Yale University Press, 1992), 190-205. For legacies in wills for the expense of substitute pilgrims, see, for example, the will of John Pygott in 1488 allocating money for a pilgrim to the BVM at Doncaster, the BVM at Walsingham, the Holy Blood at Hales, and St. Thomas at Canterbury: Joseph T. Fowler, ed., *Acts of Chapter of the Collegiate Church of SS Peter and Wilfrid, Ripon, A.D. 1452 to A.D. 1506*, SS vol. 64 (1875 for 1874), 264-5.

[4] Although Webb refers to the variety of motives for pilgrimage, including penitential sanctions, the enforced and penitential aspect of pilgrimage deserves closer investigation: Webb, *Medieval European Pilgrimage*, xiii, 49-50. For an interesting insight into motives for pilgrimage, S. Medcalf, "Motives for Pilgrimage: *The Tale of Beryn*," in *England in the Fourteenth Century*, ed. Nicholas Rogers, Harlaxton Medieval Studies vol. 3 (Stamford: Paul Watkins, 1993), 97-108.

[5] For example, for pursuing work on the Sabbath, several offenders were directed as their penance to haul slates to the parish church of Downham, inducing them to reflect on the nature and occasion for work: Alice M. Cooke, ed., *Act Book of the Ecclesiastical Court of Whalley 1510-1538*, Chetham Society new ser. vol. 44 (Manchester, 1901), 58.

[6] Pedersen, 'Demography in the Archives." By contrast, some accused might wish not to be examined and sentenced locally, to avoid shame; thus Thomas Poyner of Lillingstone Lovell, allocated a time and place in 1518 to plead his defense of self-defense in laying violent hands on a cleric in holy orders, persuaded the vicar general to change the place from Lyddington to the Old Temple in London as Lyddington was too close: Margaret Bowker, ed., *An Episcopal Court Book for the Diocese of Lincoln 1514-1520* , LRS vol. 61 (1967), 75-6.

[7]Thomas Wright, ed., *The Political Songs of England from the Reign of John to that of Edward II*, Camden Society (London, 1839), 159–the resentment here is generally against the interference of the courts rather than the distance to them.

[8]WRO 794.011 BA 2513 1 (i) (act book, 1530-1537), p. 327 (paginated not foliated): instance cause, the rector of Kempsey *c*. Richard Aston *alias* Tyler of Kempsey: "Et monuit dictum Tyler ad comparandum coram eo In ecclesia omnium sanctorum Wigorn' inter horas primam & iijam post meridiem huius die [sic] ad audiendum taxacionem expensarum in dicta causa " (1537)..

[9] In many cases, of course, absolution was received for a commuted amount of money rather than an actual journey; for such absolutions for violent laying of hands on clerks in holy orders, William Brown, ed., *The Register of Walter Giffard, Lord Archbishop of York 1266-1279*, SS vol. 109 (1904), 277-8.

[10]James Masschaele, "The Public Space of the Market Place," *Speculum* 77 (2002): 383-421. For the appearance of this form of penance in market place as well as parish church in the diocese of Worcester in 1560, Worcestershire Record Office 794.011 BA 2513 2 (i) (act book, 1557-1563), p. 193 (paginated not foliated): office cause *c*. Richard Hobbyns of Stratford upon Avon for incontinent living with Margaret Caplewoode, the daughter of his late wife whom he made pregnant: "iniunxit ei quod duobus diebus foralibus proximis stet in pleno foro ibidem nudatis pedibus et capite in lintheis tantum more penitentis cum virgula alba in manu sua" (December 6, 1560); see also the proximate causes in 1561 at pp. 202, 249 and 293 ("tribus diebus foralibus in pleno foro ville de Wych; duobus diebus in pleno foro dicte Ciuitatis [Worcester]; tribus diebus foralibus agat publicam penitenciam in pleno foro seu mercato Ciuitatis Wigorn'").

[11]Webb, *Medieval European Pilgrimage*; Duffy *The Stripping of the Altars*; but see Jonathan Sumption, *Pilgrimage: An Image of Medieval Religion* (London: Faber, 1975), 105. Note also the theoretical contrast between Victor & Edith Turner, *Image and Pilgrimage in Christian Culture: Anthropological Perspectives* (Oxford: Oxford University Press, 1978), 8-9, 31-2, and John Eade & Michael J. Sallnow, "Introducton" in *Contesting the Sacred: The Anthropology of Christian Pilgrimage* ed. Eale and Sallnow (Urbana, IL: University of Illinois Press, 1991). For journeys to Jerusalem, Sylvia Schein, "Bridget of Sweden, Margery Kempe and Women's Jerusalem Pilgrimages in the Middle Ages," *Mediterranean Historical Review* 14 (1999), 44-58 and, most recently, Colin Morris, "Pilgrimage to Jerusalem in the Late Middle Ages" in *Pilgrimage* ed. Morris and Roberts, 141-63.

[12]The most cogent discussion is still Brett, *The English Church under Henry I*, 162-4, listing evidence for Lincoln, Ely, York, Worcester, Winchester and Chichester. Brett suggested a Norman introduction at p. 164.

[13]Brett, *The English Church under Henry I*, 164 for this implication.

[14]Mary Mansfield, *The Humiliation of Sinners. Public Penance in Thirteenth-century France* (Ithaca, NY: Cornell University Press, 1995), 147-54.

[15]Sarah Hamilton, *The Practice of Penance, 900-1050* (Woodbridge: Boydell, 2001).

[16]Antonia Gransden, ed., *The Letter-Book of William of Hoo Sacrist of Bury St Edmunds 1280-1294*, Suffolk Record Society vol. 5 (1963), 41 (no. 28).

[17]Philippa M. Hoskin, ed., *English Episcopal Acta 22 Chichester 1215-1253* [*EEA*] (Oxford: Oxford University Press, 2001), 105 (no. 129). For the canonical

significance of an indulgence of forty days, Patrick Zutshi, "Collective Indulgences from Rome and Avignon in English Collections," in *Medieval Ecclesiastical Studies in Honour of Dorothy M. Owen* ed. Michael J. Franklin and Christopher Harper-Bill (Woodbridge: Boydell, 1995), 283.

[18]Hoskin, *EEA* 22, 107 (no. 31)

[19]Note, however, that in 1163, the portion of the oblations from Pentecostal processions in question related only to Devon: Frank Barlow, ed., *EEA* 11 *Exeter 1046-1184* (Oxford: Oxford University Press, 1996), 78 (no. 88).

[20]Barlow, ed., *EEA* 12 *Exeter 1186-1257* (Oxford: Oxford University Press, 1996), 170-1 (no. 188).

[21]David M. Smith, ed., *EEA* 4 *Lincoln 1186-1206* (Oxford: Oxford University Press, 1986), 66 and 165 (nos 92 and 256)

[22]Michael J. Franklin, *EEA* 16 *Coventry and Lichfield 1160-1182* (Oxford: Oxford University Press, 1998), 54 (no. 60).

[23]Smith, ed., *EEA* 1 *Lincoln 1067-1185*, xlix, 17 (no. 26), 78-9 (116-19), 93 (156).

[24]Janet Burton, ed., *EEA* 5 *York 1070-1154* (Oxford: Oxford University Press, 1988), 22-3 (no. 22).

[25]For *secunde sedes* in the early twelfth century, Brett, *The English Church*, 198-9.

[26]For the suggestion that the Pentecostal oblations were recompense for the chrism consecrated by the bishop and collected on Maundy Thursday, Barlow, *EEA* 12, 171.

[27]For the apportionment of the Pentecostal income to the *mensa* of the community or chapter, Brett, *The English Church*, 163.

[28]Michael J. Franklin, ed., *EEA* 8 *Winchester 1070-1204* (Oxford: Oxford University Press, 1993), 11 (no. 19), 92 (130), 146 (192), 198 (254).

[29]Frances M. R. Ramsey, ed., *EEA* 10 *Bath and Wells 1061-1205* (Oxford: Oxford University Press, 1995), 203 (Appx. 1, no. 36)

[30]Barlow, *EEA* 11, 78 (no. 88).

[31]For a vivid description of the occasion of the processions in "France", Mansfield, *The Humiliation of Sinners*, 147-54; George C. Homans, *English Villagers of the Thirteenth Century* (Cambridge, Mass.: Harvard University Press, 1941), 372-3 for competition in display between parishes.

[32]The continuing importance of secular minsters such as Southwell in the mundane activities of its neighbourhood society is astonishing, if barely visible: Christopher J. Holdsworth, ed., *Rufford Abbey Charters*, Thoroton Society Record Series vols. 29-30 (1972-4), passim: for example, vol. 1, 87 (no. 153), 94 (no. 167), 96 (no. 172), for the role of Southwell in afforcing and confirming charters and the use of its seal by the laity to secure charters.

[33]Mansfield, *The Humiliation of Sinners*.

[34]*The Register of John le Romayn, Lord Archbishop of York 1286-1296 Part I*, SS vol. 123 (1913), 350.

[35]CUL EDR D/2/1 fol. xxxij recto "...et pro penitencia visitabit feretrum sancte Etheldr'." For the context, Margaret Aston, *Thomas Arundel. A Study in Church Life in the Reign of Richard II* (Oxford: Oxford University Press, 1967).

[36]CUL EDR D/2/1 fols. lxij verso–lxiij recto: "iniungimus sibi quod accedat ad feretrum sancte Etheldr' ob illam causam tamen et quod vadat pedes ab ista

parte ville de Wychford' per totam villam et sic usque feretrum et offerat ibidem quatuor denarios ...et quod dictam peregrinacionem perficiat citra medium quadragesime."

[37]CUL EDR D/2/1 fol. xxxiiij verso: "super crimine grauis fornicacionis and et pro dicta contumacia iniunximus quod offerat in manus Sacriste Elien' nomine feretri sancte Etheldr' quatuor denarios..."

[38]CUL EDR D/2/1 fol. lxxxv verso: "et ibit nudis pedibus de Wilburton' ad feretrum sancte Etheldr' et ibidem offerret unum cereum duarum librarum cere..."

[39]CUL EDR D/2/1 fol. lxvj recto: "quod vadant pedes ad feretrum sancte Etheldr' in ecclesia Elien' et offerent ibidem singuli videlicet singulos denarios" ... and (to ensure interior reflection) to engage in this additional penance "humiliter peregerunt."

[40]CUL EDR D/2/1 fol. cxl recto (1380): "deponitis vestibus suis circuibit ecclesiam Elien' cum [sic] processione more penitencie deferendo in manu sua unum cereum."

[41]For this reason, circumspection is required in calculating the extent of popular devotion from the accounts of feretrars: Nilson, *Cathedral Shrines*, 144-90.

[42]Fowler, *Acts of the Chapter of the Collegiate Church of SS Peter and Wilfrid, Ripon*, 6-7.

[43]Fowler, *Acts ... Ripon*, 11-12.

[44]LRO B/C/2/2 fol. 48v.

[45]LRO B/C/2/2 fol. 56v. (*peperit proles*).

[46]HRO 21M65/C1/1 fol. 57r.

[47]Elizabeth M. Elvey, ed., *The Courts of the Archdeaconry of Buckingham 1483-1523*, Buckinghamshire Record Society vol. 19 (Buckingham, 1975), 264 (no. 352).

[48]Charles Johnson, ed., *Registrum Hamonis Hethe Diocesis Roffensis AD 1319-1352* [*Hethe*], 2 vols., CYS vols. 48-9 (1948), vol. 1, 200. For pilgrimages to Walsingham, R. P. Mander, "Pilgrimages to East Anglian Shrines," *East Anglian Magazine* 7 (1948): 223-8.

[49]*Hethe*, vol. 1, 233.

[50]*Hethe*, vol. 1, 476.

[51]*Hethe*, vol. 1, 196, 201, 217, 224, 439, 464, 472; II, 596, 598-9, 673, 827, 843, 938, 961-2, 977, 999. Bury St Edmunds was the direction for penitents sent by ecclesiastical courts in the late thirteenth century, as we know from certificates in the letter book of Adam de Hoo, sacristan of the abbey there: Gransden, *The Letter-Book of William of Hoo*, 47 and 81 (nos 38 and 150). The journey to Rome was imposed for laying violent hands on a clerk, in accord with the canonical response to this offense: *Hethe* vol. 2, 673 (1341). For voluntary pilgrimage to Compostella, Robert B. Tate, *Pilgrimage to St James of Compostella from the British Isles during the Middle Ages* (E. Allison Peers Lectures 4, Liverpool, 1990) and D. J. Birch, "Selling the Saints: Competition Among Pilgrimage Centres in the Twelfth Century," *Medieval History* 2 (1992): 20-34.

[52]For the suggestion that pilgrimage to Walsingham comprised a "milky way" associated with women: Susan Morrison, *Women Pilgrims in Late Medieval England. Private Piety as Public Performance* (London: Routledge, 2000).

[53]*Hethe*, vol. 1, 196, 217.

[54]*Hethe*, vol. 1, 201, 224.

[55]*Hethe*, vol. 1, 72, 108; II, 769.

[56]Nigel Tringham, "A Visitation of Tarvin Prebend, Cheshire, in 1317," *Journal of the Chester Archaeological Society* 73 (1994-5), 88.

[57]Arthur T. Bannister, ed., *The Register of Adam de Orleton, Bishop of Hereford (A.D. 1317-1327)*, Cantilupe Society (Hereford, 1907), 365.

[58]Bannister, *Register of Adam de Orleton*, 165-7, 170-1.

[59]William W. Capes, ed., *The Register of Richard de Swinfield, Bishop of Hereford (A.D. 1283-1317)*, Cantilupe Society (Hereford, 1909), 431.

[60]Joseph H. Parry, ed., *The Register of John de Trillek, Bishop of Hereford (A.D. 1344-1361)*, Cantilupe Society (Hereford, 1910), 80.

[61]Parry, *Register of John de Trillek*, 61.

[62]Parry, *Register of John de Trillek*, 62.

[63]Capes, *Register of Richard de Swinfield*, 337.

[64]Parry, *Register of John de Trillek*, 35.

[65]Bowker, *An Episcopal Court Book*, 3.

[66]Bowker, *An Episcopal Court Book*, 109 (1519).

[67]Elvey, *Courts of the Archdeaconry of Buckingham*, 220 (no. 304).

[68]Cooke, *Act Book ... Whalley*, 8-9, 53, 149-50, 156-6, 164, 166.

[69]Cooke, *Act Book ... Whalley*, 156-7. See also the imposition of penance first in the church of Burnley, then in the castle chapel, and then in Rossendale chapel. Unfortunately, the edition of the act book does not provide details of parish of residence.

[70]WRO 794.011 BA 2513 1(ii) (act book, 1540-50), p. 103 (paginated not foliated). "Et quod publica fama &c in diuersis parochiis dicte Ciuitatis &c"

[71]WRO 794.011 BA 2513 1 (ii), pp. 18-19, 114, 115, 118, 177, 220-1 and 237 are clear examples of penance on three Sundays in the offender's own parish church.

[72]WRO 794.011 BA 2513 1 (i) (act book, 1530-1537), p. 164 (paginated, not foliated).

[73]WRO 794.011 BA 2513 1 (i), p. 294. The penance prescribed here and elsewhere is usefully described as before the cross in the procession and to offer a candle to the priest at the offertory.

[74]For the most recent exposition of the position of the greater sanctuaries, Gervase Rosser, "Sanctuary and Social Negotiation in Medieval England," in *The Cloister and the World. Essays in Medieval History in Honour of Barbara Harvey* ed. John Blair and Brian Golding (Oxford: Oxford Univdersity Press, 1996), 57-79. For the formation of these greater franchises, Rosenwein, *Negotiating Space*.

[75]*Sanctuarium Dunelmense et Sanctuarium Beverlacense*, SS vol. 5 (1837).

[76]Hanawalt, *Crime and Conflict in English Communities 1200-1348*.

[77]Jenny Kermode, *Medieval Merchants. York, Beverley and Hull in the Later Middle Ages* (Cambridge: Cambridge University Press, 1998).

[78]The fullest exploration is Leona C. Gabel, *Benefit of Clergy in England in the Later Middle Ages* (Smith College Studies in History 14, 1928-9).

[79]WRO 716.093 BA 2922. 794.011 BA 2513 contains details of a few claimants in *c*.1544. Benefit was, of course, restricted to males at this time: Cynthia Herrup, *The Common Peace. Participation and the Criminal Law in Seventeenth-century England* (Cambridge: Cambridge University Press, 1987), 48, 50, 143.

[80]For the relationship between grand larceny and claims for benefit of clergy, Thomas Green, *Verdict According to Conscience. Perspectives on the English Criminal Trial Jury, 1200-1800* (Chicago: University of Chicago Press, 1985), 127-8.

[81]WRO 716.093 BA 2922, pp. 121-2 (paginated not foliated). The volume provides details of origin and status only inconsistently.

[82]For the social status of later claimants to benefit, Herrup, *Common Peace*, 151.

[83]Joyce Horn, ed., *The Register of Robert Hallum, Bishop of Salisbury, 1407-17*, CYS vol. 72 (1982), 148-9 (nos 1004-5).

[84]So adding to the perceptions in Hanawalt and Kobialka, *Medieval Practice of Space.*

4

"Localism" in Late-Medieval England

> To live is to live locally, and to know is first of all to know the places one is in.[1]

When, in 1470, Robert Dale made bequests in his last testament, he intended to support the fabric of the churches of Northallerton (2s.), Danby Wiske (2s.), Langton (1s.), Scrowston (1s. 8d.) and Bedale (2s.), as well as his own parish church.[2] About nineteen years later, John Elyez of Banningham in Norfolk made bequests of 3s. 4d. to each of three parish churches and 1s. 8d. to another.[3] A year previously, Henry Bylawe of Wickhampton (Norfolk), made benefactions in his will towards the maintenance of all the contiguous parish churches, that is, 1s. 8d. to the fabric of each of Freethorpe, Halvergate, Tunstall, Moulton, Southwood, Limpenhoe, Reedham, and South Burlingham–and, indeed, 4d. to the curate at each of these churches.[4] In the archdeaconry of Norwich in 1536, Anne Athowe, widow of Brisley, amongst her many devotional bequests, gave 3s. 4d. towards the maintenance of each of the adjacent parish churches of Gateley, North Elmham, Beetley, Mileham, Stanfield and Horningtoft.[5] In these selected, illustrative examples of bequests, the benefactions were directed to several churches within a locality. It was the idea of (churches within) a locality which was foremost rather than legacies to specific persons within the testator's local area. This distinction is important in contrasting these benefactions with social connections across a local area described briefly below. Ideas about "belonging" in pre-modern British history have tended (although not exclusively) to focus on place and in particular the parish and its "community"–that is, integration within a single parish.[6] Dale (and the other testators), nonetheless, can be interpreted as expressing an attachment to a locality, a nexus of parish churches, which had a significance in his life (and, prospectively, his death). Although the multitude of late-medieval parishioners concentrated on their own, single parish of residence, a small number experienced the same sentiment as Dale.[7]

We are highly familiar now with the concept of "belonging" and with equating its sense with the parish as the historical "community"–a bounded entity set against other parishes. Although, putting aside identity through group solidarity or other forms of association, attachment to place might have involved a hierarchy of places, the primary attachment to the parish in the English past seems to have been enduring. Undoubtedly for most people the sense of "belonging" was associated with their parish.[8] The trap which we might fall into is that these sorts of attachments were socially uniform.[9] Even attachment to the parish might have been the privilege of a social group within the parish, the "stayers" from kinships and the established social groups.[10] The introduction of the poor laws and the laws of settlement no doubt reinforced the claims of the poor on parishes and so may have promoted a form of "attachment" through entitlement.[11] The floating population of migrants and the poorest might well hitherto have remained excluded from association with the parish. It is at another social level, furthermore, that local attachments outside the parish can also be detected. This latter group was constituted from the more affluent parishioners and is reflected in their testamentary bequests as above. What is seen in operation here is the formation of personal *espaces vécus*, localized life-worlds beyond the parish.[12]

There were, of course, other aspects of localism. The notion of the "country" had a special resonance, signified by the Latin equivalent, *patria*.[13] With some misunderstanding, Henry Reynforth of Halifax in 1521 referred to his mortuary "after the use of the contre", although mortuaries then were exacted by canon law; his confusion was, though, understandable.[14] More lucidly, John Hardde, a husbandman of Marton, desired "that my body have honest buryall after the maner & custome of the countrey."[15] For another aspect of testamentary provision, Oliver Feyrechyld specified that his residual estate be divided amongst his children "after the custome and maner of the cuntrey."[16] So too Alexander Ellott made provision for the distribution of his residual estate "After the use and Custum of the Cuntre" and Nicholas Blowett "after the costomme And maner of ower contre."[17] In like manner, when the will of John Mylnarr of Bradbourne (Derbyshire) made provision in 1544 for the third part of his personal estate for his wife, it recited: "acordyngly to the custome of the Cuntreye."[18] The division of the personal estate of Richard Ward of Chebsey conformed to the notion of third parts, but since the whole of the will was composed in Latin, in the corresponding phrase "secundum consuetudinem patrie [according to the custom of the country]."[19] John Wole of Biddulph phrased the principle in the vernacular with emphasis: "accordyng to the custom of owr contray."[20] In 1541 Roger Rushton, of Leek, wished his son Thomas to have his heirlooms "Accordyng to the custum off thys cuntrey" and for the division of his personalty between his wife and children "Accordyng to the custum in these partyes used."[21] This affection for and association with the prevailing local usage is exhibited further in the final wish of John Dernylye: "I wyll be brogthe furthe off my nawn parte acordyng to the custom of the cuntrey."[22] The mistaken provision of Henry Reynforth was repeated by Nicholas Beynett of Glossop in 1540: his mortuary "as use & custom ys yn the Contre", an error repeated by John Stevenson of Brampton who also ordained his mortuary "as the costum of the contre ys."[23] In large measure, the desire for burial according to the custom of the country was equally misguided. For such customs did not really exist. Customs of inheritance did differ regionally and the notion of the *legitim*–the tripartite division of personal estate of the married male testator–obtained in the north Midlands as well as the far North. What is really reflected in these provisions, however, is an attachment to a particular locality and wish to conform to the practices, whether imagined or real, of that locality, the "country".

Whilst contemporaries recognized the significance of the *patria* for local customs and usages, they could not, however, demonstrate their attachment to it concretely. It existed amorphously.[24] For inhabitants of early-modern England, that experience of a wider social space, although still painstaking to elucidate, has been made more apparent. It has been demonstrated that social and kinship networks often extended over a nexus of parishes, but, again, the precise implications of that extended social geography remains imprecise. For example, Anne Mitson has revealed kinship networks across groups of parishes in southern Nottinghamshire and the importance of these "core" or "focal" families in localities–not just single parishes–has been remarked upon by Henry French.[25] Charles Phythian-Adams has inspired this search for wider levels of social relationships, endorsed recently by Keith Wrightson.[26] All these conglomerations of relationships developed out of social and kinship networks rather than attachment to a locality–although that association may, for some, have been generated by the social networks in due course. Affection for a locality *qua* local environment might be something different. For the late-medieval English population, however, we extend back into a comparatively less-well documented time, so that our discovery of the spatial experiences of people will be fragmentary.

On the other hand, it might make some sense to consider such wider horizons and a hierarchy of "belonging". Human and regional geographers have, for example, indicated that the space within which people move is not so confined. The *espace vécu* was larger than the parish and so we have a phenomenology at a different spatial level. It is with those whose *espace vécu* was more than one parish that this chapter is concerned.

The purpose is to try to understand how many people might have had a familiarity with a wider locality in late-medieval England and how that space was experienced.

These *espaces vécus* were developed through personal enterprise and experience. The solidarity of attachment with these wider spaces was enabled, however, by the character of late-medieval religious devotion. A belief in the doctrine of purgatory stimulated testators to desire intercession through prayers by the living to expedite the progress of souls through purgatory. Testators with these wider local associations might thus invoke the assistance of several local parishes with which they were associated rather than simply their own parish of domicile. Following an exposition of the evidence, in the second part consideration is given to the interpretation of what those attachments to more than one parish might mean. It is the formation of these *espaces vécus* in association with prayers and masses for the dead which is the focus. It must be emphasized, nonetheless, that the phenomenon was restricted to a small proportion of testators and an even smaller cohort of all those who died, since those who left wills remained a minority at this time.

Most of the evidence produced below is acquired from testamentary bequests. The use of this material itself poses problems, perhaps insoluble. For the time concerned–up to about 1550–will-making remained somewhat exclusive, initially in the last half of the fifteenth century reserved to a small section of the population. We are therefore dealing with the perceptions of a minority within local populations. Secondly, testamentary provision is an activity at the end of life: it may not very well reflect the earlier circumstances of the life-course. What we have through testamentary bequests is access to the perceptions of those with an accumulation of spatial experience (and social capital), not typical at all perhaps of those at different (earlier) stages in the life-course.[27] It is still worth having these understandings of the later life-course to provide a counterbalance to the notion of the parish as the *only* source of an emotion of "belonging". Having said that, however, it is undoubtedly true that the primary sense of "belonging" was associated with the parish. The bequests of most will-makers establish that. What is explored here, however, is how wider socio-spatial experience was permitted to some inhabitants of localities and how they reflected on those wider associations.[28]

Sentiments about locality were not confined, of course, to this realm of the spiritual–although in the cultural worlds of early-modern societies it is nigh on impossible to separate religious from other motives. Before and after the Reformation, charitable giving through wills might reflect allegiances to wider social areas. We might cite a few illustrative examples. In his will of 1531, William Rayne of Cottisbrooke remembered the poor of the parishes of Creeton, Holwell, Gilborough, North Toft, Naseby and Haslebeach.[29] Three years later, William Burton of Hagnaby made provision for the poor of his own parish and those of Dunsby, Morton and Repingale.[30] A further six years thereafter, the poor of his own parish of Toynton St Peter were not the only concern of Richard Newsome, for, although a yeoman, he directed in his will that 20d. be distributed to the poor in each of the parishes of Greetham, Followby, Ashby and Horncastle.[31] In the period of the Marian restoration, in 1557, Robert Thornehill of Woodhall in Holderness, expressed his attachment to places significant to him through his testamentary bequests to the poor of Walkeringham (20s.), Misterton (20s.), Beckingham (10s.), Gainsborough (20s.), Gringley (6s. 8d.), and Misson (13s. 4d.).[32]

We can return then to the commitment by Robert Dale in 1470. From a number of sample counties we have wills of a select proportion of testators who made bequests to more than three parish churches–at least the testator's own parish and two other parishes. Where a testator made a bequest to only one parish in addition to parish of habitation, it is possible that the bequest was to parish of origin. That bequest represents a complex sense of "belonging", but not necessarily attachment to a locality. Francis Whitwell, of Egford in the suburb of Lincoln, thus made a bequest to the church works of Dighton where he was born (a substantial amount of 6s. 8d.) and also remitted a further 6s. 8d. to the same church works to acquit the "wittword" of his sister, Cecily.[33]

That sentimental dualism was experienced by Thomas Cusslyn who made his will in Hingham in 1499. He specified 5s. as his mortuary to the rector of Hingham, directed 20d. to the high altar (probably for tithes "forgotten", illustrating he was a landholder in Hingham), and bequeathed 13s. 4d. for the reparation fund for Hingham church. He also made provision for the observance of his death in Hingham church. After that observance, however, his body was to be transferred to Hardingham church for the important offices and ceremony–including, no doubt, the commendation–before his burial at Hardingham beside his late wife.[34] In deciding on a baseline of bequests to parish of habitation and two other parishes, then, we are attempting to eliminate that complex sense of "belonging" of migrants to parish of origin and current parish. Although that dual sense is important, the focus here is on a sense of attachment to a locality.

Some additional refinements must also be introduced into the selection of testators. First, we have discounted bequests made to the high altar of other parishes. Directions of payments by testators to high altars probably represent the conscience of the testator about unpaid ("forgotten") tithes–in which case the testator had lands in those parishes. These payments to high altars do reflect a sense of belonging, but one complicated by landholding, not necessarily one of purely emotive association with locality, although it might have been infused with devotion to the sacrament. Similarly bequests to particular saints in churches are excluded since they might illuminate local or personal devotions, but not necessarily a sense of belonging. The evidential material is thus restricted to bequests to the churches or to the church works. Also excluded are bequests to friars or religious houses since they also reflect a different mode of association.

We cannot assume, therefore, that notions of "belonging" to a locality existed everywhere. On the other hand, where some testators did patronize more than two parishes in their wills, we do have some intimations of their intentions. Robert Halgarth, tanner of Horncastle, in his testament of 1529 bequeathed money to the parish churches of Bamborough, Thimbleby, Langton, Thornton, Dalderby, Screlby, Mering, Upper Toynton, Ashby, Scrafeld, Winceby, Spilsby, and Nether Toynton, all of which lay on his regular journeying between Horncastle and Spilsby, reflecting how his quotidian experience informed his sense of belonging to this locality.[35] In 1555, John Dyar of Kilmersden in Somerset allocated 1s. in his will to each of the seven parish churches (not named) which adjoined his own parish.[36] In 1530, Thomas Byrkeytt requested his executors to provide a bushel of malt "to every churche that marchys upon hus".[37] Four years later, John Stawper of Nettleton bequeathed 8d. to the parish church of Kelsey and 4d. to every other parish church "aboundyng on the towne of Nettylton".[38] Although not specifically directed to churches, John Huddylstone of Rowston, made provision for legacies of 3s. 4d. to each of the four "towns" "jonyng abowt" his parish.[39] The localism of some testators is reflected in their description of their bequests.

John Pudsey of Stonesby, for example, in 1544 specified 1s. to every church which "marchys on these meares", that is, a donation to all the neighboring parish churches.[40] It might be presumed that the twelve unspecified churches to which William Rychardson of Melton Mowbray also offered 1s. by his will of 1544 were contained within a concentric circle around that market town.[41] What these testators intended to elicit was remembrance within the adjacent parish churches for the benefit of their souls.

Some of the gentry, of course, astutely patronized numerous parish churches, the best example of which was Robert Jakes, of Bagworth Park, one of the retinue of Lord Hastings. Amongst his munificent gestures for the benefit of his soul, he allocated 3s. 4d. to the contiguous parish churches and chapelries of Stanton, Ibstock, Heather, Shackerstone, Swepstone, Nailstone, Markfield, Newbold Verdon, Barlestone, and Desford, and a cow for Thornton.[42] Although not quite of such elevated status, Mary

Beamont in her will of 1537, as well as arranging for burial by her husband in the chancel of Goadby parish church, assigned 1s. to each of the parish churches of Eastwell, Walton, Hose and Caldwell.[43] More generous in his provision was John Prior of Great Glen, whose status was reflected in his bequest of £1 to his parish church, his establishment of a chantry priest to sing for two years with an allowance of £10, and his burial inside the church. Prior allocated 6s. 8d. to the local parishes of Wistow, Newton Harcourt, Oadby, Great and Little Stretton, Burton Overy, the two Kibworths, Smeeton Westerby, Foxton, Lubenham and Great Bowden.[44] With an inventory valuation of £90 5s. 3d., Thomas Bradgate of Peatling Parva was similarly in a position to be fairly bountiful in his bequest of 6s. 8d. to each of the parish churches of Gilmorton, Ashby Magna, Willoughby Waterless, Peatling Magna, Bruntingthorpe, and Kimcote.

Testamentary bequests before 1550 were, of course, associated with a select proportion of society. One of the further complications is that few testators defined their status in wills before the middle of the sixteenth century. We can, nonetheless, illustrate that bequests to multiple local parishes were not restricted to those of gentry status. Rural landholders of a more modest nature were involved in this patronage. In 1529, William Hale, a yeoman of Marston Mortaine (Bedfordshire), made benefactions to three other local parishes: Flitton, Pulloxhill and Houghton Conquest.[45] Five years later, a husbandman of Grimoldby (Lincolnshire), made provision in his will for three other parish churches.[46] In 1534 also, another testator from the same village made benefactions to six other parish churches.[47] In Somerset in 1545, Thomas Othis, a yeoman, patronized his own and six other parish churches.[48] These examples are merely illustrations of donations to multiple parish churches in the testaments of yeomen and husbandmen. None of those testators belonged to the social elite of local gentry status, although all pertained to the upper echelon of rural and local small-town society. Whilst Rychardson was engaged as a tailor in Melton, Pudsey's inventory valuation amounted to £50 4s. 8d. Although we have no inventory for Rychardson, his aspirations at least are represented by his bequests: a small amount to each of the two gilds in Melton (4d.), 6s. 8d. to his parish church, 10s. for a trental (thirty masses), 10s. and a silver spoon to the local clergy, and his burial costs to constitute £1. Although Pudsey requested burial inside his parish church, Rychardson was satisfied with interment in the churchyard.

What is most apparent about the status of most of these testators, however, is their non-gentle condition. Alice Hyll, of Sharnford, whose inventory valuation amounted to £19 19s. 0d., allocated 1s. each to the parish churches of Sapcot Owene, Frolesworth, Claybrooke, and Aston Flamvile.[49] Unfortunately, only half a dozen of the wills contained an occupational description of the testator, four of whom ascribed themselves to the category of husbandman.[50] Even at the lowest level of rural society, some testators at least aspired to make benefactions to several parish churches. It is quite possible that widows or single-women without any dependants or children had the facility to make endowments to parish churches despite their insubstantial wealth. For example, Maud Gamull of Saxelby, whose inventory valuation only extended to £4 0s. 4d., expressed a desire to be buried in the parish church at the normal cost of 6s. 8d., but also to make benefactions of 5s. to Asfordby church and 1s. to each of the churches and chapels at Welby, Wartnaby, Grimston and Nether Broughton.[51] Her personal estate accounting for no more than £4 10s. 10d., Margaret Kynde of Peckleton hoped for the distribution of 6s. to the poor at her burial, 3s. 4d. in alms in Kibworth Harcourt, benefactions of 6s. 8d. to each of two parish churches, 3s. 4d. to each of four chapels and churches, a cow and a calf to her own church, and 3s. to the local clergy.[52] In like manner, the widow of Saddington, Agnes Hortone, was able to consider 2s. for the church of Shearsby and 1s. to three other churches and chapels.[53]

The strategy of some other rural parishioners with inconsiderable personal estate consisted of smaller amounts of cash to the church, such as the 4d. to each of six churches assigned by Thomas Hawson of Nether Broughton (inventory valuation £8 5s. 8d.) and the 6d. to each of seven churches by William Hardman of Welby (inventory valuation £7 3s. 1d.).[54]

Another approach to afford benefactions to multiple parish churches consisted of benefactions in kind, most usually small measures of malt which could be used to generate income for the church through church ales. Although his inventory totaled £73 5s. 11d., John Masham of Billesdon still resorted to gifts of a single bushel of malt to each of eight local parish churches–and only the same to his own parish church.[55] At least a dozen other will-makers resorted to provision of small amounts of malt (most often not exceeding a bushel) to several local parish churches.[56]Exceptionally, Thomas Walton of Hoby provided half a quarter of malt for the eight parish churches which he benefited.[57] At the other end of the spectrum, Thomas Elys of Plungar, with personal estate of merely £5 3s. 0d., could manage only a bushel for each of two parish churches, the Lady light, and St. Barbara's light.[58] Although not as impoverished, William Bardon of Cossington allocated only swarms of bees to the parish churches of Rothley and Thurcaston.[59]

For the diocese of Norwich, we have information from the register *sede vacante* of 1499 and also, for the archdeaconry of Sudbury, from the register "Baldwyne", engrossing the probate of wills between 1439 and 1461 (See Fig. 4.1).[60] In the Suffolk part of the diocese, bequests to parish churches were affected by a predilection for the friars in Cambridge, Colchester, Ipswich, Orford, Norwich and Dunwich, but most particularly those in Babwell, Thetford, Sudbury and Clare. This disposition towards the friars no doubt reduced testators' resources for making benefactions to parish churches.

A fair number of testators, however, did bequeath money to adjacent parishes, some quite notably. Amongst these exceptional benefactors was Peter Fysscher of Hepworth who, in 1439, made assignments of money to the parish churches of Fakenham Magna, Sapiston, Wordwell, West Stow, Cockfield, and Great Welnetham.[61] His actions were exceeded by John Stalour whose will of 1452 contained benefactions to the parish churches of Isleham, Moulton, Newmarket, Barton, Tuddenham, Brandon, Eriswell and Lakenheath.[62] Not greatly surpassed, Thomas Schorthose, a weaver of Sudbury, benefited the churches of Bulmer, Borley, two of the Belchamptons, Great Cornard, Great Henney, and Acton (1459).[63]

In fifteenth-century Suffolk, very many churches were being re-fashioned in perpendicular style, not least towers and south porches. Some testators obviously maintained a watchful eye on what was happening in their locality. Thus Thomas Gatle of Great Livermore, made a provision in his will of 1440 for ten marks to the fabric of the new tower of Great Barton provided the parishioners commenced the work within a year of his death.[64] That same observation of the locality stimulated Robert Honford, to allocate money to another parish: "Item I giff to the makyng off the church of Cheidell xxxiijs. iiijd. to be peid as their workis goith forward."[65]

The material for Buckinghamshire is less problematic (See Fig. 4.2 for Buckinghamshire and Bedfordshire).[66] Testators' actions here were not really affected by patronage of the mendicants. As an example of benefactions, Richard Kyne of North Marston in 1484 allocated 3s. 4d. to each of the parish churches of Oving, Pichecote, Hogston and Greenborough, and 6s. 8d. to that of Fenny Stratford.[67] In Bedfordshire, the presence of the friars, particularly in Bedford and Dunstable, interfered in the process of testamentary bequests. There too the attraction of augmenting the lights in the parishioners' own churches was strong.[68]

Remaining within the diocese of Lincoln, the evidential material for Lincolnshire is exceptional, comprising a large mass of testamentary instruments of the early sixteenth century.[69] (See Fig. 4.3) Unfortunately, the material for Somerset (Fig. 4.4) is complicated by the manner in which the testamentary material has been edited. Some assumptions therefore have to be made–that the various editions of wills do not involve any serious duplication. Here, an example of a benefactor of several churches is William Sampson of Milborn Port who in 1545 desired legacies to the parish churches of Haydon, Woborne, Pottington, Charlton Cromwell, Stawell, Hengstrege and Candill.[70]

Notions of "belonging" in the area around Leeds (comprising the parishes of Leeds, Sherburne, Batley, Methley, Whitkirk, Rothwell and so on) were quite the opposite. Between 1514 and 1537, fewer than a dozen of the 226 testators made a bequest to a parish other than their own, and then only to one other parish rather than several. For example, Alice Dyneley of Whitkirk bequeathed 6s. 8d. to Garforth church in 1527 and Richard Grave of Rothwell 2s. to Methley church. Whilst Robert Hemsworth did make benefactions to several churches, he also conferred money on their high altars for forgotten tithes, suggesting that he held lands in those parishes.[71]

For Leicestershire, more specific details can be presented.[72] Of a total of 1139 wills proved between 1522 and 1546 inclusive, just fifty-five included bequests to two or more parish churches other than the testator's own parish church (Fig. 4.5). The testators patronized a mean of four churches each. The rank order can be summarized as follows: bequests to two churches by thirteen testators; three by fourteen; four by ten; five by seven; six by four; eight by four; nine by one; and twelve by two.

Some sporadic data can be included for the diocese of Lichfield.[73] John Dyxson of Ansley, Warwickshire, for example, included a bequest of 1s. to ten "other" parish churches, as well as two wax torches (each 6s. 8d.) to his own parish church. His inventory valuation of some £44 placed him in a position to remember these churches and to request them to commemorate him.[74] With some £25 of personal estate, Thomas Brown of Croxall, could equally afford to make a bequest of 1s. not only to his own parish church but to three others.[75] Assessed with similar personal estate, just over £23, Richard Stonele of Napton on the Hill complemented the 1s. 4d. that he bequeathed to his own parish church with 4d. to each of the churches of Harbury, Lodbrooke, Southam and Hardwick.[76] In like manner, Richard Garratt of Cubbington allocated 1s. to his own parish church and five other adjacent parish churches.[77] Since his personal estate amounted to no more than £6 4s.10d., William Garlande bequeathed a ewe and lamb–in themselves symbolic–to four churches other than his own parish at Packington.[78] With particular intensity, Edmund Heyteley of Aston provided for bequests of 2s. to two other parish churches and 1s. to four others and a chapelry.[79] With similar personal estate, Richard Jude of Packington Priors, although only bequeathing his best pot and pan to his own parish church, earmarked a lamb to each of the churches of Maxstoke, Meriden and Anstey to request prayers there.[80] From his parish of Shifnall, Thomas Howlle made benefactions of two tapers to Longford church and five pounds of wax to each of the churches of Gnowsall and Forton–the wax and lights, as the lambs above, bearing particular symbolism, perhaps associated with the self-presentation of this wealthy individual.[81] John Wodwarde of Allestree wished to present local parish churches with wax torches, two to his own church, and one to Tamworth and Chorley churches, and 8d. and 4d. to Overton and Norton churches respectively.[82] Joan Hootun, despite her more modest means, made bequests of 3s. 4d. to one church and 1s. 8d. to two churches other than her own parish church (which she also liberally patronized).[83] In the case of the will of the gentleman, William Reydyng of Chilvers Coton, it is perhaps less surprising that he bequeathed to the churchwardens of the four parishes of Nuneaton, Bedworth, Exall and Astley 3s. 4d. each to perform a mass and dirige and ringing, additional to the same amount for the same purpose to the churchwardens of his own parish.[84] John Wodwarde of Allestree remembered adjacent parish churches in his will in 1535: a wax torch each to Tamworth and Chorley; 8d. to Overton; and 4d. to Norton.[85]

The same sort of devotional effervescence was exhibited by William Sambroke of Kynnersley in his will of 1536. To his own parish church and to Offley church he wished to donate a taper for a light to burn before the Easter sepulchre until the (day of the) Resurrection and then to be placed before the holy rood and to be lit at the high time of the principal feasts throughout the year. He added three flaxen sheets for his parish church, one to cover our Lady on the north side of the church, another our Lady on the south side, and one to cover St. Chad (the principal image). Not content, he instructed 6s. 8d. to be remitted for a missal and 2s. 4d. for a processional. He extended his benefactions of wax for lights: 1 lb. for a taper before St. Christopher; 1 lb. to light the image of St. Peter in Edgmond church; 1 lb to illuminate the same saint's image in Worbury church; and 1 lb for that of St. Michael in Chetwynd church. He further asked for (the profits from) a cow to be divided between Adbaston church and Sillenton chapel. It is then consistent that he wished to provide 10s. for a trental and for his year's mind. Of the four supervisors nominated by this copyholder's will, two were clergy, the rectors of his own parish and of Upton.[86]

For his funeral, Richard Elkes stipulated twelve tapers (each priced at 6d.) to burn around his body, to be distributed afterwards to six parish churches as well as his own.[87] Griffith Evans and John Edward had the same idea, the former allocating his funeral tapers to four other parish churches and Edward to three.[88] Both testators expressed their association with the same nexus of parishes in Shropshire, around Baschurch. The husbandman John Getyn also belonged to this locality, assigning tapers from his funeral to Baschurch and two other churches, Cockshutt and Fitz.[89]

In the urban context, some parishioners extended their largesse to all the parishes within the town. In the borough of Derby, for example, Roger Woodward of St. Werburgh's parish, made provision in the late 1530s for the poor in all the urban parishes, 5s. for those in St. Alkmund's parish, 3s. 4d. those in St. Michael's, 6s. 8d. those in All Saints, 5s. those in St. Peter's, and another 5s. those in St. Werburgh's. The higher amount for All Saints reflected its position as the leading urban parish because of its collegiate status and so, like many testators in Derby, Roger specifically requested the presence of the sub-dean of All Saints as well as the priests from all other parishes in the town, to attend his funeral.[90]

We can now make one further suggestion about these bequests to multiple local parishes, although one which cannot be fully substantiated but is only a strong possibility. Parochial clergy frequently made bequests to numerous local parish churches in their wills. We do not need to re-hearse these clerical testaments in detail—an example will suffice. In 1543, John Manfeld, rector of Ivelchester, made donations to the parish churches of St. Mary the More, Northover, Lymyngton, Yevilton, Ilminster, Ticknell and North Curry.[91] This clerical sentiment of association with other local parish churches had a different inspiration from lay testators', but it may have influenced those lay testators who made bequests to their local parish churches. In other words, it is possible that our lay benefactors of multiple parishes were imitating a clerical convention.

Migration for opportunities for landholding in the later middle ages may also have influenced the nature of bequests. Some of the bequests in Lincolnshire seem to reflect movement and remembering a parish of origin. Another aspect of the reorganization of the later middle ages was the accumulation of land in more than one parish and that too might have informed bequests to parish churches, although the exclusion of benefactions to the high altar will have made allowance to some extent. Another consequence of the movements might have been the distribution of kinship networks over several adjacent parishes. All these characteristics of the demography, opportunities for landholding, and migration of the later middle ages might have influenced the bequests of testators to parish churches.

In Lincolnshire—and Somerset too—a local tradition of communal activity between parishes had long been established, for inter-commoning, the exploitation of moors and marshland, and drainage and sea-banking. Almost seventy townships co-operated for sea-bank maintenance in 1345.[92] This legacy of co-operative action might have stimulated bequests by testators to several local churches rather than simply their own parish.

We should not, however, underestimate the importance of spiritual motives in bequests to multiple parishes—if not by the testator, then by the encouragement of a loved one. So Richard Hurresdysch of Ashover, although possessing personal estate valued at only £ 5 3s. 0d., left a ewe to each of the church of Matlock and a leper house by the exhortations of his wife: "Item to matcloke Chyrch that was my Wyffe mynde a3ew ... Item to burton lazers that was my wyffe mynde a3ew".'[93] The ethos of the Church universal might have encouraged a wider perception of spiritual obligations. One way in which testators with the wherewithal might accomplish their belonging to the universal church was through their patronage of several parish churches in the locality. The bequests to other parishes–defined here by donations to the church or the church works–did not ostensibly specify any counter-gift, but testators probably expected spiritual benefits from their generosity–their good works dispatching their souls through purgatory. Through this invocation of the intercession of the congregations of other parish churches for the health of the testator's soul, the testator was invoking an interdependency across a locality. The testator predicates not inter-parish rivalry, competition or hostility, but participation in a local alliance of the devotional. Of course, the relationship between testators' aspirations and the reality of response to their wishes is complicated. One cannot assume that the parishioners in these other parishes responded positively, nor, indeed, that the parishioners of the testators' own parishes had equanimity about the "alienation" of resources. Benefaction to other parish churches might evoke feelings of "betrayal"; they might stimulate sentiments of envy; they might result in reactions against the display of wealth and the "privileges" it conferred and the belief that the use of wealth could purchase salvation. Those are possibilities and potentialities. Since such recourse was not accessible to the majority, but achievable only by the few, participation in the belief as well as the action may be doubtful.[94]

We should add as an aside here too a note about the extension of spiritual benefits in wills not only to the testator's soul and souls named by the testator, but all Christian souls. We should not immediately assume that such an inclusion was foremost in the minds of testators. It may well be that this prescription was at the instigation of the drafter of the will (often clerical) rather than the testator. In this present context, we might also point out that the inclusion of all Christian souls was intended when masses were specifically ordained, but when gift-exchange was latent or implicit, as in these benefactions to other parish churches, souls were not mentioned at all. Without further substantiation, we are limited to commenting that some–and admittedly a minor proportion of–testators appealed to a wider area in their search for assurance for their souls, concomitant with their perception of "locality".[95]

We might then speculate–for it requires further consideration and substantiation–on the events of the later sixteenth century which might have disrupted this pattern of donations. One effect of the triumph of Protestantism might have been to inculcate the primacy of one's own parish. Simultaneously the formation of the Tudor state through the agency of parochial officers might have encouraged this concentration on the single parish.[96] More particularly the poor law statutes of 1597 and 1601 might have emphasized that principal responsibility to one's own parish.[97] We must not create too concrete a divide here, for late-medieval society had already developed notions of the deserving poor and one's own. In making provision for the poor in his will of 1536, Robert Thyrkill of West Walton was fairly emphatic in his restriction of the enjoyment of his alms: "Item I will that myn executours do give to x poore men within oure owen parishe to iche of them iiijd immediately after my Dethe."[98] For most late-medieval testators, the inevitable focus was their own parish, sentimentally, but also pragmatically. On the other hand, Catholic notions of purgatory provided an incentive to think more widely about one's position in a wider, if local, (life-)world, an opportunity taken by a small proportion of will-makers. Their post-mortem benefactions probably reflected their vision of their locality and it may have been one shared by others who did not have the same level of resources.

Number of parishes	Number of wills	Percentage of wills
2	81	32.53
3	58	23.29
4	42	16.87
5	24	9.64
6	16	6.43
7	9	3.61
8	7	2.81
9	4	1.61
10	3	1.2
11	1	0.4
12	1	0.4
13	2	0.8
19	1	0.4

Table 4.1   Rank Distribution of Bequests to Multiple Parishes (Excluding Leicestershire)

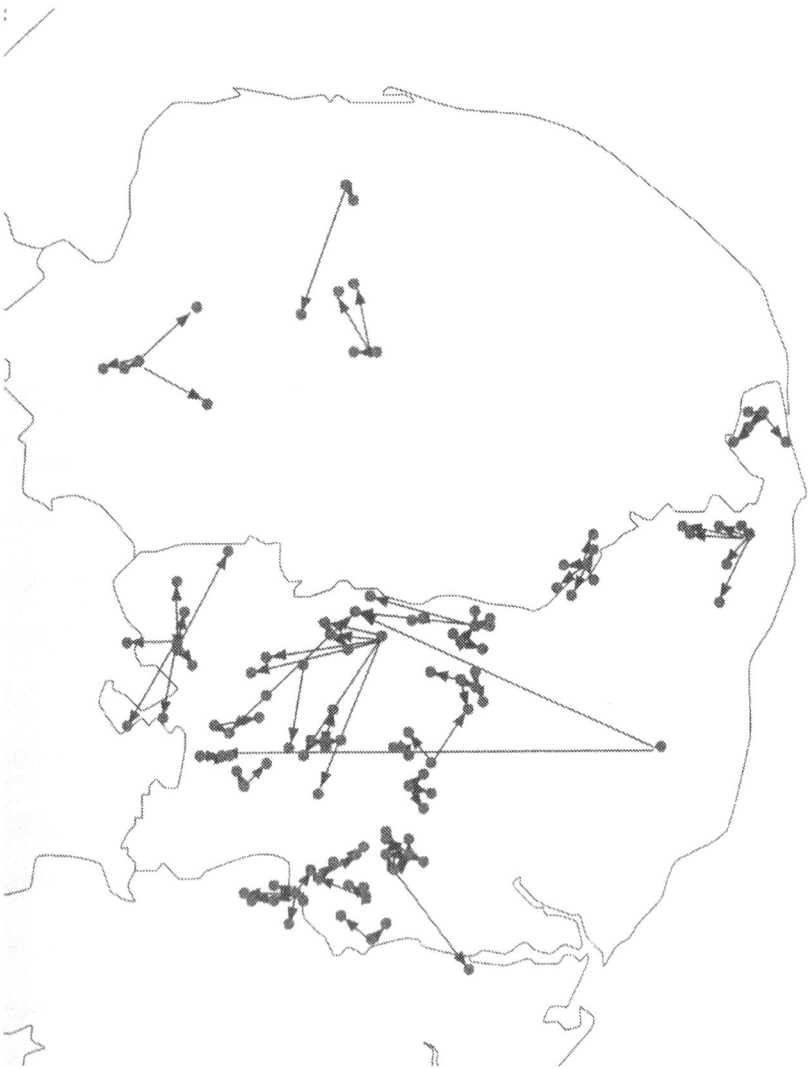

Figure 4.1   Diocese of Norwich: Testamentary Bequests to Several
Parishes

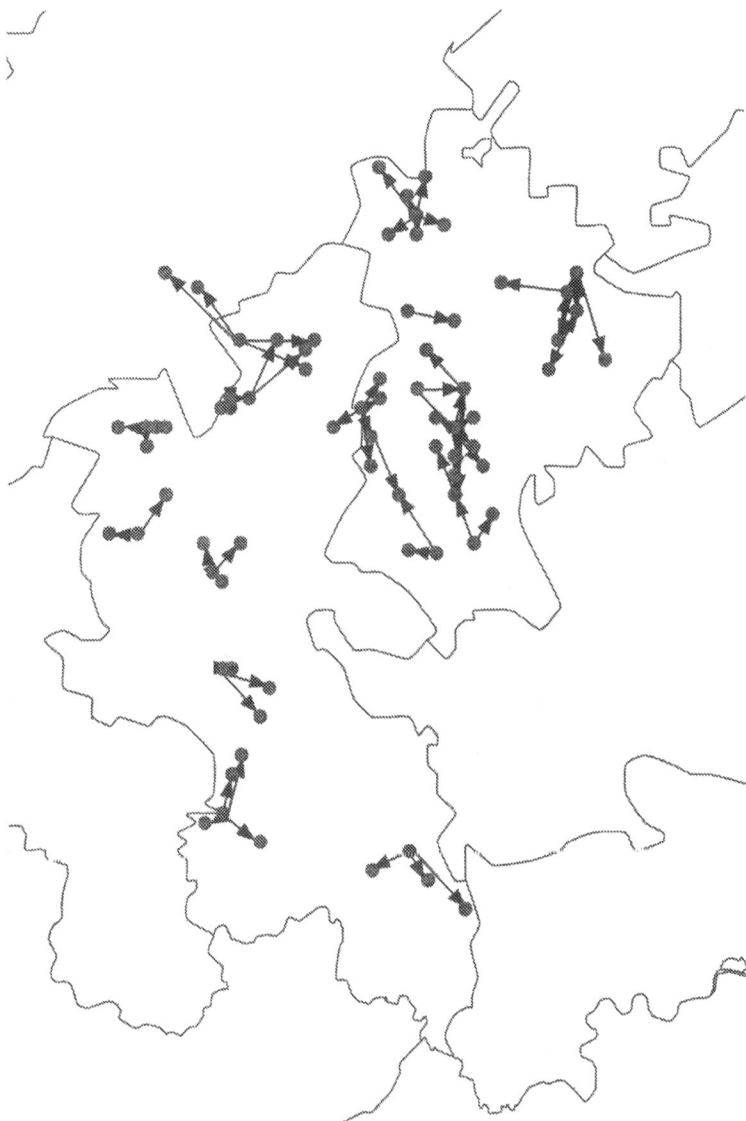

Figure 4.2   Buckinghamshire and Bedfordshire: Testamentary Bequests to Several Parishes

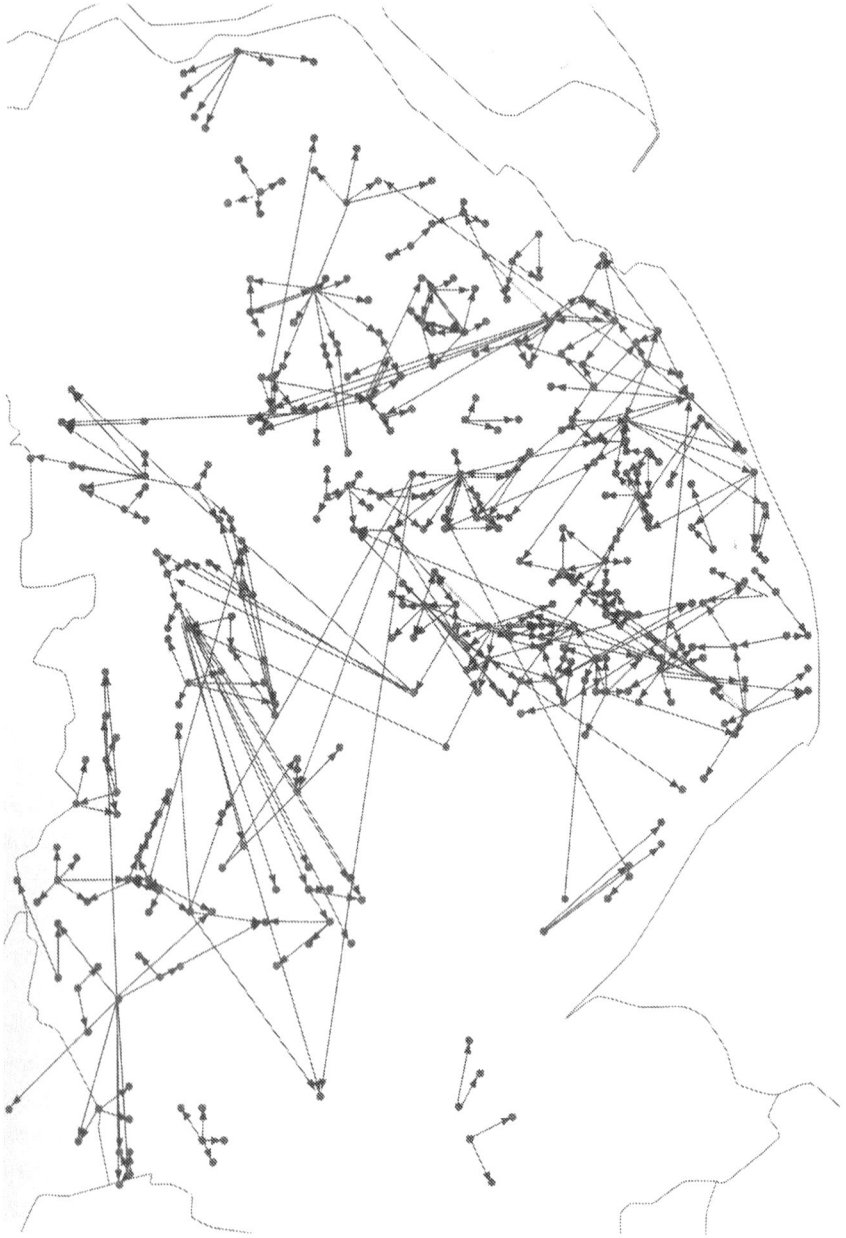

Figure 4.3   Lincolnshire: Testamentary Bequests to Several Parishes

Figure 4.4   Somerset: Testamentary Bequests to Several Parishes

Figure 4.5   Archdeaconry of Leicester: Testamentary Bequests to Several Parishes

Notes

[1]Edward Casey, "How to Get from Space to Place in a Fairly Short Stretch of Time. Phenomenological Prolegomena," in *Senses of Place* ed. Feld and Basso, 18. Whilst I am not fundamentally in agreement with this phenomenological starting point, it is a useful heuristic point of departure. Somewhere along the line, one has to engage with space and place in a hermeneutic manner to get beyond self to society. For an outline of this aspect of humanistic geography, Peet, *Modern Geographical Thought*, 37-66. For attempts to move to theoretical considerations of locale and locality, Peet, *Modern Geographical Thought*, 180-8, and, importantly, Soja, *Postmodern Geographies*, 150-2. For a succinct explanation of the return to idiographic geography and "sense of place", Crang, *Cultural Geography*, 100-12.

[2]Raine, *Wills and Inventories from the Registers of the Archdeaconry of Richmond*, 8-9 (vii). Throughout this chapter, will and testament will be used interchangeably, but technically at law a testament was restricted to the distribution of personal estate (goods and chattels), whilst the last will (*ultima voluntas*) arranged the disposition of land not directly inherited by the heir at law.

[3]NNRO Archdeaconry of Norwich Register Cook fol. 141b v.

[4]NNRO Archdeaconry of Norwich Register Cook, fols. 147r-v (1488).

[5]NNRO Archdeaconry of Norwich register of wills (microfilm 503), fols 1r-v.

[6]For notions of "belonging", Anthony P. Cohen, ed., *Belonging: Identity and Social Organisation in British Rural Cultures* (Manchester: Manchester University Press, 1982).

[7]For attachment to the parish in late-medieval England, Katherine French, *The People of the Parish: Community Life in a Late Medieval English Diocese* (Pennsyvlania: University of Pennsylvania Press, 2001); French, Gary Gibbs and Beat Kümin, eds., *The Parish in English Life, 1400-1600* (Manchester: Manchester University Press, 1997); for the conflation of religious and secular association with the "community" of the parish, Kümin, *The Shaping of a Community: The Rise and Reformation of the English Parish, c.1400-1560* (Aldershot: Ashgate, 1996).

[8]Andrew Brown, *Popular Piety in Late Medieval England. The Diocese of Salisbury 1250-1550* (Oxford: Oxford University Press, 1995), 67-158; Ken Farnhill, *Guilds and the Parish Community in Late Medieval East Anglia c.1470-1550* (Woodbridge: Boydell, 2001); French, Gibbs and Kümin, *Parish in English Life*; French, *People of the Parish*; Kümin, *Shaping of a Community*

[9]Indeed, here I must acknowledge that what follows is restricted to identity and place for those who were "(em)placed" rather than the displaced. The best introduction about the problems of place and identity is Feld and Basso, *Senses of Place*, esp. 3-11.

[10]Souden, "Movers and Stayers in Family Reconstitution Populations."

[11]The extent to which this was the case in early-modern English rural society is dissected by Hindle, *On the Parish?* See also Hindle, "A Sense of Place? Becoming and Belonging in the Rural Parish, 1550-1650," in *Communities in Early Modern England*, ed. Alexandra Shepard and Philip Withington (Manchester: Manchester University Press, 2000), 96-114, and "Dependency, Shame and Belonging: Badging the Deserving Poor, c.1550-1750," *Cultural and Social History. The Journal of the Social History Society*, 1 (2004): 6-35.

[12]Claval, *Regional Geography*, 22, 45-46.

[13]Most succinctly explained now by Wrightson, *Earthly Necessities*, 87-89, although perhaps too closely associated with the *pays*.

[14]John W. Clay and Ely W. Crossley, eds., *Halifax Wills Being Abstracts and Translations of the Wills Registered at York from the Parish of Halifax Parts I and II 1389-1544* (Halifax, 1904), 62 .

[15]LRO B/C/11 John Hardde 1542 Marton; see also Isabel Walkar, Mackworth, widow, 1542: honest sepulture after the custom and manor of the "Cowntre".

[16]LRO B/C/11 Oliver Feyrechyld 1543 Norbury.

[17]LRO B/C/11 Alexander Ellott 1544 Duffield, Nicholas Blowett 1538 Tissington (Bradbourne).

[18]LRO B/C/11 John Mylnarr 1544 Bradbourne.

[19]LRO B/C/11 Richard Ward 1537 Chebsey.

[20]LRO B/C/11 John Wole 1538 Biddulph; also Roger Wynkyll, Biddulph, 1545 (division according to the custom of our "contray").

[21]LRO B/C/11 Roger Rushton 1541 Leek.

[22]LRO B/C/11 John Dernylye 1537 Glossop.

[23]LRO B/C/11 Nicholas Beynett 1540 Glossop; John Stevenson 1535 Brampton.

[24]Compare Karen I. Blu, "'Where Do You Stay At?'" in *Senses of Place*, ed. Feld and Basso, 200.

[25]See first, however, the rather neglected essay by David Rollison, "Neighbourhood to Nation: The Trotmans: A Middlerank Kin-coalition, 1512-1712," in his *The Local Origins of Modern Society. Gloucestershire 1500-1800* (London: Routledge, 1992), 97-119, esp. 119: "The rise of the English 'bourgeoisie' was a cumulative process of territorial expansion, a conquest of space". Henry French, "Social Status, Localism and the Middling Sort of People in England, 1630-1750," *Past and Present* 166 (2000): 66-99; Anne Mitson, "The Significance of Kinship Networks in the Seventeenth century: Southwest Nottinghamshire," in *Societies, Cultures and Kinship, 1580-1850: Cultural Provinces in English Local History*, ed. Charles Phythian-Adams (London: Scolar Press, 1992), 24-76.

[26]Phythian-Adams, *Societies, Cultures and Kinship*; Phythian-Adams, *Re-thinking English Local History*, University of Leicester, Occasional Papers in English Local History 4th ser. 1 (Leicester, 1987); Wrightson, *Earthly Necessities*, 87, 93.

[27]The consideration of probate material as source has been placed on a firmer basis by Tom Arkell, Nesta Evans and Nigel Goose, eds., *When Death Do Us Part. Understanding and Interpreting the Probate Records of Early Modern England* (Oxford: Leopard's Head Press, 2000).

[28]I decline here to adopt the term *mentalité* with all its associations of structure and structuralism. Equally, I'm not completely happy with Bourdieu's notion of structuration based on social group or class experience. I'm still somewhat circumspect about Giddens' structuration theory which attempts to reconcile structure with some (limited) agency. If, as Foucault suggested, without further explanation, each discourse contains the seeds of its own resistance, then agency has some practical application. So once again, I resort to de Certeau's exposition of the ability of individuals when confronted with a dominant discourse, to confound it, if only

within the limits of their capabilities, either deliberately or inadvertently.

[29]Andrew Clark, ed., *Lincoln Diocese Documents 1450-1544*, Early English Text Society vol. 149 (Oxford, 1914), 247 (Appendix 3).

[30]David Hickman, ed., *Lincoln Wills 1532-4*, LRS vol. 89 (Lincoln, 2001), 383 (575).

[31]Clark, *Lincoln Diocese Documents*, 231 (lx).

[32]John W. Clay, ed., *North Country Wills ... 1383 to 1558*, SS vol. 116 (1908), 242.

[33]Charles W. Foster, ed., *Lincoln Wills Registered in the District Probate Registry at Lincoln*, 3 vols., LRS vols. 5, 10, 24 (Lincoln, 1914-30), vol. 1, 83.

[34]Christopher Harper-Bill, ed., *The Register of John Morton Archbishop of Canterbury 1486-1500 Volume III Norwich Sede Vacante, 1499*, CYS vol. 89 (2000), 92 (137).

[35]Foster, *Lincoln Wills II*, 127.

[36]Dorothy O. Shilton and Richard Holworthy, eds., *Medieval Wills from Wells in the Diocesan Registry, Wells, 1543-6, 1554-6* Somerset Record Society vol. 40 (Taunton, 1925), 249.

[37]Foster, *Lincoln Wills III*, 6.

[38]Hickman, *Lincoln Wills*, 362 (541).

[39]Hickman, *Lincoln Wills*, 54 (1530).

[40]ROLLR Wills 1544/98.

[41]ROLLR Wills 1544/107.

[42]ROLLR Wills 1531/23.

[43]ROLLR Wills 1537/3.

[44]ROLLR Wills 1546/14.

[45]Patricia Bell, ed., *Bedfordshire Wills 1484-1533*, Publications of the Bedfordshire Historical Record Society vol. 76 (Bedford, 1997), 147 (244).

[46]Hickman, *Lincoln Wills*, 326 (484).

[47]Hickman, *Lincoln Wills*, 340 (509).

[48]Shilton and Holworthy, *Medieval Wills from Wells*, 199.

[49]ROLLR Wills 1543/44.

[50]ROLLR Wills 1533/13, 1535/32, 1536/31, and 1538/27.

[51]ROLLR Wills 1538/30.

[52]ROLLR Wills 1543/56

[53]ROLLR Wills 1539/58.

[54]ROLLR Wills 1531/19, 1538/37.

[55]ROLLR Wills 1543/65.

[56]ROLLR Wills 1524/7, 1525/13, 1539/61, 1539/69, 1541/41, 1541/57, 1543/93, 1544/103, 1545/140, 1546/13, 1546/20, 1546/68.

[57]ROLLR Wills 1525/13.

[58]ROLLR Wills 1524/7.

[59]ROLLR Wills 1546/3.

[60]Harper-Bill, *Register of John Morton Volume III*, 35 (49), 47 (68), 53 (77), 89 (132), 94 (139), 96 (141), 106 (163), 109 (169); Peter Northeast, ed., *Wills of the Archdeaconry of Sudbury 1439-1474. Wills from the Register 'Baldwyne' Part I: 1439-1461*, Suffolk Record Society vol. 45 (Ipswich, 2001), 8 (17), 23 (57), 26 (69), 31 (87), 41 (108), 44 (116), 57 (149), 62 (162), 67 (180), 98 (271), 103 (285), 141 (369), 172 (449), 190 (492), 192 (497), 207 (548), 256 (705), 257 (708), 265 (726), 327 (920), 337 (954),

340 (960), 384 (1115), 404 (1180-1181), 410 (1200), 423 (1240), 444 (1279), 445 (1280), 506 (1462).

[61]Northeast, *Wills of the Archdeaconry of Sudbury*, 8 (17).

[62]Northeast, *Wills of the Archdeaconry of Sudbury*, 257 (708).

[63]Northeast, *Wills of the Archdeaconry of Sudbury*, 404 (481).

[64]Northeast, *Wills of the Archdeaconry of Sudbury*, 67 (180).

[65]George J. Piccope, ed., *Lancashire and Cheshire Wills and Inventories from the Ecclesiastical Court, Chester. The First Portion*, Chetham Society vol. 43 (Manchester, 1857), 5 (1527).

[66]Elvey, *The Courts of the Archdeaconry of Buckingham*, 12 (7), 52 (66), 147 (213c), 158 (227A), 159 (228A), 187 (266), 219 (303), 276 (365), 281 (371), 345 (425), 398 (483),

[67]Elvey, *The Courts of the Archdeaconry of Buckingham*, 12 (7).

[68]Duffy, *The Stripping of the Altars*.

[69]Foster, *Lincoln Wills II*; Hickman, *Lincoln Wills*.

[70]Shilton and Holworthy, *Medieval Wills from Wells*, 57.

[71]G. Denison Lumb, "Testamenta Leodiensia," *Miscellanea*, Thoresby Society vols. 9 and 11 (1900-4), vol. 9, 247 and vol. 11, 52, 55.

[72]The wills consist of those proved in the consistory court and deposited now in ROLLR. Peculiar jurisdictions are omitted. PCC wills would add only another thirty testators for Leicestershire between 1522 and 1546 inclusive: The National Archives PROB11/21-31.

[73]My research into the diocese of Lichfield probate material is in progress. To date, I have examined over 3000 probate items before 1547. LRO B/C/11.

[74]LRO B/C/11 John Dyxson 1541 Ansley.

[75]LRO B/C/11 Thomas Brown 1537 Croxall.

[76]LRO B/C/11 Richard Stonele 1546 Napton on the Hill.

[77]LRO B/C/11 Richard Garratt 1544 Cubbington (inventory valuation £17 2s. 2d.).

[78]LRO B/C/11 William Garlande 1541 Packington.

[79]LRO B/C/11 Edmund Heyteley 1538 Aston (inventory valuation £17 16s. 8d.).

[80]LRO B/C/11 Richard Jude 1538 Packington Priors (inventory valuation £13 16s. 5d.).

[81]LRO B/C/11 Thomas Howlle 1540 Shifnall (inventory valuation £78 19s. 0d.).

[82]LRO B/C/11 John Wodwarde 1535 Allestree.

[83]LRO B/C/11 Joan Hootun 1536 Wiken.

[84]LRO B/C/11 William Reydyng, Chilvers Coton.

[85]LRO B/C/11 John Wodwarde, Allestree, 1535.

[86]LRO B/C/11 William Sambroke, Kynnersley, 1536.

[87]LRO B/C/11 Richard Elkes 1541 Marton.

[88]LRO B/C/11 Griffith Evans 1536 Stanwardine (inventory valuation about £17); John Edward 1538 Baschurch (£8 7s. 4d.).

[89]LRO B/C/11 John Getyn 1541 Eaton.

[90]LRO B/C/11 Roger Wodward, Derby, 1538.

[91]Shilton and Holworthy, *Medieval Wills from Wells*, 48.

⁹²Alfred E. B. Owen, ed., *The Medieval Lindsey Marsh. Select Documents*, LRS vol. 85 (1996), 4-5. In general, A. Mary Kirkus, ed., *The Records of the Commissioners of Sewers in the Parts of Holland 1547-1603 [volume I]*, LRS vol. 64 (1959); Owen, ed., *Records of the Commissioners of Sewers [volume II]*, LRS vol. 63 (1968); Owen, ed., *Records of the Commissioners of Sewers [volume III]*, LRS vol. 71 (Lincoln, 1977).

⁹³LRO B/C/11 Richard Hurresdysch 1534 Ashover.

⁹⁴We might note here too that the distribution of doles–good works–might extend over several parishes, as the 1s. bequeathed to three other parishes by Richard Hollyar for bread doles to their poor: LRO B/C/11 Richard Hollyar 1536 Shenstoke.

⁹⁵As ever, my discussion is informed (but not exclusively) by de Certeau: *Practice of Everyday Life*; *The Writing of History* trans. T. Conley (New York: Columbia University Press, 1988); Ahearne, *Michel de Certeau*. For the importance of emotional responses, Barbalet, *Emotions and Sociology* which restores a Kantian critique of pure reason. With reference to their body, testators had a sense of "home" which it is my intention to address elsewhere.

⁹⁶Michael Braddick, *State Formation in Early Modern England c.1500-1700* (Cambridge: Cambridge University Press, 2000), 103-35.

⁹⁷Hindle, *On the Parish?*

⁹⁸NNRO Archdeaconry of Norwich register of wills (MF 503), fol. 5v. In general, Marjorie K. McIntosh, "Local Responses to the Poor in Late Medieval and Tudor England," *Continuity and Change* 3 (1988): 209-45.

5
Young People's Space:
Contours of Courtship, 1580-1640

[James Neale of Rockingham, Northants.]...presented for bringinge home to his howse one Katherine Chester of Hauerborough
and suffering hir to continue there four or five dayes at the least
thinckinge to have made hir his wiffe for the banes were asked
between them and no ympedyment hard of yet she is gone and
the match broken of which yf it should have holden he did offend
by lawe as we suppose...[1]

[William Rowell of Benefield, Northants.] ... for hauntinge the
companie of Ann Locksmyth of Brigstock ... [and found together
in a field] verie suspiciouslye[2]

Not all sexual liaisons create permanent association.[3] Much sexual activity
in the late sixteenth century and early seventeenth century was, however,
pre-marital, not simply extra-marital, although there were also desultory
sexual contacts. Whilst sexual activity of the type quoted above reveals
how people came into contact, it is only marriage formation which allows
an insight into how social and kin relationships might be permanently
established–and, importantly for this chapter, maintained over and within
localities extending outside the parish.[4]

After considerable recent investigation, social organization in early-
modern England is becoming better appreciated, if there remain some differences of interpretation.[5] The formation of social relationships is less well
perceived, although kin relationships have been elucidated. For example,
from the legacies in wills Cressy has suggested a persisting importance
of extended kinship.[6] Pursuing similar lines of inquiry, Mitson proposed
the social significance of kinship networks over groups of parishes, constituting connections across localities at the level of what later became the
"middling sort"–associations of dominant focal families over a broader

geographical area than the single parish.[7] In both projects, the focus was directed–because of the sources–to existing and established kinship linkages. Since testamentary dispositions for some time at least through the sixteenth century marked off a wealthier cohort and since the focal families belonged largely to the holders of local offices (increasingly those brokers between "state" and the very specific locality), only one segment of local society was addressed.[8] How can we achieve some understanding of the *creation* of social relationships and the degree of social interaction for the whole of local society?

Here, a return is made to the formation of marriage as one central aspect of the formation of social interaction and relationships. Since both O'Hara and Adair have recently subjected matrimonial matters to the microscope to elicit macro-level interpretations, it might be complained that further examination of nuptiality can afford no more insight.[9] Whilst conscious of that consideration, the attempt here probes the spatial aspects of the formation of marriage and through that the instantiation of social relationships. In other words, the discussion here is concerned with the spatial dimensions of everyday life. Clark produced a valuable conceptualization of migratory patterns from matrimonial causes in ecclesiastical courts.[10] That research represents, perhaps, so far so good. On the other hand, matrimonial causes can perhaps be categorized as pathological rather than normative. Such instance causes may tend to give an unusual representation of the formation of marriage, since more marital arrangements would not have been a cause of contestation. Although they might have ensued from the "normal" vagaries of marriage formation, the causes probably constitute "problem" cases which fit into a narrow and defined context. Eloquent as these causes are, they contain a certain tendentiousness.

Office causes can supplement the instance causes in an interesting manner. Thus in *contra* Edward Burneby of Morcott, he was accused "that he hath left his owne wiffe and is said to keep company with one Kinges wiffe of Glason [Glaston]."[11] The formation of the new relationship involved only a few miles between Morcott and Glaston. In 1595, Alice, who lived in Creaton committed fornication with John Osborne of Brixworth, whilst Alice Vine of Helpston engaged in the same way with Molton of Barnack, more or less adjacent parishes.[12] Nevertheless, the great deficiency of ecclesiastical court papers is their lack of quantitative data as well as their pathological context.

Since the causes do articulate so much about matrimony, it is perhaps churlish to return to another source which seemingly provides sparse information: marriage registers of 1540 to 1640. In a statistical manner, they have been employed by Souden and Wrigley and Schofield (and their critics).[13] The intention here is to deploy the data to reconstruct spatial patterns of marriage formation. From 1754, marriage registers were produced on printed forms which required detail of, *inter alia*, place of habitation at the time of marriage. During the temporary period of civil registration in the Commonwealth period after 1653, that information was also demanded. Before 1653, the amount of detail in the registers depended on the proclivity of the incumbent–although the registers were annually examined by the churchwardens so they too were complicit. Since most clergy simply recorded the minimum–names of the marriage partners (although some of the earliest registers simply entered one partner's name, usually the groom)–most registers are deficient for any reconstruction of the geography of this form of social relationship.

Fortunately–and serendipitously–some incumbents exercised a more intense curiosity, dedication and interest, in registering also the place of abode of the "strange" (exogamous) partner. (Throughout this chapter, the terms endogamy and exogamy are used with reference to place, not social group). Whilst such registers cannot guarantee a reflection of a comprehensive situation, they do amount to a purposive sample of how this particular type of social interaction extended geographically–the marriage "horizon" interpreted here as a space of social contact. The number of registers which contain this information before 1700 is erratic, so questions are therefore inevitable: whether the information is sufficiently representative in terms of quantity and geographical comprehensiveness. Moreover, it is not always the whole register before 1700 that recorded the information, but only particular incumbents, so that sometimes the information exists for only shorter periods or is discontinuous.[14]

The data are further complicated by legislative and other changes, particularly in the late seventeenth century. By 1600, there was considerable clarity about the requirements for a marriage validly registered before the church, confirmed by the Canons of 1604 (cc. 62-63 and 101-103).These alterations might have affected marriage formation and registration, although exactly how still remains to be conclusively shown. Registration might have been compromised by the introduction of civil registration in 1653, by which the partners had to seek out a justice of the peace rather than arrange celebration in their parish church. By and large, the data employed here omit the period of civil registration of 1653-60, so its effect is attenuated. One other consequence, indeed, of the provisions of 1653 was to confirm the movement of young people to seek out a justice of the peace to certify their marriage. For example, most of the marriages involving parties from Wigston Magna were performed before Justice Beaumont at Stoughton Grange Hall.[15] Partners from villages in north-east Leicestershire visited Justice Pochin at Barkby Hall. Marriage partners from Heckington made the journey to Roxham and Boston for their marriages.[16]

The marriage duty of 1695 to 1705 (6&7 William & Mary, c.6) might conceivably impinge on the final few years in the sample here. During the late seventeenth century, it has been established, there was a general problem of under-registration and "clandestine" marriage. The data here, of course, relate only to Anglican registration of marriages.[17] Since this chapter is concerned more with marriage "horizons", the issues of completeness of registration might not be severe. On the other hand, the implications of the Settlement Acts of 1662 and 1698 *could* have inhibited marriage outside the parish, but the provisions of the 1597-1601 poor law legislation might have anticipated some of these restrictions, if not all.[18]

There is, moreover, a serious difficulty of the data. The place of residence recorded by the incumbent is simply that: the current place of residence of the partners. It might have been a temporary domicile. Given the high mobility of young people (as servant in husbandry and seeking opportunities) some were likely to have no more than temporary habitations, remaining there for no more than one year if servants in husbandry. Without extensive family or biographical reconstitution, we have no certainty about their place of origin. In some cases, it might well be possible that, although one of the partners was exogamous at the time of marriage, both partners had origins and had originally met in the same place, but had become separated by distance because of the exigencies of temporary employment. If, on the other hand, we assume that marriage was only entered into when at least one partner had a settled existence (the late European marriage pattern of Hajnal), then we can take a little more confidence in the recorded locations of the partners.[19]

For those reasons, a sample of the data is presented in Table 5.1 (p. 133), which lists forty-eight parishes and registers, the periods for which the information on exogamous partners was recorded, the origins of the partners, the proportion of exogamous partners (a minimum), the proportion of exogamous partners who derived from contiguous parishes, and the total number of parishes of origin of exogamous partners. This sample is purposive, intended to include: parishes with varying numbers of marriages (and hence also demographic size) and parishes of different characteristics (rural, "sub-urban" and urban). What that listing demonstrates is a purposive sample of some fifty parishes from different areas of England, different *pays*, and for different types of settlement and parish. Displayed in the listing is the number of exogamous marriage partners recorded. Finally, the table reveals the number of different locations of habitation of exogamous marriage partners, important for two purposes: for the spatial aspects of everyday life–the field within which exogamous social relationships were created; and for expressing the relative social contexts of different forms of settlement and place.

We can abstract the data for the number of marriages as follows. The mean number of marriages per parish comprised 119 with a standard deviation of 66.77, whilst the median number of marriages per parish consisted of exactly one hundred. The total number of marriages comprised 5,720. If we consider the exogamous brides in these marriages, we have a total of 1,368, with a mean of twenty-nine from each parish (standard deviation 23.51) and median of twenty-three. By comparison, the number of exogamous grooms was (unexpectedly, perhaps) slightly higher: 1,546. For the foreign grooms, the mean was accordingly thirty-two per parish (standard deviation 22.85), with a median of twenty-seven. For these forty-eight parishes, an investigation has been made into the number and percentage of partners from contiguous parishes and the total number of parishes of origin of partners.

Reinforcing these fuller data is information from forty-seven other parishes, which have not been examined for the proportion of partners from contiguous parishes and for the number of parishes of origin (in other words, the data for columns eight and nine of Table 5.1 are omitted). These data are presented as Table 5.2 (p. 137). In these parishes 9,573 marriages were registered at a mean of 213 per parish (standard deviation 183.7) and median of 124. For these celebrations, 2,053 brides were from another parish (a mean of forty-six with standard deviation at 42.43 and median of twenty-six per parish), whilst 3,049 grooms were from outside the parish where the marriage was consummated (mean per parish sixty-eight with standard deviation of 68.7 and median of forty-five).

Overall then, the data consists of 15,293 marriages comprising 30,586 partners, 8,016 (twenty-six percent) of whom were exogamous. Of the exogamous partners, fifty-seven percent were male and forty-three percent female. Although, therefore, the celebration of the marriage was predominantly uxorilocal (at the bride's parish church), a significant proportion of marriage services was performed in the groom's parish.[20] To some extent then, these figures complicate the notion that marriages were preponderantly celebrated in the bride's parish. In the late sixteenth and seventeenth century, although most marriages were so consummated, a significant number involved the bride's travel.[21] No doubt there was a customary imperative for uxorilocal marriage which had functional aspects: the wedding feast provided by the bride's family and her dowering at her own church door if dower was involved. That propensity might well have been confirmed in the late sixteenth and early seventeenth centuries by the need to address bridal pregnancy. It was one way of establishing that the bride's family would become accountable for the child in the case of default by the parents.

Some preliminary comments should be offered about the relationship between marriage and migration. On the one hand, the continuous movement of people seeking work brought into contact partners from different locations. On the other, the very imperative to continue to migrate in search of work might lead to the collapse of spousal arrangements before marriage. There has, moreover, been something of a debate about whether women who migrated had a higher prospect of marriage than women who remained in their own parish.[22]

Immediately apparent from the detailed figures is the distinction between urban and rural marriages. The highest level of exogamous partners pertained in the urban center of Lincoln. In four of six Lincoln parishes in the dataset, exogamous brides or grooms accounted for forty-two to sixty-seven percent of marriage partners. Here it is evident that more than half the exogamous partners were male: in three representative parishes fifty-three, fifty-six and fifty-six percent.

The next level of density of exogamous partners obtained in "suburban" parishes, those parishes immediately adjacent to boroughs, but outside the borough's boundaries. Such places included around Nottingham, Gedling (seventy-three percent exogamous partners); Wilford (forty-six percent); Sneinton (fifty-seven percent); Colwick (sixty-eight percent); proximate to Leicester, Aylestone (forty-three percent); Belgrave (thirty-two percent); Humberstone (forty-four percent); and Evington (forty-eight percent, but see further below). Two further features of these "sub-urban" marriages are evident. The first is the level of intermarriage with urban partners. For example, fifty-seven of the 154 exogamous partners in Wilford came from Nottingham; sixty-one of the 155 in marriages in Sneinton; and fifty-five of the 133 in Colwick; thirty-one of the 162 in Gedling; and seventeen of the 65 in Wollaton (which was separated from Nottingham by an intervening parish). There was, then, a close interaction between the "sub-urban" parishes and the adjacent borough.

That was not, however, the exclusive characteristic. At the same time, exogamous marriage partners in marriages in these "sub-urban" parishes derived from a much larger number of foreign parishes than in marriages in most rural parishes. Such partners married in Wilford, for example, originated from sixty-nine other parishes; in Sneinton fifty-five; and Colwick forty-four. If we move even just to the next parish or so out from Nottingham, the numbers of a partners from Nottingham decline precipitately: six in Strelley (but which might have been influenced by other variables); eight in Nuthall; five in Lowdham; two in Lambley; four in Calverton; two in Epperstone; and one in Oxton.

It follows then that the numbers of exogamous marriage partners in rural parishes remained at a much lower level. Examining the data from seventy rural parishes, the mean proportion of exogamous marriage partners was twenty-two percent (standard deviation 8.49) with the median at the same level. In fact, five rural parishes had less than ten percent of exogamous partners; twelve between ten and fifteen percent; and sixteen between sixteen and twenty percent. All these figures are, of course, approximate, relying on the accuracy and consistency of the incumbent's registration; they serve as no more than guidance. Those problems permitting, we can hazard some comments about these rural parishes. The further the parish from a large urban center, the lower the proportion of exogamous partners. Even proximity to a small or market town made no considerable difference, for some of those market towns had low levels of exogamous partners: thus Bingham and Mansfield with less than twenty percent; and Wymeswold (a market vill) with about fourteen percent. Some particular locations–which had suffered late-medieval depopulation and had a deep concentration on husbandry–constituted locations still unattractive for exogamous marriages. Settlements on the Wolds or near the Wolds in Leicestershire and Lincolnshire fell especially into this category: Long Clawson; Scalford; Ashby Folville; Stathern; Nevenby; Claypole; Denton; and in the Wreake Valley Rotherby and Hoby.

What we have then–perhaps fairly predictably–is a gravity-feed model of marriage "horizons", with greater activity in and around urban centers, declining with distance from those centers. Such a mechanical model, nonetheless, does not account for all spousal arrangements. The space of marriage arrangements was punctuated by "lawless" churches, where properly "clandestine" marriages were performed. The voluminous exogamous figures for Kinoulton and Evington reflect that phenomenon. Although some of Evington's exogamy ensued from its proximity to Leicester, many partners were encouraged to resort there because of its status as a peculiar jurisdiction associated with the prebend of St. Margaret's, Leicester. Kinoulton had a completely different location, entirely rural, but had complete exemption and autonomy as a long-established manorial peculiar jurisdiction.[23] Suspicions are aroused also about Stanford upon Soar, a rectory in a parish with a low population, which, although not a peculiar jurisdiction, had a location conducive to "clandestine" marriage, precisely on the boundary between the archdeaconries of Nottingham and Leicester, the dioceses of York and Lincoln, and the parish directly north of the burgeoning early-modern urban presence of Loughborough. "Clandestine" marriages did not always remain undetected: John Sweting and his wife, Isabel, of the parish of Upminster, were detected in the archdeaconry court "that theie maried in weste Thorocke church beinge owte of there owne parishe and an exempte withoute banes or askinge or lycence."'[24]

One caveat which has been advanced about the employment of information about exogamy before more formal regulation after the 1753 Act is that a tendency might have obtained more predominantly to record the place of residence of male partners to establish settlement rights. Indeed, if that purpose had been significant before 1640, then more consistent recording of the data might have been expected. Although that issue of entitlement might have influenced the recording of this information after 1662, the recorded detail before 1640 seems to be concerned with both partners equally.[25]

Other exceptional circumstances must also be considered. Less seriously, there are contingent reasons for occasional aberrations which, although interesting, do not affect the overall information. In 1587, for example, the curate of Billingham, since he was only in deacon's orders could only preside over a marriage but not perform communion after the marriage, so he directed a couple by his license to be married at Woolston.[26] Some unions were consecrated in "foreign" parish churches for reasons of evasion: Anthony Payne of Duns Tew (Oxfordshire) had been betrothed to Ursula Fuller and the banns read three times in the parish church at Duns Tew, but he then married Alice Franckline of Oxfordshire at Hampden in Buckinghamshire in 1584.[27]

With a slightly risky presumption, we might consider that marriage partners made their personal connection within a space of regular and wider social contacts. Although their communication became a special relationship, it conformed to a broader flow within local society.

What is not attempted here is any precise definition of levels of endogamous and exogamous marriage. The reason for that exclusion is that, whilst statement of place of habitation provides positive evidence of exogamy, we cannot always assume endogamy in instances where no place of habitation is registered. In registers where exogamous partners are marked, there are inevitably numerous marriages which simply record AB and CD married. Two consequences ensue: the information is not sufficiently robust to compare levels of endogamy and exogamy; and the information about exogamy *might* be an under-recording. Apart from not addressing the issue of exogamy/endogamy, we also need to recognize that from the recorded information inferences can only be made about the minimum fields and levels of exogamous social interaction–both in terms of the number of exogamous partners and places with which social contact was sustained.

We can explore the ecclesiastical court records to confirm the spatial dimension of sexual liaisons, on the one hand those resulting in an illegitimacy and on the other those presented as incontinence. For example, John Chester of Marston (Northamptonshire.) was presented in the early seventeenth century for getting Helen Pitwaite pregnant. Helen inhabited the contiguous parish, Greetworth.[28] About the same time, an accusation was brought against Thomas Whighthing of Watford (in the same county) for sexual incontinence with Joan Crane of Flore, parishes in the same locality.[29] Some of the presentments, of course, were retrospective, in that the accusation concerned a pre-marital sexual relationship by a since-married couple, as when Catherine Orton of Maidwell was presented for incontinence with Edward Payne of Wollaston.[30]

Occasionally, the presentments of these dalliances illustrate how marriage formation might have originated in market centres, although in the cases reported the sexual liaison did not develop into marriage. Thus a cause was initiated against Susan Newett of the market town of Towcester for an incontinent liaison with William Braine of Bugbrooke, within its hinterland.[31] Isabel Feild *alias* Hartleet–because wife of Passover Hartlett now–confessed that two years before her marriage to Hartlett, she had produced a child by intercourse with Anthony Bishop, then of Wroxton, but now (alas) of her abode, Banbury. The deed had been perpetrated at the house of her father-in-law, Titus Buckingham, in Banbury. Bishop, a miller of Wroxton, was accommodated at the house when he came to Banbury on market days.[32] The illicit liaison which led to the pregnancy of Ann Frisby was also conducted in a market town. In 1602, when she was living in Ashby Folville, she confessed that she had become pregnant by Anthony Picke of Barsby some seven years previously. At that time, she dwelt with Edward Dent at Dalby Chacombe. She had met Picke on several occasions at Gulson's house in Melton Mowbray on market days where he had carnal knowledge of her.[33] Some marriage partners must have come into contact through encounters in market towns, although the data above do not strongly support that conclusion.[34] Market towns which were also statute staples for the contracts for the hiring and the employment of servants might have been more formative for the social contacts of young people.

In 1601, Thomas Pawson, a clerk aged thirty-five of Bothamsall, deposed that he had accompanied John Leverton to witness his proposal to Isota Gaskine. They journeyed from Bothamsall to a place near Mansfield where she was milking. Thomas acted as intermediary: "Maid as I heere saye there is somme good will betweene this younge man meaning the articulate John Leverton & you are willing to make him a promise of mariage..."[35] The life-course mobility of young people inevitably meant that the formation of marriage also contributed to the production of social relationships over space and between place, confirming and strengthening notions of locality. Since such liaisons were likely to be initiated within their existing information fields, the new relationship instantiated the idea of their "country".

Only in exceptional circumstances were the spatial repercussions different. In 1603, Margaret Jackson of St. Mary's parish in Leicester admitted being delivered of a child in the house of Margaret Byddle within the parish. Thomas Kingston of Shitlanger in Northamptonshire was accused of being the father, a married man and her master when she was discovered to be pregnant. She revealed her predicament to him and disclosed that she would return to her mother in Yorkshire for lying in. He offered her 15s. for her costs and promised maintenance for the child. She departed intending to return "into her owne countrey". She rested at Braybrook in an alehouse for two or three days, where she happened to meet William Middleton who transported her to Leicester on her way north. Middleton's wife asked her to remain there a short time after which she would assist her journey north. Margaret then declaimed that Middleton's wife had borrowed 14s. from her. Unable to recover it, she was compelled to remain in Leicester at Widow Byddle's, where her former master came to afford her a further 6s., sending another 5s. later.[36] It was probably an unusual encounter across a wide space and distant places. The episode reminds us of the unsettled life-course of a large proportion of young people and the especial vulnerability of some young women, to which we shall return in Chapter Ten.

Parish	Dates	Total marriages	Of which female moved for the ceremony	Of which male moved for the ceremony	Total partners	Number and percent of exogamous partners	Number and percent of exogamous partners from contiguous parishes	Number of parishes of origin of exogamous partners
Nottinghamshire								
1 Upton	1602-1700	259	60	27	518	89 (17.2)	41 (46.1)	41
2 East Bridgford	1629-1700	101	39	8	202	47 (23.3)	10 (21.3)	31
3 Elton on the Hill	1612-1683	68	5	1	136	6 (4.4)	2	6
4 Orston	1604-1639, 1660-1664	119	27	22	238	49 (20.6)	14	24
5 Upper Broughton	1571-1643, 1654-1700	135	43	10	270	53 (19.6)	14	36
6 Clifton	1657-1700	72	24	11	144	35 (24.3)	3	15
7 Wilford	1657-1700	167	76	78	334	154 (46.1)	73	69
8 Strelley	1665-1700	74	22	19	148	41 (27.7)	10	22
9 Wollaton	1654-1700	102	36	29	204	65 (31.9)	14	30
10 Nuthall	1663-1700	73	26	13	146	39 (26.7)	10	20
11 Bunny	1566-1700	375	116	29	750	145 (19.3)	39	70
12 Sneinton	1660-1700	137	78	77	274	155 (56.6)	65	55
13 Colwick	1660-1700	98	66	67	196	133 (67.9)	74	44
14 Lambley	1571-1700	168	30	23	336	53 (15.8)	18	33
15 Calverton	1617-1700	182	65	35	364	100 (27.5)	39	44

Table 5.1a   Sample of parishes with Extended Information

Parish	Dates	Total marriages	Of which female moved for the ceremony	Of which male moved for the ceremony	Total partners	Number and percent of exogamous partners	Number and percent of exogamous partners from contiguous parishes	Number of parishes of origin of exogamous partners
16 Epperstone	1636-1700	104	39	13	208	52 (25)	13	33
17 Oxton	1626-42, 1654-1700	89	31	15	178	46 (25.8)	18	27
18 Kinoulton	1658-1686	83	53	51	166	104 (62.7)	10	49
19 Rolleston cum Fiskerton	1585-1700	377	32	120	754	152	36	73
20 Averham	1616-1700	113	15	33	226	48	23	24
21 Kelham	1663-1700	87	15	32	174	47	16	32
22 Marnham	1666-1700	95	13	36	190	49	12	31
23 Cromwell	1665-1700	95	38	51	190	89	32	39
Leicestershire								
24 Long Clawson	1630-1700	108	12	21	216	33	8	26
25 Aylestone	1633-1700	110	35	59	220	94 (42.7)	30 (31.9)	47
26 Thurcaston cum Cropston and Anstey	1638-1700	132	36	42	264	78 (29.6)	18 (23.1)	38
27 Walton on the Wolds	1578-1700	107	16	57	214	73	24	44
28 Quorndon	1635-1700	84	16	19	168	27 (16.1)	10 (37)	18
29 Humberstone	1623-1700	118	46	58	236	104	54	41
30 Scalford	1637-1700	99	6	11	198	17 (8.9)	4 (23.5)	15
31 Rotherby	1597-1700	68	0	16	136	16 (11.8)	3	15

Table 5.1b　Sample of Parishes with Extended Information (continued)

Parish	Dates	Total marriages	Of which female moved for the ceremony	Of which male moved for the ceremony	Total partners	Number and percent of exogamous partners	Number and percent of exogamous partners from contiguous parishes	Number of parishes of origin of exogamous partners
32 Hoby	1613-1700	74	5	8	148	13 (8.8)	2	10
33 Barkby (incl. N. Thurmaston)	1612-1700	92	4	21	184	25 (13.6)	6 (24)	19
34 Knipton	1640-1700	73	6	18	146	24 (16.4)	2	20
35 Branston	1635-1700	72	9	23	144	32 (22.2)	10 (31.3)	25
36 Rothley	1653-1682	107	33	31	214	64	12	36
37 Wymeswold	1653-1700	94	12	14	188	26 (13.8)	9 (34.6)	16
38 Rearsby	1653-1700	98	17	40	196	57 (29.1)	16 (28.1)	36
39 Ashby Folevile cum Barsby	1634-1700	116	14	26	232	40	10	31
40 Bitteswell	1637-1700	74	13	37	148	50	20	34
41 Leire	1635-1700	74	13	38	148	51	14	36
Lincolnshire								
42 Claypole	1662-1700	97	12	20	194	32	5	23
43 Harmston	1609-1700	216	45	70	432	115	20	60
44 South Hykeham	1650-1695	72	26	24	144	50	12	26
45 Norton Disney	1649-1700	64	12	13	128	25	10	18
46 Denton	1573-1612	159	2	35	318	37	5	31
47 Boothby Graffoe	1603-1700	111	19	27	222	46	8	26
48 Fleet	1658-1700	128	18	18	256	36	13	18

Table 5.1c   Sample of Parishes with Extended Information (continued)

Parish S= "sub-urban" U= urban M= active market	Dates	Total marriages	Of which female moved for the ceremony	Of which male moved for the ceremony	Total partners	Number and percent of exogamous partners
Nottinghamshire						
1 Costock	1558-1700	97	26	15	194	41 (21.1)
2 Normanton on Soar	1625-1700	60	14	8	120	22 (18.3)
3 West Leake	1617-1700	109	44	24	218	68 (31.2)
4 Bingham (M)	1654-1658	86	22	12	172	34 (19.8)
5 Hawksworth	1586-1700	171	53	30	342	83 (24.3)
6 Whatton	1628-1700	179	43	38	358	81 (22.6)
7 Cotgrave	1628-1700	142	24	14	284	38 (13.4)
8 Farndon	1632-1666	131	27	45	224	89 (39.7)
9 Holme Pierrepont	1612-1700	112	52	49	262	73 (27.9)
10 East Stoke	1595-1700	297	91	66	594	156 (26.3)
11 Trowell	1654-1700	84	11	7	168	18 (10.7)
12 Gedling (S)	1646-1683	111	103	59	222	162 (73)
13 Lowdham	1559-1700	648	118	72	1296	190 (14.7)
14 Selston	1669-1700	74	21	15	148	36 (24.3)
15 Kirkby in Ashfield	1663-1700	70	21	23	140	44 (31.4)

Table 5.2a Sample of Parishes with Basic Information

Parish S= "sub-urban" U= urban M= active market	Dates	Total marriages	Of which female moved for the ceremony	Of which male moved for the ceremony	Total partners	Number and percent of exogamous partners
16 Mansfield Woodhouse	1677-1700	113	23	27	226	50 (22.1)
17 Sutton *cum* Lound	1539-1700	797	52	132	1594	184 (11.5)
18 Blidworth	1599-1700	152	26	55	304	81 (26.7)
19 Mansfield (M)	1617-1662, 1678-1700	672	70	188	1344	258 (19.2)
20 Hayton	1656-1690	110	18	32	220	50 (22.7)
21 Farnsfield	1616-1634, 1668-1700	93	10	23	186	33 (17.7)
22 Laxton	1657-1700	143	4	27	286	31 (10.8)
23 Plumtree	1651-1693	73	17	15	146	32 (21.9)
24 Stanford on Soar		194			388	312 (80.4)
25 Coston		119			238	49 (20.6)
26 Rolleston *cum* Fiskerton	1585-1700	377	32	120	754	152
27 Averham	1616-1700	113	15	33	226	48
Leicestershire						
28 Kirby Muxloe	1630-1700	65	18	17	130	35 (26.9)
29 Wigston Magna	1636-1700	216	26	68	432	94 (21.8)
30 Belgrave (incl. S. Thurmaston) (S)	1657-1700	84	21	33	168	54 (32.1)

Table 5.2b   Sample of Parishes with Basic Information (continued)

Parish S="sub-urban" U=urban M=active market	Dates	Total marriages	Of which female moved for the ceremony	Of which male moved for the ceremony	Total partners	Number and percent of exogamous partners
31 Tilton cum membris	1631-1700	124	26	64	248	90 (36.3)
32 Wanlip	1563-1700	79	22	46	158	68 (43)
33 Prestwold cum membris	1573-1700	413	53	192	826	245 (29.7)
34 Stathern	1658-1700	67	4	8	134	12 (9)
35 Evington	1638-1700	100	37	58	200	95 (47.5)
Lincolnshire						
36 Lincoln, St Mary, Wigford (U)	1594-1700	374	97	125	748	222 (29.7)
37 Lincoln, St Michael (U)	1579-1604, 1635-1637	244	151	176	488	327 (67)
38 Lincoln, St Martin (U)	1670-1700	282	106	134	564	240 (42.6)
39 Lincoln, St Peter at Arches (U)	1581-1700ff	498	195	248	906	443 (44.5)
40 Lincoln St Paul's (U)	1618-1666ff	415	63	306	830 f and ff	369
41 Lincoln, St Peter's Eastgate (U)	1610-1679f and ff		120	141	261	
42 Surfleet	1608-1700	323	37	54	646	91 (14.1)
43 Navenby	1663-1698	77	3	14	154	17 (11)
44 South Kelsey	1609-1655	73	7	15	146	22 (15.1)

Table 5.2c   Sample of Parishes with Basic Information (continued)

Parish S= "sub-urban" U= urban M= active market	Dates	Total marriages	Of which female moved for the ceremony	Of which male moved for the ceremony	Total partners	Number and percent of exogamous partners
45 Heckington	1609-1699	573	85	136	1146	221 (19.3)
46 Westborough	1656-1700	239	20	24	478	44 (9.2)
47 Bourne (M)	1613-1650∫		25	61	∫	86

∫ The registration of places of residence is erratic.

Table 5.2d Sample of Parishes with Basic Information (continued)

Notes

[1]NRO X611/29, fol. 18v. (1597).

[2]NRO X611/29, fols. 34v., 41r., 44v., 47v., 49r. (1597-8).

[3]The most important discussion is still Martin Ingram, *Church Courts, Sex and Marriage in England, 1570-1640* (Cambridge: Cambridge University Press, 1987).

[4]In other words, this chapter does not address issues of nuptiality such as age at marriage; parental control; "community" control of pauper marriage; seasonality of marriage; the reliability of marriage registration; and so forth. The literature on such matters is too extensive to recite. A recent short introduction is Andrew Hinde, *England's Population: A History Since the Domesday Survey* (London: Arnold, 2003), 111-27.

[5]Wrightson, "'Sorts of People' in Tudor and Stuart England"; French., "Social Status, Localism and the Middling Sort of People."

[6]David Cressy, "Kinship and Kin Interaction in Early Modern England,"*Past and Present* 113 (1986): 38-69.

[7]See Chap. 4 above.

[8]See Chap. 4 above.

[9]Diana O'Hara, *Courtship and Constraint: Rethinking the Making of Marriage in Tudor England* (Manchester: Manchester University Press, 2000); Richard Adair, *Courtship, Illegitimacy and Marriage in Early Modern England* (Manchester: Manchester University Press, 1996).

[10]Peter Clark, "Migration in England During the Late Seventeenth and Early Eighteenth Centuries," *Past and Present* 83 (1979): 57-90..

[11]NRO X614/27, fol. 64r. (visitation and correction book, 1595)

[12]NRO X614/27, fols. 61r and 63r.

[13]David Souden, "'East-west-home's best'?"; E. A. (Tony) Wrigley and Roger S. Schofield, *The Population History of England 1541-1871: A Reconstruction*, revised edn. (Cambridge: Cambridge University Press, 1989).

[14]The data are extracted from William P. W. Phillimore et al., eds., *Leicestershire Parish Registers: Marriages*, 11 vols. (London: Phillimore, 1900-1914); William P. W. Phillimore et al., eds., *Lincolnshire Parish Registers: Marriages*, 7 vols. (London: Phillimore, 1905-1914); William P. W. Phillimore et al., eds., *Nottinghamshire Parish Registers: Marriages*, 22 vols. (London: Phillimore, 1899-1938)

[15]Elliott, ed., *Leicestershire Parish Registers Marriages* vol. 12 (London: Phillimore, 1914), 139.

[16]William P. W. Phillimore and R. E. G. Cole, eds., *Lincolnshire Parish Registers Marriages* vol. 4 (London: Phillimore. 1909), 191.

[17]R. Brian Outhwaite, *Clandestine Marriage in England, 1500-1850* (London: Hambledon, 1995).

[18]For synopsis of the impact on registration of marriages, Wrigley and Schofield, *Population History of England*, 28, 42; Adair, *Courtship, Illegitimacy and*

Marriage, 139-42; for marriage formation of the poor, Hindle, *On the Parish?*, 337-60.

[19]John Hajnal, "Two Kinds of Household Formation Systems," *Population and Development Review* 8 (1982): 449-94; see now Jane Whittle, "Servants in Rural England c.1450–1650: Hired Work as a Means of Accumulating Wealth and Skills Before Marriage, " in *The Marital Economy in Scandinavia and Britain, 1400-1900*, edited by Maria Ågren and Amy Louise Erickson (Aldershot: Ashgate, 2005), 89-110.

[20]For totals of English registered marriages, Wrigley and Schofield, *Population History of England*, 494.

[21]E. A. (Tony) Wrigley, "The Effect of Migration on the Estimation of Marriage Age in Family Reconstitution," *Population Studies* 48 (1994): 81-97 at p. 96.

[22]S. Ruggles, "Migration, Marriage and Mortality: Correcting Sources of Bias in English Reconstitutions," *Population Studies* 46 (1992): 507-22; Wrigley, "The Effect of Migration on the Estimation of Marriage Age".

[23]For "lawless" churches, Outhwaite, *Clandestine Marriage*, 24-26; Gillis, *For Better, For Worse*, 90-98.

[24]ERO D/AEA9, fol. 41v.

[25]Keith D. M. Snell, "English Rural Societies and Geographical Marital Endogamy, 1700-1837," *Economic History Review*. 2nd ser. 55 (2002): 262-98.

[26]Raine, *The Injunctions and other Ecclesiastical Proceedings of Richard Barnes*, 136.

[27]Briunkworth, *Oxford Archdeaconry Court*, vol. 1, 107.

[28]NRO Peterborough Diocesan Records archdeaconry correction book, 1610-1618, p. 274.

[29]NRO Peterborough Diocesan Records archdeaconry correction book, 1610-1618, p. 286.

[30]NRO Peterborough Diocesan Records archdeaconry correction book, 1610-1618, p. 62.

[31]NRO Peterborough Diocesan Records archdeaconry correction book, 1610-1618. p. 334.

[32]E. R. C. Brinkworth [and R. K. Gilkes], eds., *The 'Bawdy Court' of Banbury: the Act Book of the Peculiar Court of Banbury, Oxfordshire and Northamptonshire 1625-1638*, Banbury Historical Society vol. 26 (Banbury, 1997), 164.

[33]ROLLR 1D41/13/26, fol. 21v.

[34]O'Hara, *Courtship and Constraint*, 138-43.

[35]UoN Dept. of MSS. AN/LB 220/2/2/4.

[36]ROLLR 1D41/13/28, fols. 37r-v.

Part II
"Sacred" Space?

6
Penitential Spaces

The survival of humiliation as an important element in penance imposed by ecclesiastical courts from the thirteenth through to the early seventeenth centuries, produced and reproduced penitential geographies, forming and representing space. Although the persistence of humiliation of sinners has been recognised in the thirteenth century–that is, explaining its continuation after the Fourth Lateran Council of 1215–its later persistence has not been fully explored, and yet its survival through the late middle ages and into the late sixteenth century presents a number of spatial problems and issues.[1] Perhaps one reason for this relative neglect is the concentration on confession in considerations of penance, for confession placed its emphasis on interiority, that is contrition.[2] Indeed, secular change in the nature of penance–from a horizontal one informed by the seven deadly sins to a vertical one based on the ten commandments–has been predicated on a transformation of confession in the late middle ages, although such an interpretation has not been unreservedly accepted.[3] As the penance of confession is largely reconstructed through the penitential manuals, it is perceived through discursive, theological and soteriological windows. Vision through the windows of the penitential manuals and confession has also suggested a general transformation from a communitarian and social environment of penance to an individual, private and personal one: until the early modern period confession was semi-public without the confidentiality of the confession box.[4] Sentences imposed by ecclesiastical courts, however, maintained a consideration also of exteriority–satisfaction. Ritual, public humiliation thus constituted a part of the sentences imposed by spiritual courts into the early seventeenth century. In this sense, considering penance as imposed by the ecclesiastical courts for sins or crimes or faults allows a phenomenological approach to penance: the ways in which it was experienced, and experienced in particular spaces and places. It also demonstrates that under the reformed church of the late sixteenth century, *imposed* penance could retain a communitarian and social response not simply a private and personal one, and a communal one played out in public space. The performance of penance in the parish church also constructed penitential spaces in the church, repetitively used for a theater of penance, and thus reconstituted as performative spaces.[5] In less continuous manner, sentences in the courts spiritual also defined penance in the market place, with its almost sole emphasis on public, ritual humiliation and example. The performance of penance–but also other social events–thus confirmed parish church and market place as public and open spaces (although there were, of course, other spaces in which penance was performed, such as churchyard and cathedral close).[6]

The chronology of penance in the market place, however, exhibits less continuity than penance in the parish church. It therefore assumes significance in the development of confessional categories and the relationships between them. Investigating the development of penance in the market place allows a window on local confessional regimes and the difference and correspondence between late-medieval traditional religion and late-sixteenth-century reformed religion.

The penitential inheritance from the Middle Ages

Neither penance in the parish church nor in the market place were innovations of the early modern period. Nevertheless, the two elements of penance followed different paths, for whilst there was continuity in the performance of penance in the parish church through the late middle ages and into the late sixteenth century, penance in the market place had a discontinuous legacy. Penance in the market place extends back until at least the end of the thirteenth century, representing that strand of satisfaction which continued after the Fourth Lateran Council's emphasis on interiority. A dislocation occurred by the early sixteenth century, however, for penance in the market place seems to have already declined in some dioceses. Penance in the market place was thus interrupted at that time and seems only to have recurred after the formation of the reformed (Calvinist) *ecclesia anglicana* in the 1560s. Simultaneous with the abandonment of the market place by the spiritual authorities was a relinquishment of corporal punishment as a disciplinary measure. Some measure of corporal element in penance had been involved in both parish church and market place–the *fustigatio* in procession in both public fora. The medieval antecedents for penance in the market place were thus associated with bodily discipline whilst those of the late sixteenth century contained no physical punishment.

The continuous implementation of physical punishment in the market place as penance imposed by the ecclesiastical courts for sexual delinquency can be summarily encapsulated.[7] In some parishes in the deanery of Thedwestry in the archdeaconry of Sudbury in the late thirteenth century, a small number of penances was directed to be performed in the market places.[8] About the same time, Oliver Sutton, bishop of Lincoln, condemned a few transgressors to beatings in the market place for serious depredations.[9] In exceptional cases, the Archbishops of York pursued a similar course of action.[10] By the end of the thirteenth century, then, beatings around the market place were employed as a discretionary disciplinary measure by ecclesiastical courts.[11] The market places of Wareham and Romney provided the sites for ecclesiastical correction in Kent in 1292/3.[12] By the early fourteenth century, satire of the church courts treated penance in parish church and market place as familiar:

At chirche ant thourh cheping ase dogge y am drive.[13]

In the register of Hamo Hethe (1319-1352) for Rochester diocese, beatings round the market place were a familiar recourse, imposed for adultery, fornication and also the non-observance of feast days.[14] A consistory court for one year, 1363-4, in the same diocese compelled ten individuals to perambulate the market as penance.[15]

The performance of penance in the market place is perhaps best illustrated by a court book for the peculiar jurisdiction of the cathedral chapter of Lincoln for the 1330s and 1340s, comprehending a number of vills in central Lincolnshire.[16] Although most penance was referred to the parish church, a significant number of sentences was enacted in the local market vills and towns, in the market places of Caistor, Market Rasen, Sleaford, Navenby, Lincoln, Alford, Ludford, Grantham, Glentham, Horncastle, and Kirton.

In the early fifteenth century, the visitation of Dean John Chandler for part of Salisbury diocese condemned sinners to the market places of Yetminster, Ramsbury, Lyme, Sherborne, Bere Regis, Preston, Netherbury, Combe, Highworth, and other places.[17] By the fifteenth century, therefore, use of the market by the ecclesiastical courts was a regular procedure for penance for sexual delinquency and indeed for other sins on occasion.

Of course, the most spectacular performance of penance in the market place concerned abjuration by heretics, Lollards. The elaborate processional procedure was itemised in almost all the prosecutions of heretics: nude except for a white sheet, barelegged and barefooted in the penitential manner; carrying a candle; marked out by the symbol of the faggot or bearing a bundle of faggots on his back (representing the deferred threat of being burnt for heretical beliefs); required to perambulate the markets or the four corners of the market; preceded by the apparitor and followed by the curate wearing a surplice and carrying a rod pointing at the penitent; and whipped and disciplined at each station of the market.[18] Such elaborate disciplining of heretics is illustrated by the acts of Thomas Langton, bishop of Salisbury, at the end of the fifteenth century, and in Lincoln diocese in the middle of the same century.[19] The heresy trials in the diocese of Norwich in 1428-31 had earlier relied on the market place as a penitential locus for abjured heretics.[20]

As it evolved in the later middle ages, public penance consequently evokes a number of inter-related issues. Market places had become cultural sites for surrounding hinterlands, in which the ritual of public penance became a cultural tie between town and country.[21] Spiritual punishment was performed in profane space, in the market place, as well as in spiritual space, the parish church. Ritual processional routes were created in both parish church and market place for the performance of humiliation. The choreography of penance thus contributed towards the production, reproduction, representation and ambivalence of space, as sacred and profane spaces were confused.[22]

The cultural hinterlands of market centers were thus informed by ecclesiastical and spiritual jurisdiction in the late middle ages. Moreover, the act book for the peculiar jurisdiction of the chapter of Lincoln in the 1330s and 1340s reveals that this cultural performance occurred in market centers of all sizes, not just the principal markets–at small places like Navenby, Alford, Ludford, Glentham, and Kirton as well as those centers like Grantham and Market Raisen. If those smaller markets were not active as economic propositions, it was still intended that they continue as sites of cultural performance in the middle of the fourteenth century. In economic terms, Ludford remained ephemeral: although it received a market charter in 1252, in 1334 the vill was assessed at just under £3, not elevating it above any other vill in the locality.[23] Alford was barely more prosperous, assessed at just under £4.[24] In the heresy trials in the diocese of Norwich, smaller markets were still cultural sites in the early fifteenth century, although some also retained an economic function–in particular Loddon, but also Acle, Bungay and Beccles.

In the late sixteenth century, however, when the ritual of public penance in the market place was restored, it was confined to the large urban markets, the principal markets in the county. The cultural hinterlands of those principal urban markets were still defined, however, by ecclesiastical jurisdiction and spiritual punishment, which continued to produce in the 1560s and 1570s a cultural tie between town and countryside.

In the late middle ages, the performance of ritual penance in public in both parish church and market place had involved bodily discipline. Punishment was inscribed on the body, not just on the soul, or it was effected on the soul through the body. Correction was thus corporal, not simply spiritual, in the ecclesiastical disciplinary regime.[25] The *fustigatio* pertained to punishment in penance in both the parish church and the market place, although the exact nature of the *fustigatio* remains unclear apart from the intention of ritual expiation through pain.[26] Since it was incorporated in penance in procession in the parish church, the spilling of blood in the sacred space of the parish church risked defilement.[27] Physical punishment was, nonetheless, part of the medieval spectacle of public penance: the marked body represented the crime and the politics of the individual and local society.

By the early sixteenth century, however, bodily punishment was being abandoned by some ecclesiastical authorities, although it continued as an important part of civil punishment. It is possible that this abandonment of corporal punishment by some ecclesiastical courts reflected the transformation of theological notions of pain in the late fifteenth century.[28]

The practice and performance of penance in the late middle ages blurred the demarcation between viewer and actor, spectator and participant, and law and drama. The mimetic performance of the drama of ritual public humiliation provided a theater of punishment in which all participated. The locus of that theater was both the market place and the parish church.

In the late sixteenth century, the market place was revived as a place for this ritual drama, but in the early sixteenth century, its employment for penance had declined, or, indeed, in some jurisdictions all but been abandoned. In six years of causes in an episcopal court book of Lincoln, between 1514 and 1520, only two causes were referred to the market place. In 1516, Amy Martynmasse of Sharnford, Leicestershire, for her fornication with the curate of Uppingham, Sir Thomas Westmoreland, was directed to the market place of Uppingham. To the market place of Stamford was appointed Humphrey Rosse in 1519, subsequently excommunicated for obduracy against performance. Both therefore might have been considered to have exceeded the bounds of tolerance. Note, however, that no corporal punishment was inflicted in either case; spiritual symbolism was highlighted, as each had to carry a lighted candle as well as be accoutered in penitential clothing.[29] In the same diocese, the archdeaconry act book for Buckinghamshire contains penance performed only in the parish church in the late fifteenth and early sixteenth century.[30] The visitation of parts of the diocese of Norwich in 1499 resulted in the imposition of penance in some eighty causes in the parish church only, although four were to involve a *fustigatio*.[31] This pattern is confirmed by the corrections *sede vacante* in 1499, for, in all fourteen cases of sexual immorality for which a sentence was imposed, the penance was to be enacted in the parish church with lighted candles.[32] Emphatically, penance in the archdeaconry of Leicester in the early sixteenth century consisted entirely of performance in spiritual, not civic, space.[33]

Similarly, the act book for the peculiar jurisdiction of Whalley between 1510 and 1538, contains very few causes directed to the market place. In the office causes, forty-six were performed in parish church alone, and merely two, it seems, in both parish church and market place. Whilst some of the penances were, incidentally, described as *penitentiales corporales*, it would seem that the interpretation here is that the humiliation was the bodily punishment, rather than any *fustigatio*.[34]

The "hiatus" of the early sixteenth century

By the early sixteenth century in particular, the character of penance had been transformed, perhaps under the influence of devotional praxis amongst the laity at that time.[35] Whilst all of the penances described below existed from an earlier time, the nature of their use in the early sixteenth century points towards a regime which was manifestly less inclined to enforce bodily discipline for error.[36] Types of penances were imposed by the courts spiritual which placed an emphasis on religious symbolism and contrition. There is ostensibly here a relationship between official doctrine and "popular" culture in the sense that the penances imposed by authority accorded with voluntary acts that parishioners might ordinarily have conducted as part of their individual piety.[37] Thus when Robert Curtebe of Oadby was sentenced for detinue of tithes, his penance was to genuflect in the middle of the choir with a lighted candle in his hand and to recite five prayers with the "O saluta beate marie" and the "credo", after which he was instructed to offer the candle to the principal image in the church.[38] John Pyllyng of Rossendale, for begetting an illegitimate child, knelt in prayer at his usual pew on Sunday in Rossendale chapel with a lighted candle in his hand during mass, after which he offered the candle at the high altar. Another penance in Rossendale chapel consisted of repetition of five Lady psalters. For fornication, John Hepe knelt during mass and then, genuflecting, offered a candle to the principal image in the church.[39] Offering candles to the principal image in the parish church was a frequent penance in the early sixteenth century.[40] The alternative was to offer the candle to the priest at the end of mass in a gesture of submission and reconciliation.[41] A woman who had fornicated carried a light to mass and offered it into the priest's hands desiring him to explain the cause of her penance, whilst John Crawford who had had sexual knowledge of a woman was given the penance of symbolically loading gravel at the seven ashes, which was both penitential at a penitential time and also a retributive good work.[42] Similarly good works were included in 1539 in the penance of William Ashebye for fornication, for, as well as processing before the cross with a light, kneeling before the choir door during mass, and offering his candle into the hands of the curate, he was also directed to lay twenty loads of gravel "wher as most need is In the way" before Whitsunday.[43] Recitation of the seven penitential psalms was also frequently imposed as penance.[44]

Another interesting intersection between the official doctrine of penance and popular devotional culture consisted of the prescription of pilgrimage as penance. Imposed penitential pilgrimages had an earlier existence, but form part of a regime which in the early sixteenth century relied less on bodily punishment. Accused of carnal knowledge of Joan Clarke, Giles Mawyer of Chalfont St Giles received a penance of pilgrimage on five feast days of the Virgin to Missenden.[45] Pilgrimage was not simply then voluntarism; it was also coercive as an official imposition. In view of this coercion, pilgrimage cannot have represented only liberation from profane social structures through access to a sacred space which was timeless and "liminal", for it was not always enacted voluntarily. Forced pilgrimage might thus have contributed to an ambiguous reception of pilgrimage and sacred space.

It appears then that there was a transformation in the character of penance imposed by ecclesiastical courts by the early sixteenth century which abandoned some of the earlier emphases on satisfaction, such as the market place and the *fustigatio*, and tended more towards fulfilling the requirements of contrition, of internal sorrow and repentance, although the process was a gradual one which extended over the late middle ages and the pattern of abandonment varied by diocese.[46] It is therefore not suggested that the penitential impositions described here were new, but that in the early sixteenth century their singular use gave a different character to medieval penance.

Penance in the early-modern market place

The timing of the reintroduction of penance in the market place in some ecclesiastical jurisdictions coincides with the influence of "Godly" regimes, as will be demonstrated below. Whilst Godly religion required a strong measure of interiority, the Godly apparently resorted to public, communitarian enforcement of penance. Consequently, the restoration of public penance in the market place might be considered a disciplinary aspect of Godly religion which was enforced through public humiliation not interior reformation. These undercurrents then raise the issues of the nature of disciplinary regimes and also the relationship between the official discourse of penance and popular culture. First, however, it must be explained how public penance in the market place underwent those transitions.

From 1551-1553, Bishop Hooper instituted a regime in the diocese of Gloucester which included penance performed at the High Cross in Gloucester on Saturdays based on a cell in the market place. Penitents from rural places were required to travel into Gloucester to perform their penance, although some were allowed to enact their penance in other market centers. No commutation of this penalty was allowed under any circumstances. Hooper's regime, no doubt modelled on his experience of continental Reformed practice, was, however, short-lived.[47]

Renewal of penance in the market place in the late sixteenth century exhibited a differential geography, which seems to reflect the intensity of Godly influence. There remained, for example, several ecclesiastical jurisdictions in which penance in the market place, although occasionally used as a discretionary punishment, hardly otherwise existed (see below). In others, nevertheless, the imposition of humiliation in the market place was adopted as an important strategy for the reformation of character and morality. This re-adoption of this approach was, however, transient, confined to the 1560s to 1580s; thereafter, although it was used in a discretionary manner, it receded again. The re-imposition of penance in the market place is thus associated with a generation of religious change in certain eclesiastical jurisdictions.

Its transience is illustrated by events in the archdeaconry of Leicester. The revival of penance in the market place had been established by 1561 from which date the act books of the archdeaconry court survive after a long hiatus. In the act book of 1561-1563, fourteen office causes incurred penance in a market place as well as in the parish church–that is, the sentence in cases of sexual incontinence and fornication imposed penance in the parish church and also in the market place.[48] The policy, nevertheless, was not pursued exclusively, for some such causes received only penance in the parish church, although only a minority. There was thus some consistency in enforcing a penance which consisted of both parish church and market place in 1561-1563. Between 1563 and 1576, however, the policy appears to have lapsed.[49] By 1576, penance had been re-instituted in the market place as well as parish church.[50] In the period covered by this act book in 1576-1577, eighteen penances were imposed as a combined penance in parish church and market place. The office act book for 1581 contains a further seven impositions which included the market place.[51] Subsequently, penance in the market place was used intermittently as a discretionary punishment in five cases in 1582-1585 and two cases in 1585-1588.[52] The punishment was invoked again for a fornicator in 1597 when, to ensure the visibility of the penitent, the offender had to stand "upon a skaffold a yard from the ground" in Loughborough market on a Thursday.[53] This episode was, however, just that, not a part of a regular sequence.

When penance in the market place was reintroduced by 1561, it involved some severity. Thus Henry Byggyn of Buckminster, for adultery with his *famula* (servant) Agnes, performed three penances in his parish church and three in Melton market. Richard Peke, convicted of the same crime with his servant, Isabel Wyldman, was sentenced not only to three days in Loughborough market, nearest to his domicile in Thorpe Hawker, but also another penance *circa villam Leic'*. Then also John Harfar, for his betrayal of trust in getting his servant, Agnes Wylde, with child, was also sentenced to three days in Melton market as well as three in Saxby church.[54] The severity is only partly explicable by exploitation of a female servant, however, for Richard Tete was also subjected to three penances in Loughborough market for his dalliance with Joan Bothon of Quorn, she also being sentenced to penance *circa villam Leic'*.[55] So also, Richard Eglott's adultery which incurred penance of three days in Hathern church and three in Loughborough market, was committed with Margaret Strett of Hathern, not ostensibly a servant.[56] No doubt therefore the abuse of trust of protection of a servant in a patriarchal society was regarded with intense disdain, but that was not the sole reason for the intensity of some of the penances imposed in 1561-1563. Occasionally in later cases, penance was imposed in two markets: Mary Blanckney of Wymeswold, who confessed to having eloped for a week with John Ferne of Thringston in 1586, performed penance in the markets of both Loughborough and Mountsorrel; the servant (Elizabeth) of John Whyte of Stapleton, who was implicated in adultery with her master, was sentenced to penance in both Hinckley and Leicester markets; and John Done of Ashby Folville for fornication with Margaret Martyn, suffered the humiliations of Leicester and Melton markets.[57] The discretionary levels of these punishments must be related to some particularly heinous aspect of the sins.

In one office cause, the intention of referring penance to the theatre of the market place is made explicit: in the public market of Melton Mowbray on Tuesday when the throng of people is there.[58] That purpose of the authorities in the late sixteenth century was reinforced in the archdeaconry of Nottingham, where from the 1560s penance in the market place was consistently and unwaveringly applied with a distinct and purposeful intention. Although most of the sentences simply refer to public penance in a specified market place on a specified number of days, the office act books of the archdeaconry of Nottingham contain occasional detail of the nature of that penance imposed. From the survival of the act books in 1566 the following examples are descriptive of the process.

> That thaie shall goo this present Daie about the market of Retford he bare headed, bare legged, and bare footed in his shirt onlye, and a sheite about his mydle with a white rod in his hand and she bare legged, bare footed, and a kirchiff caste lowse upon her heade in one petycot and a sheit about her mydle with a white rod in her hand after the manner of penytentes.[59]

> That upon Satourdaie next he shall goo about the market place of nott' at xij of the clock the same Daie bare headed, bare footed and bare legged in his shirt and dublet onlye, and a sheite about his myddle with a white Rod in his hande, after the manner of a penytent And John Crane the apparitor shall goo before him, and se him Doo the saide penaunce, and so declare unto the people whye and wherefore the said Ferneley Dothe the saide penance.[60]

The policy of penance extracted in both parish church and market place was consistently applied in all cases in Nottingham archdeaconry court between 1566 and 1579. It is feasible that its architect was Archdeacon Lowth (1565-1590), who possibly intended to extend his influence through this policy of reform in his ecclesiastical court.[61]

An interesting aspect of the ritual of penance in Nottingham is the (re)construction of a penitential processional route between St. Mary's church and the market place. By May 8, 1568, this processional arrangement had become clearly defined: the day as Saturday, the principal market day in Nottingham; the time limited to between eleven and one o'clock when the most intense activity occurred in the market place; the penitents first attending St. Mary's church, then processing to the market place, perambulating it preceded by the apparitor, and then processing back to St. Mary's. Church and market place and the processional route between them were thus clearly delineated in the ritual of public humiliation of penitents and located in time to provide the maximum public spectacle.

Referring only to the market place of Nottingham–that is, discounting the other markets in Nottinghamshire–the regularity of this procedure was marked. At least an average of one penance per month was performed in most years, but in some years up to an average of four each month. The spectacle of penance was thus a regular one. There was some discretion in sentencing, penitents being required to attend in the market place from one to four days, presumably depending on the nature of the crime and the character of the sinner. After 1579, however, the imposition of penance in the market place declined, apparently used only as a discretionary punishment.

The re-introduction of penance in the market place in the archdeaconries of Essex and Colchester followed a similar pattern to that in Nottingham archdeaconry. In the first extant act book for Essex archdeaconry after the accession of Elizabeth, that of 1560-1562, penance in the market place was invoked; the first few cases involved, it seems, failed purgation, but sporadically sexual offences were encompassed. Through these two years therefore, penance in the parish church only remained more frequent than that in both parish church and market. The first instance occurred in 1560 when John Goose of Alveley failed in purgation; he was ordered

> to comme into the Market place of Alveleie there standing with a whyte shete one hower confessing his fallt and the next Sunday after to comme into the churche of Alveley In forma predicta confessinge as aforsaide.[62]

The frequency of the imposition of penance in the market place in the archdeaconry of Essex is tabulated below (Table 6.1).

The required demeanour of the penitents can be elicited from occasional entries in the act books for Essex archdeaconry:

> To stand in the marquet place of Brentwood in a whitt sheat <in the marq> when the people are most there with a paper upon his had & the Detection written in the same.[63]

> that on saterdaie next in the marquett place of horndon on the hil when the most people are there the both parties abouesaid to stand upon ij stoles with a whitt shete <a whitt rodd in ther handes> seueralle about them and ... to remaine the space of iij houres.[64]

> That upon frydaye next he shall stand <at Chelmsford> in a sheit more penitentie [sic] openly at the marquet cross there from x of the clocke in the fore none <of the same Daye> until xij of the same Day And ther confesse his fault openly and penitently & to certifie it under the handes of the parson and vj of the honest men of the same parishe.[65]

The general context for the attraction for public, ritual humiliation in the archdeaconry of Essex was a pervasive attachment to the reformed religion in the county. That disposition is even more evident in the archdeaconry of Colchester and the activities of the archdeaconry court in office causes might be attributed to George Withers, the second town preacher in Colchester, who later became archdeacon of Colchester.[66] There was indeed cohesion between magistracy and clergy as from May 1566 a new tribunal was established in Colchester, comprising bailiffs and archdeacon, which expressly ordained that fornicators should be whipped on the back of a cart. Further it was promulgated that moral offenders should walk the length of the market place and then stand in front of the Moot Hall door to proclaim their offence.[67] Clearly visible here is the arrangement by which the magistracy permitted the clergy to use the public, civic facility of the market place to promote spiritual (and concomitantly social) reformation. The background is even more interesting, however, because Withers had in June 1568 defended at the University of Heidelberg a doctoral thesis arguing for the necessity of the consistorial order established in Geneva, that is for an independent church consistory alone. In this endeavour, he came into direct argument with Thomas Liebler (Erastus) at the University who argued against Withers and in favour of the authority of civil authority over the clergy. Withers was thus marked out as a "Disciplinist".[68]

The extent of the adoption of the market place of Colchester as a penitential space can be illustrated from the first earliest extant office act books for the archdeaconry, for in these years of 1569 to February 1572 twenty-four causes of sexual indiscretion were adjudicated; of these twenty-four, eleven were sentenced to penance in both the parish church and market place, but thirteen to the market place alone with no reference to the parish church.[69] Through until 1579, sentences to penance in the market place continued at a high level (see Table 6.2). In the decade 1570 to 1579, from Earls Colne alone twelve convicted sexual delinquents were sentenced to penance in Colchester market place.[70]

Despite the enthusiasm for public humiliation in the market place in these ecclesiastical jurisdictions considered above, not all courts spiritual adopted this approach in the 1560s and 1570s. Some, like Ely, applied this punishment in several cases, but not consistently, whilst others, like Peterborough and Lichfield, used it rarely, that is as a discretionary instrument. There are very few instances of its application in the diocese of Peterborough, but in 1583 Agnes Simons of Preston was to perform penance on Saturdays in Oakham and Uppingham markets for being unlawfully with child and about a month later Eusebius Billingworth was sentenced to Thrapston market place for begetting a bastard child.[71] Six years earlier, the consistory court of Peterborough directed William

Billing of Brigstock to Kettering market place, Cuthbert Miller of Castor to Peterborough market place, and Bartholomew Hawley of Harringworth to Uppingham market place.[72] In this diocese, however, penance was normatively in the parish church. In the Oxfordshire archdeaconry court in 1584, only one penance involved the market place, a perambulation of Woodstock market.[73] Four penances in the market place were imposed on sinners before Bishop Still of Bath and Wells on his visitation in 1594.[74] Infrequent too were penances in the market place in the act books of the consistory court of Winchester acting for the archdeaconry of Winchester. The most prominent example occurred in isolation in 1568 when Richard Ayling was directed to the markets of Winchester, Alton, Basingstoke and Andover on their market days, for having got pregnant his servant, Alice Mill, with whom he cohabited rather than with his wife. The offense was thus deemed particularly heinous.[75] The pattern of application in Lichfield diocese is similar, but even later. In the act book of January 1582/3 to October 1589, two penitents were directed to both the parish church and the market place.[76] At the end of 1591, John Robertes of Newport was despatched to the market place of Newport for carnal knowledge of Barbara Pete.[77] Whereas the market was rarely employed before 1600, in the act book of December 1601 to January 1602/3 and thus covering approximately twelve months, four penitents were referred to both the market place and parish church, two to the market place only, and twenty-five to the parish church only.[78]

From the diocese of Ely, there are some dramatic prescriptions for the nature of penance in the market place, but it was nonetheless deployed intermittently as a discretionary punishment. The initial cause in the court concerned absolution from excommunication through penance at the *stacio* in the markets at Ely and Cambridge in February 1568/9.[79] The second cause in the consistory court, entered in July 1570, reflects this florid description of the sentence:

> to stand <the next> ij market dayes at Cambridge market crosse in a white shete a white wand in his hand & ij papers wrytten with great letters for abhominable Adultrye on upon his brest & another upon his backe...[80]

Not until almost three years later was another penitent referred to the market place, but the penance prescribed was equally demonstrative:

> once in Elye market Crosse in a shete, haveinge a whyte wand in his hand, and ij papers wrytten with greate lettres <with this po-esye viz. for Fylthye lyveinge & shameless bragginge in the same> one of them pynned upon his brest & The other upon his backe.[81]

In this cause, this enhanced punishment was exacted for the multiple sins of the defendant who had not only dismissed his wife, but also engaged in slanderous and lewd language. In the same year, a similar penance was imposed on Richard Lawrence and Elizabeth Syblye of Ely for reason "That they haue committed the abhomynable synne of Incest togither she beinge his former wyves brothers daughter."

Their penance thus involved:

To stand at ye market Crosse in Elye upon Saterdaye beinge the xxxjth [sic] of Januarye 1572 from x of the clocke before noone until ij of the clocke in the after noone clothed in whyte shetes holdinge ij whyte wands in theyre hands haveinge eche of them ij papers wrytten with great lettres with this poesye for abhomynable synne of Incest pynned one upon theyre backs and the other upon theyre brests &c[82]

Where penance of this nature was implemented in the diocese of Ely, it was almost universally for offences of an intolerable or recidivist nature. When, thus, in 1576/7 Robert Hardinge and Elizabeth Soomerfyeld received their penance in the public market place of Ely, the cause was "for lyveinge togither worse than they did before".[83] Despite pleading in mitigation in November 1577 "That she was and is verye nere the tyme of hir delueraunce", because she was pronounced contumacious and excommunicated Elizabeth Hoode of West Wratting became an example to others:

uppon Satterdaye next comminge beinge the xvjth of November 1577 to stand at ye Bull ringe in Cambrydge clothed in a white shete downe to ye grownd holdinge a white rood or wand in hir hand & haveinge a paper written with great lettres pynned uppon hir brest & ye lyke paper uppon hir backe Declareinge hir offence from x of ye clocke in the forenoone until twoe in ye after none &c.[84]

Finally, in the sequence, in April 1581, Agnes Haseldon of Barrington produced a certificate that she had performed her penance at the bull ring in Cambridge market for adultery.[85] The imposition of penance in the market place in the Ely consistory court was thus limited in incidence, if florid in performance. What is apparent overall, however, is the different response in different ecclesiastical jurisdictions in the late sixteenth century to the possibility of a retributive justice in the form of penance in the market place alongside that in the parish church. More enthusiastic for its regular imposition were Godly jurisdictions, whilst other courts spiritual employed it more sparingly as an exemplary and discretionary device against excessive or particularly heinous crimes.[86]

Responses and meanings

Although, however, the intentionality of penance in the market place is clear–to engender humiliation and shaming–its authorial intent and meaning were compromised by how it was received and interpreted. Firstly, its deployment depended on a collaboration between magisterial and ecclesiastical authorities. Secondly there is the complex interrelationship between official culture–the disciplinary regime–and "popular" culture–the shared belief in humiliation and shaming rituals.[87] At a much simpler level, however, resistance to authority was possible, and rejection of any deep meaning in performing ritual.[88]

Avoidance was one such strategy. Thus Alice Barker, pregnant by Robert East of Holme, Nottinghamshire, had been harboured by Richard Levers of Emneth, and fled instead of performing penance, whilst leaving the township of Emneth 10s. towards the maintenance of her abandoned child, perhaps indicating the township's complicity.[89] Accused and convicted of whoredom, Alice Mepoole of Girton fled and then returned to avoid detection of not having performed her penance.[90] In 1578/9, it was detected that Richard Androwe of Ashton "carried and conveighed away one Ales Deacon from Lilford to thende she should not Doe the pennaunce which was enioyned unto her and besides that he is suspected to haue gotten her with child."[91]

Remaining obdurate in excommunication exhibited more defiance of the imposition of penance, so that William James of Whittlesea in July 1577 "…had penaunce enioyned & deliuered to him twoe seuerall tymes, and for that he did yt not he was excommunicate, & so remaynethe."[92] A similar tactic was employed by John Byrd of Hinton who, in January 1576/7, was suspended for not performing his penance, but still introduced himself back into the congregation, berating the minister for performing his duty.[93] Simple omission was a constant occurrence, as when Bridget Browne of Romford was presented again because "she dyd not her pennaunc as she was appointed" or when William Warren was cited again for not acquitting his penance in Alveley market.[94] Outright and outraged recrimination was another response, as when John Tayler of Stanton St Michael professed, in railing against the incumbent, that he would see the parson hanged before he would perform penance.[95] Initial bravery led Robert Maxwell in April 1580 to refuse the apparitor citing his wife, resulting in his excommunication and seeking absolution with great sorrow (*tristitia magna*).[96]

Equally, the ritual might be performed without subscription to its intended meaning, in a hollow manner. Perhaps that dissembling or compliance sustained Richard Sneathe in 1582, who was directed to redo his penance because it was suspected that it was not enacted with "inward sorrowe" nor "penitentlie".[97] As explicitly, because she did not enact her penance penitently the first time, Joan Turneley of Eakring was commanded to

> come to Newarke on Wednesday next and there to be carted with a pan ronge before her and lyckwyse to doe her penaunce at Eykeringe on Sunday next standinge on a seyte in the middest of the churche ad (sic) service tyme her face turned towardes the people.[98]

In this instance not only did empty performance of the ritual incur a higher sanction of penance, but in rough music is particularly apparent the relationship between official doctrine and popular culture.

Bravado or insouciance was another reaction, verging on the blasphemous. Thomas Brayne, curate of Cranham, alleged that he heard Henry Parker

> affirme that he had slandered the widowe Doore in sayeing that he had abused her bodye and for so reporting he had xxs. given him and also the same Parker offered to laye xs. that he shold Doe no more or other penaunce.[99]

Resistance to the ecclesiastical process was not, however, a discovery of the late sixteenth century. Although it is less visible in the records, it certainly existed earlier. In 1359, the apparitor of the bishop of Carlisle was attacked and prevented from performing his office in the market of Brampton, perhaps for issuing citations.[100] An outrage was perpetrated against the apparitors of the deanery of Pontebury in 1316 when they were performing their duties in the town of Montgomery; they were beaten to bloodshed and the culprits were denounced by the Bishop of Hereford.[101] When cited for adultery with Cecily *domina* of Staunton in 1299, William de Bredon forced the archbishop's messenger to eat the citation and was consequently excommunicated.[102] The excessive demands of apparitors were heavily criticised in the fourteenth century.[103]

Refusal to perform penance at an earlier time, however, could incur a very heavy price. In 1378, John son of Adam Joseph declined to perform penance for adultery and incest by which he fathered four children by Alice wife of John Cooper. The penance of *fustigationes* of three days around three local churches and two days round each of the markets of Cambridge, Linton and Icklington, reflected the seriousness of the crime. On his refusal, John was excommunicated and, since he remained obdurate, the secular arm was invoked to arrest him. Detained by the sheriff, he was incarcerated in Cambridge gaol for four days, but finally released on bail of £30 advanced by four friends. He subsequently performed the penance.[104]

For others the humiliation of the market place was something to be avoided and its authorial intent was subscribed. Accordingly, Ambrose Stone, who had completed his penance in Bury and Horringer churches, persuaded Sir Ambrose Jermyn, knight, to write to the Commissary requesting lenience for Stone, exonerating him from penance of standing in the market the whole time of the market.[105] Since Stone was a gentleman, however, honor and social status was also implicated in avoiding the dishonor of penance in the market place.

It is not perhaps surprising that the ritual elicited such different responses, reflecting its polyvalency. Whilst Michael Drayton and Henry Arthington reflected at the end of the sixteenth century on the humiliation of penance–Drayton in an historical context–John Ashmore in 1621 conveyed a profoundly dismissive message at least about the interiority of penance and about its subversion:

A Priest, for Penance, one enioyned to take
A iourney with three Pease loose in his shoo:
Which he, devoutly given, did not forsake,
But fram'd himself his Penance straight to doo:
Yet, that he might perform it with more ease,
His wit did serve him, first to boyl the Pease.[106]

From different perspectives, both Martin Ingram and Christopher Haigh have questioned the significance of penance in the late sixteenth and early seventeenth centuries. Haigh, on the one hand, suggested, from his evidence in Lancashire, that penance was most often commuted or redeemed in the late sixteenth century.[107] Emendation through private tariffs had long featured in the penitential manuals, however, and remained a consistent feature of act books of the later middle ages, although not usually encompassing a preponderance of penances. In the London consistory court in the early sixteenth century, merely 40 percent of penances, it has been suggested, were performed, a figure which seems particularly low, the remainder being commuted.[108] In a court book for the peculiar jurisdiction of the cathedral chapter of Lincoln, comprehending parts of mid Lincolnshire in the 1330s and 1340s, a proportion of the sentences was commuted, both by grace and negotiation, although the almost standard tariff of 1d. in redemption of a "beating" suggests some form of regularization.[109] In the late fifteenth century, indeed, the parishioners of Boston complained to the Vicar-General of Lincoln about the frequency of pecuniary penance which resulted in only the very poor performing public penance.[110] Indicated there is the issue of status in relation to penance, since the ecclesiastical courts were careful not to undermine social position and ordering by enforcing humiliating penance against those of higher social status. Nor was there clarity about the relationship between commutation and corporal penance or about the jurisdictional abilities to redeem penance in the late middle ages.[111]

In the Godly regimes of the *ecclesia anglicana* in the 1560s and 1570s, penance in the market place was rarely emended. In some other regimes where it was emended, the price was occasionally very high. In 1588/9, William Madder had to deliver ten marks to the poor for commutation of his penance during divine service and at the reading of the homily.[112] In 1568/9, Thomas Russell was assessed at £3 6s. 8d. for commutation of penance and Richard Phypers at £5 6s. 8d., both making downpayments (20s. and 40s.) and taking out bonds for the payment of the remainder, whilst still having to acknowledge their fault in church.[113]

In his analysis of the early seventeenth century, Ingram correctly perceived that penance, which was by then by and large confined to the parish church, might have had no significant impact on social regulation. Before then, however, a different regime had obtained in the 1560s and 1570s in some ecclesiastical jurisdictions, which enforced an intense public humiliation. Although even then, responses to penance were multivocal, the influence of this regime was perhaps still quite pervasive in its disciplinary impact.

Broader implications

To the extent that this chapter has concentrated on evidence from English ecclesiastical courts, it presents a rather localised process. In fact, however, it is entirely possible that the processes established in some of these English ecclesiastical fora in the 1560s and 1570s belonged to a much wider imposition of Reformed standards throughout parts of Europe.[114] Margo Todd, for example, has brilliantly described the disciplinary processes enforced by consistories of the Scottish Kirk, emphasising the public and communal aspects in penance in the parish church, to the extent that she enunciates the anthropological notions of "community" of Victor Turner and Oliver Tambiah which have also been inferred in late medieval religious observance.[115] Differences there were, particularly in the manner in which the market place was enforced as a place of public humiliation, for in Scotland the magistracy alone implemented that aspect. Moreover, it appears that the vigor of Scottish discipline continued after some weakening of English punishment from the 1580s.[116]

Taking an even wider perspective, other Protestant churches in parts of Europe introduced a similar penitential regime informed by confessional requirements and social ordering which engendered a communal focus.[117] The "community-building function" of the discipline of penance was evident in the Dutch Reformed church whilst the French Reformed consistories acted in a disciplinary manner which had "a decidedly communal ring".[118] Networks of exiled reformed clergy presumably communicated information about these processes across Europe.[119]

Penance thus exhibits the confusion and ambiguity of space. Through the late middle ages and into the early seventeenth century, the parish church was both a spiritual space and a space of ritual, public humiliation. In the late middle ages too the market place, although a secular forum, was employed as a site of spiritual correction. In both fora, even in the parish church, spiritual correction involved some form of bodily discipline.[120] In these spaces too official doctrine and popular culture intersected, as ritual public humiliation and shaming provided a shared strategy and tactic, if not shared values.[121] Humiliation in public ritual form persisted over the *longue durée* as a prominent element in penance imposed by ecclesiastical courts, especially for sexual delinquency. Spiritual correction was performed in the public forum, the market place. Godly regimes deployed public ritual humiliation in the market place, a communitarian and social disciplining alongside an emphasis on interior, private contrition, so that spiritual correction was also influenced by social ordering. In the decades of the 1560s and 1570s, moreover, through penance it can be uncovered how differently the "birthpangs" of Protestant England were experienced *in different jurisdictions*.[122]

Dates of act book	No. of cases of penance in the market place
1560–2	6
1563–5	22
1565–6	4
1567–8	13
1569–70	6
1572	9
1573–5	8
1577–8	2
1579–80	0
1584	2
1586–8	3
1590	1

Table 6.1   Frequency of Penance in Market Places, Essex Archdeaconry

Dates of act book	No. of cases of penance in the market place
1560–2	6
1563–5	22
1565–6	4
1567–8	13
1569–70	6
1572	9
1573–5	8
1577–8	2
1579–80	0
1584	2
1586–8	3
1590	1

Table 6.2   Frequency of Penance in Market Places, Colchester Archdea-conry

Notes

[1]Mansfield, *The Humiliation of Sinners*, provides analogous confirmation in a slightly different context.

[2]For the differences of satisfaction/contrition and discipline/consolation, Thomas Tentler, *Sin and Confession on the Eve of the Reformation* (Princeton, NJ: Princeton University Press, 1977), 16-22.

[3]John Bossy, "The Social History of Confession in the Age of the Reformation," *TRHS* 5th ser. 25 (1975): 21-38, and "Moral Arithmetic: Seven Sins into Ten Commandments," in *Conscience and Casuistry in Early Modern Europe*, ed. Edmund Leites (Cambridge: Cambridge University Press, 1988), 214-34. For equivocation, Raymond A. Mentzer, "Notions of Sin and Penitence within the French Reformed Community," in *Penitence in the Age of Reformations* ed. Katharine Jackson Lualdi and Anne T. Thayer (Aldershot: Ashgate, 2000), 84-100 at pp. 87-89, esp. p. 88 n. 8.

[4]Bossy, "The Social History."

[5]The processional aspect of these spaces in parish churches is perhaps best illustrated by Cooke, *Act Book of the Ecclesiastical Court of Whalley*, 74, 113, 133, 134, 154, 156, 300: *circuat; ad circuendum; circuat processionaliter*; to process before the cross at the head of the procession. For the early-modern period, the performative nature has been beautifully illustrated by Professor Margo Todd in her paper ("Performing Penance in Early-modern Scotland") at the seminar series on "Religion in the British Isles 1400-1700" at Oxford on May 3, 2001. See now Todd, *The Culture of Protestantism in Early Modern Scotland* (New Haven: Yale University Press, 2002), Chapter 3 ("Performing Repentance").

[6]"& the one not to frequent and use the cumpanye of another but openlye & publyquelye, as in market Fayre churche and open congregation": CUL EDR D/2/9c, fol. 151r; correspondingly, all other spaces which were not open were represented as *loca suspecta*: CUL EDR D/2/1, fols lxxxvjr and lxxxvijr-v. See also the INTRODUCTION.

[7]Masschaele, "The Public Space of the Market Place."

[8]Antonia Gransden, "Some Late Thirteenth-century Records of an Ecclesiastical Court in the Archdeaconry of Sudbury," *Bulletin of the Institute of Historical Research* 32 (1959): 62-69.

[9]Rosalind M. T. Hill, "Public Penance: Some Problems of a Thirteenth-century Bishop," *History* xxxvi (1951): 213-26 at pp. 219-20 (debauchery of a nun; infraction of sanctuary). Sutton more generally resorted to excommunication.

[10]William Brown, ed., *The Registers of John le Romeyn Archbishop of York 1286-1296 Part II and of Henry of Newark Lord Archbishop of York 1296-1299*, SS vol. 128 (1917 for 1916) (Cecily, lady of Staunton, for adultery, in the markets of Nottingham and Bingham; and two males directed to the markets of Retford and Nottingham).

[11]For penance imposed in the market place of Darlington for serial adultery, Thomas D. Hardy, ed., *The Register of Richard de Kellawe Lord Palatine and Bishop of Durham 1311-1316*, Rolls Series (London, 1873), 417-18 (1313); for penance imposed in the market place of Beverley in 1303/4, Arthur F. Leach, ed., *Memorials of Beverley Minster: The Chapter Act Book of the Collegiate Church of St John of Beverley A.D. 1286-*

1347, SS vols. 98 and 108 (1898-1903), vol. 1, 5.

[12]C. Eveleigh Woodruff, "Some Early Visitation Rolls Preserved at Canterbury," *Archaeologia Cantiana* 32 (1917), 150, 154, 156 and 164.

[13]Thomas Wright, ed., *Political Songs of England from the Reign of John to that of Edward II*, Camden (London, 1834), 159.

[14]Charles Johnson, ed., *Registrum Hamonis Hethe, Diocesis Roffensis, AD 1319-1352*, CYS vol. 49 (1948), vol. 2, 946, 965, 980, 993, 997-9, 1008, 1015, 1027 and 1043.

[15]S. L. Parker and L. Poos, "A Consistory Court from the Diocese of Rochester, 1363-4," *English Historical Review* 106 (1991): 652-65 at pp. 657-9 and 663.

[16]LAO MS D&C A/2/24. I am indebted to Professor Larry Poos for allowing me to read his transcription of this volume before its publication by the British Academy Records of Social and Economic History. See now Laurence R. Poos, ed., *Lower Ecclesiastical Jurisdiction in Late-medieval England. The Courts of the Dean and Chapter of Lincoln, 1336-1349 and the Deanery of Wisbech, 1458-1484*, British Academy Records of Social and Economic History n.s. vol. 32 (Oxford: Oxford University Press, 2001).

[17]T. C. B. Timmins, ed., *The Register of John Chandler, Dean of Salisbury, 1404-1417*, Wiltshire Record Society vol. 39 (1984), 18, 35, 74, 79, 84, 106-11, 113, 115, 118, 124 and 126. For impositions of penance in the market place in the same diocese in the late fourteenth century, *The Register of John Waltham, Bishop of Salisbury, 1388-1395*, CYS vol. 80 (1994), 116-17 and 179.

[18]Apparently, however, the market place was not a site for penance by heretics in the early sixteenth century: J. Fines, "Heresy Trials in the Diocese of Coventry and Lichfield, 1511-12," *Journal of Ecclesiastical History* 14 (1963): 160-74 at p. 170. For the fifteenth century, John A. F. Thomson, *The Later Lollards 1414-1520* (Oxford: Oxford University Press, 1965), 231.

[19]*The Register of Thomas Langton, Bishop of Salisbury, 1485-1493*, CYS vol. 74 (1985), 51 (no. 420) , 71 (no. 485), 73-7 (nos. 487-91) and 81 (no. 500); for the background, Brown, *Popular Piety in Late Medieval England*; the penitent heretics were directed to multiple large markets to emphasize the humiliation and correction. Clark, *Lincoln Diocesan Documents 1450-1454*, 101 (I owe this reference to Professor Charles Phythian-Adams).

[20]Norman Tanner, ed., *Heresy Trials in the Diocese of Norwich, 1428-31*, Camden 4th ser., vol. 20 (1977), passim.

[21]For the framing of this question of the cultural relationship between town and country in the early modern period, MacLean, Landry, and Ward, *The Country and the City Revisited*, esp. "Introduction" at 1-23.

[22]Douglas, *Purity and Danger*; Tim Unwin, "A Waste of Space? Towards a Critique of the Social Production of Space ..,"*Transactions of the Institute of British Geographers* n.s. 25 (2000): 11-29; Soja,*Postmodern Geographies*; Lefebvre, *Production of Space*; Sibley, *Geographies of Exclusion*.

[23]For the markets in Lincolnshire, Graham Platts, *Land and People in Medieval Lincolnshire*, History of Lincolnshire vol. 4 (Lincoln 1985), 137, 194-5; for the assessments in 1334, Robin E. Glasscock, ed.,*The Lay Subsidy of 1334*, British Academy Records of Social and Economic History new ser. vol. 2 (Oxford: Oxford University Press, 1975), 174, 181 and 184.

[24]For the nature of marketing at this time, James Masschaele, "The Multiplicity of Medieval Markets Reconsidered," *Journal of Historical Geography* 20 (1994): 255-71, and *Peasants, Merchants and Markets*; Jane Laughton and Christopher Dyer, "Small Towns in the East and West Midlands in the Later Middle Ages: A Comparison,"*Midland History* 24 (1999): 24-52.

[25]It is possible to construe this as either the more general pre-modern physical disciplinary regime of Foucault or as the bodily training involved in religious praxis described by Mauss and recently re-phrased by Talal Asad. Since it continued in civil punishment, however, it seems likely that the change was not informed by the evolution of civility in the Elias/Spierenburg paradigm. Michel Foucault, *Discipline and Punish: The Birth of the Prison* (London: Penguin, 1977); Pieter Spierenburg, *The Spectacle of Suffering: Executions and the Evolution of Repression* (Cambridge: Cambridge University Press, 1984). For some of these approaches, BrianTurner, *The Body and Society: Explorations in Social Theory* (Oxford: Blackwell, 1984); Talal Asad, "Remarks on the Anthropology of the Body," in *Religion and the Body*, ed. Sarah Coakley (Cambridge: Cambridge University Press, 1997), 42-52. For spectacle, however, Seth Lerer, "'Represented now in yower syght'. The Culture of Spectatorship in Fifteenth-century England," in *Bodies and Disciplines: Intersections of Literature and History in Fifteenth-century England,* ed. Barbara Hanawalt and David Wallace (Minnesota: University of Minnesota Press, 1996), 29-62. For how England diverged from the continent in the restrained approach to and abandonment of bodily discipline, M. Flynn, "The Spectacle of Suffering in Spanish Streets," in *City and Spectacle in Medieval Europe*, ed. Barbara Hanawalt and Katherine L. Reyerson (London, 1994), 153-68.

[26]For a recent contribution to the body in late medieval and early modern society, Darryll Grantley and Nina Taunton, eds., *The Body in Late Medieval and Early Modern Culture* (Aldershot: Ashgate, 2001).

[27]See, however, Arthur F. Leach, ed., *Memorials of Beverley Minster. The Chapter Act Book … AD 1286-1347*, SS vol. 98 (1898), vol. 1, 262-3 (1310) penance "cum percussionibus virgarum" for disturbing the peace of St. John.

[28]Esther Cohen, "The Animated Pain of the Body," *American Historical Review* 105 (2000): 36-68 and *The Crossroads of Justice: Law and Culture in Late Medieval France* (Leiden: Brill, 1993), 150-6.

[29]Margaret Bowker, ed., *An Episcopal Court Book for the Diocese of Lincoln, 1514-1520*, LRS vol. 61 (1967), 3 and 86-87.

[30]Elvey, *The Courts of the Archdeaconry of Buckingham.*

[31]Edward D. Stone, ed., *Norwich Consistory Court Depositions 1499-1512 and 1518-1530*, Norfolk Record Society vol. 10 (Norwich, 1938); see also Christopher Harper-Bill, "A Late Medieval Visitation: The Diocese of Norwich in 1499," *Proceedings of the Suffolk Institute of Archaeology* 34 (1980): 35-47 at pp. 38-39. Penance is not prescribed in R. W. Dunning, "The Wells Consistory Court in the Fifteenth Century," *Proceedings of the Somerset Archaeological and Natural History Society* 106 (1962): 46-61.

[32]Christopher Harper-Bill, ed., *The Register of John Morton Archbishop of Canterbury 1486-1500 Volume III Norwich sede vacante, 1499*, CYS vol. 89 (2000), 148-61 (nos 234-92), the pattern of the penance confirmed by the sporadic corrections in the visitations in the register.

[33]Arthur P. Moore, "Proceedings of the Ecclesiastical Courts in the Archdea-conry of Leicester, 1516-1535", *Associated Architectural Society Reports* 28 (1905), at, for example, 612, 623, 637 and 649.

[34]Cooke *Act Book...Whalley.*

[35]For one perception of the development of late medieval devotion, Duffy, *The Stripping of the Altars*; see also John Bossy, "Prayers", *TRHS* 6th ser. 1 (1991): 137-50.

[36]Brian L. Woodcock, *Medieval Ecclesiastical Courts in the Diocese of Canterbury* (Oxford: Oxford University Press, 1952), 97-98, suggests the decline of corporal punishment occurred over a very long time.

[37]For one perception, Duffy, *The Stripping of the Altars.*

[38]ROLLR 1D41/13/1, fol. 4v (1520s).

[39]Cooke, *Act Book...Whalley*, 23, 45, 58, 154 and 178.

[40]HRO 21M65/C1/1, fols. 79v, 81r, 84r, 123r, 123v.

[41]LRO B/C/2/3, fol. 5v (1528/9): "Quo die comparuit Thomas tayliour et fa-tetur se cognouisse carnaliter Elenam buttelar deinde dominus iniunxit sibi peni-tenciam subscriptam videlicet quod die dominica xxviijo die mensis Junii nudis pedibus et tibiis capite discooperte cum candela precii unius Denarii una manu & preculis in altera incedat ante crucem tempore processionis more penitentis et quod genuflectet se coram summo altari cum candela accensa in manu sua usque ad offertorium et postea offeret candelam manu sacerdotis et genuflectet usque finem misse." See also fol. 76: to carry a candle to the step before the altar where he shall kneel towards the offertory and offer the candle to the curate; fol. 21r a candle of 1 lb. offered to the "ymago" of St. Peter (1529).

[42]ERO D/ACA 1, fols. 100r and 101r (1540-2).

[43]CUL EDR D2/2, fol. 42v.

[44]For these psalms, Alexandra Barratt, ed., *The Seven Psalms: A Commentary on the Penitential Psalms Translated from French into English by Dame Eleanor Hall,* Early English Text Society vol. 307 (Oxford: Oxford University Press, 1995). For an example of this penance, LRO B/C/1/A, fol. 143r. For similar penances, Woodcock, *Medieval Ecclesiastical Courts*, 98.

[45] Bowker, *An Episcopal Court Book...Lincoln*, 109. For further examples and elucidation, chapter 3 above.

[46]There are, nevertheless, problems in the poor survival of court books from this time, which might be a reflection of the problems of the church courts then, and also in the cursory nature of sentences. For the problems of the courts, Richard H. Helmholz, *Roman Canon Law in Reformation England* (Cambridge: Cambridge University Press, 1990), 28-41.

[47]F. Douglas Price, "Gloucester Diocese under Bishop Hooper 1551-3," *Trans-actions of the Bristol and Gloucestershire Archaeological Society* 60 (1938): 51-151 at pp. 90-93. For the implications for the clergy of the diocese, D. G. Newcombe, "John Hooper's Visitation and Examination of the Clergy in the Diocese of Gloucester, 1551," in *Reformations Old and New: Essays on the Socio-economic Impact of Religious Change* ed. Beat A. Kümin (Aldershot: Ashgate, 1996), 57-70.

[48]ROLLR 1D41/13/3, fols. 9r, 12v, 13v, 14r, 14v (bis), 26r (bis), 34v (3), 35r, 36r (bis), and 43r (3).

[49]ROLLR 1D41/13/5-8 (1569-73). In all cases, penance for such offences was restricted to the parish church only, not parish church and market.

[50]ROLLR 1D41/13/9 (1576-7), fols. 4r, 8v, 9r (bis), 12r, 15r, 22r, 23r-v, 24r, 28r, 30r, 32r, 33r, 39r, 41v, 42r and 45r.

[51]ROLLR 1D41/13/10 (1581), fols. 38r, 50r (bis), 126v, 129r-v, 134v.

[52]ROLLR 1D41/13/11, fols. 87v, 126v, 129r-v (bis), 134v; 1D41/13/12, fols. 5r and 17v. 1D41/13/13 (1589) contains no instances.

[53]ROLLR 1D41/13/22, fol. 34v.

[54]ROLLR 1D41/13/3, fols. 13v, 14r and 43r.

[55]ROLLR 1D41/13/3, fol. 44r.

[56]ROLLR 1D41/13/3, fol. 43r.

[57]ROLLR 1D41/13/9, fols. 12r and 28r (1576); 1D41/13/12, fol. 17v (1586).

[58]ROLLR 1D41/13/11 (1582-5), fol. 134v (*c*. John Bodell for adultery with Alice Byard): "in foro publico de Melton Maubre et populi multitudo intersit Die martis".

[59]UoN Dept. of MSS. Archdeaconry A1 (unfoliated), *c*. Giles Raynor and Elizabeth Walton of Selston, 1566.

[60]UoN Dept. of MSS. Archdeaconry A1 (unfoliated), *c*. Ferneleye 20 July 1566.

[61]For the context of the archdeaconry and for Lowth, Robin A. Marchant, *The Church under the Law: Justice, Administration and Discipline in the Diocese of York 1560-1640* (Cambridge, Cambridge University Press, 1969), ch. 5 and Marchant, *The Puritans and the Church Courts in the Diocese of York 1560-1642* (London: Longmans, 1960), 132-6.

[62]ERO D/AEA 1A, fol. 14r.

[63]ERO D/AEA 7, fol. 53v *c*. Sutton of Great Warley (1572)

[64]ERO D/AEA 7, fol. 54r *c*. Nicholas Raynold and his *famula* (1572).

[65]ERO D/AEA 7, fol. 149r *c*. William Pery alias Straittes (1572)

[66]Laquita M. Higgs, *Godliness and Governance in Tudor Colchester* (Ann Arbor, MI: University of Michigan Press, 1998), 216.

[67]Mark S. Byford, "The Price of Protestantism: Assessing the Impact of Religious Change in Elizabethan Essex," unpublished D.Phil diss. (University of Oxford, 1988), 319-400 and "The Birth of a Protestant Town: The Process of Reformation in Tudor Colchester," in *The Reformation in English Towns 1500-1640* ed. Patrick Collinson and John Craig (Basingstoke: Palgrave, 1998), 23-47, esp. 43. An example of processing the length of the market and then confessing at the Moot Hall door is provided by Pressey, "The Records of the Archdeaconries of Essex and Colchester", 17.

[68]Christopher J. Burchill, "On the Consolation of a Christian scholar: Zacharias Ursinus (1534-83) and the Reformation in Heidelberg," *Journal of Ecclesiastical History* 37 (1986): 565-83 at p. 573; Euan Cameron, *The European Reformation* (Oxford: Blackwell, 1991), 415.

[69]ERO D/AC/A3-A4.

[70]<Http://www-earlscolne.socanth.cam.ac.uk/index.html>

[71]NRO PDR consistory court office act book 18, fols. 11r and 12r. I have examined all the other act books through to 1620.

[72]NRO PDR consistory court act book 14, fols. 21r, 34v, and 60r (all 1577).

[73]Edwin R. Brinkworth, ed., *The Archdeacon's Court:* Liber Actorum 1584, Ox-

fordshire Record Society vols. 23-4 (1941-2), vol. 1, 15. Here, as in other act books, the brevity of sentences makes certainty elusive.

[74]Derek Shorrocks, ed., *Bishop Still's Visitation 1594*, Somerset Record Society vol. 84 (1998), 32, 85, 110, and 112 (the markets were Frome, Dunster, Glastonbury, and Wells). The preponderance of causes of sexual delinquency, however, were dealt with by penance in the parish church.

[75]HRO 21M65/C1/12, fol. 3r. I have sampled the act books.

[76]LRO B/C/3/10 (unfoliated; at the end of the volume): *c.* Dadley of Solihull (Solihull market); *c.* Baker of Chilvers Coton (Nuneaton market).

[77]LRO B/C/3/1 unfoliated *c.* John Robertes (5 Dec 1591).

[78]LRO B/C/3/10 unfoliated (markets of Stafford, Leek, Woolshall, Newport and Uttoxeter). I have searched through all the act books into the early seventeenth century. The principal problems are the lack of sentences and also the declaration of penance according to a schedule with no further detail.

[79]CUL EDR D2/8, fol. 14r. Some examples of these penances have been printed by H. Hall, "Some Elizabethan Penances in the Diocese of Ely," *TRHS* 3rd ser. i (1907): 263-77 at pp. 274-5.

[80]CUL EDR D2/8, fol. 100r *c.* Alan Canom of Bampton.

[81]CUL EDR D2/9b, fol. 112v *c* Robert Knevett.

[82]CUL EDR D2/9, fol. 31v.

[83]CUL EDR D2/9c, fol. 187v (6 March 1576/7).

[84]CUL EDR D2/10, fol. 86.

[85]CUL EDR D2/10, fol. 239v. I have examined all the act books through to the early seventeenth century. The problem as always is the frequent summary format of penance as in the schedule without further information.

[86]For the stigmatising, consequential effects of punishment, Robin A. Duff and David Garland, eds., *A Reader on Punishment* (Oxford: Oxford University Press, 1994), 14; for communicative justice intending reformation of the individual and reconciliation into the "community": 15. For the social theory of punishment, see, in general, David Garland, *Punishment and Modern Society: A Study in Social Theory* (Chicago: University of Chicago Press, 1990).

[87]Tim Harris, ed., *Popular Culture in England, c.1500-1850* (Basingstoke: Palgrave, 1995), esp. 1-27.

[88]Here, overt resistance to authority is included in refusal, not only "the hidden transcript" of James C. Scott, *Domination and the Arts of Resistance: Hidden Transcripts* (New Haven: Yale University Press, 1990). For resistance in the performance of ritual, Maurice Bloch, "Symbols, Song, Dance and Features of Articulation: Is Religion an Extreme Form of Traditional Authority?' in his *Ritual, History and Power: Selected Papers in Anthropology* (London: Athlone, 1989), 19-45; Edward Muir, *Ritual in Early Modern Europe* (Cambridge: Cambridge University Press, 1997); for the polyvalency inherent in ritual, Catherine Bell, *Ritual Theory, Ritual Practice* (Oxford: Oxford University Press, 1992), and Caroline Humphrey and James Laidlaw, *The Archetypal Actions of Ritual: A Theory of Ritual Illustrated by the Jain Rite of Worship* (Oxford: Oxford University Press, 1994).

[89]CUL EDR D2/9a, fol. 71r 7 November 1573. "And that she did not hir penaunce that she was enioyned to Doe but instede of hir penaunce Doinge she gaue to the Towne of Emmeth towards the bringinge up of hir chylde xs."

[90]CUL EDR D2/10, fol. 27r: "...she being excommunicated for whoredome, did flee the Towne, & ys since returned, as yet not punished for hir offence."

[91]NRO Peterborough Diocesan consistory court act book 14, fol. 116.

[92]CUL EDR D2/9c, fol. 192v.

[93]CUL EDR D2/10, fol. 11r: "He was suspended for that he did not his penaunce which was enioyned him sithens which suspension he hathe intruded him self into ye congregacion. And he speakethe evell of the Minister there for doeinge his dwetye."

[94]ERO D/AE/A5, fol. 5 (1569) and D/AEA 1A, fol. 73v (1562).

[95]CUL EDR D2/10, fol. 242r (1581): "he abused him selfe in the parishe churche there after service tyme uppon Wednesdaye before Easter 1581 with undecent and unsemely speches towards the parson there (Mr Howgreave) sayeinge that he woulde see him (meaninge and speakinge of Mr Howgreave parsone there) hanged before that he woulde doe enye penaunce."

[96]CUL EDR D2/10, fol. 215r.

[97]ROLLR 1D41/13/11, fol. 26r.

[98]UoN Dept. of MSS. A3/1/3 unfoliated (Jan. 1576/7).

[99]ERO D/AEA 11, fol. 90r (Dec. 1579).

[100]Robin L. Storey, ed., *The Register of Gilbert Welton Bishop of Carlisle 1353-1362*, CYS vol. 88 (1999), 46 (no. 247):"As you have had some of us called before the bishop's ministers, take them these gifts."

[101]William W. Capes, ed., *Registrum Ricardi de Swinfield*, CYS vol. 6 (1909), 512-13 (it happened on a Wednesday).

[102]*Register of John le Romeyn...Part I*, 243-6.

[103]See most recently, Michael Haren, *Sin and Society in Fourteenth-century England: A Study of the* Memoriale Presbitorum (Oxford: Oxford University Press, 2000), 108-9, but also Louis A. Haselmayer, "The Apparitor and Chaucer's Summoner," *Speculum* 12 (1937): 43-57.

[104]CUL EDR D/2/1, fols. lxxxxvijr-v.

[105]Ralph A. Houlbrooke, ed., *The Letter Book of John Parkhurst Bishop of Norwich Compiled During the Years 1571-5*, Norfolk Record Society vol. 43 (1974-5), 121 (no. 75).

[106]*English Poetry: The English Poetry Full-text Database* (Chadwyck-Healey Ltd, 1995). The poem of Ashmore (fl. 1621) is entitled *In Sacrificium quondam*. Drayton referred back to the sorcery of Dame Eleanor, duchess of Gloucester, a motif which recurred in Shakespeare and other plays. Arthington (fl. 1592-1607) declaimed: "Or yf I should be dayly whypt in open market place/ to warne all people to beware how they abuse thy grace," which presumably alludes to penance rather than civic punishment.

[107]Christopher Haigh, *Reformation and Resistance in Tudor Lancashire* (Cambridge: Cambridge University Press, 1975), 229-33.

[108]Richard Wunderli, *London Church Courts on the Eve of the Reformation* (Cambridge, Mass.: Medieval Society of America, 1981), 52 (the term is *composuit*). See also, Woodcock, *Medieval Ecclesiastical Courts*, 98.

[109]LAO D&C A/2/24, fol. 9v (the terminology is *vel redimeret penitenciam* and *redimet*, so there is a difference between the option of redemption and actual redemption).

[110]Margaret Bowker, *The Secular Clergy in the Diocese of Lincoln 1495-1520* (Cambridge: Cambridge University Press, 1968), 36.

[111]Haren, *Sin and Society*, 96-97. Canonically, only consistory courts, not archidiaconal ones, could commute to pecuniary penalties.

[112]LRO B/C/3/10 unfoliated (at end).

[113]CUL EDR D2/8, fols. 3v and 31v. There were other similar amounts in the Ely court.

[114]The whole of this section is informed by comments by Professor Diarmaid MacCulloch.

[115]Todd, "Performing repentance". Dr. Christopher Haigh also made comments at the seminar which have helped to improve my paper.

[116]This point was made to me by Professor Todd.

[117]In particular, Lualdi and Thayer, *Penitence in the Age of Reformations*, the editors referring, for example, to communal solidarity and social stability inherent in these reforms (at 2, 4, and 6-7). Although the volume is largely concerned with confession, in consistorial organisation of these churches, there was a continuum from confession to inquisitorial jurisdiction. I owe the reference to this volume to Professor MacCulloch.

[118]Charles H. Parker, "The Rituals of Reconciliation: Admonition, Confession and Community in the Dutch Reformed Church," in *Penitence in the Age of Reformations*, 101-15 at p. 103 and in the same volume, Raymond A. Mentzer, "Notions of Sin and Penitence," 84-100 at p. 99.

[119]For example, Parker, "The Rituals of Reconciliation," 104. For the continental experience of Withers, particularly at Heidelberg, Higgs, *Godliness and Governance*, 204.

[120]Perhaps most clearly enunciated in Cooke, *Act Book...Whalley*, 126, 133, 164 et al.: *penitentie corporales*.

[121]For the difference of strategies and tactics in relation to space and in relation to power, de Certeau, *The Practice of Everyday Life*, 29-30; Martin Ingram, "Juridical Folklore in England Illustrated by Rough Music,' in *Communities and Courts in Britain 1150-1900* ed. Christopher Brooks and Michael Lobban (London: Hambledon, 1997), 61-82, and "Ridings, Rough Music and Mocking Rhymes in Early Modern England," in *Popular Culture in Seventeenth-century England* ed. Barry Reay (London: Croom Helm, 1985), 166-95. For a suggestion about entitlement to the use of public space, however, Peter G. Goheen, "The Ritual of the Streets in Mid-19th-century Toronto," *Society and Space* 11 (1993): 127-45.

[122]Patrick Collinson, *The Birthpangs of Protestant England: Religious and Cultural Change in the Sixteenth and Seventeenth Centuries* (London: Macmillan, 1988); for recent interpretations of the impact of the reformed *ecclesia anglicana*, Christopher Marsh, *Popular Religion in Sixteenth-century England: Holding Their Peace* (London: Macmillan, 1998); Judith Maltby, *Prayer Book and People in Elizabethan and Early Stuart England* (Cambridge: Cambridge University Press, 1998), 1-82.

7
Church Space and Contingency

In some respects, the religious transformations of the sixteenth century produced changes in the organization of and attitudes towards church space in English parish churches. We should, nevertheless, be wary of dismissing continuities of proprieties. The Introduction recounts, for example, the potential for "sacralization" of Calvinist church space through the late sixteenth century. To anticipate an inevitable derogation of church space after the middle of the sixteenth century can be premature. The legislation of Edward VI was anxious to retain orderliness and good conduct in parish churches. Its provisions were intermittently reiterated.[1]

> That if any person or persons whatsoeuer shall after the first daye of Maye next followinge, strike, smyte, or Laye violent hand uppon any other eyther in a Church or Churchyard then ipso facto Every person soe offendinge shalbe deemed Excommunicated and Excluded from the Congregation of Christian people.[2]

The occasion for this repetition was the response to a particular event in the parish church of Swaffham in 1618, which will be examined in more detail below. What becomes clear from this occasion is how attitudes to church space were complicated and inconsistent.[3]

We can illustrate how these infractions of the decorum of church space punctuated medieval parish life. Two aspects can be considered here: theft from churches; and violent disruption of church space resulting from dispute. The first issue is expanded upon below, but we can here mention one case. In the Newgate sessions of 1531 a case was discussed which involved the theft of a valuable pyx from a parish church, the pyx allegedly valued at £20: "en que le precious corps de nostre seigniour Jhesu Chryste fuit contenus."[4]

One final aspect of violation of church space was the perpetration of theft from churches. It was a not infrequent occurrence in the late middle ages, as attested by indictments at sessions. Accusations of theft, nevertheless, have some ambiguity. Confusion about ownership undoubtedly led to misunderstandings when churchwardens or clergy were involved, not least because of the increasing numbers of private chantries in parish churches and bequests under wills. Moreover, Lollardy accounted for some, although probably small, proportion of the larcenies. Even so, despoliation of church vessels and furnishings, including the pyx, was in many cases actual theft, which imputes some measure of skepticism about religion to the offenders.[5]

Indictments for theft from churches featured regularly at Crown Pleas and in assizes, a minor incident of such an offense committed by Robert Lad who purloined a chalice from Eynsford parish church in the middle of the fourteenth century.[6] Towards the end of that century Peter de Shirbourn, chapman, and others were indicted for robbery of the church of Haugham.[7] Neither infraction compared with the violation of the church of the Holy Cross at Holywell in 1393, for which Robert Baron, chaplain, alias Savage, Matthew Silvestre, William Bysshop alias Brunne, John Chaunflour alias White, Adam Barbour alias Gilbert Englyssh of Ireland, and Stephen Richard were presented. The six absconded with two missals, two gold chalices, a processional, a psalter, two surplices, a bed cover, two blankets, four towels, a pair of sheets, and other *impedimenta*. All six were found guilty, but five proved clergy, whilst the unfortunate sixth was condemned to be hanged. Nevertheless, their status as itinerant thieves was confirmed by the accusation against them of burglary of the house of Thomas Skynner at Deddington, from which they extracted high-status clothing, and Chaunflour's subsequent capture at Banbury with stolen property and the appeal against him by Edward Draper of Tetbury in Gloucestershire for another theft.[8] In an attempt to recover items stolen from their church, the churchwardens of Peterborough in 1476 made payments of 10s. to a man of Oundle and 6s.8d. to an inhabitant of Apethorpe.[9]

Disputes over seating allocation and the consequent turmoil inside the church could be presented equally at quarter sessions as in the ecclesiastical forum, so the justices of Somerset in 1610 demanded a recognizance for good behavior against one of the adversaries in a case over a seat in a parish church who had uttered "outrageous audacious and disgraceful" words in church.[10] Such outbursts and contestations were as much a concern for public order as abuses of spiritual space.[11] This contention over seating in church existed before the profusely researched disputes of the late sixteenth and early seventeenth centuries.[12] Indeed, isolated contests were taken to the highest judicial forum.

Altercations within the parish church were not always provoked by the laity. The letter book of John Parkhurst, bishop of Norwich, recorded that the parson of Beccles, Mr Buckley, caused the arrest of four of his parishioners "upon a Saboth daye openly in the church in seruice tyme" upon process which he had prosecuted against them in King's Bench in the 1570s.[13] Some individuals, of course, managed partially to restrain themselves, as John Gadburye partly suppressed his anger when, whilst he was ringing the bells for the anniversary of the Queen in 1584, the parson, finding Gadburye's hat on the font, threw it outside. Gadburye limited his reaction to a verbal assault, responding that he would have boxed the parson's ears had it occurred in another place.[14]

Irritation and cholera accounted for the reaction of John Tayler of Stanton St Michael in April 1581 when

he abused him selfe in the parish churche there after service tyme uppon the wednesdaye before Easter 1581 with undecent and unsemely speches towards the parson there (Mr Howgreave) sayeinge that he woulde see him (meaninge & speakinge of Mr Howgreave parsone there) hanged before that he woulde doe enye penaunce.[15]

Such contention within the spaces of parish churches in the reformed era might, nonetheless, pale into relative insignificance in comparison with some of the violent infractions of this space in the pre-Reformation parish church. Indeed, it is possible to some extent to quantify the frequency of the violation of the space of the medieval parish church. In an enormous diocese such as Lincoln, the ordinary was compelled to rely on delegating authority to other agents to reconcile parish churches and churchyards which had been defiled or polluted by the spilling of blood. Unfortunately, the analysis is only possible where the bishop of necessity devolved the responsibility, for the episcopal registers rarely record reconciliation by the bishop himself. Happily for us, from 1290 it was frequently necessary for Bishop Sutton of Lincoln to license others to re-consecrate defiled spaces. Some impression of the occasions of defilement through blood-pollution can be represented in Figure 7.1. Bearing in mind that this representation will be minimal, since the bishop himself will have performed many absolutions, it is apparent how frequent was the pollution of "sacred" space.

Although details of the causation are often elusive, the general tenor of violation can be perceived. Scuffles in the parish church occurred with some frequency, sometimes provoked by the implementation of legal orders. Now, despite the premeditation, it might be concluded that such examples merely demonstrate an incorrigible sprinkling of rogues unable to manage or control their emotions and with reprobate habits. Certainly the failure of some individuals to manage their emotions presented one occasion. Other occasions of the defilement of the space of parish churches, however, reinforce the social politics of emotions, by which individuals or groups of people, through a direct display of their emotions, expressed dissatisfaction about power or personal animosity with scant regard for the sanctity of the location.[16]

In 1339/40, an inquisition was ordered in Sandal in the composite manor of Wakefield to determine whether John Shephird and his three sons had assaulted Thomas de Ketilthorp on the feast of St. Andrew the Apostle in the church at Sandal.[17] Now, on the same manor in 1309, another description of the violation of church space invokes the notion of the regularity of church attendance enabling premeditation. At the tourn court at the township of Birton, it was presented that Richard de Bello Monte had engaged in battery with the spilling of the blood of another male, but further that Richard frequently came to the church at Birton to seek quarrels–on the assumption, no doubt, that he was certain to find prospective antagonists.[18]

Where individuals were involved and collided in church, the result could be catastrophic, as is intimated by the pollution by blood of churches which needed to be reconciled. At their most extreme, these affrays ended in death and the assassination was committed in the holiest of holies, the sanctuary. So Robert Mabson the elder of Braceby rushed into the church of Haceby with two knives with which he assaulted the chaplain reciting divine service. In this case, then, the miracle of the mass was hardly a social one.[19]

Such infractions of church space were, furthermore, not always merely contretemps between a couple of parishioners. Collective forcible occupation, fortification and defense of the parish church happened and occurred over long periods of time. An extreme example was the illegal sequestration of the prebendal church of Thame in 1293. Disputing the institution of a new prebendary, a group of parishioners occupied the church and forcibly defended it by fortifying it, for the most part of 1293. On December 15, 1293, Bishop Sutton of Lincoln issued a mandate to all archdeacons of the whole diocese to excommunicate in every church, chapel, chapter and meeting of the clergy upon every Sunday and feast day except Christmas Day, the ringleaders of the attack, naming fifteen men.[20]

The full impact of violent eruptions inside the parish church is available through a copy of the proceedings concerning a contretemps in the parish church of Swaffham in 1618.[21] When the proceedings were complete, the costs of one of the parties were assessed at £6 14s. 4d., after the case had endured to the summer of 1623 before its resolution.[22] What had transpired is that Bodham was accused of laying violent hands on William Harvye during the offertory. Harvye's deposition imparts one *ex parte* understanding. A tanner, Harvey was aged about thirty-five and had lived in Swaffham for more than twenty years. As a fellow of some local credit, he was requested by one of the churchwardens, Aubrey Canham, to assist with the collection, the other warden being absent. Harvye had collected some of the money in his hat when, he alleged, Bodham violently snatched some of it from the hat. The narrative was elaborated by the deposition of one of the witnesses, Richard Starke, aged about fifty, who had also inhabited Swaffham for about twenty years. According to Starke, Bodham approached Harvye and demanded "what he ment to medle with the said Collection", to which Harvye responded that "he was intreated soe to do by the said Abred Canham", whereupon Bodham scooped the money out of the crown of Harvye's hat and made off.[23] More of both the altercation and the context was furnished by another witness, Christopher Bensley, blacksmith, who had also, it seems, been domiciled there for twenty years, and he was aged about fifty-two. Bodham purloined the money, Bensley alleged, "uttringe these wordes videlicet: I will haue this." The context, however, became more complicated as Bensley's deposition unfolded for Canham, it transpired, was the vicar's churchwarden, and Bodham had been elected warden by the body of parishioners there called the Twelve, no doubt a select vestry.[24] Whatever the ramifications and the animus involved, the event presented to all the congregation an unseemly and undignified tussle between two men of status within the parish.

In considerations of church space in medieval and particularly early-modern England a number of conceptualizations of space have been emphasized. In primary position is the structural distinction between sacred and profane space, marking off ecclesiastical space. Within that categorization is the representation of the zoning of space within sacred space, from holiest–the sanctuary–to the more peripheral zones. Between sacred and profane, the suggestion is made, existed liminal spaces– particularly the south porch–where passage between spaces occurred. Such then has been the concern for the representation of space. For later medievalists and early-modernists, the representation of those spaces has been informed also by practices of space, but again in a structured manner: the re-creation of the social order within the parish church, whether through seating, burial, or different access to the liturgy.[25] Consistent within these discussions are the representation of space and its structuring.

As has been demonstrated, seating became a particular cause of contention within parish churches in the late sixteenth and early seventeenth centuries, occasioning disputes about social place and precedence which threatened not only "sacred" space but also the whole social order. It equally provided an opportunity for retribution, since the occupant of the seat could be anticipated. It was alleged in the archdeaconry court of Nottingham that human excrement ("mannes dunge") had been littered on the seats of Lady Leake and the alderman's wife in Newark church in 1615. Since the seats were locked, suspicion was directed to Simon Rainer who had been responsible for cleaning the seats. It was suggested that "the said Simon haddest taken some discontentment against them." Rainer defended himself that he had not had the task of cleaning the seats for some time since he was prohibited by Sir Francis Leake's servants, although he had had access to the key until a month ago.[26]

One result was the imposition of a new form of penance in causes of defamation. The reprobate was sentenced, like Joan Mylnes of Blyth in 1585:

> she shall in the parych church uppon Sunday next come to the seat at the tyme of Dyvine servyce wher he sytteth and ther aske forgyvnes and pay hym his charges.[27]

One aspect of the appropriation of space in the parish church involved the formalizing of public aspects of conveyancing, which extend into the middle of the sixteenth century. The church of Clapham was the location for the signing of a marriage settlement in the 1540s and its livery of seisin, but such private arrangements extended back much further.[28]

> To all the faithful of Christ who will see or hear the present writing Walter le Welshe of Goring sends greetings in the Lord forever. Know that I have on Sunday on the eve of St Peter in Chains 23 Edward I in the burial ground at Goring examined, heard and in all things understood well the charter of feoffment of Gilbert de Chalcote which I lately made to him in free marriage ...[29]

In the case of Walter *le Welshe* in the churchyard of Goring, a parishioner appropriated the consecrated space around the church as a place to make a public declaration acknowledging a charter which he had previously made to a beneficiary, an in-law. Since the *maritagium*–dowry–was usually transferred in the south porch of the parish church where the marriage ceremony was celebrated, the use of the churchyard for this declaration appears at first sight a logical extension of space. In this particular case, nonetheless, there also appears to be an interrupted process. The charter had already been completed and the livery of the *maritagium* presumably completed, for what Walter was performing in the churchyard was a later examination of the charter–an *inspeximus*. There is the possibility therefore that two distinct actions have taken place–separate in time–in the second of which Walter adopted the churchyard as a public space to make a public declaration of his acknowledgment of the charter. Concomitantly, he appropriated that "sacred" space to provide determinacy to his secular transaction.

When Lemmar de Walpol, his wife and her son, alienated twenty-three acres in Walpole to Lewes Priory, he made an oath for performance in the church of St. Nicholas in Lynn and then in the churchyard of St. James of Acre in the presence of a number of laymen.[30] Oath-making in the conventual church or chapter house was impeded in this case by distance, so local consecrated places were employed to ensure the inviolability of the oath.

What seems to have been effectively a gage of meadow about 1233 also involved redemption in a parish church. If at the end of a term of nine years John wished to "purchase" back the meadow, a consideration of eight marks 8s. 4d. was due, William or his assigns coming to the church to receive the money before the worthy men of the township.[31] By another agreement–of 1257–forty of the sixty marks owed as consideration for a croft and other tenements in Cockerington were to be acquitted in St. Herefrith's parish church, Louth.[32]

Another example may enlighten this process of using spiritual space for secular purposes–although oath-taking, of course, had spiritual implications. At the very end of the thirteenth century, Thomas le Verly and his wife, Alice, daughter of John Pake, quitclaimed to John de Melkeleye their right in the dower held by Agnes, widow of John Pake–that is, Alice renounced any right of dower in this land. To guarantee that renunciation, Alice made her oath on the high altar of the parish church. The agreement, however, was between secular persons and did not involve any religious beneficiary, although it may be that these parties appropriated the practice involved when benefactions were made to the religious.[33]

Although it did involve an ecclesiastical dignitary, the transaction at Weston on 20 June 2 Edward III was effectively simply a mortgage by which Sir Robert de Knapton, knight, gaged his manor and advowson of Misterton to the bishop of Ely. To redeem, Sir Robert or one of his heirs needed to enter the parish church of Solihull at the specified time of the day a year from the next Michaelmas to pay the bishop's attorney 160 marks and costs.[34] The venue for the payment of eighty marks of rent from several manors by Robert Spencer and his wife, the countess of Wiltshire, to other lay dignitaries, was at "le Rode" in the north door of St. Paul's in London.[35]

Perhaps more informally, James Kertton of Ripon, it was deposed by William Forsett in a case of *fidei laesio* invoked in the ecclesiastical court in 1460, had promised to his creditor in the nave of the church of Ripon near the font to deliver 3s. at Michaelmas next to acquit a debt–all of which Forsett, the witness, had overheard.[36] Athough it might have been a spontaneous promise, it is perhaps as plausible that it was also exacted in that place to give force to the commitment.

Thomas, duke of Exeter, made an arrangement with trustees, involving the payment to him of £280 annually during his life in St. Paul's cathedral, London, at the altar by the shrine of St. Erkenwald, April 29, 2 Henry VI.[37] William Potter and Margaret Baker granted to Robert Levyshoth and John a Donne a messuage in Wadhurst (Sussex) for £19 13s. 4d. to be paid in half-yearly instalments in Begham church, December 12, 1 Edward IV.[38]

Perhaps it should not be surprising, then, that in the late sixteenth century the settlement of financial obligations was regularly associated with the church porch. When, in 1592, Nicholas Bacon and an associate entered into a bond with George Downing, gentleman of Norwich, the £100 at issue was to be redeemed on April 1, 1593 between one and three o'clock in the afternoon in the north porch of the parish church of St. Simon in Norwich.[39] On the renewal of the obligation on April 1, 1593, instead of its liquidation, the place for future redemption was specified as the north porch of the parish church of St. Michael Coslany in the City.[40] Now, that did not conclude the affair, for there was a further renewal on October 1, 1593, when the principal had become £105 now to be redeemed at Lady Day 1594 in the north porch of St. Clement's parish church in the City.[41]

Appropriation of church space to authenticate deeds implied some degree of status, although "middling" as much as the highest degree. Those belonging to that latter category might deploy their influence in church space even more assertively. In 1360, for example, the bishop of Carlisle issued a mandate to the dean of Carlisle.[42] The bishop had been informed by William Lengleys, knight, that William had released a falcon at Brunstock Beck, but it escaped. At his instance, the bishop required an order to be announced in all churches for the return of the falcon within eight days under pain of excommunication.

Two forms of appropriation of ecclesiastical spaces can then be detected: a personal act, sometimes to elicit a public forum, and institutional use of the space. Institutional use of church space as distinctive from personal appropriation of space entailed two aspects: often it involved the humiliation of a parishioner before the congregation; and *ipso facto* the action was insinuated into the interior and body of the church. Particular use of the parish church for the secular business of the local society was necessitated by the relationship between early-modern state formation and the localities, although it was essentially a relative rather than an absolute transformation.

Provision for the poor before the legislation of 1597-1601 had involved the churchwardens in meetings within the parish church, but the frequency and importance of these business affairs were regularized by the new responsibilities of the late Elizabethan statutes.

Whereas this Court Was this day informed by Mr Norborne being of Councell with the Inhabitantes of Bremble Within this County That there hath bin an aunccient agreement betweene the said Inhabitantes of Bremble and the Inhabitantes of Foxham being a hamlet beinge Within the said parish of Bremble That the Inhabitantes of Bremble should mayneteyne theire poore people inhabiting Within theire said parish Without the contribucion or assistance of the Inhabitantes of Foxham And that the Inhabitantes of Foxham should mayneteyne their poore people Without the helpe or Contribucion of the Inhabitantes of Bremble and that the ouerseers of the poore of the seuerall places <yielding> yielded up seuerall accomptes accordinglie until of late a bastard Child Was borne Within the said hamlet of Foxham by reason Whereof the said Inhabitantes of Foxham beinge somethinge hard taxed refused to stand to theire old Composicion & agreement And Whereas this court Was like Wise then enformed that Mr John Hungerford one of the Justices of the peace of this County and other the Inhabitantes of Bremble and of Foxham aforesaid having land lyinge Within the hamlet of Foxham and parish of Bremble are behinde & haue not paid theire rates to the poore many yeares last past as they ought to haue done This Court doth therefore desire Sir Edward Baynton bte (sic) And the said Mr Hungerford to meete on Sonday next Come Seavennight being the Twelueth day of this instant October in the parish Church of Bremble aforesaid after eveninge prayers are there ended And this Court doth likewise order That the Inhabitantes of Bremble and Foxham aforesaid shall likewise there attend the said Sr Edward Baynton and the said Mr Hungerford and there sett downe there reasons Why they should not continewe theire old Composicion & agreement as aforesaid And alsoe sett downe what monneyes there is behind either by the said Mr Hungerford or from any of the Inhabitantes of Bremble and Foxham aforesaid in any rate towards the relief of the poore of the said parish and hamlet

aforesaid And yf it shall then appeare That he said Mr Hungerford
or any other are behind in any the rates aforesaid And shall refuse
to pay the same Then this Court doeth desire that the said Sir
Edward Baynton Togeather With seuerall of the overseers of the
poore of the said parish of Bremble or hamlet of Foxham shall at
the next Sessions of the peace to be holden in for this County of
Wiltes Certifye the same unto his Majesties Justices of the peace
then & there assembled That further order may be taken therein
as to lawe & equity shall seeme meeke[43]

Such then are examples of the two forms of social activity deployed
in church space, derived from quite different times and contexts. Private
response to the use of church space is both eclectic and contingent, but
frequent. Institutional assumption of that space had reference to changing
contexts, in which the relationship between civic and secular authority
and ecclesiastical jurisdiction became fore-grounded in the late sixteenth
and seventeenth centuries.

The churchwardens were, moreover, usually the officers responsible
for supervising the maintenance of bastard children and the father's
contribution was frequently made directly to them. Nevertheless, the
justices had a commensurate jurisdiction over bastardy and actively
intervened. Indeed, in these cases of maintenance, the bench sometimes
decided that the maintenance should be delivered to the churchwardens,
significantly inside the parish church, in the center of "sacred space", at an
important liturgical time. The Somerset justices promulgated an order in
1627/8 for the maintenance of Thomas Fryday alias Vyne of Bruham, this
reputed father to pay 9d. weekly every Sunday after evening prayer in the
church porch of the parish of Bruham.[44]

Another order pronounced by the same bench in December 1628 for
the maintenance of Richard Samson a base child born at Yeovil, demanded
that the reputed father pay 8d. weekly, commencing on the next Sunday
in the church porch of Yeovil after evening prayer.[45] The miller, William
Lycheat of Wedmore, the reputed father of the child of Margery Chalcrofte,
was directed by the Somerset bench in 1608 to pay 6d. weekly to the
churchwardens and overseers every Sunday after morning prayer.[46] For
the maintenance of another bastard child born at West Buckland–also in
1608–the bench commanded 9d. to be delivered weekly by the suspected
father to the churchwardens every Sunday after divine service, deposited
at or upon the communion table of the church.[47] A year later, the same
bench reached the same conclusion in the case of a bastard child in
Sampford Courtenay, ordering the alleged father to pay up weekly to the
churchwardens on Sunday after divine service on the communion table.[48]

These justices provided for the maintenance of another bastard child by the father contributing on the communion table of the parish church of Wellington on Sunday after divine service.[49] In 1614, they required a father to pay maintenance of 1s. weekly on Sunday after morning prayer to churchwardens and overseers.[50] Three other fathers who came before this bench were also ordered to pay maintenance on Sunday after morning prayer.[51]

The occasion of these payments ordered by the bench exacted maximum publicity for the humiliation of the fathers, but also coincided in some instances with statutory parochial arrangements. Legislation required the churchwardens to meet regularly on Sundays to deliberate about poor relief, an obligation enforced by the justices.[52]

Accordingly, the Hertfordshire bench in 1618 received the presentment against the overseers of the poor of Hemel Hempstead for not assembling in the parish church on Sunday afternoon after divine service to consider means for the relief of the poor.[53] In conformity with the same law, the Lancashire bench in 1602 demanded that the negligent overseers of the parish of Manchester meet in the church a week on Sunday to take order for the relief of the poor and once a month afterwards.[54]

More intriguing, perhaps, are those, admittedly infrequent, decisions when justices directed their critics to the parish church to perform a kind of penance imposed by the civil authority, to humiliate the offender, to be exemplary to the congregation, and to satisfy the justice and exonerate his reputation and honor. Perhaps extraordinarily, William Kenytye received a punishment in 1601 to stand on Sunday next and remain in the church of Oldham near the choir door during divine service and at noon naked from the waist up with papers on his head: "This person is punished for disobeying the justice of the peace and constable."[55]

Then we have the discretionary use made of the church by the justices for communication. When, in 1670, the magistracy of Cambridgeshire discovered that excessive wages were being demanded, that the contracts between masters and servants were not being registered at the statute sessions, and that servants were departing from their employment without testimonials, they issued new orders: "And the rates for wages hereto annexed bee with all convenient speed read & published in the seuerall parish Churches within the said County imediately after divine service & preaching is ended ..."[56]

In some parishes, it seems, the church doubled as a lock up, sometimes subjected to infraction by the local "overmighty". At the Essex sessions in the late sixteenth century, Francis Smith of Blackmore, gentleman, was presented by the churchwardens for striking with his sword at the constable at the church gate, and delivering John Reve of Blackmore out of the church where he had been locked up by the constable.[57]

For more benign purposes, the justices appointed the parish church as the place for notification of briefs for unfortunate inhabitants of their counties. Justices issued orders for ministers to proclaim these misfortunes and to ask for assistance–for Christian and social charity. Between 1638 and 1644, the West Riding bench issued a number of such orders, sometimes to the ministers of parishes within specified wapentakes, sometimes through the county. In 1638, the magistrates received the petition of Elizabeth Hodge that her house had been burgled whilst she was away, the felons not having been apprehended, and she by this loss reduced to poverty. The court requested that the ministers and curates of the churches and chapels of the wapentake of Osgodcross publish the contents of this order in their churches and chapels on a Sunday and the churchwardens collect the benevolence of the congregation for her relief.[58] Another woman, the widow Dorothy Burgoyne, experienced a fire in her barn, of five bays of building, by which she lost 300 sheaves of corn and twelve loads of hay and all farm implements, to a value in excess of £100. Convinced of the demonstrable need of Dorothy and her six children, the bench appealed to the ministers throughout the West Riding in 1638 to make a similar promulgation from their pulpits. All these actions might be encompassed within that general notion of charity and *caritas* associated with the spiritual as well as social sphere.

Finally, there were those disrespectful events which were entirely contingent violations of "sacred" space. In 1618, it was alleged that Richard Hawgood had attended church at Slapton drunk on Shrove Tuesday and had vomited during divine service.[59] The churchwardens of Chipping Warden were reprimanded for neglecting their duty by not reporting "certain disorders" in the church on St. Stephen's day "as throwinge mattes aboute the church and fightinge in the church."[60] The parishioners of Cropredy were as unfortunate in 1620, for, to their annoyance, William Tompson became inebriated in the alehouse before attending church in the time of prayer, so that he too vomited in church.[61] A decade earlier, the congregation at Banbury was probably horrified by Henry Glover "making water" in the parish church.[62] It was reported that Richard Love also could not contain himself and "made water" in Wisbech St. Peter during divine service in 1639.[63] The pew doors at Bere Regis were damaged in play by a servant in 1599.[64]

An outrageous desecration occurred in the cathedral church of Ely, as reported at the visitation of 1639, for it was alleged that a great noise and disturbance disrupted divine service on new year's day on the occasion that a cat was roasted on a spit by William Smith in the church, attracting a large alternative congregation, profaning both the day and the place.[65] In the early seventeenth century too–in 1613–some scholars (presumably young boys) not only brought their cocks into the church on Shrove Tuesday, but held a cockfight in the building.[66] Whilst the chancel of Coddenham parish church remained in decay in 1597, beggars surreptitiously gained entry to the church through the windows and slept in the chancel.[67]

One of the ultimate effects of the Reformation was the proscription of plays within churches, hitherto a site for religious performances.[68] On occasion, however, post-Reformation secular ludic entertainment strayed into the parish church.[69] One St. Stephen's Day in the early seventeenth century, Thomas Dawkyn the younger and eight neighbors organized a play at night in the house of the elder Thomas Dawkyn. Having advertised its performance beforehand, "a greate companye" gathered in the house during the play, with the consequence that there was insufficient room for the players. As the church door was open for bell-ringing, they all resorted to the church to complete the play, without the permission of the churchwardens.[70] In contrast, the two churchwardens of West Ham admitted to turning a blind eye to a play organized by some of their parishioners in the parish church, including standing on the communion table, because the cause was a charitable purpose, to assist a poor man.[71]

At Lyme Regis in 1558, the Queen's Majesty's players performed in the church.[72] In another Dorset borough, Poole, another company of players acted in the church in 1551.[73] Dartmouth parish church was the venue for the Earl of Leicester's players in 1569-1570.[74] In 1559, the mayor of Plymouth authorized Lord Dudley's players to perform in the parish church, which was again the venue for other players in 1565 and 1573-1574.[75] In nearby Plymstock, the performance was enacted in the parish church in 1568.[76] A seat was damaged in Tewkesbury church during a play in 1575.[77] Subsequently, however, definite proscriptions were directed against plays in churches, epitomized by the repetition of their forbiddance in visitation articles.[78] That prohibition was perhaps the first stage in the demise of provincial theater.[79]

On many occasions, what was occurring was the importing of disputes into the parish church, perhaps because it was predictable that the adversary would be there at a certain time. It was recounted in the archdeaconry court of Essex that William Rooke of West Ham:

> pulled awaye a mans hatt and threw it from him and would not suffer him to sitt in his seate at t in the tyme of devyne service but molested him whereby all the whole parishe was disquieted in the service tyme and the minister was compelled to stay his service thoroughe his Rudenes which he sondry tymes hathe and dothe use in the Church service tyme...[80]

Nor was the cathedral itself immune from scuffles between its servants and officers. When a peremptory admonition was delivered in 1606, the occasion was the complaint of Arthur Jackson, the epistolar, against Mr. Sadlington, the gospeller, for striking him in the church and defaming him and the rest of the choir as rogues and rascals.[81] In the choir, during divine service, John Carlton allegedly abused Thomas Askew, a peti-canon, referring to him as an ass, fool and dunce. When sentenced to acknowledge his fault the next morning before the lesson, Carlton remained obdurate, with the result that he was suspended from the choir until he did perform his penance.[82]

Moreover, it was not unusual for divine service in the Cathedral to be accompanied by noise. In 1596, the Chancellor was compelled to issue instructions that during divine service, the two sextons and the verger should strive to abate the noise "wherby the service may be the more quietly perfourmed."[83] One of the disruptions might have been the struggle for seats in the choir before 1599 when the members of the choir were assigned seats for "the reformation of a greate disorder committed in the church by the sayd quire for places in tyme of service"–a sort of non-musical chairs.[84] Two points at least can be observed here. First, the cathedral officers and servants were as implicated in disruption in the great church as any lay person. Secondly, the aural landscape of the post-Reformation church of metrical psalms and barking and scurrying dogs was exacerbated at Norwich by a scramble for seats in the choir.[85]

A few years later, divine service in the cathedral was–it was alleged–disrupted more portentously by the arrest of one of the canons by the sheriff in one of those regular acrimonious disputes between urban officials and cathedral authority which erupted from time to time both before and after the Reformation. The Norwich assembly disclaimed its authorizing the action and offered to bring its officers to account.[86]

Contretemps with the churchwardens happened inside the church, frequently when the wardens attempted to collect lays and assessments. Stephen Underwood was presented in 1613

> for rayleinge miscallinge & utteringe manie & outragious & uncivill speeches against Thomas Jefferey one of the Church wardens in their Churche at Burton upon sonday the xjth Day of June last imediatly after evening prayer in the hereenge & preseince of a greate congregacion.[87]

Within the church, as has been profusely demonstrated, the social hierarchy was represented and duplicated, producing a "social map" of the parish within the church, particularly through pew assignments.[88] The social hierarchy was also narrated back to the congregation through the differences in wine for the communion and the order of the kissing of the pax.[89] Social position was mapped out in detail in the seating arrangements in the parish church.

The differentiation by seating is reflected in the amounts collected in pew rents. The churchwardens of St. Michael's in Worcester itemised 126 payments of seats in 1595, at varying levels of 6d., 9d., and 1s. per seat; unsurprisingly, women's seats were valued at only 6d.[90] These distinctions already had a long existence, for, when twenty-nine payments for seats were collected in Walsall parish church in 1495-1496, twenty-two consisted of 4d., but the others at 6d., 8d., and 1s.[91]

The introduction of seating, moreover, enabled the formation of personal space, not only during life, but for the body afterwards too. Some testators expressed their intention to be buried inside the church by their seats. The eruption of that aspiration to be associated with a seat after death was manifest quite soon after the appearance of seating.

The intense localization of space within the church was assisted from the fifteenth century by the insertion of seating. In particular, social space in the nave was reconfigured. Whereas the congregation had previously stood as a mingled crowd, the introduction of seating allowed further the reproduction of the local social hierarchy inside the church. As seating became regulated and allocated by the churchwardens, that intrusion of social hierarchy into spiritual space increased. People were assigned to place and the space of the nave came to reflect social hierarchy within parochial society and the congregation.

No doubt too processional routes had been impeded by an unorganized standing congregation, whilst the rigid formation of aisles or "alleys" by seating facilitated the progress of processions around and through the nave. Processions performed various purposes, principally linking the spaces and people within the church, perhaps, but also demonstrating again the hierarchy of both clerical and lay elements.

Another effect which seating had on spatial experience in the church was the inhibition of people in urban places running from church to church to see each elevation, about which the humanist critics complained. Seating required some of the congregation to endure the whole service, immobilizing them. Initially, since seats were probably not provided for all, those at the back might have continued to rush into and out of urban parish churches to witness successive elevations.

The demand for seating thus came from different directions: privileged arrangements for some; organizing the congregation into gender, status and hierarchy; and promoting liturgical arrangements. Much of the requirement was thus to meet the differentiation of clerical and lay people within local spiritual society which no doubt replicated those distinctions being introduced in higher status spaces.

One egalitarian consequence, however, was to enable greater access–that is, visibility–of the principal liturgical performances, not least the elevation of the host at mass. Daily sight of the elevated host had for many an important resonance and meaning. Standing congregations obstructed vision so that the congregation at this important juncture became a crowd. Regulated seating re-opened at least some of the vistas to the chancel. As usual, nonetheless, matters were not that simple. Social differences resulted in unregulated seating–discussed below–so that the seating too impeded sight of the actions in the chancel. Those higher up the local hierarchy might be allocated pews closer to and with easier vision of the host, whilst the less fortunate were assigned to seats behind nave columns, in the aisles, and where sight through the rood screen and chancel arch and door was difficult.

All these developments and issues confirm the need to consider in detail the progress of the introduction of seating into parish churches. The manner in which it was achieved assumes a special importance for people in liturgical space.

We should not assume that it was impossible to represent social status within the nave previously, when congregations stood, but seating allowed the fundamental ordering of the whole congregation. Nor was social place fixed and immutable with seating: it could be renegotiated or contested. Nor should we assume that the impact of seating was cataclysmic, a once-for-all reorganization of the whole of the nave. There is sufficient evidence that the installation of pews and benches occurred incrementally, as seats were deemed necessary, as finances allowed, and as numbers of the congregation expanded. In some churches, we therefore perceive stages in the insertion of seating, so that the nave constituted for a time a hybrid space of both regulation (seating) and disorganization (standing). That too involved a marking off in the congregation between those provided with seating and those compelled to continue to stand. On the whole, however, pewing transformed the social implications of the space of the nave, ultimately organizing the whole of the congregation in the body of the church by office, status and gender.

We can perceive too that the initial seating was not permanent, that is, not fixed to the floor, but removable, allowing events within the body of the church, such as religious plays. The introduction of fixed seating was thus likely to promote contention.

Whilst structuration theory attempts to negotiate a pathway between structure and agency, its concern is with repetitive actions which are consistent with and contribute to a recognizable context: a limited repertoire of responses within a field or *habitus*.[92] The role of agency was restrained. Structuralism, however, ostensibly did not allow for individual action. What is suggested in this chapter is that even within such an apparently (but superficially) structured or structurated space as the church, individual actions were not bounded or constrained, but revealed contingent practices. In some cases, those contingent actions resulted from a loss of self-control, a submission to emotion, a failure to manage an emotional response. By itself structuring time, however, attendance at church provided the opportunity for premeditation, predictive of people's movements at certain times, so that the object of animosity could predictably be located. Furthermore, representation of space implied a privileged position, a perception denied to many people. The ability to represent space and define its character proceeded only with authority. Attempts to re-create the social hierarchy within church space produced conflict. The suggestion that the church promoted (the restoration of) social harmony in a society riven by social and kinship conflict begins to look rather compromised.[93] Attitudes to church space were revealed through contingent acts of hostility. For some–the elite–representation of space might have equated to their reality, but for many reality existed as contingency. Definition of space by the elite–its representation–served to preserve a social order and social harmony which they predicated, but in that process rendered space hierarchical and exclusive. Those who were not involved in inventing or promoting this representation of space could not *continuously* conform to or identify with that organization of space. Their social lives and practices were informed by exigency.

Appendix

Essex Record Office D/AEA 8, fol. 283 (old foliation 284) [1575]
Officium Domini contra Vincentium Honcottes et Willelmum Rookes nuper gardianos De Westham

Excommunicati sunt in compare[n]d' &c Comperta et facta per eos fide &c Dominus absoluit et restituit eos &c Et tunc Dominus eis obijcit that whilest theie were there Churchwardens theie suffered and caused in lent last past ij sonderie hollidaies ~~there~~ there was ij playes kepte in the Church by Comon players the one upon the sondaie before our ladie and the other one ~~our~~ our ladie Daie laste paste and the people were suffered to stand upon the Communion table Diuerse of them, the same ~~vi~~ Vincent Honicottes and William Rookes confessed the same to be true and Dnyed that ~~it was~~ the same playes were suffered for that theie ~~might~~ had a poore man in Decay and had seane ... less of the same players to the use of the same Poore man Dominus acceptauit eorum confessiones the same William Rookes affirmed that he comminge into the Church perseved that the players went about to playe he spekinge to them Declared that he wold not give his consent that theie shold not play there and he wold not be blamed for them but he tarried & hard the play ~~Dominus~~ & there in he consented to the play Dominus eis iniunxit that upon Sondaie nexte theie shall confesse that theie ~~were~~ are sorie that theie Did suffer the Church to be prophaned and in there necligence there in he the same Vincent to give vs and William Rookes to give ijs vjd et ad respondendum in proxima

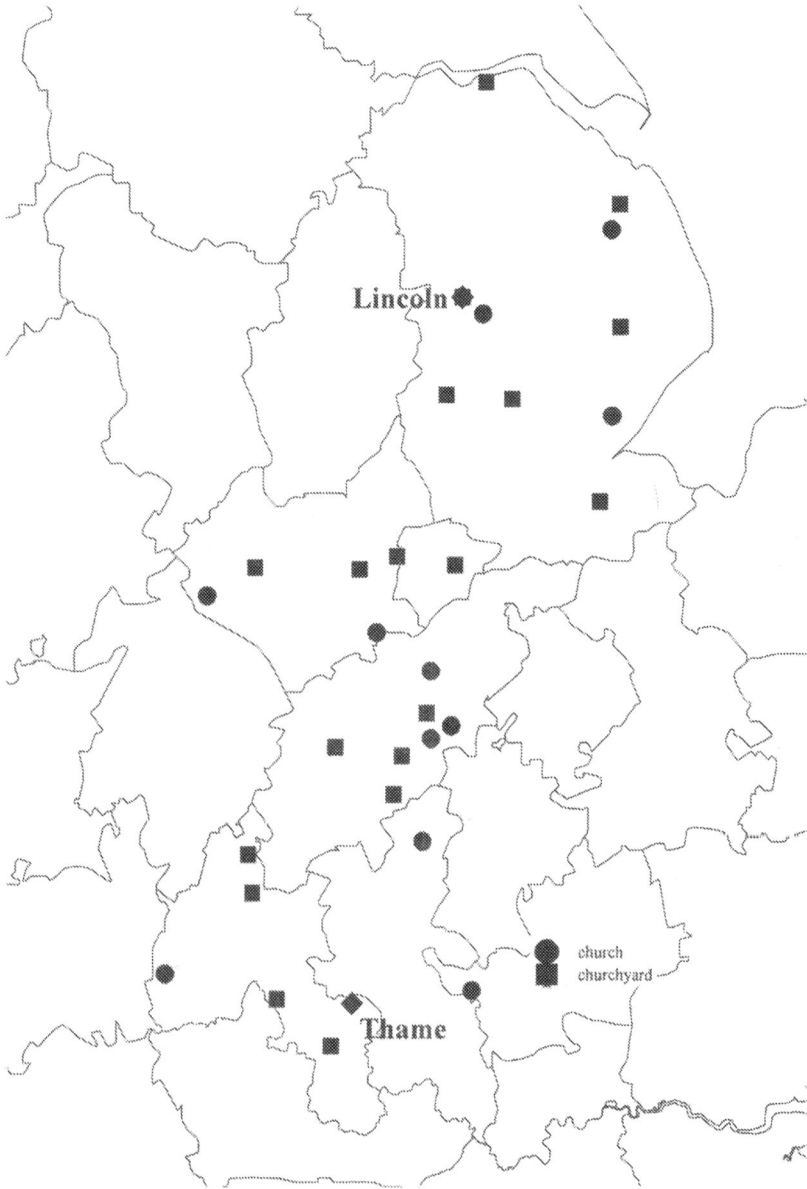

Figure 7.1   Reconciliation of Churches and Churchyards by Commission, Diocese of Lincoln, 1290-1297

Notes

[1] For the more expansive space of the cathedral, Patrick Collinson, "The Protestant Cathedral, 1541-1660" in *A History of Canterbury Cathedral* ed. Collinson, Nigel Ramsay, and Margaret Sparks (Oxford: Oxford University Press, 1995), 177-8.

[2] NNRO ANF/9/1, fol. 44v.

[3] Compare Marsh, "Sacred Space in England, 1560-1640: The View from the Pew.".

[4] John H. Baker, ed., *Reports of Cases from the Time of King Henry VIII*, vol. 2, Selden Society vol. 121 (London, 2004), 381 (no. 23).

[5] Susan Reynolds, "Social Mentalities and the Case of Medieval Scepticism," *Transactions of the Royal Historical Society* 6th ser. 1 (1991): 21-41; John H. Arnold, *Belief and Unbelief in Medieval Europe* (London: Hodder Arnold, 2005), extends the argument.

[6] *Chancery Miscellanea* Part 4, List & Index Society vol. 38 (London, 1968): bundle 64/file 9/298.

[7] *Chancery Misc.* 4, bundle 67/file 7/295.

[8] Elizabeth G. Kimball, ed., *Oxfordshire Sessions of the Peace in the Reign of Richard II*, Oxfordshire Record Society vol. 53 (Oxford, 1983 for 1979-80), 135-6.

[9] William T. Mellows, ed., *Peterborough Local Administration* volume I, Northamptonshire Record Society vol. 9(Kettering , 1930), pp. 21, 22.

[10] Edward H. Bates, ed.,*Quarter Sessions Records for the County of Somerset*, vol. I, Somerset Record Society vol. 23 (Taunton, 1907), 55.

[11] See the frequent use of the term "disordre" in such causes in the Oxford archdeaconry court in 1584: Brinkworth, *The Archdeacon's Court. Liber Actorum 1584*, vol. 1, 5, 27.

[12] For just one example in the church courts, Brinkworth, *The Archdeacon's Court, Liber Actorum 1584*, II, 170-1, between two women in St. Ebbe's parish church in Oxford in 1584.

[13] Houlbrooke, *The Letter Book of John Parkhurst*, 254.

[14] Brinkworth, *The Archdeacon's Court*, Liber Actorum *1584*, vol. 1, 89.

[15] CUL D2/10, fol. 242r.

[16] The management and manipulation of emotion is remarkably encapsulated in Barbara Rosenwein, "Worrying About Emotions in History,' *American Historical Review* 107 (2002): 821-45.

[17] K. M. Troup, ed., *The Court Rolls of the Manor of Wakefield from October 1338 to September 1340*, Yorkshire Archaeological Society (Leeds, 1999), 56.

[18] William Paley, ed., *Court Rolls of the Manor of Wakefield* volume II *1297 to 1309*, Yorkshire Archaeological Society vol. 36 (Leeds, 1906), 212.

[19] John Bossy, "The Mass as a Social Institution, 1200-1700," *Past and Present* 100 (1983): 29-61.

[20] Rosalind M. T. Hill, ed., *The Rolls and Register of Bishop Oliver Sutton, 1280-1299* vol. 4, LRS vol. 52 (1958), 135, 150: it is worth emphasizing the length of the occupation and recalcitrance.

[21] NNRO ANF/9/1, fols. 44v-84v.

[22] NNRO ANF/9/1, fols. 83r-84v: "Expense Thome Bodham in negotio

Correctionis contra eum per Abreham Canham promoto facto."

[23]NNRO ANF/9/1, fol. 58r.

[24]NNRO ANF/9/1, fols. 59v-61v.

[25]For the order of precedence before and after the Reformation, Kümin, *The Shaping of a Community* ..., 232-3, 237-40: the order of kissing the pax; pew allocations; select vestries; and dissent by a minority of parishioners; John Craig, "Co-operation and Initiatives: Elizabethan Churchwardens and the Parish Accounts of Mildenhall," *Social History* 18 (1993): 357-80: kissing the pax; difference of communion wine. For different interpretations of the question of hierarchy in seating and the periodic contests which it caused, see Christopher Marsh, "Order and Place in England, 1580-1640: The View from the Pew," *Journal of British Studies* 44 (2005): 3-26. The most complete investigation remains Kevin Dillow, "The Social and Ecclesiastical Significance of Church Seating Arrangements and Pew Disputes, 1500-1740," unpublished D.Phil. dissertation (University of Oxford, 1990). It's possible that much of the seating before the seventeenth century was moveable rather than fixed: Paul W. White, "'Drama in the Church': Church-playing in Tudor England," *Medieval and Renaissance Drama in England* 6 (1993): 15-35. Seating for urban dignitaries in churches can be considered by allusion to Robert Tittler, "Seats of Honor, Seats of Power: The Symbolism of Public Seating in the English Urban Community, c.1560-1620," *Albion* 24 (1992): 205-23.

[26]UoN Dept. of MSS. AN/LB 222/5/12/1-2.

[27]UoN Dept. of MSS. AN/LB 216/5/1/7.

[28]*Catalogue of Ancient Deeds*, vol. I (London, 1890), 156 (A.1387).

[29]Bodleian Library MS Charters Oxon d1, no. 41: "Omnibus Christi fidelibus presens scriptum visuris uel Audituris Walterus le Welshe de Garingges salutem in domino sempiternam Noueritis me die dominica in vigilia sancti Petri aduincula Anno Regni Regis Edwardi filii Regis Henrici vicesimo tercio in Cymiterio apud Garingges inspexisse Audiuisse et bene in omnibus intellexisse Cartam feoffamenti Gilberti de Chalcote quam eidem de libero maritagio nuper feci..."

[30]*Cat. Ancient Deeds* vol. 2 (London, 1898), 135 (A2934).

[31]*Cat. Ancient Deeds*, vol. 2, 71 (A.2380).

[32]Alfred E. B. Owen, ed., *The Medieval Lindsey Marsh. Select Documents*, LRS vol. 85 (Lincoln, 1996), 58-59 (25).

[33]*Cat. Ancient Deeds*, vol. 1, 118 (A1016).

[34]*Cat. Ancient Deeds*, vol. 1, 159-60 (A1419).

[35]*Cat. Ancient Deeds*, vol.1, 477, 502, 558 (C913, C1170, C1700).

[36]Fowler, *Acts of Chapter of the Collegiate Church of SS. Peter and Wilfrid, Ripon*, 91-92.

[37]*Cat Ancient Deeds*, vol. 3 (London, 1900), 382 (C3563)

[38]*Cat Ancient Deeds*, vol. 3, 40 (A4194).

[39]A. Hassell Smith and G. M. Baker, eds., *The Papers of Nathaniel Bacon of Stiffkey* volume III *1586-1595*, Norfolk Record Society vol. 53 (Norwich, 1987-8), 214.

[40]Hassell Smith and Baker, *Papers of Nathaniel Bacon*, vol. 3, 244.

[41]Hassell Smith and Baker, *Papers of Nathaniel Bacon*, vol. 3, 251.

[42]Storey, *Register of Gilbert Welton*, 64 (354).

[43]WSRO Quarter Sessions A1/150/6 (unfoliated and unpaginated; Michaelmas sessions, 4 Charles I).

[44]E. H. B. Harbin, ed., *Quarter Sessions Records for the County of Somerset*, vol. 2, Somerset Record Society vol. 24(1908), 68.

[45]Harbin, *Somerset*, vol. 2, 91.

[46]Harbin, *Somerset*, vol. 2, 18.

[47]Harbin, *Somerset*, vol. 2, 19.

[48]Harbin, *Somerset*, vol. 2, 52-3.

[49]Harbin, *Somerset* II, 169.

[50]Harbin, *Somerset* II, 119.

[51]Harbin, *Somerset* II, 132, 148, 156.

[52]43-44 Eliz c2 §1.

[53]William J. Hardy, ed., *Notes and Extracts from the Sessions Rolls 1581-1698*, Hertford County Records vol. I (Hertford, 1905), 45.

[54]James Tait, ed, *Lancashire Quarter Sessions Records vol. 1 1590-1606*, Chetham Society n.s. vol. 77 (Manchester, 1917), 153.

[55]Tait, *Lancashire Quarter Sessions Records* vol 1, 97. One wonders here, however, if the intention was for the second part (at noon, naked etc.) to be performed in the market place on some market day.

[56]Cambridgeshire Record Office Q/SO1, p. 166.

[57]ERO Q/SR 106/28.

[58]John Lister ed., *West Riding Sessions Records* vol. 2, Yorkshire Archaeological Society Record Series vol. 54 (Leeds, 1915), 99-100, 143, 196, 199, 202-3, 223, 234-5, 244-5, 317-18, 344-5, 379-80.

[59]NRO Diocese of Peterborough Correction Book 1610-1618, 386.

[60]NRO Diocese of Peterborough Correction Book 1610-1618, 357, 371.

[61]Sidney A. Peyton, ed., *The Churchwardens' Presentments in the Oxfordshire Peculiars of Dorchester, Thame and Banbury*, Oxfordshire Record Society vol. 10 (Oxford, 1928), 246.

[62]Peyton, *Churchwardens' Presentments*, 205.

[63]William M. Palmer, *Episcopal Visitation Returns for Cambridgeshire: Matthew Wren, Bishop of Ely, 1638-1665*, Cambridgeshire and Huntingdonshire Archaeological Society (Cambridge, 1930), 68.

[64]Rosalind Conklin Hays and C. E. McGee, eds, *Records of Early English Drama. Dorset* (Toronto: University of Toronto Press, 1999), 125.

[65]Palmer, *Episcopal Visitation Returns for Cambridgeshire*, 49.

[66]ROLLR 1D41/13/38, fol. 80v.

[67]John F. Williams, ed., *Bishop Redman's Visitation 1597*, Norfolk Record Society vol. 18 (Norwich, 1946), 147.

[68]See, for example, J. Alan Somerset, "Local Drama and Playing Places at Shrewsbury: New Findings from Borough Records," *Medieval and Renaissance Drama in England* 2 (1985), 3.

[69]White, "'Drama in the Church'", but whose examples generally occurred before the 1560s.

[70]ROLLR 1D41/13/38, fol. 45v. (presentment, 1613).

[71]See the Appendix to this chapter for the text; the event is mentioned by White, "'Drama in the Church'", 23.

[72]Hays and McGee, *Records of Early English Drama. Dorset*..

[73]Hays and McGee, *Records of Early English Drama. Dorset*, 241.

[74]John M. Wasson, ed., *Records of Early English Drama. Devon* (Toronto: University of Toronto, 1986), 67.

[75]Wasson, *Records of Early English Drama. Devon,* 234, 237, 242.

[76]Wasson, *Records of Early English Drama. Devon,* 277.

[77]Audrey Douglas and Peter Greenfield, eds., *Records of Early English Drama. Cumberland. Westmorland. Gloucestershire* (Toronto: University of Toronto, 1986), 336.

[78]Douglas and Greenfield, *Records of Early English Drama. Cumberland. Westmorland. Gloucestershire,* 345-6 (for examples only).

[79]John Coldewey, "Carnival's End: Puritan Ideology and the Decline of English Provincial Theatre," in *Festive Drama* ed. Meg Twycross (Cambridge: D. S. Brewer, 1996), 279-86.

[80]ERO D/AEA 10, fol. 76v.

[81]John F. Williams & Basil Cozens-Hardy, eds., *Extracts from the Two Earliest Minute Books of the Dean and Chapter of Norwich Cathedral, 1566-1649,* Norfolk Record Society vol. 24 (Norwich, 1953), 42.

[82]Williams and Cozen-Hardy, *Extracts ... Dean and Chapter of Norwich Cathedral,* 47 (1614).

[83]Williams and Cozen-Hardy, *Extracts ... Dean and Chapter of Norwich Cathedral,* 38.

[84]Williams and Cozen-Hardy, *Extracts ... Dean and Chapter of Norwich Cathedral,* 39.

[85]The other aural sensibilities have been explored by John Craig, "Psalms, Groans and Dogwhippers: The Soundscape of Worship in the English Parish Church, 1547-1642," in *Sacred Space in Early Modern England,* ed. Coster and Spicer, 104-23.

[86]NNRO NCR case 16 shelf c no. 5, fol. 350v.: "Whereas an arrest was lately made uppon Mr Carleton one of the Cannons of Christes Churche by the shreives offycers within the churche in the tyme of diuyne service as was informed and published at <A> Ceane on tewsday last past to all the clergy men there that the Cittie <& Cittizeins> were agentes in that arrest and done with ther pryties [sic] to deface the churche and Churche men ..." (May 4, 5 James I).

[87]ROLLR 1D41/13/38, fol. 125v.

[88]Flather, *Gender and Space in Early Modern England,* will address this issue extensively.

[89]As n. 24 above.

[90]John Amphlett, ed., *The Churchwardens' Accounts of St Michael's in Bedwardine, Worcester, from 1539 to 1603,* Worcestershire Historical Society (Worcester, 1896), 121-2.

[91]G. P. Mander, ed., "Churchwardens' accounts of All Saints church Walsall 1462-1531," *Collections for a History of Staffordshire* (Kendal: Titus Wilson and Son for The William Salt Archaeological Society, 1930 for 1928), 232-3.

[92]Parker, *Structuration;* Graves, "Social Space in the English Medieval Parish Church."

[93]Bossy, "The Mass as a Social Institution, 1200-1700."

8
Micro-spaces: Church Porches

Church porches: Openings

Openings are problematic spaces. Most dangerous are the orifices of the body, which, although they have purposes, also allow access for impurities and pollution.[1] Openings into the spaces of "public" buildings do not engender the same degree of peril, but they are inherently ambiguous. Apertures in some circumstances become punctures. To some extent, they are also micro-spaces between larger spaces. Spaces can also, however, be represented as having meanings and expected uses and purposes. In the context of spaces, conceiving representation and reality as dichotomous may be a false binary. In the first place, the representation of space has a discursive impact on the experience of some people some of the time. Consciousness of the representation of the space influences their actions. The relationship between representation and reality of spaces can thus be "dialogic". On the other hand, unless these spaces are closely monitored and regulated (confined to the official, symbolic and expected), spaces can be subverted and appropriated, and no less is that pertinent to micro-spaces.[2] An element of agency inhered in the capacity to appropriate the space, but also to reject its symbolism. Regulation of the space might be exerted by officialdom and authority, but order might also be imposed in the space by surveillance, including self-discipline.[3] That self-restraint depended on control of the emotions within the space, but occasionally emotional responses to situations resulted in the subversion of the space, an unreflexive repudiation of its representation and symbolism. In fact, these micro-spaces, because of their ambiguous location as transitions between two different and larger spaces, were perhaps more susceptible to "irregularity".

Doorways into parish churches had specific meanings and uses. The entrance most associated with the laity was the south door and porch, through which parishioners normally had access to their "own" space in the church, the nave and aisles. Accordingly, the south porch became a site of lay activity, both through ritualized procedures condoned or liturgically and canonically prescribed or approved, or through appropriation of that space by some of the laity. The south porch was thus developed as the largest of the porches in parish churches, especially for the conduct of the medieval marriage ceremony (see below). Equally, it was transformed into a particular type of space. It is tempting to perceive the south porch above all as a liminal or transitional space, between the "profane" (secular world) and the (putative) "sacred" (holy).[4] The liminal aspect of the south porch is, indeed, confirmed by the usual location of the baptismal font near to it, signifying, for baptism, the reception of the child into the Christian community, a ritual taking place near the entrance to the church, not in the central space of the congregation. To some extent, that transition obtained, but structuring of this kind can be taken to excess, for it fails to take into account the fuzzy, messy, unselfconscious and ambiguous use of space, by groups of people and by individuals. Furthermore, some characteristically secular transactions were enacted in the south porch presumably to invoke the witness of the holy to these secular activities–the payment of legacies and debts. Nor is it entirely satisfactory to consider this space as only "public space". For, although some of the personal transactions made there were enacted because of its "public" (that is, openly visible) character, in other circumstances–not least as occasional shelter–it remained an intensely contingent space.[5] The following exploration of the use of the space of the (south) porch of the parish church is thus divided into two parts: ritualized procedures; and appropriation of space.

As explored in Chapter 7 above and the INTRODUCTION, changes during the sixteenth century transformed the parish church from a site of the encounter with the holy, a "sacred" space, to a place for meeting for prayer and praise, a "sacralized" space. Reverence for the space remained an issue, however.

Consciousness of space

First, we should establish how the representation of this micro-space entered the consciousness of parishioners. There is a complication with the space of the church porch, since it mediated transition not between binary opposed spaces, but between churchyard and church. Doctrinally, the churchyard belonged to the same holy conspectus as the church. In practice, however, parishioners did not admit the churchyard to the same level of holiness as the church, and often treated it in practical terms as an ambiguous space.[6] It was the site of many secular activities and episcopal and archidiaconal visitations frequently commented on the lack of enclosure, separating off and protection of the space, and its constant use for grazing animals.[7] The church porch thus in practice assumed a significance in "popular" consciousness which it did not have doctrinally.

The internalization of the representation of space can be illustrated by litigation in the archdeaconry court of Nottingham, Foster *c.* Greene and the counter-cause of Greene & Revel *c.* Foster. The background to the dispute was acrimony between previous and current churchwardens, which occasioned an altercation as two of the parties exited their parish church of Annesley. Foster refused to contribute to the current church rate (and also objected to the manner of the election of one of current churchwardens, Revel).[8] The examination of Robert Hill, husbandman, aged about fifty-six, reveals the details of the contention in the church porch in 1617.[9]

That uppon a Sabaoth daye within one quarter or thereabouts he this deponent beinge comminge forth of the Church of Annesley articulat immediatlye after the readinge of Morninge prayer did heere the articulat Godfrie Greene beinge then goinge out of the church & enteringe the Church porche saye to the articulat Christopher Foster Thou lyest & thou lyest in the throate of thee & the said Christopher Foster sayinge unto the said Godfree Thou knowest wheere thou speakest this or els thou woldest not give me the lye & then the said Godfrie beinge in the Churchyard theare answeared; whie then thou maist followe me...

Whilst the witness acknowledged that he owed the party producing him £10, the basic circumstances can be accepted as accurate, if not the interpretation of them. The witness alleged further that he heard that the two parties 'have not binne freinds anie tyme this twelue moneth and more' and that too explains the simmering acrimony which erupted in the church porch. Another testimony, that of John Gelsthrop of Annesley, husbandman, aged about thirty-five, articulated that the dispute arose when Foster, a former churchwarden, asked Greene, one of the current churchwardens, for a copy of the lay (church rate), to which Greene responded "paye me for it & you shall have one." The witness proceeded:

... & afterwards reasoninge further in the church porch, the said Christopher said to Godfrie Greene articulat paye me that thou owest me to whome the said Godfrie answered I owe thee nothinge, & then the said Christopher replied, then Breedon saith not true, & then uppon other words which this deponent doth not remember spoken by the said Greene the said Christopher said Yf thou waste out of this place thou wouldest not saye these words, whereupon the said Green said, Then followe me forth of the churchyard ... [and]

that he doth not beleeve that this suite is followed of malice but doth thincke that there is somme unkyndenes betweene the said Christopher & Godfrie..

The critical conclusion of the disagreement was confirmed (if not impartially) by the third witness, Richard Revell of Annesley, yeoman, aged about fifty-three, the other current churchwarden.

[Foster to Greene:] Greene Thou art a proude fellowe ... Thou owest me iijs to whome the said Godfrie said it is not so it is a lye, & then the said Christopher said Thou knowest wheere thou arte or els thou wouldest not saye so to me wheereupon the said Godfrie said I am goinge forthe of the Church yarde Yf thou wille have anie thinge with me Followe me ...

[and heard Foster say about Greene] I will undoe him & more of his neighbours ...

Behind the immediate dispute, then, was a long period of tension, perhaps emanating from the previous years when Greene and Foster had been co-churchwardens. Finally, the mutual dislike erupted in an abrupt exchange of words. They were, nonetheless, able to restrain their emotions in recognition of the special character of the space.

Official space

Ritualized Procedures
Keeping definitions as succinct as possible, the ritualized procedures discussed below were simply recursive or repetitive practices which had a performative element (dramatic action) and symbolic meanings. Two of the practices–the first two explored–were associated with life-course events. For the purposes here, there is no need to become involved further in interpretation of ritual and ritualization.[10] What *is* important is that the representation and use of the space was officially authorized and sanctioned and so entered into "popular" consciousness.

Marriage

Before the Reformation, marriage was a sacrament but, as its basis was consensual (consent between the parties) in canon law (*Dignum est* 1152), the church did not have control over marriage. Marriage formation was possible by two processes outside the church: words of present consent between the parties (*verba de presenti* such "I do take thee for my wife") and words of future consent (*verba de futuro* such as "I will take thee for my wife"), the latter when consummated by sexual intercourse. Marriage in the church (*in facie ecclesie*) was not necessary. In recognition of this essentially lay aspect of marriage, the ceremony when conducted by a priest might occur outside the church, usually in the south porch, which is one reason why the south porch is so large: to accommodate the wedding party. The priest could perform this ceremony in the porch. There too the ring could be placed by the groom for the priest to bless and hallow (sprinkle with holy water). Only after this ceremony in the porch might the party move into the church, to the first step before the altar for the nuptial mass and blessing.

By the late fifteenth and early sixteenth centuries, it is possible that, in London at least, marriages *in facie ecclesie* were performed inside the church.[11] In the North, however, there was at least some understanding that marriage took place at the church door. Thus, in a matrimonial cause in the Durham ecclesiastical court in 1452, the male party, William [Will], was alleged to have proclaimed: "I Will sall wed the Janet at the kirk dore."[12]

In fact, the south porch was mentioned as the "wedding porch door" in several other contexts. Thus the priest of Frome, David Thomas, desired to be buried at the wedding porch door near Sir John Clarke, by his will of 1545.[13]

After the Reformation, marriage was no longer a sacrament, but the ecclesiastical authorities exercised more control over it so that informal marriage outside the church was not tolerated. The ceremony now took place inside the church, at the devotional center, in the face of God, despite it not being a sacrament. The important part was that it was a public ceremony, performed by the priest before the congregation. The porch continued to be used only in a residual way for the conferment of dower.[14]

Churching

Practice

Without considering the meanings elicited by this life-course ritual, its practice can be described as follows. After childbirth, a mother was normatively required to attend the parish church for a ceremony. That ceremony again normally occurred forty days after the birth. [Leviticus 12:4-5 prescribed thirty-three days after the birth of a male child and sixty-six after the birth of a female child].

Pre-Reformation

The woman attended church accompanied by two married women. She was veiled and carried a lighted candle. At the church porch, she was met by the priest who accepted the white chrism cloth in which the child had been baptized. In the porch, before she could enter the church, she was sprinkled with holy water by the priest and only then allowed into the church, where she was ritually readmitted to the communion (mass) and to the community of the faithful by the priest reciting Psalm 120 (121) over her. The porch thus acted as a liminal, marginal locus before reintegration into the community, in one interpretation at least.

Post-Reformation

The liminal space of the porch was removed and the woman processed directly into the church. In the Prayer Book of 1549, she was allowed to enter straight into the church to the choir door to kneel and be churched. From 1552, she was allowed to process right to the (putative) sacred space in the church to kneel before the table for the ritual. Moreover, after the Reformation she was no longer required to be veiled nor to carry a lighted candle.[15]

Penance

In this context, penance is restricted to that imposed in office causes in the ecclesiastical court, not penance imposed after confession before a priest. It is therefore penance which involves an element of satisfaction (exterior penance) as well as contrition (interior penance) and thus involves public ritual performance of penance, one space for which was the parish church. Lay persons sentenced to perform penance in the parish church were usually required to wait outside the church in the porch before being admitted to perform their penance, thus in a liminal, marginal locus outside the "community" of the parish (now the congregation inside the church) and outside the communion. Penance specified in the Ely diocesan court illustrates the procedure. In 1570, Sybil Carton of Gamlingay was directed to stand in the church porch in the accouterments of the penitent: white sheet and with a white wand in her hand. She was ordered to perform this action on three successive Sundays from the second peal of the bells declaring morning prayer. After the reading of the lesson, the vicar would collect her from the porch and bring her to the head of the congregation. About the same time, Thomas Wasse of Graveley was to undergo the same ignominy, the timing replicated: to stand in the porch from the second peal announcing morning prayer on Sunday until the reading of the second lesson.[16]

Clerical penitents, however, were not placed in such an extreme liminal position, but waited at the font, inside the church, but at its margins. There was a symbolic difference in this use of space. Lay penitents were excluded from the community of the church and the house of the Lord, removed to the porch. The performance of their penance then replicated their readmission to the community, congregation and communion. Clerical penitents, in contrast, were not excluded from the community and house, but placed inside at its margin. Thus the chaplain, Robert Segefeld, accused of fornication, for his penance waited at the font reading the psalter.[17]

Examples

[1] that she shuld stand in the church dore of Wawlcamstow the next sonday all the service tyme in a whit sheit bare fott with a white rod in hir hand & to Desier all the people going into the church to pray for hir[18]

[2] Salutem in christo yow shall receave John Nafare of Linshebye to do penaunce after thys sorte Fyrste one sondaye nexte he muste come to Thurnebye churche and theyre stande in ye churche porche from ye second pele tyll ye laste havyng nothyng apon hym butt all bare savyng hys sherte & A heyre clothe A lofte of ytt with asshes throne apon hys {A} hedde & A whyte Rodde in hys hande & so comme into ye churche when yow begyn servys and stande in ye myddle yle with hys face to the people all servis tyme & yow rede ye homelye of adulterie y^t beyng done he shall fall flatt one ye grownde and saye with A lowde voyce y^t all ye people maye here hym My Sowle clevethe to ye duste, O Lorde qwycken thow me accordyng to thye woorde & declare to ye people ye cause why he dothe those penaunce [sic] and desyre all the bothe yownge and olde to take example at hym & praye for hym, thys done yow muste certifie ye maner of hys doyng, whether he do ytt penitently or no youres John gote Registre[19]

Although thus the location of the first stage of penance, the space of the porch could as easily be subverted for unrepentant contrary idling, for Thomas Fuller of Kennington departed from the church during preaching and sat idly in the porch.[20]

Social space

Partly influenced by the need to accommodate the marriage party, the size of some porches also proceeded from the use of space for associational (guild) or parochial functions, as at Clare. In 1440 a dispute erupted between the parishioners of the church of St Nicholas in Gloucester and the rector, the Prior of the Hospital of St. Bartholomew about the use of a chamber over the porch of St. Nicholas. The parishioners' claim–denied by the Prior–revolved around a customary use of the chamber as a base for maintenance and repair of the church. The dispute was resolved by a lease of the chamber to the parishioners for a term of forty years from 1440.[21]

Parishioners might have regarded the porch (as well as the tower) as a communal resource; at least that is the implication of bequests under wills not to the fabric of the church in general, but specifically to the porch. In some cases, of course, the legacy coincided with a re-building of the porch in the middle of the fifteenth century, a not unusual occurrence in Suffolk. Testators bequeathed small amounts for the porches at Woolpit, Nayland, Boxford (although one legacy amounted to as much as five marks), Stoke by Nayland, Bardwell, Wickham, Ousden and Cowlinge.[22] Paving Rodmersham church porch was intended by a legacy from William Foxtone.[23] For All Saints, Bristol, William Wytteney furnished a cloth, the Dance of Pauls, at a cost of £18, which was intended to remind parishioners of their own mortality.[24] This depiction was suspended from a battlement constructed each year at the appropriate times (St. James and, appropriately, All Hallows) in front of the south door.[25] As indicated above, however, bequests for the maintenance of the porch usually consisted of much smaller amounts, such as the half a quarter of malt bequeathed by a parishioner of Eaton Socon in 1500.[26]

The communal resource of the porch sometimes extended to the space above the porch itself. Where an upper space existed, it was often dedicated to fraternities, their chapels, schools, and stores.[27] A testator of Northill thus in 1504 made a bequest of 10s. to the priest celebrating in the chapel of St. Anne constructed over the south porch of his parish church.[28] Following this example, William Tychmers devoted a quarter of a mark to help support a priest for a year in the same chapel above the porch.[29] Within a year, the same chapel above the porch received the proceeds of the leasing out of a heifer towards the priest's stipend.[30] Interest in this upper space confirms the communal attachment to the porch as parishioners' space.

Personal appropriation

In contrast with the ritualized practices described above, personal appropriation of the space of church porches was irregular and contingent. That intrusion into the space had, moreover, no authorization or sanction. Some (although not all) of these acts of appropriation were, furthermore, unselfconscious and unreflexive in the sense that the perpetrators did not always consider closely the nature of the space nor the consequences of their intrusion into the space. In this context, then, these interventions may reveal more about attitudes to the space than ritualized practices.

Perhaps it should not be surprising that in the late sixteenth century the settlement of financial obligations occasionally occurred in the church porch. When, in 1592, Nicholas Bacon and an associate entered into a bond with George Downing, gentleman of Norwich, the £100 at issue was to be redeemed on April 1, 1593 between one and three o'clock in the afternoon in the north porch of the parish church of St. Simon in Norwich.[31] On the renewal of the obligation on April 1, 1593, instead of its liquidation, the place for future redemption was specified as the north porch of the parish church of St. Michael Coslany in the city.[32] That arrangement did not conclude the affair, for there was a further renewal on October 1, 1593, when the principal had become £105, now to be redeemed at Lady Day 1594 in the north porch of St. Clement's parish church in the city.[33]

Numerous testators requested in their wills the payment of legacies in cash in the south porch of the parish church, usually on a specified date and at a specified time. Again, the designation of this small space depended on its "public" aspect (in all senses of that word) for this purpose and perhaps too an invocation of the holy to attest to the act.[34] It was stipulated under the will of William Cartewrighte of Ossington, Nottinghamshire, esquire, in 1602 that a yearly rent of £100 should be delivered in the church porch of Ossington.[35] By three instalments in 1589, 1592, and 1595, £180 was to be delivered to Constance, daughter of Adam Wilson of Tideswell, yeoman, under his will of 1586: the venue specified in his will was the church porch, at Michaelmas.[36]

We have fairly comprehensive evidence of testators' intentions for the payment of legacies in parish church porches in early-seventeenth-century Suffolk. Parish churches where at least one legacy was to be liquidated in the porch in the first four decades of the seventeenth century are represented in Figure 8.1 (below, page 217). The density is evident, comprehending very many parishes.[37] Even within a short period of five years, more than one testator specified the transfer of legacies in some parish church porches in the archdeaconry of Suffolk (coterminous with "East Suffolk"): two in each of Laxfield, Ashfield, Wissett, Orford, Beccles,

Monk Soham, and Worlingworth. In fact, only just under fifty out of 783 testators in this archdeaconry between 1620 and 1624 specified the payment of legacies in church porches, but they were sufficient to mean that this action occurred in over forty different parish churches. It is, of course, quite possible that other executors acquitted legacies in church porches without specific direction in wills to do so.

The same pattern can be observed in the archdeaconry of Sudbury (co-extensive with "West Suffolk") in the six years between 1630 and 1635 (also Figure 8.1).[38] In these years in this jurisdiction, although only thirty-three testators specifically directed payment in a parish church porch, twenty-eight different parishes were involved. As in the archdeaconry of Sudbury, some porches hosted more than one transaction within the six years: Thelnetham three and Chevington, Hopton and Mendlesham two each.

For some legacies, moreover, the action in the porch was repetitive over many years. For example, William Gooch, yeoman of Ringsfield, in 1618 made provision of an annuity of £20 for life to his wife, Rebecca, to be delivered each year in instalments at four terms in the church porch of Fressingfield.[39] A similar annuity of £32 at two terms was expected in the church porch at Sproughton.[40] Numerous forward payments of legacies–years ahead–were specified by Robert Burnditch, boatwright of Holbrook, to be remitted in the parish church porch, starting five years after his decease, and dependent on recipients attaining their age of majority.[41] The iterative nature was more complex still under the will of Henry Cole, yeoman of Offton, requesting an annuity of 20s. for each of his daughters Joan and Sarah, and legacies to his other daughter, Thomasine, his five grandchildren, and his son, Robert, all to be liquidated in the "great south porch" of Hadleigh church.[42] A similar complexity was encompassed in the will (1628) of Hugh Largent of Kirtling, whose copyhold tenement passed to his son Robert as next heir. Robert was obliged to defray several legacies, all in the local parish church porch over a number of years, no doubt staggered to allow him to raise the money from the issues of the tenement: an annuity of 20s. to the testator's wife, payable quarterly; 40s. to the testator's daughter, Margaret, within two years of Hugh's decease; 40s. to another daughter, Alice, within three years; £4 to the other son, Richard, within five years; 40s. to another daughter, Frances, within six years, and the same to the remaining daughter, Mary, within seven years; and thereafter 40s. to the testator's grandchildren. Robert's visits to the church porch to make payments would have been frequent over the years.[43]

Although not consistently specified, it was usually the south porch where these amounts of money were transmitted. Merely as examples, wills designated the south porch at Battisford, Rumburgh, Syleham,

Worlingworth, Chevington, Clare, Eye, Thurston, Hitcham, Boxford, Cavendish, Mildenhall, Lawshall and Mendlesham.[44] The south porch constituted that visible, public space, at the intersection of secular and (putative) sacred, where the transaction could be attested by passing parishioners and the sight of God or the numinous, for images or symbols of saints were positioned in porches.[45] It is quite likely, moreover, that the payments were intended to be made in the south porch before or after service time as the congregation entered or departed from the church, adding to the public visibility of the transactions.

The common alternative–although not often mentioned in wills–was delivery in houses. By comparison with the church porch, the other "public space", the market place, did not seem to be favoured as a place for delivery of legacies: a Rushmere testator in 1621 designated Beccles market cross; and the corn market cross at Ipswich was the location for transfer of a bequest of 40s. in a will of 1622.[46] Otherwise, the market place did not feature in this way.

Justices of the Peace frequently specified ecclesiastical space for the payment of secular debts. This particular locus–the church porch–*could*, in other contexts, be interpreted as a liminal space between secular and spiritual space, but the action involved here belonged purely to the secular realm. The church porch was presumably selected as a public, visible place where such a transaction was open and verifiable.

In 1601, the Lancashire bench ordered Ellen Blundell to deliver to Thomas Boyes £18 by three half-yearly instalments, Thomas renouncing to Ellen his interest in a tenement in Scarisbrick; the justices further ordered the payments to be made in the porch of Ormskirk church.[47] When the same justices in 1604 required John Lyvesey, of Plesington, to pay to Anne Gaket 8d. a week in the porch of Blackburn church between the hours of ten and noon for the maintenance of a bastard child, however, some ambiguity is involved.[48] The justices of the North Riding in 1608 required a recognizance for the payment of 40s. to Jane Lumley on Easter Wednesday in the church porch at Ainderby for the maintenance of her bastard child.[49] Sexual immorality was an offense determinable in the courts spiritual. Moreover, the churchwardens were usually the officers responsible for supervising the maintenance of bastard children and the father's contribution was frequently made directly to them. Nevertheless, the justices had a commensurate jurisdiction over bastardy and actively intervened. Indeed, in these cases of maintenance, the bench sometimes decided that the maintenance should be delivered to the churchwardens, significantly inside the parish church, in the center of (putative) "sacred space", at an important liturgical time.[50]

The Somerset justices promulgated an order in 1628 for the maintenance of Thomas Fryday alias Vyne of Bruham, his reputed father to pay
9d. weekly every Sunday after evening prayer in the church porch of the
parish of Bruham.[51] Another order pronounced by the same bench in December 1628 for the maintenance of Richard Samson a base child born
at Yeovil, demanded that the alleged father pay 8d. weekly, commencing
on the next Sunday in the church porch of Yeovil after evening prayer.[52]
The costs, amounting to £3 10s., of the interim maintenance of a bastard
child in Earls Colne were to be defrayed in the church porch on the feast
of St. John the Baptist between 1 and 4 p.m., by the direction of the Essex
magistrates.[53]

Burial in the south porch can be considered another personal appropriation of this space. In 1497-9 several East Anglian testators had mani-
fested this desire: Robert Stronge to be buried in the south porch of Cromer
church (allocating 6s. 8d. to its repair); John Usher in the south porch of
Foulsham church; William Laade of Terrington "beneath" the porch; William Mynot who in his will referred to the stone which he had seen which
covered the grave of John Gordon in the porch of Dedham church; and
John Reynold, grocer of Norwich, before the porch of St. Andrew, Norwich.[54] Mynot subsequently allocated 40s. in his will for the construction
of a porch at Our Lady of Grace chapel in Ipswich for the poor to sit in,
with images of his grandfather, father and mother in the east window and
of himself and his two wives in the west.[55]

After the Elizabethan settlement of religion, some testators desired
burial in the church porch of Great Chesterfield (1560), and the south porch
of Great Cranfield (a husbandman in 1562). Other Essex testators opted
for the churchyard, but near the church door at St Osyth, on the west side
of the porch at Feering, and in the case of William Thayer, a husbandman
of Great Baddow, burial by the path leading to the south porch.[56]

Many West Riding will-makers had the same predilection: Edward
Bekardyke in 1530 in the churchyard before the church porch; in 1539,
Anthony Kirkbie burial in the porch of Sherburn parish church near his
wife; Henry Scott of Wortley to be interred in the churchyard at the south
church door in 1541; Margaret Berry of Wakefield in the church porch in
1543; Nicholas Wilson of Sherburn-in-Elmet in 1548 near his wife "at the
churche porche"; Thomas Booreman of South Milford in the churchyard
"ne unto the troyghe ende by the porche dore" in that year; the following
year Robert Roger of Cookridge in the churchyard of Adel near the church
door; another year on, William Poole in the church porch of Saxton; in
1552 William Wattes of Wakefield, smith, inside the church against the
south church door.[57]

If interment in the south porch was not within access of a testator, burial in the churchyard near the porch was an alternative. Although to be interred in the churchyard, Robert Walton of Pontefract wished his grave to be located "right overthwarte the churche porche" (1557).[58] In that same year, a yeoman of Rothwell Haigh, Edmund Parker, expressed his desire to be buried in Rothwell churchyard "foranempste the saide church porche".[59] William Pepwall, of Halesowen, expressed his desire to be buried in Hales churchyard before the porch under the stone where his first wife was interred.[60] At Newton Kyme, William Greene, who made his will in that year, required his body to be interred in the churchyard near the south porch, as also then did Robert Ward of Methley: in the church-yard "neyre unto the southe churche doore".[61] In the following year, Alice Boswell asked for burial in the south porch of Sherburn church and John Milner of Pontefract, a weaver, in the churchyard but "over against the south church doore."[62]

The number of examples could be multiplied to tediousness, but it is perhaps important to cite two further instances: the desire of Edward Robuck, a saddler of Pontefract, who in 1546 directed burial "withoute the procession doore of the south side within the parishe church yerde of Allhallowes in Pontefracte"; and the prescription of the clerk, Thomas Wrangham, that he be buried in St. Andrew Auckland "at the going in of the churche dore of Sainte Androwes churche within the portche"; for both requests indicate the motive for burial in this location.[63] Testators wished to have the benefit of remembrance by parishioners when they entered and left church and when they formed processions at significant times of the liturgical year.

The impetus to burial in a porch is reflected in the will of William Lendall of Chislehurst (Kent) who, in 1549, asked in his will to be buried in the church porch and bequeathed 3s.4d. to the churchwardens for repairs "so that they suffer me to lye in the church porche."[64] At nearby High Halstow, Robert Luddesden, aspiring to burial in the porch, allocated 6s.8d. to pave the porch, with a further 3s.4d. if necessary for a proper job.[65]

We can recapitulate then that the attraction of burial in the south porch was the flow of the congregation into and out of church for all services. As related above, furthermore, the south porch was traditionally where marriages took place, so that Simon Symms of Greenwich in his will of 1548 hoped for burial in the south aisle "before the weddinge dore."[66] An-other allurement in some cases was the location of the holy water stoop in the south porch, which influenced the decision, for example, of Richard Mikylhalf of Gravesend in 1500.[67] John Smart of Plumstead (Kent) went a stage further, in 1526 requesting burial in the porch by the holy water stoop, but with a stone and writing on it "testifying who lyeth there", thus purposely placed and advertised to demand attention.[68] A Somerset parson elected to be buried in the church porch by the holy water bucket, renouncing his right to be interred in the chancel.[69]

Although predominantly preferring the south porch, some testators wished for interment by other porches. At Toddington, Thomas Turner in 1496 expressed his desire to be buried outside the north porch of his parish church.[70] So also Harry Est of Marston requested burial "afore the north dore."[71] In this case, we might surmise that the focus was on the door through which the clergy entered the church, an association with the parishioners' ghostly father.

Although mentioned less frequently, the west door was favored by some testators as it was the processional door, so in 1461 Thomas Benet of Snodland earmarked four marks towards the maintenance of the west porch with his body for burial there.[72] So, in 1457, John Kempston, mayor of Bedford, selected burial in the churchyard before the west door of St. Paul, Bedford, perhaps equating the processional west door with the dignity of his office and status.[73]

Not only did Thomas Reade of Newcastle request burial in the church porch of St. Nicholas church, he specified that it should be St. George's porch, and allocated 20s. for the porch's maintenance.[74] Here, however, we encounter a problem of medieval terminology. More usually the Middle English term for an aisle was "alley", but occasionally porch included not only the porch but also the adjacent aisle. This wider interpretation might account for a number of burials which were not actually in the porch, but in an aisle. Ralph Constable, gent., thus desired burial in the Lady porch of his parish church of Ainderby in 1554.[75] Burial in the porch of St. John in Richmond church was requested in 1560 by Sir William Loftus, clerk, formerly chaplain to the gild of St. John there.[76] In St. Nicholas, Newcastle, there was a St. George's porch where Johns Lassells and Mittforth, both merchants, asked to be interred in 1582 and 1623.[77] Richard Thompson also expressed his wish to be buried near a porch, St. John's.[78] In Newton parish church, there was a space commonly called the "Walleses Porch" where John Wallis of Coupland expected to be buried in 1611, perhaps a proprietary aisle or space within the church.[79] We might interpret in the same manner the "Braidforth porch" in Balmborough parish church where Peter Bradforth was contented to rest in 1647.[80]

Although, therefore, not a locus of profuse burials, the south porch was selected as the spot for interment by a number of parishioners. We might infer that these inhabitants wished to be interred in a place where the secular world encountered the sacred, in a symbolically liminal place where passage from one space to another occurred. As importantly, their interment was situated in a place where the local society of the parish frequently passed, so that they would be remembered.[81] There too, their bodies were close to some communal activities of the parish, as, in a sense, the porch was a space appropriated by the parish for its secular activities. Some, who did not expect to be buried in the porch, but in the churchyard, hoped for burial near the south porch where the parishioners congregated and passed. Whether in the expectation of intercession by the the local society of the parish in traditional (Catholic) religion or simple remembrance in the reformed (Protestant) confession, some parishioners desired to be buried in the south porch.

As an entrance, the church porch was susceptible to appropriation for display and social honor. The porches of some parish churches thus displayed the armorial bearings and rebus of local notables, as the de Vere arms over the south porch of Lavenham parish church.[82] This sort of annexation was reserved for the more magnificent and largest parish churches–as also for the gatehouses of monastic houses. In effect, this appropriation also constituted a secularization of a (putative) "sacred" space, for the gable of the porch was usually reserved for a niche for the statue of patronal saint of the parish or some emblem representative of the dedication. In some parishes, moreover, especially in late-medieval Suffolk, investment in the porch was intended to enhance the honor and dignity of the parish and its parishioners. The perpendicular porches of many larger Suffolk parishes belong to this category. Many are two-storeyed, with a large elevation.[83] In 1482-3, more than £11 was expended on the new porch for Walberswick parish church.[84] Included in the re-modeling of the perpendicular churches of Suffolk "wool" towns and parishes then was an emphasis on the porch as a symbol of an entrance into holy space and a depiction of parochial integrity.

In complete contrast, the porches of small parish churches or chapels were as likely to be neglected and fall into dereliction. The churchwardens of the chapelry of Hoath complained that the porch (as well as the church house) "lakkithe reparacione" in the early sixteenth century.[85] At Ham, the porch was denuded of tiles.[86] The churchwardens of Iwade lamented that their church had no porch at all.[87] On the other hand, preference for burial in the porch might have been inspired by the invasion of churchyards by animals, as the pigs which apparently dug up graves in the churchyard of Mersham.[88] As in other respects, then, the appropriation of space was socially mediated.

For individuals, the parish church might adventitiously provide a place of succor not through its charitable provision, but merely as a physical place of shelter. Poor itinerants depended on the south porch for lodging. In 1569, "a stranger who dyed in the Church porche" was interred at Tamworth.[89] It was reported to the council of Norwich in 1652 that a poor widow had lain in the church porch for three months, having no house and unable to pay rent.[90] The court of mayoralty of the same city was advised that Samuel Hubbard would not or could not provide for his wife who lies in the porch of St. Augustine's church and that Samuel himself had lodged in a church porch.[91] When examined as a vagrant in Norwich, Robert Stokay from Lincolnshire, recounted how he had journeyed to Norwich, but on his arrival his money had expired, so he lay in the church porch where he was arrested.[92] James Latimer was presented by the churchwardens of Draughton (Northamptonshire) "for lyinge this moneth in our Churche porche."[93] At Brixworth in the same county, the register of burials recorded in August 1595: "A poore boye that Dyed in the Church porch."[94] Hindle has discovered numerous other examples of the poor inhabiting the church porch, occasionally in the form of dead bodies. He also intimates that occupying the porch might have constituted a tactic to solicit alms.[95] The destitute, consequently, appropriated church space for their direct needs. In the process, they might further derogate the space of the church, as did the four vagrants, discovered by the constables of North Damerham, playing cards for money in the church porch.[96] Accordingly, the tithingman of Stourton was presented at Quarter Sessions for not preventing beggars from lying in the church porch, drinking and smoking, to the dishonor of God's house and disturbance of the parish.[97] In his will of 1528, Thomas Polley of Eynesford (Kent) made a bequest of 3s.4d. towards the maintenance of the young child found in the church porch.[98]

On the other hand, some testators elevated the south porch as a site of succor for unfortunate people. By his will of 1625, Peter Glover of Darlington allocated £4 to be distributed at the church door to the poor of the town.[99]

We can really place into context burial in the church porch, however, by reference to those parish clergy who elected to be buried in the porch. The vicar of Farningham, Mr. Gilbert Carleton, made alternative suggestions for his burial in his will of 1500: under the high altar so that his feet were under those of the celebrant at mass, the traditional privilege of the clergy (rectors more than vicars); "orells under the steppe comyng yn att the church dore, so that euery creature comyng yn att the same dore may trede upon my buriall", by which he expressed humility but also anticipated prayers for his salvation.[100] Perhaps the same motivation resided in the election of Sir Ralph Staff, vicar of Barnham, to be interred "without the Church Porch of Barnam with a Tombe."[101]

Another hazard for the porch was defecation. The practice of grazing animals in the churchyard occasionally led to mess in the porch. Fouling the porch also happened in urban churches, so that when the great door of

All Saints, Bristol, which opened onto Broad Street, was repaired in 1525, a penny of the cost was expended in removing dung at the door.[102] In like manner, the churchwardens of St. Mary Bredin complained that because Agnes Sheldwiche did not fence a vacant plot next to the church door, the parishioners were inconvenienced by a dunghill.[103] More drastically, the porch at Upton Scudamore was so polluted by sheep dung that the parishioners complained that they trod it into the parish church.[104] Even worse, the defective porch and door at Seham allowed swine and other animals into the church in 1579.[105] Degradation by animals–pigs–was an urban phenomenon too, compounded by the irreverent actions of some townspeople, such as Humphrey Ayre who dressed or killed a beast in the south porch of St. Nicholas, Nottingham, in 1620.[106]

We can now return to Foster c. Greene. In their altercation, the particular nature of the space of the church porch (and the churchyard, indeed) was recognized. Observation of this space did not always happen. At Moulton, in the early seventeenth century, Emma Dawes allegedly scolded and railed at Ann Harrington in the church porch on a Sunday.[107] More seriously, Robert Bett failed to restrain himself in the church porch of Kingsthorpe in the last decade of the sixteenth century: "...being moved to Choller and nothing regarding the Daunger of the lawes did Brawle with one Mr Rise curat of Kingsthorpe in the church porche of Kingsthorpe aforesaid one monday at the evening."[108] The porch was a place where parishioners were likely to encounter each other and the incumbent and where such incidents would result.

Church porches: Closing

By considering both structured and contingent actions in church porches, we begin to understand the variety of responses to (micro-)spaces in medieval and early-modern England. Some of the structured changes were introduced as part of the reformation of the liturgy and canonical rites. That official ordering of space, however, should perhaps not be viewed in isolation, but placed alongside unstructured and contingent lay use of church porches which, to some extent, traduced the authorized representation of space. Although spatial representation and practice were inter-related, they were also in tension, and the church porch illustrates that very well.

Controversy over the social production of space and the representation of space is not completely irreconcilable.[109] Whilst the representation of space–a symbolism imposed through dominance–influenced how people normatively acted, it was always open to subversion.[110] Indeed, subversion is not the *mot juste*. In the alternative use of the church porch, the actors did not consciously transgress the space. They had, indeed, no consciousness of the official meaning of the space. Use of the space was in some cases intimately bound up with the conditions of their life. Beggars were not choosers. In some cases, the adoption of the space by the impotent was simply a matter of de Certeau's meandering and wandering and inadvertence. When physical violence demeaned the space, it happened because people–usually, but not exclusively men–lost control over their emotions, ignorant of or oblivious to any meaning of the space.[111] Conscious appropriation of space, on the other hand, was instigated by the powerful, like the de Vere family.

Space was not necessarily unitary. A space had multiple meanings and was used–consciously, but also unconsciously–in many ways. Even such a small space as a church porch was the *locus* of multiple activities and actions which were inconsistent and often contradictory. We do not have to revert to the Kantian idea of space as container, but we should be aware that neither was space *just* represented or *just* socially produced. Life is and was more complicated and complex than that when we examine its empirical details.

Figure 8.1   Payment of Legacies in Parish Church Porches in the Archdeaconries of Suffolk, Early Seventeenth Century

Notes

¹Douglas, *Purity and Danger*. For an example, the presentment of the church-wardens of Graveney that the door from the chancel to the churchyard was in disrepair so that the church might be robbed: Kathleen L. Wood-Legh, ed., *Kentish Visitations of Archbishop William Warham and his Deputies, 1511-1512*, Kent Records vol. 24 (1984), 243. Bill Miller, however, has also reminded us that our own orifices are the source of our pollution of the outside: Miller, *The Anatomy of Disgust*.

²The problem of maintaining order in populated (putative) "sacred" spaces is well addressed by John Eade, "Order and Power at Lourdes: Lay Helpers and the Organization of a Pilgrimage Shrine," in *Contesting the Sacred*, ed. Eade and Sallnow, 57-58.

³There is no single influence on the comments here, rather a bricolage of Foucault, Elias, Giddens, Bourdieu, Bakhtin ("dialogic") and Erving Goffman.

⁴Here, I assume the structural approach to (putative) sacred space to follow firstly Mircea Eliade and secondly Mary Douglas: Eliade, *The Sacred and the Profane*, esp. chap. 1 ("Sacred Space and Making the World Sacred"); Douglas, *Purity and Danger*. A structurational (rather than structuralist) consideration, derived from both Bourdieu and Giddens, is contained in Graves, "Social Space in the English Medieval Parish Church". My interpretation here is informed by phenomenology on the one part and by Michel de Certeau on the other. Rather than seeking recursion and habitus in the intersection of secular and (putative) sacred in the formation of space in the parish church in the manner of Graves, my intention is to illustrate hermeneutically how contingent social practices (the uncontrolled, the erratic, and the unconsciously subversive) reflect perceptions of space–fuzzy, ambiguous and unstable: de Certeau, The *Practice of Everyday Life*, esp. 97-102.

⁵Reference here is purely to "public space" in the sense of "openly visible". No attempt is made here to associate this visible openness with the "communicative action" of the Habermasian "public sphere". In ecclesiastical courts, the contemporary definition was to proscribe nefarious activity in *loca suspecta*, that is, out of public view (See the "Introduction"). I do not intend here any dichotomy or binary opposition between public and private space.

⁶For the "problem" of the dead, their interment, and "popular" customs surrounding burial in early-modern England, see now Peter Marshall, *Beliefs and the Dead in Reformation England* (Oxford: Oxford University Press, 2002).

⁷Wood-Legh, *Kentish Visitations*, passim, has many examples.

⁸UoN Dept. of MSS. 223/2/15/2 and also 223/2/15/3/1-5.

⁹UoN Dept. of MSS. AN/LB 223/2/1/1/1-2.

¹⁰The literature about ritual and ritualization has burgeoned so greatly that it is hardly possible to know where to start.   Perhaps the most useful point of departure is now Catherine Bell, *Ritual. Perspectives and Dimensions* (Oxford: Oxford University Press, 1997).

¹¹I am grateful here for the expert advice of Shannon McSheffrey.

¹²Raine, *Depositions and other Ecclesiastical Proceedings from the Courts of Durham...*, 33.

¹³Shilton and Holworthy, *Medieval Wills from Wells Deposited in the Diocesan Registry, Wells*, 216.

[14]Richard M. Smith, "Marriage Processes in the English Past: Some Continuities," in *The World We Have Gained. Histories of Population and Social Structure,* ed. Bonfield, Smith, and Wrighton, 43-99; Eric Carlson, *Marriage and the English Reformation* (Oxford: Blackwell, 1994); Richard H. Helmholz, *Marriage Litigation in Medieval England* (Cambridge: Cambridge University Press, 1974); John Gillis, *For Better, For Worse. British Marriages, 1600 to the Present* (Oxford: Oxford University Press, 1985); David Cressy, *Birth, Marriage and Death. Ritual, Religion, and the Life-cycle in Tudor and Stuart England* (Oxford: Oxford University Press, 1997); Christine Peters, "Gender, Sacrament and Ritual: The Making and Meaning of Marriage in Late Medieval and Early Modern England," *Past and Present* 169 (2000): 63-96.

[15]Gail Gibson, "Blessing from Sun and Moon: Churching as Women's Theater," in *Bodies and Disciplines,* ed. Hanawalt and Wallace, 139-54; Will Coster, "Purity, Profanity and Puritanism: The Churching of Women 1500-1700," in *Women in the Church* ed. William J. Sheils and Diana Wood, Studies in Church History vol. 27 (Oxford: Blackwell, 1990), 377-87; David Cressy, "Purification, Thanksgiving and the Churching of Women in Post-Reformation England," *Past and Present* 141 (1993): 106-46; Cressy, *Birth, Marriage and Death,* 197-229.

[16]CUL EDR D2/8, fols. 123v, 131r.

[17]Raine, *Depositions and other Ecclesistical Proceedings from the Courts of Durham...,* 35.

[18]ERO D/AEA 2, fol. 36v c. Bridget famula of Thos Bryghte of Walthamstow for sexual incontinence.

[19]ROLLR 1D41/13/9, fol. 8a [single, loose leaf] [instruction to the parish incumbent, n.d., but 1576] c. John Nafare for adultery.

[20]Wood-Legh, *Kentish Visitations,* 205.

[21]William H. Stevenson, ed., *Calendar of the Records of the Corporation of Gloucester* (Gloucester, 1893), 393 (1115).

[22]Northeast, *Wills of the Archdeaconry of Sudbury 1439-1474,* 24 (60), 41 (108), 95 (261), 118 (316), 145 (380), 176 (458), 180 (469), 207 (548), 230 (619), 331 (930), 376 (1089), 420 (1231), 441 (1273), 448 (1285), 479 (1386).

[23]Wood-Legh, *Kentish Visitations,* 254.

[24]Clive Burgess, ed., *The Pre-Reformation Records of All Saints', Bristol. Part 1,* Bristol Record Society vol. 46 (Bristol, 1995), 14.

[25]Burgess, ed., *The Pre-Reformation Records of All Saints' Church, Bristol. Part 2,* Bristol Record Society vol. 53 (Bristol, 2000), 93, 117.

[26]Patricia Bell, ed., *Bedfordshire Wills 1480-1519,* Bedfordshire Historical Record Society vol. 45 (Bedford, 1966), 9 (20).

[27]See generally Joseph Bettey, *Church and Parish* (London: Batsford, 1987), 63.

[28]Bell, *Bedfordshire Wills 1480-1519,* 44 (98).

[29]Bell, *Bedfordshire Wills 1480-1519,* 59 (125).

[30]Bell, *Bedfordshire Wills 1480-1519,* 68 (141).

[31]Hassell Smith and Baker, *The Papers of Nathaniel Bacon of Stiffkey vol. III,* 214.

[32]Hassell Smith and Baker, *Papers of Nathaniel Bacon III,* 244.

[33]Hassell Smith and Baker, *Papers of Nathaniel Bacon III,* 251.

[34]Nesta Evans, ed., *The Wills of the Archdeaconry of Sudbury, 1630-1635,* Suffolk Record Society vol. 29 (1987). See further below.

[35]John W. Clay, *North Country Wills*, SS vols.116 and 121 (1908 and 1912) II, 193 (cliv).

[36]David G. Edwards, ed., *Derbyshire Wills Proved in the Prerogative Court of Canterbury 1575-1601*, Derbyshire Record Society vol. 31 (2003), 79 (158).

[37]Marion E. Allen, ed., *Wills of the Archdeaconry of Suffolk 1620-4*, Suffolk Record Society vol. 31 (1989), 7 (9), 26 (42), 28 (46), 37 (65), 57 (95), 60 (99), 81 (136), 82 (140), 87 (150), 111 (194), 113 (200), 115 (203), 116 (204), 118 (209), 123 (219), 126 (222), 140 (247), 158 (276), 161 (281), 168 (292, 294), 182 (313), 201 (352), 208 (367), 225 (405), 263 (471), 268 (477), 500), 279 (501), 315 (558), 327 (578), 331 (581, 592), 339 (593), 344 (598), 351 (610), 353 (620), 365 (637), 370 (649), 381 (665), 392 (682), 396 (688), 433 (752), 442 (767), 448 (788).

[38]Evans, *Wills of the Archdeaconry of Sudbury 1630-1635*, 29 (72), 54 (127), 59 (137), 62-3, 66 (153), 68 (156), 119 (272), 123 (282), 180 (428), 187 (447), 188 (450), 249 (597), 255 (612), 619 (259), 271 (643), 275 (653), 280 (664), 282 (670), 286 (678), 288 (682), 288 (683), 291 (689), 294 (728), 310 (736), 335 (795), 355 (844), 356 (846), 361 (861-2), 376 (894).

[39]Allen, *Wills of the Archdeaconry of Suffolk 1620-4*, 161 (281).

[40]Allen, *Wills of the Archdeaconry of Suffolk 1620-4*, 353 (620).

[41]Allen, *Wills of the Archdeaconry of Suffolk 1620-4*, 442 (767).

[42]Allen, *Wills of the Archdeaconry of Suffolk 1620-4*, 433 (752).

[43]Evans, *Wills of the Archdeaconry of Sudbury, 1630-1635*, 180 (428).

[44]Allen, *Wills of the Archdeaconry of Suffolk 1620-4*, 201 (352), 263 (471), 277-8 (500), 448 (788); Evans, *Wills of the Archdeaconry of Sudbury, 1630-1635*, 54 (127), 59 (137), 62-3, 119 (272), 180 (428), 187 (447), 255 (612), 280 (664), 294 (697), 306 (728), 310 (733), 355 (844), 376 (894).

[45]See, for example, Foster, *Lincoln Wills Volume II A.D. 1505 to May, 1530*, 107: a bequest of wax to the image in the church porch at Scalford, 1529. The lily motif (the symbol of the Virgin (the parochial dedication)) in the porch at Warmington (Northamptonshire) is another example.

[46]Allen, *Wills of the Archdeaconry of Suffolk 1620-4*, 110 (193), 195 (338).

[47]Tait, *Lancashire Quarter Sessions*, 107.

[48]Tait, *Lancashire Quarter Sessions*, 220.

[49]John C. Atkinson, ed., *Quarter Sessions Records Volume 1*, North Riding Record Society (1884), 109.

[50]For payments inside the church, including on the communion table, Bates, *Quarter Sessions ... Somerset*, vol. 1, 18, 19, 52-3, 119, 132, 148, 156, 169.

[51]Harbin, *Quarter Sessions Records for the County of Somerset*, vol. 2, 68.

[52]Harbin, *Quarter Sessions ... Somerset*, vol. 2, 91.

[53]ERO Q/SR 109/19.

[54]Harper-Bill, *Register of John Morton*, 38 (55), 40 (57), 56 (83), 74 (109), 95 (140).

[55]Harper-Bill, *Register of John Morton*, 40 (57).

[56]Frederick G. Emmison, ed., *Essex Wills. The Commissary Court, 1558-1569* (Chelmsford: Essex County Council, 1993), 60 (269), 62 (277), 150 (713), 151 (722), 226 (1050).

[57]Lumb, *Testamenta Leodiensia ... 1539 to 1553*, 7, 36, 101, 211, 221, 229, 258, 331; *Wills and Administrations from the Knaresborough Court Rolls* vol. I, SS vol. 104 (1902), 24.

[58]Lumb, *Testamenta Leodiensia ... 1553 to 1561*, 21.

[59]Lumb, *Testamenta Leodiensia ... 1553 to 1561*, 109.

[60]WRO: will of Pepwall.

[61]Lumb, *Testamenta Leodiensia ... 1553 to 1561*, 136, 205.

[62]Lumb, *Testamenta Leodiensia ... 1553 to 1561*, 238, 246.

[63]Lumb, *Testamenta Leodiensia ... 1539 to 1553*, 177; Clark, *North Country Wills 1383 to 1558*, 244 (cxciv) (1565).

[64]Leland L. Duncan, *Testamenta Cantiana: A Series of Extracts from Fifteenth and Sixteenth Century Wills Relating to Church Building and Topography. West Kent*, Kent Archaeological Society (London, 1906), 12.

[65]Duncan, *Testamenta Cantiana*, 35.

[66]Duncan, *Testamenta Cantiana*, 32.

[67]Duncan, *Testamenta Cantiana*, 28.

[68]Duncan, *Testamenta Cantiana*, 60.

[69]Shilton and Holworthy, *Medieval Wills from Wells*, 84 (1545).

[70]Bell, *Bedfordshire Wills 1480-1519*, 49 (105).

[71]Alan F. Cirket, *English Wills, 1498-1526. [From the First Surviving Register of Wills Proved in the Court of the Archdeacon of Bedford]*, Bedfordshire Historical Record Society vol. 37 (Bedford, 1957), 36.

[72]Duncan, *Testamenta Cantiana*, 70.

[73]Margaret McGregor, ed., *Bedfordshire Wills proved in the Prerogative Court of Canterbury 1383-1548*, Bedfordshire Historical Record Society vol. 58 (1979), 18 (14). Although John Holdern intended to be buried inside the church of Dunstable in his will of 1530, the location was near the west door: 135 (108).

[74]Clay, *North Country Wills*, 142 (cii).

[75]James Raine, ed., *Wills and Inventories from the Registry of the Archdeaconry of Richmond ...*, SS vol. 26 (1853), 82 (lxxvii).

[76]Raine, *Wills and Inventories from the Registry of the Archdeaconry of Richmond ...*, 144 (cxxi).

[77]John C. Hodgson, ed., *Wills and Inventories from the Registry at Durham Part III*, SS vol. 112 (1906), 92; Herbert M. Wood, ed., *Wills and Inventories from the Registry at Durham Part IV*, SS vol. 142 (1929), 168.

[78]Raine, *Wills and Inventories from the Registry of the Archdeaconry of Richmond ...*, 232 (clxxiii).

[79]Wood, *Wills and Inventories from the Registry at Durham Part IV*, 48.

[80]Wood, *Wills and Inventories from the Registry at Durham Part IV*, 314.

[81]For what the "community" of the parish actually meant, Beat Kümin, *The Shaping of a Community: The Rise and Reformation of the English Parish 1400-1560* (Aldershot: Ashgate, 1996).

[82]Nicklaus Pevsner, *The Buildings of England: Suffolk*, 2nd edn., rev. by E. Radcliffe (Harmondsworth: Penguin, 1996), 323.

[83]Pevsner, *Buildings of England: Suffolk*, 91, 431, and illustrations 10(a) and 11(a-b).

[84]R. W. M. Lewis, ed., *Walberswick Churchwardens' Accounts, A.D. 1450-1499* (London: Headley Brothers, 1947), 173.

[85]Wood-Legh, *Kentish Visitations*, 77.

[86]Wood-Legh, *Kentish Visitations*, 95.

[87]Wood-Legh, *Kentish Visitations*, 262.

[88]Wood-Legh, *Kentish Visitations*, 157.

[89]*Tamworth Parish Registers I*, Staffordshire Parish Registers Society (1917), 31.

[90]D. E. Howell James, ed., *Norfolk Quarter Sessions Order Book 1650-1657*, Norfolk Record Society vol. 26 (1955), 47.

[91]William L. Sachse, ed., *Minutes of the Norwich Court of Mayoralty 1632-1635*, Norfolk Record Society vol. 36 (1967), 19.

[92]NNRO NCR Case 12a/1a, fol. 126r. (1553).

[93]NRO Peterborough Diocesan Records Archdeaconry correction book 41, 1610-1618, 184.

[94]NRO 50P/1.

[95]Hindle, *On the Parish?* 319-20, 415.

[96]B. Howard Cunnington, ed., *Records of the County of Wiltshire* (Devizes: Simpson & Co., 1932), 113.

[97]Cunnington, *Records of the County of Wiltshire*, 134.

[98]Duncan, *Testamenta Cantiana*, 23.

[99]J. A. Atkinson, B. Flynn, V. Portass, K. Singlehurst, and H. J. Smith, eds, *Darlington Wills and Inventories 1600-1625*, SS vol. 201 (1993), 204 (58).

[100]Duncan, *Testamenta Cantiana*, 26.

[101]Walter H. Godfrey. ed., *Transcripts of Sussex Wills as far as they Relate to Ecclesiological and Parochial Subjects, up to the Year 1560* / Transcribed and Classified by the Late R. Garraway Rice, Sussex Record Society vols. 41-43 (Lewes, 1935-38), I, 75.

[102]Burgess, *Pre-Reformation Records of All Saints ... Part 2*, 310.

[103]Wood-Legh, *Kentish Visitations*, 68.

[104]Bettey, *Church and Parish*, 80.

[105]Raine, *The Injunctions and Other Ecclesiastical Proceedings of Richard Barnes*, 118.

[106]R. F. B. Hodgkinson, "Extracts from the Act Books of the Archdeacons of Nottingham," *Transactions of the Thoroton Society* 30 (1926), 55.

[107]NRO Peterborough Diocesan Records correction book 1610-1618, 154, 172.

[108]NRO Peterborough Diocesan Records X610/24, fol. 185r.

[109]Unwin, "A Waste of Space?" directed at Lefebvre, *The Production of Space*.

[110]Sibley, *Geographies of Exclusion*, on the impact of the representation of space as dichotomous, after Douglas, *Purity and Danger*, so that other uses of space are categorized or even stigmatized as transgressive and intrusive.

[111]No attempt has been made here to engage with the idea of "emotional communities" suggested by Rosenwein, "Worrying about Emotions in History," esp. 844-5, or with space as the locus of group memory, delineated recently by Hebbert, "The Street as Locus of Collective Memory."

Part III
In and Out of Place

9
The Politics of Urban Habitation, 1550-1640: Immigration, Poverty and Urban Space[1]

> God forbid for what would people say, then they would say that gentlemen came to the City to buy up the houses and to pull down poor folks' houses to the intent that they would not have poor people dwell near unto them ...'[2] (1563)

Recently, it has been proposed that the post-Reformation acquisition and management of urban property provided further opportunities for urban corporations to development an urban political culture.[3] The ownership of urban property also facilitated some influence over the urban environment through control over some at least of the urban tenements. Nevertheless, the built urban area experienced contrasting vicissitudes during the sixteenth century, which presented urban authorities with almost insurmountable problems.[4] The urban fabric was important for urban corporations not only for their own enjoyment, but also to represent the borough or City to the external world. Managing that external perception of the urban place had long exercised the collective consideration of mayors, aldermen and councils. To that end, constant endeavors were made by corporate authorities to ensure a "commodious" environment.

The urban built environment was a constant source of anxiety for urban authorities because it represented the dignity of the borough or town and of the urban authority and elite. Surveillance and influence over the urban environment, the built environment, and the building process remained a particular concern. That propensity to regulate involved action over the reality and representation of the urban and urbanity. Control over the real entailed regulating and maintaining buildings, whilst representation evolved out of the power of the urban elite to depict space and to present its image as well as, or, indeed, set against, its reality.

By the late sixteenth century, however, the expression against incommodious housing was not about the decay of building through its disappearance, but its deterioration in accommodating an increasing population–new, smaller tenements and fragmentation of existing housing which resulted in a meaner urban environment.[5]

As has been illustrated for Warwick and Norwich, for example, the demographic upturn in provincial urban centres at the end of the six-teenth century was ambiguously a demonstration of the reviving fortunes of urban places simply because of the increase of poverty.[6] Complaints about impoverished urban parishes at this time were not only rhetoric. Of course, attaining a realistic idea of the problems confronting urban places is compounded by rhetorical enunciation inspired to persuade. Com-plaints by urban authorities were often designed at least partly by those motives. Even the obiter dicta of urban justices in urban quarter sessions were directed towards an audience.

For urban authorities, the decay of housing stock did, however, re-main an intractable, internal problem. It was generally associated with the invigorated influx of immigration into urban centres. Whilst inwards mi-gration to boroughs was a constant demographic phenomenon, in the late sixteenth century it exacerbated increasing urban problems.[7] The urban magistracy was genuinely disconcerted about the impact on the urban en-vironment. Equally, however, the association of enhanced immigration of impoverished strangers, adding to the difficulties presented by the indig-enous poor, with decay of the housing stock, had a further relationship with other urban issues.

> Alsoe whereas by experience heretofore and especially in the tyme of this present visitac[i]on it appeareth very evidently that diverse auncient dwellinge howses within this citie beinge here-tofore used severally to be inhabbited only with one howsehoulde and noe moore are nowe of late tyme made and converted into many severall cottages and dwellinge howses and there fower or moore severall howshouldes dwellinge and abidinge in many of the same auncient howses and diverse straungers and forriners admitted to be inmates ...[8]

Elements of scapegoating, rhetoric and stereotyping were no doubt contained within this complaint, but there was undoubtedly an equal element of reality. The argument that the alms available to the indigenous poor were diminished and traduced was perhaps exaggerated, as also the manner in which the strangers "growe obstinate and cannot be remooved." On the other hand, it is apparent that "great discommodity" did ensue and the prescription to compel landlords to install only one family in each "ancient" tenement was a realistic attempt to preserve the urban fabric.

Whilst an outbreak of pestilence was thus the occasion of the above measure, real concerns were felt and expressed about the deterioration of the urban environment. So, whilst another immediate context for the regulation of strangers was times of national security (during internal upheaval and external threat: 1569 and 1588 and their rumors and aftermath), the long-standing concerns were the burden of poverty and the maintenance of the fabric of the urban environment as "commodious" as possible. For those reasons, the penalty for infraction of the order at Chester was as severe as disfranchisement of burgesses.[9]

Perhaps the real extent–as opposed to the rhetoric–of the issue was reflected in the accusation against George Vause, feltmaker, that he had converted a kiln and an adjacent building near the walls by the Newgate into housing for poor strangers. Vause had been previously ordered to evict these undertenants but had neglected to do so. It further transpired that Vause had no title to the new building–which belonged to the City.[10]

A considerable proportion of the evidence adduced here derives from the presentments of the constables to the justices in Nottingham, which revealed practical action on the ground. The presentments exhibit not merely the performance of their required responsibilities by the constables, but also an insight into their concerns which can be assumed to reflect the anxiety of at least some other burgesses. For the most part, the presentments of the constables were not contaminated by rhetorical purpose. On the other hand, urban authorities frequently reprimanded constables for imperfection and avoidance in the performance of their duties. Inference from the constables' presentments for Nottingham, however, suggests a large degree of diligence, even initiative, from the constables, and that exhortation was not a one-way traffic. It was not beyond the constables to demand action from and to criticize the urban authorities.

Perhaps we should consider first how that played out in practice in Nottingham, not for the uniqueness of the constables' activity there, but from the perspective of one of the few occasions where constables' concerns become apparent rather than reported in the sessions rolls. What exists at Nottingham in the sessions rolls are the original presentments of the constables. Although scrappy in format, these written responses were constantly purposeful and not mediated by redaction by officialdom.[11]

(William Hall) ... for that he is readie to harbor in his howsse everie vagabounde & bad fellowes <people> that commith to the town and sufferith them to begg which Doth greatlie trobell men in their markettes.[12]

We present Mr Aldarman clark For byldyng a sort of pawltrie howses wych hath downe grat Hurt to ower towne.

We present Mr <Andrew> Jackson For the lyke Howses kepyng in Hys handes.[13]

(John Mather) ...taking an inmate in to his house and thei are poor folkes and the wyf lyes in chyld bed.[14]

(William Wydoson) ...for taking tennentes which is chargable to the parish the hous is in the uper end of hongot.[15]

(Robert Sherwyn) ...for takinge many and dyvers innmates into his howse at the broad marshe end to the number of iij or iiij in that howse.[16]

The urgency of the constables of the wards of Nottingham in their presentments foregrounds two of the inter-related issues which confronted and challenged urban officialdom in early-modern England: the influx of migrants and transients into urban places and the consequent anxiety about the character of the housing stock and the urban environment.

What exist therefore are sporadic complaints of urban authorities about the work of the constables and directions for improvement counterbalanced by the Nottingham bills' illustration of largely effective action by the constables in matters reflecting the concerns of established townspeople.[17] It therefore becomes necessary to consider further these aspects: the occasional, dismissive remarks by authority; the efficacy of the constables on the ground; and, indeed, the organization of the constables in Nottingham. By pursuing the details of Nottingham, what is at issue is not just an exemplar of activity, but a window onto the performance of the constables more often concealed. As a point of further clarification, the bills of presentments are not concerned at all with the detection of felonious activity (theft, burglary) but only with those concerns about order and disorder which prevailed in urban (and rural) populations.

As has been exemplified with quotations from the constables' presentments for Nottingham, the immigration of strangers and the expansion of poor housing to accommodate them, presented urban authorities with a mighty challenge. Here, however, it is necessary to exercise some caution, since not all urban authorities had at hand the ability to prevent unregulated housing. In particular, in developing towns like Sheffield with no corporate authority and a fragmented landownership, the division of tenements for multiple occupancy could proceed virtually uninhibited. At the opposite end of the spectrum, incorporated boroughs had a stronger–but not uncontested–hand in attempting–usually ex post facto–to prevent fragmentation of urban property for poor strangers' accommodation.

Before considering the wider issue of the reception of strangers and inmates, the concerns expressed by the constables about housing must be dissected. Of course, this issue was an integral part of the regulation and exclusion of strangers and immigrants, but hospitality of strangers was provided either by receiving them into existing households or the fragmentation of housing for their accommodation and the decline of housing standards. Mention should, however, be made that in Nottingham the real concern about strangers seems to have been exacerbated about 1590, for the bills then first incorporated a survey of five strangers' households, where they were received, their marital status, and the number of their children.[18]

As to reporting deleterious building for urban immigrants, in 1612 three burgesses were presented for building cottages to accommodate strangers.[19] In the following few months, Leonard Nyxe was reported

for Receavinge of Strangers wyth Charge of Chylldren into his newe Ereckted Cottages in the broad lane before the swyne greene, whearof one of his tenantes hath iiij smale Chylldren.[20]

Aggravated by these infractions, the constables requested the issue of orders about new buildings and the receiving of inmates in the same year.[21] Immediately thereafter, they had to bring the finger of accusation against Will Frost "for making thre tenamentes of one."[22] In 1620 the constables complained to the urban authorities about the extensive harboring of people in "new erected houses."[23] At that very time, their attention was attracted by Richard Wightman who had allowed a tenant "into a poore habytacion" which had not previously been let.[24] The authorization to the constables was codified again in 1612 in response to the

daylye experyence thatt by the contynuall buildinge and erectinge of newe cottages and poor habytacions and by the transferringe of barnes and such lyke buildinges into cottages and habytacions

for the accommodation of the rural poor entering the borough. In future the conversion of any barn or other building into cottages would require the license of the mayor, recorder and aldermen.[25]

Now the concerns of Nottingham's constables about deterioration of the housing stock to accommodate immigrants seem to have come into real prominence later than in some other urban centres. In the small, but vibrant market town of Banbury, the corporation determined in 1564, in promulgating new ordinances, to grasp this particular nettle. The section with the rubric "The taking of inmates" prohibited any inhabitant of the borough from taking any inmate or undertenant without the license of the bailiff and a borough justice, on pain of a fine of 6s.8d. and two days incarcerated in the gaol. If unlicensed inmates or undertenants were entertained for more than twelve days, the fine was increased to £2 and loss of the freedom.[26] Whilst this restriction should not necessarily be adduced as another instance of the erosion of hospitality–for such urban impediment to newcomers had a long history–there was a demonstrable inhibition to receiving sojourners.[27]

In their response to this aggravated problem, borough and urban authorities had recourse to a number of inter-related strategies. Through regular inspection and surveys, there could at least be an attempt to regulate numbers. Such investigation allowed urban authorities to advance to the second stage: general ordinances promulgated against offending landlords or direct orders to landlords and to inmates to vacate the tenements and the borough or town. One other solution was available only to those urban authorities which had acquired large amounts of urban property: direct prohibition of the fragmentation of some at least of the housing stock.

Surveys

The wardens in York were delegated in 1576 to inspect the housing for the strange poor.[28] From 1586, the corporation of St Albans introduced surveys of wards by nominated aldermen with their constables to root out impoverished newcomers. In 1589, the corporation of Oxford resolved "with all convenient speede" to compile a register of householders and inmates in all the wards. The collection of information was charged to the constables. All those not having residence for three years were to be returned to their place of origin if the mayor and aldermen did not accept them as "fytt inhabytaunts." With the assistance of the register, the exercise was to be repeated annually.[29] Salisbury's concern about strangers resulted in household surveys in 1580 and 1597 and subsequently regulations against undertenants in 1611.[30] At least by 1597, the council of Bristol demanded that churchwardens and constables of parishes conduct weekly surveys–on Thursdays–to list strangers and to report the list to the mayor.[31]

By the end of the 1570s, the mayor of Salisbury assigned named aldermen to address the problem of the overcrowding of the housing stock more specifically:

...shall take vewe of suche howses and dwellinges as are within this cittye And where they shall fynde any howses oppresside with more tenauntes or inhabitantes then are to be thought convenyent in Respecte of the howses not onlye to geve them warninge forth-wyth to provide them selves ells wheare And to have no more tenauntes or Inhabitantes in those howses then shalbe thought mete or appoynted by the persons appoyntede to make <vewe> the said vewe in euerye of the said wardes uppon payne of euerye hedd tenaunt & undertenaunt to Incurre suche punishment and payne as shall followe unto them But also that they do certifye the names of all suche head tenauntes and undertenauntes inhabit-inge within those howses where the same oppression shalbe to the mayor of this cittye wherby he maye with suche other helpe and assistaunce as shalbe requisite take suche further order for the performans of the trewe meanynge of this order that shalbe Convenyent...[32]

Perhaps a decade later, the mayor and corporation of Leicester insti-gated a survey of all inmates inhabiting the borough–their lodging and, where possible, their place of origin and length of inhabiting the bor-ough.[33] Over fifty houses contained suspected inmates. The concern was expressed in some of the entries:

M Moris Harris house Richard flude and his wife and a childe allis Deakin and Kester her husbandes son and catern nele all in one house

Wm More laborer estraunger cam to Leic' iiij yeres past his child dothe begge in the towne

That survey did not, however, resolve the problems of the borough; nor did subsequent action against inmates in the early seventeenth century.[34]

Ordinances and orders

Through the late sixteenth century, numerous boroughs introduced ordinances to prevent the fragmentation and deterioration of the urban building stock through the accommodation of inmates. The issue became manifest by the middle of the sixteenth century. In 1545 the Mayor and his brethren of Guildford determined that

... no landlorde nor tenaunt suffer in any howse of therse any moo
tenauntes in one proper house but only one ... that ys to saye he
shall fyrst take any house within the towne of any owner shalnott
Retayn Reseyve nor by any coller or meanys take in any person or
persons to inhabyte or dwell under hym or them that fyrst shall
take any suche house nott above the space of one night and one
day ...[35]

More pertinently, the strictures of the burgesses of Wakefield in 1556
defined the issue there and in many other expanding, but unincorporated,
boroughs. The burgess court demanded that chief tenants expell "anye
tennants of theire baksydes", the meaning of which referred to the practice of building small cottages at the back of traditional tenements as the
sixteenth century progressed.[36] Another early injunction against providing accommodation for inmates in the backsides of tenements was promulgated in the view of frankpledge for Liverpool in 1562.[37] In 1582, the
corporation of Oxford enunciated that:

all and everie such person or persons as have receaved any coo-
ples undertenant or undertenants commonly called inmakes [sic]
or any others into their dwellinge howse or howses within the
said Citie or liberties theareof, shall avoyd and amove the same
...'[38]

In 1566, a similar admonition was directed by the authority of Maidstone to the lessors of small tenements to eject any tenants who had not
inhabited the borough for three years unless the lessor entered into a
bond for assurance to indemnify the borough against persons becoming
chargeable.[39] Similar measures were invoked by the assembly of Norwich
in December 1600 in injunctions to churchwardens and overseers which
comprised in total eleven articles.[40] Amongst these eleven, article nine was
directed towards maintenance of the urban housing stock.[41]

9 Item you shall give knowledg unto the Inhabitantes of your parishe that whosoeuer shall offende in lettyng thir house or houses
to any Inmates as is aforesaid in the first Article He or she is to
forfite by the Lawes of this Citye for the firsst wieke xxs. And for
euery weke after vs.

At Chester, a few years earlier, the consequences were graphically described within general injunctions in the time of a visitation of "plague"
(1604), as noted above. Five years subsequently the chamber (council) of

the city of Worcester concluded too "that ... there are of late many smale cottages erected and bilded", particularly by Mr. Jennings, but also others, and especially in the Foregate. The landlords, consequently, were ordered to make security for the discharge of the parishes and city and their refusal would incur imprisonment.[42]

In Bristol, the responsibility of enforcement rested with the City's justices, to inhibit the poor's occupation of housing and its dilapidation. They attempted to achieve this end by action against chief tenants. Continuously in the 1620s, the magistrates targeted tenants who provided housing for the poor and compelled them to enter into bonds.[43] Illustrative of one type of obligation is the bond imposed on William Dale:

> The condicion of this present Recognizaunce ys such That whereas Elizabeth streate ys nowe Dwellinge as an <under> tenaunte in a howse of his within the parishe of Redclyffe <y> and hath dyvers other <under> tenauntes <beinge> <straungers> <within this Cyty> yf therefore the above bounden William Dale his heires executours and assignes and euery of them shall & Doe from tyme to tyme & at all tymes hereafter Dischardge and save harmeles the inhabitantes within the said Cytie and all the parishes within the same from the kepinge <and> releyvinge and maynteyninge of the said Elizabeth streate or any other of his said Tenauntes That then &c...[44]

More frequently, however, the chief tenants were ordered to evict the undertenants by a specified, imminent date under pain of a weekly fine. So

> The Court ordereth that Bartholomew Russell Smith shall pay vs. per week to the poore untill he remove undertenauntes beinge al strangers...[45]

and

> The Court order that Alexander Kerswell shall pay xiijs. iiijd. untill he remove his 3 undertenauntes Miles a tailor Thomas Warren & their wives & Welthian a welshwoman in fortnight next...[46]

In 1624 the court decided to introduce a general preventive injunction rather than taking retrospective action against individuals.

> An order in Sessions made that noe Inhabitantes shall receave anie undertenant strangers unles he first give sufficient security

<to> accordinge to law to cleare the parish of the Charg on paine
that every such LandLord for <so> soe receaving into every such
his tenement shall <forfeit for every one> stand asseissed for every
week soe keeping his undertenaunt xijd. and beside to be bound
to free the parish from the Charg at all times after.[47]

Indeed in 1627 Charles Rich was committed to the Bridewell until he removed his undertenant, his wife and four children.[48]

Similarly, the justices of the West Riding in session at Pontefract in
1614 intervened on complaint by some of the inhabitants of Selby who alleged that four or five families of inmates or undertenants occupied some
houses. As a consequence, the better sort deserted the town because of the
high rates. The remedy proposed by the justices was to lay the assessment
on those who received inmates.[49]

Failure to comply with these local ordinances might elsewhere incur
substantial fines. The 1582 injunction at Oxford determined a fine of 10s.
for every month when the ordinance was not observed. The pecuniary
penalty at Norwich was not the final deterrent, for those landlords who
were unable to acquit the fines would be additionally whipped or sent to
the Bridewell. At St Albans the fine imposed was 2s. for every day over six
days that a town-dweller lodged a stranger.[50]

Nevertheless, anxiety about deterioration of the housing stock persisted at Norwich into the middle of the seventeenth century, epitomized
by a motion by Mr. Steward in 1632 demanding regulations for

good governance especially when men dwelling in the Country
doe lett their howses to poore people which are chargeable to the
City.[51]

The alderman rhetorically–but inaccurately–pointed to a divide between urban and rural, but also indicated that authority's control over the
urban environment was limited by property ownership. The anxiety about
strangers and the fragmentation of tenements endured from at least 1584
through to the listings of the urban population in the 1620s and 1630s.[52]

In unincorporated Manchester, recourse was had to the court leet in
1582 to legislate bylaws against the social problems of immigrants. No
inhabitant of the town should provide accommodation for inmates unless
the incomers had dwelt in the town for at least three years. The constables were charged with making monthly inspections.[53] The view of frankpledge too was the forum for promulgation for Stratford-upon-Avon.
Commencing in 1554 with an injunction for all persons having inmates
to evict them, the ordinance against inmates was repeated at every court.

Nevertheless, after the re-imposition of the order in 1556 on pain of 40s., eight inhabitants were presented at the court of April 30, 1557, for harboring inmates.[54]

In Evesham, the fine for unlawfully providing accommodation for inmates was established as high as £5 per month of the offense from 1611. As in the case of Selby, the grievance concentrated on the dissatisfaction of the better sort–their "utter undoinge." The ordinance promulgated in 1611 required all those who had received inmates or had converted barns or outhouses into housing for inmates during the last seven years, to evacuate those sojourners.[55]

A general ordinance was proclaimed by the Assembly of Northampton in 1600 disallowing owners of a messuage or house to add to the building or to build in the garden except for their own use or otherwise to give an assurance that the new building would be occupied by a tenant suitable to be assessed to a subsidy at the rate of 20s. for lands or £3 in goods, on pain for default of £5 for every quarter. The validation of the wealth of the tenant was to be made before two justices of the quorum of the borough. Additionally, the order was confirmed not to receive inmates or undertenants on pain of a fine of £1 per month.[56] It should be remarked, however, that the Assembly had been as diligent some twenty years earlier (1581) in attempting to preclude inmates.

> Forasmoche as of Late yeres Dyverse and sondrye poore householders with ther famylies have Repaire to this towne and byn Indwellers together three or fowre howseholders in one smalle howse or Cotage whereby ther hathe growen Dyverse Enormities MisDemeanors Daungers & inconvenyences to the greate hurte and Slaunder of this towne For Reformacion wherof yt ys ordeyned ... that hensfourthe ther Shalbe but one howseholder in one howse, that ys to saye A man his wyffe and famylie ...[57]

All those who had entered the borough within the last three years were to be evicted and expelled, landlords to be fined 6s. 8d. for every quarter.

Borough property

Whilst local ordinances provided one measure in attempting to maintain the integrity of the urban housing stock, ownership of substantial urban property allowed a tighter control of the borough authority over at least some of the urban environment. The borough authority in Chippenham could thus limit the disastrous consequences for the housing stock by prohibiting the division of tenements which belonged to the borough lands, as enunciated in a decree of 1609 by which any changes to the internal structure of houses had to be registered with the bailiffs. Indeed a survey was conducted into recent structural changes.[58] At least one important lease allowed by the corporation of Southampton in the 1590s contained covenants not to divide the buildings into smaller tenements or to sub-let to several tenants and in 1607 a court of survey was commissioned to survey town lands and compile a new register book.[59]

Indeed, the proper management of burghal property developed into one of the principal responsibilities of councillors. Moreover, administration of property initiated the introduction of a system of committees for specific purposes. At Norwich, the delegated responsibility for administering the property belonged to the chamberlain and "his counsellors" (four named advisers) who were regularly delegated to examine properties before leases were contracted and who were occasionally also commissioned to undertake a more extensive survey when they

> shall peruse and sett downe the couenauntes for all these leassys which wer shewyd furth this <yer> daye

in advance of the next meeting of the assembly.[60]

Whilst some councils managed to achieve a satisfactory supervision of their properties, others were confronted by greater difficulty. Illustrative of the vicissitudes experienced by some urban authorities was the City of Worcester.[61] The chamber addressed the real problem at that time, by issuing an ordinance to prevent the sub-letting of the lower-level tenements to poor immigrants.[62] In the mid 1570s in Salisbury, the two chamberlains and nominated burgesses were ordained a committee to make a general survey of all the lands and produce a new rental.[63] Shortly thereafter (1580), the council resolved to increase the housing stock through its own efforts through the "reedification" of tenements. Twenty plots were identified for rebuilding decayed housing or buildings in disrepair.[64]

Although the view was repeated in 1596, it obviously did not resolve these issues.[65] Seven years later, the council issued another order on September 16 for a full survey of its lands, requiring all lessees to bring their leases to the council house for inspection, the chamberlains to examine the leased lands and tenements before this audit scheduled for October 12.[66] The council further took the position, however, that its own official action could not contain the problem and that every member of the councils should exercise individual vigilance in their localities:

Also at this Assemblye it is ordered and agreed that as manye as be of the number of the .xxiiij.ti shall euerye man seuerallye <and> or Joyntlye in and nere the stretes where they dwell, calle unto them suche of the number of the .xlviij.ti as doo dwell in the same stretes or nerest the same streetes to view and take notice of all newe incommers & straungers contrarye to the lawes and of all base borne Children and disordered houses as Tiplers and suche like as also for the streetes and watercourses which be very noysome And that everye man of this Companye doo returne certificatt and information what they have doen herein to Mr Maior and the Justices by Ashe Wensday next being the ixth of Februarye nexte for the helpe and better gouernment of this Citie...⁶⁷

From August 1619, the council of Cambridge introduced this covenant into its leases: to save the parish harmless from incumbrances caused by reason of any tenant.⁶⁸ More specific detail of those clauses is contained in the lease of a tenement (surprisingly for the longer term of sixty years) in April 1621:

And a provisoe that if any tenaunt be herafter placed in the premises whoe shalbe chargeable to the said parishe [St Andrew's] and that uppon complaynt made unto the mayor by the Churchwardens of the saide parishe noe redresse be had after one monthes warninge then this indenture of Demyse to be voyd.⁶⁹

Corresponding clauses were inserted both to inhibit sub-letting and to prevent the fragmentation of domestic buildings. The intention of one covenant was to prohibit the building of more than one tenement on a traditional plot.⁷⁰ Alternatively, a clause might be inserted to retain the lease in the hands of burgesses–that is, to limit to burgesses any assignments.⁷¹
The most common response, as indicated above, was the general injunction to chief tenants to evict their sub-tenants. The leet court of Salford adopted this remedy on several occasions.⁷² Another frequent injunction inhibited the sub-letting of tenements without the consent of the urban authority, so that the corporation of Thetford in 1578 prohibited any urban inhabitant to lease to any poor person without the approval of the mayor and "most part of" the burgesses.⁷³ Addressing the direct issue–poor strangers–the intermittent–indeed, regular, weekly–survey of newcomers became de rigueur in urban centres. Thus the constables of York were notified to make a return every Thursday of the names of those who came to live in their parishes and those constables who neglected to do so were amerced 1s. "without mitigac[i]on."⁷⁴ There existed then regular strategies

which might be adopted separately or as a battery to address the problem. Furthermore, those issues affected urban places of all sizes–from civic York through expanding Salford to decaying Thetford. Whilst reaction at the lower end of the urban hierarchy might have been imitative, it seems fairly certain that the impact of poor outsiders on the urban environment was a generalized and contentious feature. Confronted with the immense difficulties imposed by their indigenous poor, urban authorities protested their incapacity to cope with those of incoming indigents.[75]

Not everyone of status concurred with this policy of exclusion by pro-hibiting housing to the poor. In a long critique of various Elizabethan leg-islation, Nathaniel Bacon was moved to complain privately:

> The statute also made for the provicion of the poore is greatlie defrawded, and in effect made utterlie voyd, for that the hows-es to sett the poore people in [in] everie limitte are not buylded nor provided according to the statute ... as it nowe standeth the poore are greatlie disapoynted, both of releif and habitacion, and in shorte tyme are lyke to perishe for that verie manye townes doe make bylawes in their lordes courtes that none shall under a great payne take in or house anie ...

concluding:

> The statute agaynst innmates also a verie great ponishment to the poore and great trouble to the townes ...[76]

No doubt Bacon was alluding to the Cottages Acts for the provision of housing for the rural poor, but his remarks were perhaps ill-informed and inappropriate to the urban context. Whilst these two associated issues had an impact in rural townships, their effect in urban places was exacer-bated. Indeed, a fine dividing line was maintained between authorized and unauthorized sojourn, eviction and hospitality, for the urban bailiffs and constables could commandeer lodging for the licensed poor for the night. Fines were imposed on those who refused to provide this hospital-ity for the poor at the constables' request. Indeed, in 1597, the borough au-thority of Chippenham demanded that every tippler within the borough maintain at least one bed to sustain strangers or "wayfareinge" people brought to them by the constables "according to the lawes prescribed & ordered of charyte."[77]

The impact of the migrant poor confronted all authorities with con-stant and contentious dilemmas, practical and moral. Issues of inclusion and exclusion evoked anxious responses. Whilst in the rural context questions of housing caused a politics of the cottage, the politics of the urban environment had wider dimensions. Provision for the poor was only one–if, indeed, an immense–aspect. Urban authorities had also to contend with preserving the dignity of civic stature and status. How was the urban center perceived outside and how did it represent itself to the rest of society, particularly the world of civic and institutional honor? In that ideological context, the fabric of the urban environment was paramount. Civic honor in part derived from urban propriety. To maintain the fabric of the built environment was inter-related with the preservation of the urban civic and social fabric: the politics of the poor were inseparable from the politics of the building process and external politics.

Notes

[1]For geographical considerations of urban spatial differentiation: Roger M. Pritchard, *Housing and the Spatial Structure of the City* (Cambridge: Cambridge University Press, 1976); Richard Dennis, *English Industrial Cities of the Nineteenth Century. A Social Geography* (Cambridge: Cambridge University Press, 1984); for the early-modern period, John (Jack) Langton, "Residential Patterns in Pre-industrial Cities: Some Case Studies from Seventeenth-century Britain," repr. in *The Tudor and Stuart Town. A Reader in English Urban History 1530-1688* ed. Jonathan Barry (Harlow: Longman, 1990), 166-205. Here, however, issue is taken with those cultural geographers who assume a structural approach to the representation of urban space, such as Sibley, *Geographies of Exclusion*, following Douglas, *Purity and Danger*; for how that approach might influence spatial interpretation of the early-modern City: Steven Mullaney, *The Place of the Stage. License, Play, and Power in Renaissance England* (Chicago: Chicago University Press, 1988).

[2]Walter Rye, ed., *Depositions Taken Before the Mayor and Aldermen of Norwich 1549-1567* (Norwich, 1905), 70; see also NNRO NCR Case 12a/1c, fols. 18r-19v which is the full context for this quotation.

[3]Robert Tittler, *The Reformation and the Towns. Politics and Political Culture c.1540-1640* (Oxford: Oxford University Press, 1998); see also Jonathan Barry, "Provincial Town Culture, 1640-1680: Urbane or Civic," in *Interpretation and Cultural History* ed. Joan Pittock and Andrew Wear (Basingstoke: Palgrave, 1991), 198-234.

[4]The most recent interpretation of the general predicament of late-sixteenth-century towns is Paul Slack, *From Reformation to Improvement. Public Welfare in Early Modern England* (Oxford: Oxford University Press, 1999); see also Griffiths, Landers, Pelling, and Tyson, "Population and Disease, Estrangement and Belonging."

[5]Nigel Goose, "Household Size and Structure in Early Stuart Cambridge," *Social History* 5 (1980), 350-1, 357, 379-80 made perceptive comments about the transformation of concerns. See also for here and below, Paul Slack, *Poverty and Policy in Tudor and Stuart England* (London: Longman, 1988), 67-69.

[6]Beier, "The Social Problems of an Elizabethan County Town"; Margaret Pelling, *The Common Lot. Sickness, Medical Occupations and the Urban Poor in Early and*

Modern England (London: Longman, 1998), for Norwich; Jeremy Boulton, "Residential Mobility in Seventeenth-century Southwark," *Urban History Yearbook* (1986): 1-14; Peter Clark, "The Migrant in Kentish Towns, 1580-1640," in *Crisis and Order in English Towns 1500-1700* ed. Clark and Paul Slack (London: Routledge and Kegan Paul, 1972), 117-63..

[7]In general, Beier, *Masterless Men.*

[8]Margaret Grombridge, ed., *A Calendar of the Chester City Council Minutes 1603-1642*, Record Society of Lancashire and Cheshire vol. 106 (Manchester, 1956), 9-10.

[9]See further the complaint that the infection was spread by families living in cellars and rooms in houses and selling ale and beer there: Grombridge, *Calendar of the Chester City Council Minutes*, 20. For repetition of the climate and response when pestilence recurred in 1625, Grombridge, *Calendar of the Chester City Council Minutes*, 134-5.

[10]Grombridge, *Calendar of the Chester City Council Minutes*, 160.

[11]NARO CA1 series. The principal problem is that, because the papers are original bills, they almost consistently lack dating for each presentment, so that the researcher is forced to rely on the outside dates of the sessions roll (usually several months, up to six months) for their chronology. For that reason, tabulating the data becomes an insurmountable problem, resulting here perhaps in excessive citation of examples.

[12]NARO CA1/51b/10 (constables' presentments to the borough justices, October 1589-July 1590).

[13]NARO CA1/52b/14 (April-July 1593).

[14]NARO CA1/53 (1594).

[15]NARO CA1/53 (Houndgate).

[16]NARO CA1/63/48 (October 1610-July 1611).

[17]Constables delinquent in reporting inmates and strangers were summarily treated, as the 20s. fine imposed on Thomas Johnson for his "contempt" in not making the return: Stephen K. Roberts, ed., *Evesham Borough Records of the Seventeenth Century 1605-1687*, Worcestershire Historical Society n.s. vol. 14 (Worcester, 1994), 12 (51).

[18]NARO CA1/51b/22 (October 1589-July 1590).

[19]NARO CA1/65

[20]NARO CA1/65.

[21]NARO CA1/65/65

[22]NARO CA1/66/21.

[23]NARO CA1/69/33.

[24]NARO CA1/69/30.

[25]William H. Stevenson, ed., *Records of the Borough of Nottingham* vol. 4 (Nottingham, 1889), 304-6.

[26]Gibson & Brinkworth, *Banbury Corporation Records*, 38.

[27]Heal, *Hospitality.*

[28]Angelo Raine, ed., *York Civic Records* 7, Yorkshire Archaeological Society Record Series vol. 115 (Leeds, 1949-50), 114; the constables reported to the wardens in normal years the undersettles in their parish: *York Civic Records VIII*, YASRS vol. 119 (Leeds, 1952-3), 134.

[29]Herbert E. Salter, ed., *Oxford Council Acts 1583-1626*, Oxford Historical Society vol. 87 (Oxford, 1928), 32.

[30]Susan J. Wright, "Sojourners and Lodgers in a Provincial Town: The Evidence from Eighteenth-century Ludlow," *Urban History Yearbook* 17 (1990), 20.

[31]Maureen Stanford, ed., *The Ordinances of Bristol 1506-1598*, Bristol Record Society vol. 41 (Bristol, 1990), 101-2.

[32]WSRO G23/1/3, fol. 62r.

[33]ROLLR BRII/12/7/5. For the ordinance behind this survey, Helen Stocks, ed., *Records of the Borough of Leicester* vol. 2 (Cambridge,1923), 156-7.

[34]Stocks, *Records of the Borough of Leicester*, 199-200.

[35]Enid M. Dance, ed., *Guildford Borough Records 1514-1546*, Surrey Record Society vol. 24 (Guildford, 1958), 83.

[36]J. Walker, "The Burges [sic] Courts, Wakefield," in *Miscellanea II*, Yorkshire Archaeological Society Record Series vol. 74 (Leeds, 1929), 22. The same infilling of small cottages at the back of traditional tenements is evident too in the leases of the Church Burgesses in Sheffield: Sheffield Archives Office CB.

[37]Jesse A. Twemlow, ed., *Liverpool Town Books Volume 1 1550-1571* (Liverpool: University of Liverpool, 1918), 193.

[38]William H. Turner, ed., *Selections from the Records of the City of Oxford* ([S.l.] : [s.n.], 1880), 422.

[39]*Records of Maidstone* (Maidstone, 1926), 22 (reiterated in 1586 at p. 29 and in 1608 at p. 65).

[40]NNRO NCR case 16 shelf c no. 5 (assembly minute book, 1585-1613), fols. 244r-245r.

[41]NNRO NCR case 16 shelf c no. 5, fol. 245r.

[42]Sheila Bond, ed., *The Chamber Order Book of Worcester 1602-1650*, Worcestershire Historical Society n.s. vol. 8 (Worcester, 1974), 103.

[43]Bristol Record Office [BRO] JQS/M/2, fols. 22r-24v, 77r, 78r, 86r-v, 127r, 131r-v, 141r.

[44]BRO JQS/M/2, fol. 99r.

[45]BRO JQS/M/2, fol. 22r.

[46]BRO JQS/M/2, fol. 24v.

[47]BRO JQS/M/2, fol. 76v.

[48]BRO JQS/M/2, fol. 141v.

[49]John Lister, ed., *West Riding Sessions Records Volume II*, Yorkshire Archaeological Society Record Series vol. 54 (Leeds, 1915), 13.

[50]A. Gibbs, ed., *The Corporation Records of St Albans* (St Albans, 1890), 73.

[51]Sachse, *Minutes of the Norwich Court of Mayoralty 1632-1635*, 47. On December 5, 1600, the new articles promulgated by the Norwich assembly authorized a new survey of "Inmates or borders" who were immigrants, who were likely to become chargeable to parishes, and who have not dwelt in the City for more than a year: NNRO NCR case 16 shelf c no. 5, fol. 244r. (The variable interpretation of the residential qualification is interesting).

[52]Goose, "Household size and structure," 350-1.

[53]J. Harland, ed., *A Volume of Court Leet Records of the Manor of Manchester in the Sixteenth Century*, Chetham Society (Manchester, 1864), 154.

[54]R. Savage, ed., *Minutes and Accounts of the Corporation of Stratford-upon-Avon Other Records 1553-1620* vol. 1, Dugdale Society (Warwick, 1921), 28, 53, 59-61.

[55]Roberts, *Evesham Borough Records*, 11.

[56]NRO NBR 3/1, pp. 550-1 (paginated).

[57]NRO NBR 3/1, p. 391.

[58]Goldney, *Records of Chippenham*, 36; see also 34.

[59]T. B. James, ed., *The Third Book of Remembrance of Southampton 1514-1602 Volume IV (1590-1602)*, Southampton Record Series vol. 22 (Southampton, 1979), 21 (no. 442); William J. Connor, *The Southampton Mayor's Book 1606-1608*, Southampton Record Series vol. 21 (Southampton, 1978), 74 (129).

[60]NNRO NCR case 16 shelf c no. 5, fol. 20v. For similar activity, fol. 254v.

[61]For the general context of Worcester, Alan Dyer, *The City of Worcester in the Sixteenth Century* (Leicester: Leicester University Press, 1973).

[62]WRO BA 9360/A14 496.5, fol. 88r.: "Item Hit is agreed That no person within this Citie havinge howses or tenementes of the yerely rente of xs and under shall take to their tenauntes any straungers or forren pore Folkes into the same without the assent of the Bailiffes Aldermen and Chamberlaynes for the tyme beinge Apon peyne of xxs For every defaute."

[63]WSRO G23/1/3, fol. 32v. For earlier attempts to reinvigorate the urban environment by the construction of a "'Tenanttable" house on borough property in 1522: Dance, *Guildford Borough Records 1514-1546*, 8.

[64]Details of each plot are listed at WSRO G23/1/3, fols. 62r-v.

[65]WSRO G23/1/3, fol. 150v.

[66]WSRO G23/1/3, fol. 174r.

[67]WSRO G23/1/3, fol. 153v.

[68]Cambridgeshire Record Office [C. R. O.] City Archives Common Day Book 1610-1646, fol. 93r.

[69]C.R.O. City Archives Common Day Book 1610-1646, fol. 105v.

[70]C.R.O. City Archives Common Day Book 1610-1646, fols. 119v, 137r, 147r, 197r, 214v: "not to build or make any more tenementes or dwellinge howses theron uppon payne of forfeiture" (1623);"and that he shall build no more Tenementes then is builded there alreadye" (1626); "with a provisoe not to erect any cottage or dwellinge house upon the premises" (1633).

[71]C.R.O. City Archives Common Day Book 1610-1646, fol. 165r (from 1627).

[72]J. G. de T. Mandley, ed., *The Portmote or Court Leet Records of the Borough or Town and Royal Manor of Salford* vol. II, Chetham Society new ser. vol. 48 (Manchester, 1902), 13, 25, 33.

[73]W. Macray, "The MSS of the Corporation of Thetford," in *Historical Manuscripts Commission Report on MSS in Various Collections* vol. viii (London, 1914), 133.

[74]Deborah Sutton, ed., *York Civic Records 9*, YASRS vol. 138 (Leeds, 1976), 41, 54 (1589).

[75]Staffordshire Record Office D1721/1/4, fol. 158r: an estimate in 1622 of the extent of the problem in Stafford attributed to Thomas Worswick, the Mayor: "The whole number [of inhabitants] 1560/ Whereof the poore are 390."

[76]Victor Morgan, Jane Key and Barry Taylor, eds., *The Papers of Nathaniel Bacon of Stiffkey, vol. 4*, Norfolk Record Society vol. 69 (Norwich, 2000), 35.

[77]Goldney, *Records of Chippenham*, 10.

10
Marginal Geographies:
Poor Single Mothers, 1560-1640[1]

Some migrations

> That hir name ys Alyce Barker And that she confessed to him that
> one Robert East of Howme in Com. Nottingham begott hir with
> chylde otherwyse she cannot tell And that she did not hir penaunce
> that she was enioyned to Doe but instede of hir penaunce Doinge
> she gave to the Towne of Emmeth towards the bringinge up of hir
> chylde xs. And that she ys nowe gon awaye Whether he knoweth
> not.[2]

When Richard Levers of Emneth (just south of Wisbech) appeared to
answer an office cause in the consistory court of Ely why he had harbored
a woman with child, he described the unfortunate consequences which
ensued from the sexual incontinence of Alice Barker, compelled to migrate
from Holme Pierrepont in Nottinghamshire to Emneth and then, desert-
ing her child, to move on again. The explanation by Levers was offered
on the November 7, 1573.[3] Almost six years later to the day, Francis Gib-
bons was summoned to attend the same court with the same allegation.
Although slightly more convoluted in his defense, he recounted a similar
tale of the compulsory migration of a pregnant female.

> that he had suche a one in his house whose name was Elizabeth
> & that he tooke hir at the first to have ben a mayde with whome
> he had covenaunted that she shoulde have ben his mayde ser-
> vant for a yere & when xij or xiij wekes or thereaboute after hir
> first commyng to him yt was evydentlye & playnely seene & perc-
> eyved that she was with childe whereuppon he beinge unwillinge
> to harbore or meynteyne enye suche lewde persone in his howse

put hir awaye & where she is he knoweth not but as he hath hard
she went to Ipswich from whense she came[4]

Women suffered the consequences of their own actions, but also those
of their menfolk. To escape the common fame of their "country", they were
obliged to relocate–sometimes over long distances.[5] Both young women
above journeyed over fifty miles, one substantially more.

That same result was exhibited in the flight of Eleanor Rugg, who,
as a maidservant in Banbury (Oxfordshire) had been made pregnant by
her master's son. Her absconding in 1627 took her to Stow-on-the-Wold
(Gloucestershire), not only outside the peculiar jurisdiction of Banbury,
but also from the archdeaconry and diocese of Oxford and the county.
She probably traveled about twenty miles in her endeavor to remain undetected.[6] Despite movement over such a distance, she could not avoid
presentment in the ecclesiastical court.

Indeed, movement over such long distances *did* occur; flight was not
always confined to the locality. When a certain Ralph of Great Baddow was
corrected for "that he harbored one Alice Wodnett harlott in his howse"
and that she was "by his meanes conveyed awaye unponished", Ralph admitted her presence, but denied he had knowledge that she was a harlot.
It transpired that Alice had exited London to deliver her child. When she
"was broughte abed" in Ralph's house, she was almost thirty miles distant
from the capital.[7]

The experiences of these young women might then be collectively described as uprooted–deracinated–removed from their familiar surround-
ings, compelled to travel, and dependent on their own limited resources
as single persons. Certainly that was one experience of pregnant singlewomen. How individual women survived that experience depended on
their own resolve and internal resource and what succor might be contin-
gently afforded them in the face of institutional conditions which regulated against help.

Contexts

Some recent discussions of the position of early-modern women in
local societies have reflected the variable experiences of women and the
variable impact of patriarchy, according to social status, life-course and
the contingency of time.[8] Others have pointed towards those interstitial
spaces where women could formulate their own social networks.[9] Yet others have attributed to women some, if limited, agency within the ideological structure of patriarchy, indicating how some women might negotiate

their roles.[10] Some recent research has, indeed, attributed to singlewomen a very positive role of practical independence and autonomy in local societies.[11] If, however, we are fully to understand the potential impact of patriarchy, perhaps we should consider the "worst-case scenario", the situation of those women at the bottom of the social and cultural heap.[12] Only by assessing its most extreme impact can it be appreciated how ideology might determine the lives of some women, even if its impact was mitigated in the case of most women through a negotiated experience. The most vulnerable women in local societies were poor, unmarried mothers, most poignantly immediately before, at the point of, and immediately after their coming to term. Patriarchy and parturition combined to impose a truly drastic regime on these pregnant singlewomen, both through the actions of individual men, but also the pervasive influence of patriarchal values through local society, affecting the attitudes of women towards women as well as between the genders.

In 1596, Thomas Campion recounted to the court of the archdeaconry of Colchester that his servant, Mary,

> was begotten with child in his service and unknowen' to hym' she departed ... to his brothers where she was delivered of a child and that one John Campion his <ma> late man servaunt was the father of the same Child as he hath herd yt reported, Denying that sythence she was at any tyme at his house or any Waye Intiynteyned by hym and he saythe that the sayd mary is nowe at Canterburye.[13]

The long-distance migration of this unfortunate young woman was exacerbated by multiple moves enforced by her pregnancy and delivery. Her quitting service was abrupt, according to the male narrative of self-exoneration.

Investigations of early-modern migration have asserted a variety of issues. Predominant aspects of migration have been revealed as the extent of rural-urban movement, and the influence of kin in the initial reception of migrants.[14] In general migration was localized, often within the same *pays* or "country", governed by opportunities for accustomed work, and remaining embedded within a local culture. A considerable amount of movement in early-modern England conformed to and exhibited these characteristics. For the most part, migrants lived in small worlds. For example, marriage horizons were contained.[15] Yet it was not the only experience of migration and movement in early-modern England, for the social, cultural and economic disruption of these times–1540-1640– engendered an underside of long-distance wandering, meandering and traipsing. Moreover, since Ravenstein hazarded his model of patterns and processes of migration, one predicate has persisted that whilst females were more "at risk" of migrating, the distances of their migration were even more circumscribed and that the primary motivation was economic.[16] Historically, the archetypal status associated with this pattern of female migration was employment in servanthood.[17] Unfortunately, many young women were by this means placed in vulnerable positions which resulted in further non-economic migration. In 1617, the servant of John Hardwick of Northampton–later identified as Mary Dickenson–became pregnant by William Dowes the younger. Servanthood had placed her at risk. On the other hand, she was fortunate in returning home to her father in Ravensthorpe (Northants.).[18]

Whilst the migration of the vast proportion of women might have conformed to that idea, some other young women were then susceptible to a very different experience of migration.[19] Their migration–although technically "voluntary"–was tantamount to expulsion from the local society, even from their kinship support. The reason for the office cause against Richard Wymout of Arthingworth (Northants.) in 1617 was allegedly "for suffering Susan his sister to departe awaie from his house being greate with childe before pennance."[20] As well as deprived of her familial support, she was compelled to escape local ignomity both through her daily existence there, her delivery, and the sanction of penance. In such cases of flight before penance, the young woman was frequently chastised in the act book for not performing satisfaction to the congregation, the parishioners. Demonstrative shaming in her local society made it imperative for a young pregnant singlewoman to sacrifice security and migrate into an alien society without the prospect of support.[21]

It is the experience of these unfortunate young women that is examined here, reflecting on the spaces that they inhabited, although, in their single status and pregnancy virtually all spaces were ideologically denied to them. In this sense, they were–at the point of detection of their pregnancy–always out of place. Their commission of sin gave offense to their own host local society to which they could be (partly) reconciled only through penitential submission, often construed as punishment and satisfaction. They thus suffered a level of ostracism. Their reception into other local societies was inhibited by fear of their offspring becoming chargeable to the parish. They became, therefore, women of no place, spatially excluded.

For the most part, the material (below) about these young, placeless women is derived from the ecclesiastical courts of Essex: the archdeaconry court of Colchester and that of Essex. The problems–rhetorical and practical–of this evidence are discussed further below in various places. One deficiency which is not explored is the relationship between jurisdictions–between the ecclesiastical courts and the magistrates, between ecclesiastical sanction and civil punishment. Flight by these women may well have been instigated by fear of secular punishment–whipping in the market place–but it is only in the spiritual forum that we learn much of their predicament in any detail.

How far the two ecclesiastical jurisdictions in Essex represented the dilemma of these women more widely cannot be resolved, except by reference to some evidence from other jurisdictions. Essex had certainly succumbed to "godly" influence, but how far that domination produced a different disciplinary regime in the late sixteenth century is unresolved.[22] The best estimate might be that in Essex the attention given to pregnant singlewomen was highly vigilant, but that these women were perceived to be a "problem" everywhere and some comparisons are made below with what is already known about this "phenomenon" in Wiltshire and Leicestershire.[23] To balance the Essex material further, comparative information is also presented from the correction act books of the diocese of Peterborough and also its constituent archdeaconry of Northampton. The extent of bastardy in this archdeaconry can be illustrated by the presentment of singlewomen with children at the single court of Thursday, November 18, 1596 for the bishop's correction in the eastern deaneries of his diocese, those of Oundle, Weldon, Peterborough and Rutland. Twelve women from eight different parishes were cited for illicit offspring, only one of whom married the father of the child after parturition.[24]

Of course, the proportion of women constrained to take this action was low. In each of the two visitations of the archdeaconry of Northampton in 1590-1593 and 1595, fewer than a handful of such singlewomen were presented for correction.[25] On the other hand, it was a recourse familiar in local society, as is implied by an injunction to the churchwardens of Dodford in 1617 that "they are to Certifie the names of such woemen as have gone away from their parishe unlawfullie begotten with childe ... [and] to make presentment of the said crimes and to perfect their Certificate..."[26] No doubt the archdeacon's official had in mind the presentment of Dorothy Holmes in 1616 "that she was begotten with Childe by William Ives of Bozeat and that she was brought to bed at Turvie in the Countie of Bedford."[27]

Although it might be considered that the performance of penance was hardly a strong motive on the part of the woman for leaving, that explanation was taken seriously by ecclesiastical courts in Essex.[28] When Michael Willowes of Ashdon was cited in 1588 for secretly keeping Nancy Flock in his house whilst she was begotten with child, the condemnation was that he acted "to avoyd her penaunce <of> or punishment wherbye she being sowght for to be cyted to receyve punishment she colde not be mett at all..."[29] Of course, the court's perception of the reasons for evasion might not have coincided with those of the offenders, but this concern of the courts in Essex with the avoidance of punishment was emphatic and is considered further below.

Another discomforting aspect was the haste with which such decisions had to be implemented, so that suspicion was aroused about Elizabeth Hospitall because "she went suddainlie out our towne beinge with Child as the fame goeth."[30] Helen Butcher, a servant in Oxford, vanished in 1584 when she realized she was pregnant, no one allegedly knowing of her destination.[31] No doubt such professed common knowledge, rumor and social criticism precipitated her decision. That local repudiation also affected Elizabeth Cleydon of Byfield since "the common fame went that she was with child before her departure out of the towne by whom we knowe not & whether she is gone we knowe not."[32] In disputing a cause brought against him for harboring an unmarried woman delivered of a child in his house, Thomas Benvowe of West Ham maintained that he had employed one Joan as a servant who had come from East Ham, but she was delivered in his house and "ran awaie in the night time unknowen" to him.[33] When Francis Gallant–perhaps not meeting the expectations of his name–was summoned before the ecclesiastical court, he responded rather disparagingly that Helen Sefford was the name of the "wenche which was begotten with childe", but that she had left his service without his knowledge.[34] After admitting being with child, according to the churchwardens of Barnwell St Andrew in 1597, Margery Figger made flight: "but so sone as it was knowne she Departed away from hir Master Henrie Billington."[35] Whilst such pleadings in ecclesiastical courts involved a rhetoric of male self-justification or -exoneration, some element of fact might have obtained on occasion. Unfortunately, the terseness of the recording in the office act books does not allow penetration through the words portraying mitigating circumstances.[36]

Kinship issues: Complication and complexity

Moreover, the decision to migrate might not have always been entirely that of the young woman. Kin support might be instrumental, but also encourage migration, for whatever reason, presumably to avoid shame on the whole family. Thus, in 1595, when Agnes Smith fell pregnant by an unknown man in adultery, the office cause was introduced against her father, Libeus Smith, for the reasons "that he Alice his wiffe and Henry Smith have conveyed the said Agnes from place to place to the end to Conceale it and to escape punishment and also vehementlie suspected to take money and rewardes to consent to her filthy liffe and to conceale thinges worthy of punishment."[37] Only on rare occasions was the male partner implicated, as when proceedings were initiated against Hugh Gumbrey of Yardley Hastings in Northamptonshire who had illicit sexual relations with his wife before marriage and then took her to Leicester for the delivery.[38]

The demands of kinship were not, however, accepted as reasonable defense by the courts, so that John Dam of Stanford le Hore suffered presentment for harboring in his house Alice Cotton, his sister-in-law, unmarried and delivered of a child in 1590.[39] As with many other men who offended in this way, he was ordered to produce the singlewoman in court for her sentencing. He subsequently returned into court to confess that, despite diligent effort, he had been unable to find Alice. For his failure, he was sentenced to penance in the parish church.[40] Whether through gallantry to protect Alice, obligation to his wife, or genuine inability to discover Alice, he incurred the ritual of humiliation, but mitigated since his confession was to be performed before only the minister and churchwardens, not the entire congregation.[41] John Briant *alias* Dixe was also brought into court for allowing his daughter to depart before doing penance.[42]

Nor was William Donkyn of Eastwood exonerated in 1591 for harboring his daughter when she was pregnant. He explained to the court that she had become pregnant whilst in service in Ashford in Kent, so returned home. Within three days of her return, he was admonished by the constable "to putt her awaye bycause she was suspected to be with child & so he putt her awaye incontinentlye not suspecting untill then that she was with child" whereupon, he reported, she had returned into Kent where she had received punishment.[43] Widow Barnard of Hatfield Peverel was also admonished for harboring her pregnant daughter.[44]

Penance too was imposed on William Vixar of Fyfield for keeping his daughter in his house, unmarried and delivered of a child, and permitting her to leave without punishment. Although he responded with an obvious subterfuge, "that she went awaye withoute his knoweledge...", he was ordered to confess in church "that he hath offended god & the congregation in harbouring his daughter and suffering her to depart unpunished..."[45] Prescient of this attitude of the court, perhaps, Thomas Miller of Barking explained that his wife had received into their house the unmarried, pregnant mother, as she was her sister, "without his consent or privitie and that she departed not beinge delivered..." with the imputation that he had intervened to dissolve the obligation of kinship.[46]

As illustrated above, the involvement of kin might, however, compel the temporary movement of the young female out of the parish to avoid embarrassment, to a place of lying-in. In response to the accusation that he had provided succor to a singlewoman who came to term in his house,

William Rich of Elmstead maintained that the young woman, named Pertree, had been brought to his victualing house by her mother and father from Terling, that she remained there only about four days, that the child died without baptism, and that Pertree reimbursed the costs of the sojourn.[47]

Male imperative to migrate

More despicable, perhaps, was the imputed reaction of Mr. Bellingham who arranged for the conveyance away of the woman of his dalliance in 1584. When an office cause was initiated against John Garratt of St. Mary Magdalen parish in Oxford, John confessed that he had taken Margaret, great with child, to Dumbleton, but he maintained that he did so at the request of Hugh, a servant of Mr. Bellingham. Margaret was brought to John on Botley Hill in the route between Botley and Evesham and Hugh offered John a *douceur* of 40s. to take her to Dumbleton. It transpired that Margaret exclaimed to John that Bellingham was the child's father. Whether she consented or not, Margaret appears more passive rather than an active agent in this transaction.[48]

Men were often instrumental then either in the decision for women to abscond or in arranging their movement. This complicity between men is illustrated by the response of William Matterdye *alias* Pole of Walthamstow to the charge of "harboring of a woman which was in his house Delivered of a child...", for he proclaimed that "at the request of one Mr leacock in southwark he received one Alice her name he knoweth not her husbandes name..." As in many other similar instances, Matterdye was admonished to bring the woman into court to prove whether she was married or not.[49] When he appeared again, Matterdye, without the woman, maintained that "the husband of the said Alice is called John Freesdike about norwiche", from which the court deduced that Alice had conceived the child through fornication.[50] The arrangement between the men thus consisted only of a subterfuge to conceal the illegitimate birth.

Without any ambiguity, Samuel Ramsey was accused "that he hathe conveyed out of the parishe a woman with childe being Late servaunt to Richard Durraunt which woman as the common fame goeth was bigot with childe by the said Ramsey." In fact, it was revealed that Ramsey and the woman, Mary Clarke, had been Durrant's servants.[51] The instrumentality of men in the (compulsory) movement of a singlewoman featured here too. That was not the end of this episode. Shortly thereafter proceeding was initiated against Thomas Fullam of Waltham, cited to bring Mary into court. He responded that "she lyeth in childe bedd in his howse and that his wife receyved her she beinge sicke and all and the nether beinge cold for charitie sake." When further interrogated, however, Fullam confessed that Mary had lain in his house for nine weeks, for only three of which had she been sick, and further that Samuel Ramsey, the presumed father, had promised to pay Fullam 4d. a week for Mary's lodging.[52]

In that particular case, a variety of motives was presented. At one stage, Fullam represented the reception of Mary as charitable hospitality on the part of his wife and himself, but more particularly his wife, implying on the one hand female solidarity, but on the other his own innocence. William Callis of Barking alleged that "unknowen to him, his wife did receive her into his house...", again intimating female support.[53] Occasionally then, the court's attention was directed to women implicated in assisting singlewomen. The official of the archdeacon of Essex admonished John Hamond and his wife for providing hospitality to a pregnant woman.[54] In similar fashion, office causes were brought against Thomas Addam and his wife of Alverley, Thomas Benson and his wife of Wanstead, and Christopher Smythe and his wife, Elizabeth, of West Ham, but the preponderance of respondents were men.[55] At the bottom, then, was an arrangement perpetrated between men.

How that prescriptive movement organized by men might work out was further illustrated by the events surrounding the migration of Mary Kinge of Rochford in Essex. Cited to the court of the archdeaconry of Essex she responded

for that she is with Childe and that she saieth that Richard Peverell of Rochford taylor and a widower is the father therof and that he gave her xijd. after she came last to the towne, and that the said Marrie Dwelt with one John Eve till Michaelmas last and that he the said John Eve late her master receyved her into his howse and hath placed her with one Edward armiger of ortowne promisinge he- him for her howse roome betwixt this and Midsomer next xvjs. and theron hath geven the said Edward Armiger in Earnest xijd.[56]

Michael Pott of Chigwell implicated Mr. Sherburne when he was cited for lodging a woman in his house who was, in the most common euphemism, brought abed. Pott recounted that her name was Elizabeth Jackson, formerly the servant of Mr. Sherburne in Newington, implying Sherburne's role as "he knoweth not whoe was the father therof [of the child] but she was plased thereof by the same Mr Shereborne."[57] Similar details of an arrangement were revealed on the citation of Edward Badcock of Railey in 1589 for conveying away his ~~late~~ mothers late servaunte beinge with child as the common fame is by the said Edward Badcocke and also gave to goodman Phillipson ijs. for her charges and gave her iijs. iiijd. in her purse and so sent her away by George Pannet.[58]

It was revealed, for example, that when Henry Barnard of Rawreth was cited for incontinence with his maid servant, Dorothy Skott, he had removed her from his house to Philip Barnard's at Rainham.[59] On the child-birth of Margaret Orton in his house in Barking, Henry Bennel confessed his involvement in accepting and collecting her for she was the servant of W. Worster in Newgate Market Way where she was made pregnant by Clement Skidmor, nephew of Mr Skidmore in Cheapside.[60] In the case of Beatrice Ford of Rathwinter, begotten with child by John Cocksshott, it was reported that "she is at mistres Threshams of Fambridg and Georg Pawle brought her thither."[61] More serious was the result of the arrangements made in Dodham in 1589, which resulted in the presentment of John Rushebrook. It was reported that a singlewoman had been delivered of a child there, enigmatically "by the Counsell of the sayd John & Robert Rushebrook", the woman departing "secretly away from littell bromly most unnaturallye leaving hir Child behind hir at the Charges of the towne of littell bromly."[62]

The trope of suspicion of male collusion might thus explain the action against Edward Pettet of Layton in 1614 when Ursula Freeman, his niece, was delivered of a child in the house of William Oakman in Chingford. In the citation of him it was alleged "that he knoweth where the said Ursula now Dwelleth and the parties name who is the Father of her Childe and that she was placed in the said Oakman his howse by his meanes."[63] Whether honestly or otherwise, Pettet denied the accusation that he placed her at Oakman's, or that he knew her present whereabouts or the putative father. He and his kinsman, Thomas Freeman, had merely provided kin support in their obligation to save the parish of Chingford harmless for the child. The complaint in the cause, nonetheless, suggests an expectation that men took a very close interest in controlling the lives of pregnant singlewomen.

The convoluted and, frankly, aggressive reaction of some men towards pregnant singlewomen is illustrated by the events apparently surrounding Judith Haswell. She had lived in the service of Mr Bowne, parson, but, when he suspected her to be with child, he arranged that she was "sent awaye in night" with Dick Berkwell, his late servant (now inhabiting Colne) and John Morcott, now the sexton. Immediately afterwards, Bowne raised the hue and cry against Judith, alleging theft of some silver spoons by her. Judith was conveyed to Billericay or Horndon, where she gave birth. Murcott then conveyed Judith to Bungay in Suffolk, "as yt is thought."[64] Here is a detailed instance of the collusion and complicity of men in the compulsory migration of a young female, from place to place and out of the jurisdiction.

What is interesting about many of these narratives is that they were pronounced by males to implicate other men. Such was the case too when office proceedings were brought in the archdeaconry court of Colchester against William Barry of Saffron Walden in the early 1580s. On his citation because Elizabeth Smythe, his late servant, had become pregnant whilst in his house, he responded that she had been brought to him a year ago at Candlemas by Thomas Harrison of the same place "who gave his worde for hir that she was honest." On perceiving shortly afterwards, however, that she was with child, he interrogated her and she accused one Robert Frenche, a scholar who boarded there, to be the child's father, whereupon Barry delivered her back to Harrison–presumably for her breach of integrity for which he had vouched–and he "carried her away whether he knowethe not."[65] As in this case, for the most part these responses were propagated by males who revealed the collusion between men in arranging the fates of young, unmarried pregnant women.

Male involvement then usually entailed assisting or enforcing the migration of the female, receiving the female into a new location, often for a pecuniary benefit, and dispatching the young woman on her way after delivery. For whatever reason, for example, even the incumbent of Gainford facilitated in 1586 the sending away of a pregnant "wench", providing her with his own horse–although, indeed, this Sir Ralph Smith was presented by the churchwardens for other alleged dereliction.[66]

Penance/punishment and satisfaction

Sadly, movement did not evade detection and presentment, but perhaps made the humiliation less intolerable since it was in the face of strangers. Thus, Isabel Sare was presented at Grendon "that she came out of Bedfordshire with child begott in fornicacion as the fame goeth & is at the howse of one John Byas."[67] It was almost impossible to escape reputation, since a woman alone expecting a child was directly associated with illegal sexual intercourse. Better, however, to suffer retribution before strangers in a foreign parish than one's own.[68] (Also demonstrated by Isabel's movement is the intention to evade jurisdiction: in her case from both the archdeaconry and the county of Bedford).

The tenor of the court's concern is illustrated by the language deployed in the accusation against William Goodwin of West Mersey not only for harboring a woman in his house who was delivered of a child, but she "did departe & made no satisfaction to the Congregation", as a result of which William was ordered to undergo public penance.[69] The court at least envisioned that this form of punishment would not be experienced lightly and some of the unmarried mothers may well have shared that perception.

Now, Robert Peace was enjoined by the archdeaconry court to bring Elizabeth Byrch into church on the next Sunday at morning prayer for her shaming. A principal objective of the archdeaconry court of Essex was to ensure the punishment of the female offender. In the four cases of single-women who escaped the court's reach in the act book of 1573-1575, the final complaint was that "[she] went a waie unponished" or "for that he conveied her away without punishment."[70] The avoidance of humiliation by the mother was the constant refrain of the courts: "for that one Catherine Massie was Delivered of a Childe begotten of her body in fornicacion and was by them harbored conveyed awaye and the Childe christened before she the said Catherine was punished"; Henry Higlett of Rettenden was presented for harboring an unmarried woman delivered of a child "and gone awaie without ponishment" and the cause against Richard White at the same time and of the same parish also concentrated on the fact that the woman brought abed in his house "has gone without punishment"; John Tanner's offense was to allow Lucy Noke to be begotten with child in his house in Great Waltham and not to prevent her departing without punishment; the cause against William Hutt of Malden emphasized "Detected for sufferinge of his woman servant beinge with childe to goe awaie without punishment"; Thomas Addam and his wife in Alverley were "Detected for kepeinge evell rule in ~~his~~ theire howse in receyvinge a suspected woman into there howse whoe was delivered there of a childe and suffered her to departe and not ponished"; and William Glascocke of Daubeney "that he had a maide which was begotten with childe in his howse and is gon and conveyed awaie from him without punishment" in 1584.[71] In 1588 Richard Turner of Audley End was cited for sending away unpunished a maid begotten with child in his house.[72] Six years later, Robert Griggs was arraigned for allowing Elizabeth Nelson, delivered of an illegitimate child, to abscond without performing penance.[73] When, moreover, John Marshe was presented, his error had been to allow his maid servant to leave "without satisfaccion to the Congregacion", a more emphatic description of the act required.[74] The churchwardens of Wing (Rutland) expressed their real concern when presenting in 1597 that Joan Singer had had a base child "and is unpunished to there knowledg."[75]

Female tactics

Recalcitrance and obstinacy in the face of local condemnation were rare. Catherine Allen of Blatherwick who was pregnant by an unknown partner in sin, already had a reputation for being obstreperous as a slanderous person, reportedly "& maketh no accompt what she saieth because she saieth she hath nothinge to loose but a boy."[76] On the other hand, the sympathy of neighbors could be aroused by a distressed, solicitous young mother. Having engaged Janet Spence as his servant over a year, Robert Warde disposed of her service and evicted her from his house in Hurworth when she became pregnant, although Janet consistently maintained he was the father of her child. Although she initially departed from Hurworth, she returned near term and lodged, sitting and crying, at his door. Some of the wives took pity on her and, at the instance of the incumbent, Sir George Taylyer, took her inside for the delivery.[77]

Indignant mothers might support their daughter's cause more than the daughter. So in 1628 Widow Saunders was excommunicated in the peculiar court of Banbury for bringing her daughter's bastard child into the church during divine service to "trouble" the congregation. In this case, we are probably witnessing the subversive action and resistance of the poorer "sort" within a local society, for her sentence defined her as "pauper".[78] When Thomas Hakins of Hornby protested that "he cannot compell her to com to the Court to receave such punishment as by lawe she deservethe", he was ordered to bring the dissident young woman to the next court at Brentwood.[79] In like manner, Cornelius van Lewthen complained "that he hath don his indevor to bring her the said Joane into this Couort to receave suche punishment as by the same shalbe imposed upon her for the offence but he cannot bring her as yet..."[80]

Superficially, some women seemed able to take advantage of some situations, if testimony and depositions can be accepted as representing some material evidence. When she discovered she was pregnant, Alice Stidman departed from her service position in Norwich, traveled to Yarmouth, then Lowestoft, and finally to London, after brief sojourns in each place. Arthur Amys, of Norwich, deposed that he encountered her at Doggs Head where they drank together. She was well appareled and had 30s. in coin. Asked by Amys if the child was Mr Towne's, she allegedly responded: "naye, yt was one worth xx of Towne"–Master Button's. Moreover, according to Amys, she maintained "that she coulde want no moneys."[81]

Harboring: compassion or commerce?

When exiled, the young women managed to procure lodging, some-times as a genuine servant until their position became visible, or collu-sively as a pretended servant. So in 1575, Richard Skoott of Chingford was brought before the archdeaconry court of Essex because he had enter-tained a singlewoman in his house as his servant who was brought "abed" in his service.[82] Attempting ingenuity first, William Peace was compelled to admit the real basis on which he had taken in Elizabeth Byrch:

> that the same Eliz. was browght a bed in his howse but when she came First to his howse he thoughte that she was a married wieff but before she was browghte a bedd understood she was unmar-ried and there was one Robert Yreland Did ly ij nightes in his howse which Robert Did saie that he was the father of her Child and he confessed that he was paid for the kepinge of her.[83]

The implication is that in many cases, the domicile was arranged by the men involved who paid compensation to the host.

Suspicion: Implications for women

Wider imprecations followed, for all women. The detection of pregnant singlewomen had collateral consequences. All women out of place and pregnant fell under suspicion. Married women were thus brought into contact with the court to certify their marriages. Whilst some men no doubt genuinely believed they were providing succor for married women, this ambiguity about status also allowed an argument for mitigation: the man's *belief* that the woman was married.[84] When the churchwardens pre-sented Henry Perciman of West Ham in 1577 for receiving a woman who was brought abed in his house and "it is not knowne that she was lawfully maried or not", he retorted that she was "the lawful wif of John Moore & [he] was lawfully maried to her in Westham Church..."[85]

Of course, the question of marriage was compounded by the instabil-ity of marriage formation at this time.[86] William Weytherel of Chadwell, when examined, admitted that he had received Elizabeth Rainschcroft into his house when she was made pregnant by John Bouldrove of Lon-don, as alleged by Elizabeth to him. He continued that Elizabeth had con-firmed that she was betrothed to John and they were to be married in the near future. For that explanation, Weytherel was absolved, but Elizabeth, although unable to attend the court because of sickness, was ordered to perform penance in the parish church of Chadwell.[87]

Suspected by the churchwardens, Elizabeth Pangham *alias* Jones, resident in the house of Edward Vaughan of Bucking, was the reason Edward was subjected to a citation in 1586. She was perceived to be unmarried, but pregnant. On Edward's behalf James Vaughan explained in court that Elizabeth had been married two years previously in Develing to Robert Jones, now in service with Sydney in Flanders. Since the court recognized Mr. James Vaughan "is reputed and taken to be an honest gentleman", the cause against Edward was dismissed.[88] What is evident, however, is how any woman out of place and pregnant might fall under mistrust of being a singlewoman with a bastard child.

That suspicion fell in 1587 upon Elizabeth Willson, whom John Atkynson of Barking was accused of harboring when she was brought abed in his house and then allowed to depart unpunished. Responding, John alleged that she was the lawful wife of Christopher Willson, that she came by chance to his house in labor and was churched in his house, all of which was accepted when Christopher brought into court a certificate of the marriage.[89]

Accused of the same complicity in 1579, Roger Thompson of Hornchurch responded to the charge that it was not known "whether she be married or not", that the woman who was "great with child" in his house was in fact "a married wife", the wife of William Thompson, his kinsman, conjoined with William since last Michaelmas, but William "is nowe in the North countrye and is not able to kepe house as yet and for kindred sacke sake consideringe their povertie he suffereth them to remaine in his house until she is delivered..."[90]

In 1591 Edward Benbricke of West Ham offered a complicated defense to the official of the archdeacon of Essex. He had indeed entertained a pregnant woman, but this Martha Thompson was the widow of Phoenix Thompson of Rochford who died about last Christmas and his widow carried his child. At the request of John Johnson of Bow, Edward's brother-in-law, because Edward maintained a victualing house and "onely upon compassion that he bare to the estate of the poore woman", Edward received Martha who came "very bare and was very neare her delivery." As part of this arrangement, Martha had promised to pay 6d. a week for room, which she honored in part before her departure. Edward only accepted her into his house upon receipt of a certificate from the parish of Rochford that she was indeed a married woman. During her sojourn of eight weeks, she was delivered of her child and gave thanks for her delivery and had her child baptized before she departed. The cause was accordingly dismissed.[91] The office cause against Elizabeth Boylane, resident then in Great Burstead, occasioned a similar response, although she was ordered to produce proof of her defense "that she was married to one

Mr Fox in Studborow in Suffolke and that the childe whereof she was Delivered was begotten and borne in Lawfull matrimonye and that her husband Departed this life iij wieckes before St James tyde laste."[92]

Another consequence then entailed the suspicion of any woman on her own. Setting aside any rhetorical self-justification, the response of William Mootham might illustrate this misunderstanding. He maintained that he and his wife had provided hospitality for Rose for only one night and that Rose was now a servant to the Lady Morris's daughter in Ireland. Moreover, he specified, "she ys not with Child neyther ever had anye child butt is a trewe mayden and so accompted and [he] promised to bring the sayd Rose ad iudicium so soone as she cometh home to hir mother or to hir husboundes howse..."[93] Allowing the accuracy of the basic elements of his statement, not only was his position impugned, but the sexual honesty of a woman was placed in doubt not by defamation, but by the church-wardens and the court.[94]

As the intensity of anguish increased during the 1590s, another conse-quence was the tendency to label unmarried mothers as sexually deviant. In the office cause against Laurence Arnold for allowing his two servants to live incontinently, but more importantly to depart, the woman involved, begotten with child, was described as Grace Arnolde "the harlott". Grace, expelled, sought refuge with her brother Arnold in Ardley and then drift-ed into Colchester.[95] The court subsequently arraigned Robert Arnold and Nicholas Arnold of Ardley for receiving "and hyding" their sister, Grace Arnold, a harlot begotten with child.[96]

Male self-exoneration

Men drawn into court thus had an explanation at hand. In 1588 Robert Ruicke of Woodford, presented for permitting Katherine Archdaile to be delivered of a child in his house when unmarried, claimed that she was indeed married.[97] Rather lamely, perhaps, Thomas Hall of Chigwell, when accused of harboring a suspect woman who was delivered of a child in his house, proclaimed: "he thinketh [she] is a maried wife"; not unrea-sonably, he was ordered to prove his allegation.[98] Perspicaciously, Richard Sell of Barking in 1587 combined this defense with a demonstration of contrition before the court. He allowed Dorothy Kyndersley *alias* Gellie hospitality in his house where her child was born. According to Richard, she had affirmed to him that she was the wife of John Kyndersley "and for that she was a maried wife he was content to let hir be churched in the howse she beinge verie weake..." When interrogated further, he re-sponded "but whether the same Dorothie was a maried woman or no he canne tell but by the report of hir..." Judiciously, he appealed to the clemency of the court "...for his owne parte he is sorie that he haithe offended the lawe in takinge any suche person into his howse..."[99] John Bateman of Rainham relied on this defense, "[she] said that she was maried to a prentyse...", but he also presented himself as innocent "that he kepeth a vitailinge howse besides the ferry at Rainham and that the said Margarett came to his howse late in the Evening ~~& so as~~ as a guest & she was delivered the next daye ..."[100]

On the other hand, this explanation was undoubtedly a subterfuge in many cases, one which did not escape the court's vigilance. Thomas Johnson, victualer, and his wife, Joan, of Great Chesterford, were admonished

for recyving and howsing of suspected persons in their howse as ij strangers which were single persons and named them selves man and wyfe dyd Lye in naked bed to gethers manye nightes they knowing that the sayd Straungers were not married...[101]

A different reaction concerned protecting a male servant, so that John Watson of Little Waltham was proceeded against for "that he perswaded Margery Carter to burden some other man then his servante to be the father of her Child", but further conveyed away his man without punishment (that is, sentence and penance).[102] In like manner, William Grimes of Wormingford was cited to appear in 1588 for conveying away his son, William, to avoid punishment for getting their maid with child.[103] Whilst such instances of male protection of males through their removal crept into the ecclesiastical office act books, they remained infrequent by comparison with the number of occasions when men colluded to remove females.

In one of those few cases where women were involved in the harboring of singlewomen, Eleanor Gwin was accused of being a baud to her daughter and "that she hathe receyved and comforted her daughter in her sayd whoredome." Explaining that her daughter had had an illegitimate child, Eleanor was ordered not to allow her daughter to go "owt of the Contrye" unpunished.[104] When Susan Lyvvice of Elmstead was also presented, the accusation elucidated "for retayning a harlot in hir house", delivered of a child and departed.[105]

Another result was to complicate the lives of a few men, even those of some status. So it eventuated that Mr. Bartholomew Brock, late of Holy Trinity, Colchester, was summoned to explain the position of Catherine, a pregnant woman. He responded that she "was never his servaunt but that she was hyrd by his Late wyfe to watche hir in hir sicknes by the space of v weekes or there boutes..." During that time, she had resided at the house of Edmund Greene, tailor, in St. Peter's parish, where she had been made pregnant by a fellow who dwelt at Greene's, from whence she departed about Easter.[106]

Eloquent, tragic, and sadly romantic testimony was divulged in the experience of Joan Weekes of Wootton Bassett (Wiltshire) in the office cause initiated against her in the archdeaconry court of Wiltshire in the summer of 1601.[107]

> that she was maried about xiiij yeares agon unto one Griffin Davis a Welcheman & lived with him in St Mellens neere Cardiff in Wales until about 3 yeares past that she was brought out of Wales home to Wotton Basset by force of the Statute in that case provided by cause that her said husband havinge killed a man was enforced to leave her and his countrie insomuch that she sawe him not from that tyme which is for 7 yeares past until the Thursday in the Whitson weeke last past was xij monethes at what tyme she saith he her husband came to Wotton unto her in secret suite and laie with her that night & did then beget her with child & the next morneinge befor daie departed from her but where he is she yet knowth not ... And that she was delivered of that child the friday befor Shrove Sonday last & that no man man [sic] living ever had any carnall knowledge of her body but her said husband[108]

Confusion too resulted then in the prolonged harassment of women and men who provided shelter. It was purported in court that William Hayword of Chagwell had provided hospitality for an unmarried mother whose pregnancy came to term in his house "without lawful warrant", but William was able to respond that he had accepted her into his house "by the appointment and consent" of a named JP.[109] The detection brought against John Clemente of Duddinghurst for sheltering a woman brought abed in his house was nullified when he explained that he had been requested to take her in by the high constable and his neighbors.[110] On the other hand, John Darbye of South Beanfield was probably foolish, even reckless, for giving hospitality to a woman (Margaret) brought abed in his house in 1563 "& he being a swoorne man", compounded by his failure to present her and she remaining unpunished.[111] Perhaps Thomas Briges exhibited equal dereliction for his housing Agnes Barret who was made pregnant by "the party" who "usiethe to come to the saide Barret and that he herd of her evill lyvinge before she came to his hous."[112]

Concluding remarks

Although complicit arrangements between men explained a large number of these receptions of pregnant singlewomen, other motives existed: kinship and compassion–if the responses in court can be accepted as having some fact within their narrative rhetoric. The imputation of (occasional) female solidarity has been mentioned above. The reciprocity required of kinship also informed decisions.

Although the singlewomen received the greatest disadvantage from their pregnancies, the men implicated did not always escape the consequences of their own actions. Male protection of males mitigated the impact on alleged fathers, but did not allow complete immunity. Secondly, males who provided hospitality for pregnant singlewomen paid a price, even if they argued that their actions were promoted by compassion or the demands of kinship. When Francis Nox was suspected of incontinent living, his father, William of Bromfield, conveyed him away to evade punishment, to Maldon.[113] The attempt to avoid sentence of penance was not only unsuccessful, but had enforced migration of the young man.

On the detection of Christopher Smythe and his wife, Elizabeth, of the notorious West Ham, he was not only inducted into the ecclesiastical forum, but also punished by the JPs. The two of them

> did receive a woman with a childe upon Christenmas daie last paste called Marie Veall and remained theire until New yeares daie with a man lieinge in the howse suspiciouslye and the band and the hatt of the said man was found in the foresaid woman hir chamber suspiciouslie And also the foresaid Smythe received a woman into his howse beinge great with childe the morerowe after new yeares daie and remained there aboute vj or vij daies untill such tyme as the Constable broughte him befor the Justices and banished the towne of the woman and laid the said Smythe bie his feete [in the stocks].[114]

For his confession to conveying away an unmarried woman who had been delivered of a child before she had performed penance, John Burton of Hornchurch was excommunicated.[115]

In terms of the geography of forced, female migration, although long-distance movement was occasionally manifest–to remove oneself completely from the gaze of local society–short-distance movement was important at the boundaries of jurisdictions. Paramount in the intentions of these young women was to escape jurisdictions–whether civil or ecclesiastical. One particular space inhabited by these women was the immediate hinterland of London–to avoid detection by the City authorities. The preponderance of office causes about these young women in the archdeaconry of Essex thus congregated in the south of the county, adjacent to the City. West Ham in particular constituted a refuge for them. In the north of Essex, although fewer women were involved, transfer across the boundary between the counties of East Anglia remained an important feature, so that, for example, Agnes Rayner of Frinton was accused of receiving a woman who "came owte of Norfolke or Suffolke", lately delivered of a child, the father unknown.[116]

The sometimes tragic circumstances of young, poor, pregnant women is perhaps encapsulated by the predicament of Anne Pollard. According to the response of Robert Browne, accused in 1595 of housing her and allowing her departure, she remained with him only four or five days. She had, he maintained, been delivered of her child a fortnight before arriving with him, in East Street in St. James' parish, the child dying without baptism. He finally reported that Anne was now engaged as a servant to Mr. Maior in Sudbury in his household.[117] The illicit liaison of Anne and her pregnancy had compelled her continuous migration over a period of time, culminating in a movement to another county and ecclesiastical jurisdiction.

Men of status took advantage of poor servant girls, as Middleton denounced:

> *Sordido* Troth I think, master, if the truth were known,
> You never shot at any but the kitchen-wench,
> And that was a she-woodcock, a mere innocent,
> That was oft lost and cried, at eight and twenty.[118]

In those circumstances, men of superior status were often implicated in compelling the migration of poor pregnant women, arranging the details of the movement. As frequently, the encounter which caused the pregnancy was between equals, in which some of the women migrated to avoid humiliation. Some of the culpable men were protected by other males. Some men departed, but others considered the punishment and the event not inconsistent with their notion of masculinity, it would seem.[119] We should also note, however, that these unfortunate young women were, by and large, abandoned by their gender, apparently shunned–except in a few recorded examples of generosity and empathy–by other women, presumably under the pressures of a patriarchal society.[120]

Explanations of the movement of these young, uprooted singlewomen are complicated. Their circumstances accord with the "politics of uncertainty". Those with resources pushed responsibility onto those without the means to withstand disadvantage: "a process which is fundamental to the management of uncertainty: the use of power and resources to displace the costs of uncertainties onto others weaker than oneself."[121] In other words, some men tried to absolve themselves of the uncertainty of an illegitimate pregnancy by using their resources to pass that uncertainty onto the young pregnant women. The "politics of uncertainty" thus corresponded with the politics of gender. Despite the facts that some young men became embroiled in the circumstances and some young women could take (limited) advantage of their situation, the principal casualties of the "politics of uncertainty" were the young women.

Appendix

Penance imposed on Susan Willson of West Ham for an illicit pregnancy.

ERO D/AEA 25, fol. 361r-v (1611)

On the Tuesday of Easter week before the beginning of morning prayer in the vestry of the parish church before the vicar, Mr Jeninges, and the churchwardens: "humblye and penitentlie upon her knees confesse her said fault scilicet for beinge begotten with Childe in fornicacion by the said John Cam and she the said Suzan Willson shall then and there aske allmightie god and all others whom she hath offended by her evill example hartelye (*sic*) forgivnes and she shall further intreat the said Mr Jeninges and the said Churchwardens to praye with her unto allmightie god that it wold please him of his great mercie to pardon and forgive her the same offence and to graunt unto her his grace that she never fall into the like sinne again"

Notes

[1]For the circumstances of pregnancy, see now Gowing, *Common Bodies*, 111-48. For the contexts of single women, Judith Bennett and Amy Froide, eds., *Singlewomen in the European Past 1250-1800* (Chicago: University of Chicago Press, 1999).

[2]CUL EDR D2/9a, fol. 71r.

[3]Material from the diocese of Ely has been exploited in a wider context by Adair, *Courtship, Illegitimacy and Marriage in Early Modern England*, in which he alludes also (pp. 84-86) to the migration of pregnant women.

[4]CUL EDR D2/10, fol. 197v.

[5]Whyte, *Migration and Society in Britain*, 52-53 makes this assertion.

[6]Edwin R. C. Brinkworth [and R. K. Gilkes], eds., *The 'Bawdy Court' of Banbury:*

the Act Book of the Peculiar Court of Banbury, Oxfordshire and Northamptonshire 1625-1638, Banbury Historical Society vol. 26 (Banbury, 1997), 82.

[7]ERO D/AEA 8, fol. 89r.

[8]Anthony Fletcher, *Gender, Sex and Subordination in England 1500-1800* (New Haven and London: Yale University Press, 1995).

[9]Capp, *When Gossips Meet.*

[10]Mendelson and Crawford, *Women in Early Modern England.* What is meant by agency, of course, remains an open question, in relation to structures, ideologies, discourses, and within structuration theory and *habitus*; in general, now, Barry Barnes, *Understanding Agency. Social Theory and Responsible Action* (London, Routledge, 2000); Parker, *Structuration.*

[11]Amy Froide, *Never Married. Singlewomen in Early Modern England* (Oxford: Oxford University Press, 2005).

[12]For an epistemological approach which emphasizes the persistent formative impact of patriarchy, Judith M. Bennett, "Feminism and History," *Gender and History* 1 (1989): 251-72.

[13]ERO D/ACA 22, fol. 230r.

[14]Clark and Souden, "Introduction" in *Migration and Society in Early Modern England*, 11-48.

[15]Diana O'Hara, *Courtship and Constraint. Rethinking the Making of Marriage in Tudor England* (Manchester: Manchester University Press, 2000), 122-57.

[16]D. B. Grigg, "E. G. Ravenstein and the 'Laws of Migration'" in *Time, Family and Community. Perspectives on Family and Community History* ed. Michael Drake (Oxford: Open University Press, 1994), 147-64.

[17]Goldberg, *Women, Work and Life Cycle in a Medieval Economy.*

[18]NRO Peterborough Diocesan Records (PDR) archdeaconry correction book, 1610-1618, p. 316.

[19]For pregnant young women who became vagrants, Beier, *Masterless Men*, 53-54.

[20]NRO PDR archdeaconry correction book, 1610-1618, p. 280 (and again in 1617–p. 313).

[21]On the other hand, there were consequences for not performing penance: the vicar of Cressing refused to church Thomasine Stookes because she did not have a certificate of penance performed, although he was presented for this refusal: ERO D/ACA 18, fol. 202v. For penance and its context generally, Ingram, *Church Courts, Sex and Marriage in England.*.

[22]Compare Keith Wrightson and David Levine, *Poverty and Piety in an English Village. Terling, 1525-1700*, 2nd edn. (Oxford: Oxford University Press, 1995, including the Postscript by Wrightson) with McIntosh, *Controlling Misbehavior in England.* Specifically for Essex, Higgs, *Godliness and Governance in Tudor Colchester*; Byford, "The Price of Protestantism"; Hunt, *The Puritan Movement.*

[23]Richard H. Helmholz, "Harboring Sexual Offenders: Ecclesiastical Courts and Controlling Misbehavior," *Journal of British Studies*, 37 (1998): 258-68, confirms also that the harboring of sexual delinquents and their prosecution was not a "new" action associated with the "godly" of the late sixteenth century. His paper explores the whole range of sexual delinquency (for example, bawds and prostitutes), not just pregnant singlewomen.

[24]NRO PDR Episcopal Correction Book X611/28, fol. 55r.

[25]NRO PDR X610/24 and X610/27. To add to the other causes noted in the text, Agnes Stockwell "as the fame goeth was gotten with child in her mothers howse by whom we knowe not, she is gone out of the towne." (X610/24, fol. 120r).

[26]NRO PDR archdeaconry correction book, 1610-1618, p. 159.

[27]NRO PDR archdeaconry correction book, 1610-1618, p. 110.

[28]Ingram, *Church Courts, Sex and Marriage*, 290-1. For a rather bleak dramatization of the compromising of moral obligations towards sexuality in the early seventeenth century, Thomas Middleton, *Women Beware Women* ed. James R. Mulryne (Manchester: Manchester University Press, 1975, repr. 1988), and the editor's comments at pp. liv-lvii.

[29]ERO D/ACA 15, fol. 35v.

[30]NRO PDR archdeaconry correction book, 1610-1618, p. 146.

[31]Brinkworth, *The Archdeacon's Court. Liber Actorum, 1584*, vol. 1, 70.

[32]NRO PDR X610/24.

[33]ERO D/AEA 14, fol. 218r.

[34]ERO D/ACA 18, fol. 81r.

[35]NRO PDR X611/29, fols. 26r, 34r, 40v.

[36]Laura Gowing, *Domestic Dangers. Women, Words, and Sex in Early Modern London* (Oxford: Oxford University Press, 1996), 232-62. Although Gowing's causes were instance, the same tropes and tactics probably obtained in office causes.

[37]NRO PDR X610/27, fol. 47v.

[38]NRO PDR X610/27, fol. 62r.

[39]ERO D/AEA 14 fol. 39v.

[40]ERO D/AEA 14, fol. 74r.

[41]The rhetoric of outrage was directed against Henry Oldefellde, bellfounder, of Long Row in Nottingham in 1575 for "mayntynynge A Dowghtar of his as A common hore or strumpett within his Dwellinge howse which Dowghter is well knowne at this present tyme to be with childe which is bothe odius unto god & his people of this towne": NARO CA1/49, m. 8.

[42]ERO D/ACA 21, fol. 253v (1596).

[43]ERO D/AEA 15, fol. 55r.

[44]ERO D/ACA 27, fol. 196v (1605).

[45]ERO D/AEA 17, fol. 253 (loose leaf).

[46]ERO D/AEA 26, fol. 61r (1611).

[47]ERO D/ACA 24, fol. 388v. See also D/ACA 25, fol. 169v, apparently constituting another instance of a father taking his daughter from Terling to Rich's house in 1602.

[48]Brinkworth, *The Archdeacon's Court. Liber Actorum, 1584*, vol. 2, 167.

[49]ERO D/AEA 18, fol. 189r.

[50]ERO D/AEA 18, fol. 282r.

[51]ERO D/AEA 22, fol. 247r.

[52]ERO D/AEA 22, fol. 286v.

[53]ERO D/AEA 17, fol. 147r (1596).

[54]ERO D/AEA 22, fol. 217r (1604).

[55]ERO D/AEA 12, fol. 65v; 13, fol. 184r (1578); 14, fol. 22r.

[56]ERO D/AEA 23, fol. 306r.

[57]ERO D/AEA 10, fol. 85r.

[58]ERO D/AEA 14, fol. 101v.

[59]ERO D/AEA 17, fol. 158r.

[60]ERO D/AEA 10, fol. 44r.

[61]ERO D/ACA 15, fol. 35v (1588).

[62]ERO D/ACA 18, fol. 35r.

[63]ERO D/AEA 27, fol. 147v.

[64]ERO D/ACA 24, fol. 323r.

[65]ERO D/ACA 13, fol. 48v.

[66]James Raine, ed., *The Injunctions and other Ecclesiastical Proceedings of Richard Barnes, Bishop of Durham, from 1575 to 1587*, SS vol. 22 (1850), 131.

[67]NRO PDR X610/24, fol. 114v.

[68]For an example of penance imposed, see the Appendix.

[69]ERO D/ACA 21, fol. 288v. (1594); D/ACA 27, fol. 183v ("satisfaction to the Congregation").

[70]ERO D/AEA 8, fols. 89r, 189r, 283r.

[71]ERO D/AEA 12, fols. 80r, 95r, 202r, 265r; 14, fol. 22r; 22, fol. 217r (1604); D/ACA 27, fol. 196v (1605).

[72]ERO D/ACA 15, fol. 57r. For other examples from the numerous instances, D/ACA 18, fol. 212v (Agnes Filde of Cressing left without performing penance having had a base child); D/ACA 20, fol. 292r (Thomas Kinge of Great Tootham presented for allowing his maid, having had a child, to depart without punishment); D/ACA 24, fol. 1r (John Hopkins allowed a young woman delivered of a child in his house to depart within a month of her delivery without doing any penance, 1595).

[73]ERO D/ACA 21, fol. 325v.

[74]ERO D/ACA 25, fol. 74v.

[75]NRO PDR X611/29, fol. 12r.

[76]NRO PDR X610/24, fol. 121r.

[77]Raine, *Depositions and other Ecclesiastical Proceedings from the Courts of Durham*, 302-4 (cccxix).

[78]Brinkworth, *'Bawdy Court' of Banbury*, 92, 105, 111, 117. Wrightson, "'Sorts of People' in Tudor and Stuart England."

[79]ERO D/AEA 16, fol. 40r.

[80]ERO D/AEA 16, fol. 72r.

[81]NNRO NCR case 12a/1d (unfoliated).

[82]ERO D/AEA 8, fol. 283r.

[83]ERO D/AEA 8, fol. 277v.

[84]For example, the sequence of such claims at ERO D/AEA 16, fol. 37r.

[85]ERO D/AEA 10, fol. 39r.

[86]Adair, *Courtship, Illegitimacy and Marriage*.

[87]ERO D/AEA 12, fol. 329r.

[88]ERO D/AEA 12, fol. 367r.

[89]ERO D/AEA 13, fol. 140v.

[90]ERO D/AEA 11, fol. 78r.

[91]ERO D/AEA 15, fol. 201v.

[92]ERO D/AEA 25, fol. 234v.

[93]ERO D/ACA 24, fol. 112v.

[94]Gowing, *Domestic Dangers*, for the implications of defamation for women's sexual reputation.

[95]ERO D/ACA 24, fol. 303v.

[96]ERO D/ACA 24, fol. 306r.

[97]ERO D/AEA 14, fol. 18v.

[98]ERO D/AEA 13, fol. 48v.

[99]ERO D/AEA 13, fol. 59a.

[100]ERO D/AEA 18, fol. 20r.

[101]ERO D/ACA 15, fol. 35r.

[102]ERO D/AEA 8, fol. 124r.

[103]ERO D/ACA 16, fol. 79r.

[104]ERO D/ACA 15, fol. 70v.

[105]ERO D/ACA 21, fol. 28r (1596).

[106]ERO D/ACA 24, fol. 87v.

[107]The general context in Wiltshire is explored by Ingram, *Church Courts, Sex and Marriage*, 238-81. For some instances from Leicestershire, Capp, *When Gossips Meet*, 147-8.

[108]WSRO D3/4/1, fol. 20r.

[109]ERO D/AEA 13, fol. 34v.

[110]ERO D/AEA 14, fol. 123v.

[111]ERO D/AEA 2, fol. 101r.

[112]ERO D/AEA 1, fol. 61v (1560).

[113]ERO D/AEA 10, fol. 93v.

[114]ERO D/AEA 12, fol. 65v.

[115]ERO D/AEA 10, fol. 76v.

[116]ERO D/ACA 26, fol. 93r.

[117]ERO D/ACA 24, fol. 55v.

[118]Thomas Middleton, *Women Beware Women*, Act III, scene iv, lines 20-23.

[119]Attracted as I am by the notion of "hegemonic masculinity", of one variety of masculinity being in a position to discipline those with variant ideas of masculinity, there is a sense in which the disciplining simply gives prestige and value to the variant masculinity, *pace* Robert W. Connell, *Masculinities* (Cambridge: Polity Press, 1995). So, as well as the "patriarchal dividend" of hegemonic masculinity by which all males are advantaged by the actions of a minority, the disciplining of other masculinities by that minority may in the process valorize those other masculinities or be taken subversively to do so. The alacrity with which Thomas Cole of Barleythorpe (Rutland) confessed to be a "notorius adulteror" in 1597 begs little belief: "that he hath commytted adulterie with Divers and sundrye women of Okham and likewise hath hade Carnale knowledge of the bodyes of many other women in the country and Denieth to rehearse there names to us although we have earnestly required the same." NRO PDR X611/29, fol. 22v. See also the allegation "that the said Calcroft bragged & told her that Hewgh Stanidg his second Child of Bottesford was his And further that the said Calcroft bragged & told her that he had Carnall knowledg of the body of Mathew Raven his wife and his maide ...": ROLLR 1D41/11/37, fol. 73R Calcroft *c*. Gibson in defamation, 1605.

[120]See also Capp, *When Gossips Meet*, 147-8.

[121]Peter Marris, *The Politics of Uncertainty. Attachment in Private and Public Life* (London: Routledge, 1996), 14.

11
"Community": Reflections on
The Established and the Outsiders

The Established and the Outsiders displays all the hallmarks of Elias's core epistemologies: the significance of (con)figurations and attention to social proprieties.[1] Those aspects, indeed, comprised the focal points of the later gloss which Elias composed, subscribed "March 1976 Amsterdam".[2] We ought really to concentrate then on those elements of the book. We might, nonetheless, consider another impact *The Established and the Outsiders* ought to have made on its first publication in 1965. It followed by eight years Willmott's and Young's examination of a traditional working-class community and preceded Frankenberg's synopsis of community by four years.[3] Six years after "Winston Parva", Bell and Newby produced another synthesis of community studies, although Newby was yet to introduce a more skeptical tone in *The Deferential Worker*.[4] This attention to community studies had perhaps been initiated by Rees's evocation of life in the Welsh countryside in 1951.[5] Five years later–in 1956–the traditional close-knit local society of the north of England was narrated by Williams and in 1963 he described the sublime existence in a traditional (but pseudonymous) west country village.[6] Although not the only sociological studies of community, these descriptions quickly came to compose the "classic" community studies, and, indeed, most of the others exerted the same wistful appeal. One dissenting voice was that of Stacy, who had a more critical attitude in her dissection of Banbury and four years after "Winston Parva" ventured a more robust critique.[7] With the exception of Stacy, most studies conformed to the warm-glow exemplification of community. Predominantly, the classic community study concentrated on the rural–traditional village life. Exceptions were only Willmott's and Brown's urban focus, who yet exuded the warm glow, and Stacy, who approached a larger entity in the process of transformation into a late-twentieth-century urban society. It is within this context that *The Established and the Outsiders* intruded. Its impact on "community" studies did not–it seems in retrospect–meet its full potential, perhaps because its title was a diversion, the magical word community only occurring in the subtitle. Had the subtitle been the title perhaps the impact would have been maximized: *A Sociological Enquiry into Community Problems.*

The purpose of this chapter is to stimulate further discussion about the concept of "community", although it may come across as didactic and prescriptive. Some recent sociological and historical discussion has intended to redeem the term as simply a term of art, suggesting some finality and resolution to the "problems" of "community". The intention here is to ask that the discussion be continued a tad longer before closure. "Winston Parva" is placed at the center of this reinvestigation because of its potential lessons forty years after its first publication, which it cele- brates. This article is a short "thought piece".

What constituted those problems? The discordant elements were pre- cisely those that some writers now tend to assert are simply inherent in community. What Elias and Scotson demonstrated, however, is that those issues were much more than merely problems within community, but problems *for* community and *about* community.

At this point, however, we might also compare different currents in sociological thinking which existed in the 1960s. The classic community studies converged very closely with functionalism and, in particular, the structural-functionalism and systems analysis of Talcott Parsons. The principal premiss was the consensual basis of society, induced through the interdependence between and reciprocity across social groups, and the propensity for the restoration of harmony. Functionalism is perhaps most critically addressed in *TE & TO* in chapter seven, in which the norma- tive integrating function of gossip is challenged. Structural-functionalism composed a similar anthropological paradigm, not least through the influ- ence of the Manchester School of Gluckman. Whilst Gluckman's approach was largely confined to fieldwork research into (allegedly) acephalous African tribal societies, however, this strand of structural-functionalism achieved its apogee in the more diffuse discussion of anti-structure and *communitas* by the Manchester emigré, Victor Turner (and, in some con- tributions, such as on pilgrimage, jointly with his wife, Edith).[8] The first point to be made here is repetition of an insight provided by Eric Dun- ning: that Elias perceived the error of the Gluckman way when Elias held an academic position in Africa: these societies were not acephalous, but a limited dialogue with colonial surveillance, a complaint made clearer by Diamond (Diamond, 1971).[9]

Dissections of ritual, community and local social relations have moved on since then, but the odour of functionalism lingers. Ritual has been so frequently revisited recently that it is difficult to know where to start: expressions of ideological and linguistic oppression; practical oppression; a *carte blanche* or empty vessel on which the participant imposes her own meaning; a return to neo-functionalism; and a pragmatic phenomenology.[10]

To place these considerations into the historians' context, these expositions had an influence and may, indeed, continue to do so. It is commonly understood, for example, that the Toronto School of social historians of medieval England embraced something of the Parsonian systems analysis by perceiving reciprocity across a peasant social hierarchy (for example, DeWindt 1972).[11] That approach has received some critical comment without abandoning the term "community".[12]

More recently, nonetheless, although the noun "community" has proliferated in the title of historical monographs and articles, many historians have attempted to accept "community" as a purely descriptive term or variable concept (after Craig Colqhuoun).[13] It would be tedious to recite all these adoptions of "community" in historical works and invidious to mention a select few. Their existence is well known. Here, however, we encounter a conundrum of the philosophy of language. Is it possible to maintain "community" as a purely lexicographical and neutral noun divested of any emotive content?[14]

One further comment might be hazarded here: social networks are not equivalent to communities. The epistemological principle of social network analysis is to dissolve society and to build upwards from contacts and common attribute data. As a consequence, and despite Granovetteer's counter-statement of the *potential* importance of weak links, social network analysis is more concerned with matters of density, for example, which are less important for conceptualizations of community.[15]

Here, of course, we encounter semantic difficulties. The most perceptive historians contend that "community" is not structure, but process–in that the terms of "community" are constantly (re-)negotiated. That perception is, indeed, a welcome movement away from the structural-functionalist assessment of community as static. The semantic difficulty occurs, however, because some social network analysts refer to networks as *structure*.[16] "We will refer to the presence of regular patterns in relationship as *structure*. Throughout this book, we will refer to quantities that measure structure as *structural variables*."[17] "Community" does not exclude network analysis nor network analysis "community", but they are not necessarily commensurate. The conclusion might be that the network structure constituted a clique rather than a community and there are, indeed, network statistical techniques concerned with the former as a technical term. Indeed, one is tempted to suggest that social network analysis is a statistical extrapolation of "figurational" analysis, not least in the earlier social network analysis such as by Boissevain.[18] This digression should, however, be curtailed at this point.

Returning to Elias and Scotson, other minds were at work at their time, nonetheless, travailing not only independently but with independence: perhaps solitary, perhaps counter-intuitively to the 1960s. One important convergence here with Elias was Erving Goffman's *Stigma. Notes on the Management of Spoiled Identity*.[19] In exactly the same year–1963–was published the first edition of Howard Becker's *Outsiders*, although much of Becker's book had been anticipated in his earlier articles in journals.[20] These great sociological minds (Goffman, Becker, Elias) were independently, but concurrently, visiting highly significant issues–and, one might add, pre-Foucault–independently because the work of none appears in the work of another.

To return to "Winston Parva", we might place at its center a figurational concentration of participation–or power, as Elias and Scotson had it–in the form of control over the ability to stigmatize a large sector of "Winston Parva" as deviant. No other community study had perceived that triangulation. As an aside, it is necessary also to mention class. Although Elias (and Scotson) dismissed the divisions of class–and Elias did this particularly so in his postscript of 1976–class *was* important in "Winston Parva", if in a negative sense. For a discussion of consciousness of class (or not) in a "traditional" English village, there is, of course, now Bell's *Childerley*; more important for the experience of class in a decaying industrial town (Rotherham) is Charlesworth's *A Phenomenology of Working Class Experience*.[21] As Elias and Scotson demonstrated, the middle-class element of the village was really detached from the community, self-excluding; it was not involved in community affairs nor did it strive to participate; its social networks–or figurations, if you will–were outside the village.[22] The internal divisions within the "community" existed between the self-nominated "respectable" working class and the stigmatized "non-respectable" working class: "respectable" pervades *TE & TO*.[23] In other words, the conflict was, as the two authors indicated, between the established working class and the incoming working class, but it also involved the long-established dimension of the segregation of the working class into "respectable" and "rough".[24] Whilst figuration was explanatory, the breach occurred along traditional distinctions within the working class, whether rural laborers or, more particularly, urban artisans and laborers.

We can illustrate that point in a rural context.

> Borrowers were another nuisance. Most of the women borrowed at some time, and a few families lived entirely on borrowing the day before pay-day. There would come a shy, low-down, little

knock at the door, and when it was opened, a child's voice would say, 'Oh, please Mrs So-and-So, could you oblige me mother with a spoonful of tea [or a cup of sugar, or half a loaf] till me dad gets his money?' If the required article could not be spared at the first house, she would go from door to door repeating her request until she got what she wanted, for such were her instructions. The borrowings were usually repaid, or there would soon have been nowhere to borrow from; but often an insufficient quantity or an inferior quality were returned, and the result was a smouldering resentment against the habitual borrowers. But no word of complaint was directly uttered. Had it been, the borrowers might have taken offence, and the women wished above all things to be on good terms with their neighbours. Laura's mother detested the borrowing habit. She said that when she had first set up housekeeping she had made it her rule when a borrower came to the door to say, 'Tell your mother I never borrow myself and I never lend. But here's the tea. I don't want it back again. Tell your mother she's welcome to it.' The plan did not work. The same borrower came again and again until she had to say, 'Tell your mother I must have it back this time.' Again the plan did not work. Laura once heard her mother say to Queenie, 'Here's half a loaf, Queenie, if it's any good to you. But I won't deceive you about it; it's one that Mrs Knowles sent back that she'd borrowed from me, and I can't fancy it myself, out of her house. If you don't have it, it'll have to go into the pig-tub[25]

Compare the comment about such events in "Winston Parva":

Perhaps they came to ask for help without the right formulas, or borrowed things without bringing them back.[26]

Let's move on, nonetheless. What Elias and Scotson perceived that other community studies–because the nature of their communities obscured it–was that outsiders would not necessarily be simply "foreigners" making temporary visits as anonymous and fragmented groups, but could be permanent residents and, not only that, but a mass of people. We are, of course, familiar with the isolation of the individual in-comer, who, not having had the time to formulate social networks, remains an outsider, down the pecking order, or, in Elias's and Scotson's terms, the status order.[27]

'My mistake,' replied Mr Price, gruffly. 'Six an' seven, ma'am. Next please,' he banged the money down while Mrs Dorbell's hovering claw gathered it together. Meanwhile a wave of restlessness animated the customers. All pushed and squeezed, loudly proclaiming that they were next to be served. And Mrs Nattle, being the loudest voiced, the most domineering character and the most plausible liar present, prevailed, silencing, ultimately, a tiny woman by the name of Mrs Jike, a transplanted sprig of London Pride from Whitechapel, who, extra to other accomplishments, was gifted oracularly, being able to read the future in teacups and playing cards. Mrs Jike wore a man's cap and a late Victorian bodice and skirt; she was an inexpert performer upon the concertina, a student of the Court and Personal column of her penny daily and dated the passing of the world's decay from the time of the passing of Victoria the Good. She complained, to Mrs Nattle: 'Shime on y' …Y'know my bloke wownt gow to work till he gets money for his dinner beer. Yaah, measly old 'ooman, y' … Gow to Pedney.[28]

Compare again the situation in "Winston Parva".

Perhaps they spoke with a different accent ...[29]

What was distinctive about "Winston Parva" was the exclusion and stigmatization of the larger part of the community.

We can assess the fundamental difference in approach by comparing two community studies based on data collected in the 1960s, Elmdon (Essex) and "Winston Parva". What distinguishes the two are precisely the points that Elias and Scotson made about the relative influence, authority and cohesion of the established and the outsiders in their different contexts.

Elmdon

According to Strathern, the paradigmatic feature of Elmdon was "kinship at the core": the genealogically core families who had inhabited the village from at least the eighteenth century.[30] There were half a dozen such families, but principally the Hammonds, Hayes, Hoyes and the Reeves. These families were the "real" or "old" Elmdon people, who regarded themselves as the permanent residents and were so regarded by the in-comers in the early 1960s. Elmdon was "represented" by and reified through these families.The families were not affluent, but had existed as agricultural laborers. [Note, however, that by 1979 all these kinship groups had disappeared except one].

The real difference within Elmdon was between "real villagers" and "outsiders". "Real villagers" basically consisted of the core families. The outsiders consisted of families which had in-migrated into the village during the last hundred years. Although this division also occurred along class lines, between middle and working class, the substance of the difference was "belonging" to the village and being an in-comer. Thus a symbolic boundary was constructed within the "community". On the other hand, leadership, as initiative for change, lay elsewhere. In terms of welfare provision, it was the in-comers who dominated. The "real" Elmdoners remained largely passive. The in-comers, nonetheless, recognized the significance of "real" Elmdoners and were concerned for provision for them. The "real" Elmdoners regarded this interference as patronizing. "Real" Elmdoners were more involved only in sports, cricket and football. Despite the symbolic boundary erected between "real" Elmdoners–the "villagers"–and outsiders/newcomers, Strathern et al. concluded that what was at issue was only "a community within a community".

"Winston Parva"

By contrast, the elementary process in "Winston" was the representation of all the inhabitants of Zone Three–according to the characteristics of the worst elements–as deprived and depraved, but the representation of all inhabitants of Zones Two and One by the characteristics of their best elements. This "stigmatization" of all in Zone Three by the two other zones, including Zone Two, revolved around allegations of superiority and inferiority, respectable and rough. Exclusion extended the distinction further: the exclusion of anyone from Zone Three from the public sphere, from offices in voluntary associations or local politics. Representation as "outsiders" superseded duration in the community, even though some inhabitants of Zone Three had been there as long as occupants in Zones One and Two. Those dwelling in Zone Three were all stigmatized as the "cockney colony" although by the 1960s it also included many immigrants from Durham, Lancashire, Wales and Ireland. The heterogeneity and new in-migration into Zone 3 caused social fragmentation and division. Those in Zone Three were symbolically relegated to a separate pub, establishing physical as well as symbolic boundaries. Conformity remained an issue–the coercion of "community"–for the "established" expected the "in-comers" to conform to their customs and ways of life. On the contrary, the initial incoming Londoners refused to adapt to these requirements, but maintained their own culture and ways of life (music hall style of life, boisterousness). The result of not conforming was general ostracism and social division.

By contrasting these two community studies, we can highlight the importance of figurational complexities. At Elmdon, the in-comers were composed of middle-class households which dominated the local politics and cultural affairs of Elmdon, but respected the Elmdon-born as "real" Elmdon. In "Winston Parva", conversely, the established not only retained the symbolism of the real villagers, but also the ability and cohesion to stigmatize the newcomers. One examination suggests the positive ideal of "community", the other a more critical dissection. That critical dimension to community came to be fully recognized only in the decade following *TE & TO*. Despite recent attempts to exonerate the concept of community by asserting that the problems are simply inherent ("natural") in community but do not detract from community as a sociological category, we might still ponder whether such emphatic difficulties nullify the concept altogether.[31] After all the attempts to douse the warm glow and maintain community as a neutral social imperative, might we not question whether the consensual social relations anticipated by community are nothing more than a rhetorical ideal? That seems the enduring lesson of *TE & TO* –that conflict in local social relations has, indeed, elements of the pathological.

So, now to bring us closer to the present, some sociologists have reacted to what they have assumed to be a dominance of the constructed or imagined community to demand the reinsertion of the social into community–an action-centered approach.[32] As an aside, it is interesting that the request by Amit et al. that we consider again those intermittent actions which recollect "community"–that "community" is intermittently and temporarily realized through actions–bears a close of resemblance to Rosser's adaptation of Taylor in his conclusion about medieval urban Westminster: "First it is not a continuous state, but is realized momentarily at particular conjunctures".[33] This reassertion of the social alongside the cultural and the symbolic is surely to be welcomed, a position also advocated by Susan Wright in 1992.[34] Equally, however, the politics of local society demand consideration, which is where we return to Elias and Scotson. Sadly, not one author within Amit's collection of essays, *Realizing Community*, refers to "Winston Parva". That is a shame.

Some historians might retort: well, community is simply a term of convenience, and with what should we replace the term? Unfortunately, however much we profess that it is purely neutral and descriptive, "community" does not escape the positive emotive sentiment. It retains the tinge of functionalism reinforced by the political appropriation of the term in the 1970s and 1980s. What deserves a more expansive treatment than allowed here, but which has profound importance, is the coercion of "community" and those sanctions used in the process–the pressure to conform, which was a salient component of *TE & TO*. The risk that one runs, of course, is the charge of cynicism rather than realism (whatever realism is in our current condition). One solution is inadvertently supplied by Crow and Allan: the *Community Life* of their title is *not* commensurate with the *local social relations* of their sub-title. To the contrary, we might adopt the phrase local social relations to replace "community", since local social relations is a term not infected by emotive content. Similarly, for "place-community", we might be more specific: parish social relations, village social relations, neighborhood social relations and so on. We *can* jettison "community" as an umbrella, reductive, descriptive or heuristic term by less weighted categories–and that, admittedly, is what Elias and Scotson ought to have done: place place-"community" in quotation marks and then have moved to an exploration of the social relations of Winston Parva without reiterating the "c"-word. They almost got there: "What matters is the recognition that the types of interdependencies, of structures and functions, to be found in residential groups in home-making families with a degree of permanence raise certain problems of their own and that the clarification of these problems is central for the understanding of the specific character of a *community qua community*–if one may continue to use the term in a specialised sense."[35]

Notes

[1]I am grateful for discussion over a decade ago with Richard Smith who provides ever-constant support, John Scott, Stanley Wasserman, and Martin Everett, the last not only for advice, but for introducing me to the complexities of Ucinet IV many years ago. Eric Dunning has been a constant source of information about Elias and "Winston Parva" (South Wigston) and Barbara Misztal and the late Anne Witz (to whom I dedicate this chapter) have been a source of inspiration. Audrey Larrivé allowed me to see inside housing in "Winston" (South Wigston). I am grateful to the other contributors to our panel at the Elias conference in Leicester for suggestive insights, not least Daniel Bloyce, and the comments of the audience, especially John Goodwin. The thoughts of Charles Phythian-Adams, who reflects so deeply about these matters of social relationships and place, have been an ever-present stimulus. Elias, whilst a sociologist, performed his sociology very much in historical contexts; I hope that his colleagues and former students will forgive an "historian" (one admittedly informed by sociological ideas and troubled by what constitutes a "discipline" of history) for interfering in these matters. More detailed references are given in Chapter 12.

[2]Norbert Elias and John Scotson, The Established and the Outsiders. A Sociological Enquiry into Community Problems, new edn. (London: Sage, 1994), xv-lii.

[3]Michael Young and Peter Willmott, Family and Kinship in East London (London: Routledge and Kegan Paul, 1957); Ronald Frankenberg, Village on the Border. A Social Study of Religion, Politics and Football in a North Wales Community (London: Cohen and West, 1957); Frankenberg, Communities in Britain. Social Life in Town and Country (Harmondsworth: Penguin, 1969).

[4]Colin Bell and Howard Newby, eds., Community Studies. An Introduction to the Study of the Local Community (London: George Allen and Unwin, 1971); Newby, The Deferential Worker. A Study of Farm Workers in East Anglia (London: Allen Lane, 1977).

[5]Alwyn D. Rees, Life in a Welsh Countryside. A Social Study of Llanfihangel yng Ngwynfa (Cardiff: University of Wales Press, 1951).

[6]William M. Williams, A West Country Village. Ashworthy (London: Routledge and Kegan Paul, 1963); Williams, The Sociology of an English Village. Gosforth (London: Routledge and Kegan Paul, 1956)

[7]Margaret Stacy, Tradition and Change. A Study of Banbury (London: Oxford University Press, 1969); Stacy, "The Myth of Community Studies," British Journal of Sociology 20 (1969): 134-47.

[8]Victor Turner, The Ritual Process. Structure and Anti-Structure (Ithaca, N.Y.: Cornell University Press, 1969); Victor and Edith Turner, Image and Pilgrimage in Christian Culture.

[9]Arthur S. Diamond, Primitive Law. Past and Present (London: Methuen, 1971)

[10]Bloch, "Symbol, Song and Dance and Features of Articulation";de Certeau, The Writing of History, 185-91; Humphrey and Laidlaw, The Archetypal Actions of Ritual; Roy Rappaport, Ritual and Religion in the Making of Humanity (Cambridge: Cambridge University Press, 1999); William I. Miller, Faking It (Cambridge: Cambridge University Press, 2003), 58-76.

[11]Edwin B. DeWindt, Land and People in Holywell-cum-Needingworth. Structures of Tenure and Patterns of Social Organization in an East Midlands Village 1252-1457 (Toronto: Toronto University Press, 1972).

[12]Richard M. Smith, "Kin and Neighbors in a Thirteenth-century Suffolk Community," Journal of Social History 4 (1979): 139-55; Maryanne Kowaleski, "Introduction", Journal of British Studies 33 (1994): 337-9 (introduction to a special issue on medieval community) which comprises papers collectively entitled: "Vill, Guild, and Gentry: Forces of Community in Later Medieval England," reflecting differing approaches to meanings of the term "community".

[13]Alexandra Shepard and Philip Withington, eds., Community in Early Modern England (Manchester: Manchester University Press, 2000), 1-15.

[14]Maurice W. Cranston, Philosophy and Language (Toronto: Canadian Broadcasting Corp., 1969).

[15]Mark Granovetteer, "The Strength of Weak Ties," American Sociological Journal 78 (1973): 1360-80; Steven D. Berkowitz, An Introduction to Structural Analysis. The Network Approach to Social Research (Toronto: Butterworths, 1982); Jeremy Boissev-

ain, *Friends of Friends. Networks, Manipulators and Coalitions* (Oxford: Blackwell, 1974); Per Hage and Frank Harary, *Structural Models in Anthropology* (Cambridge: Cambridge University Press, 1983); E. Litwak and N. Babchuk, "Primary Group Structures and their Function: Kin, Neighbors and Friends," *American Sociological Review* 34 (1969): 465-81; John Scott, *Social Network Analysis. A Handbook* (London: Sage, 1991); Stanley Wasserman and Katherine Faust, *Social Network Analysis. Methods and Applications* (Cambridge: Cambridge University Press, 1994).

[16]Hage and Harary, *Structural Models in Anthropology.*

[17]Wasserman and Faust, *Social Network Analysis,* 3. Wasserman and Faust provide the methodological bible, but Scott, *Social Network Analysis,* the most succinct introduction.

[18]Boissevain, *Friends of Friends.*

[19]Erving Goffman, *Stigma. Notes on the Management of Spoiled Identity* (repr. Harmondsworth: Penguin, 1990: original 1963).

[20]Howard Becker, *Outsiders. Studies in the Sociology of Deviance* (New York: Free Press, 1963).

[21]Michael Bell, *Childerley. Nature and Morality in a Country Village* (Chicago: University of Chicago Press, 1994), 27-50; Simon Charlesworth, *A Phenomenology of Working Class Experience* (Cambridge: Cambridge University Press, 2000) [Rotherham].

[22]Elias and Scotson, *The Established and the Outsiders,* 25-26.

[23]Elias and Scotson, *The Established and the Outsiders,* 54, 56, for example.

[24]F. M. L. (Michael) Thompson, *The Rise of Respectable Society. A Social History of Victorian Britain, 1830-1900* (Harmondsworth: Penguin, 1988), 197-204, 353-4, but which only addresses the "respectable working man", ignoring the possibility of the rhetorical content of that term as deployed by the middle class, and not really approaching the counterpoint of the "rough" working class.

[25]Flora Thompson, *Lark Rise to Candleford* (Harmondsworth: Penguin, 1973; originally Oxford 1939).

[26]Elias and Scotson, *The Established and the Outsiders,* 73.

[27]Elias and Scotson, *The Established and the Outsiders,* 39-42.

[28]Walter Greenwood, *Love on the Dole* (London: Verso, 1993, originally London 1933), 37-38.

[29]Elias and Scotson, *The Established and the Outsiders,* 73.

[30]Marilyn Strathern, *Kinship at the Core. An Anthropology of Elmdon, a Village in North-West Essex in the Nineteen-sixties* (Cambridge: Cambridge University Press, 1981).

[31]Graham Crow and Graham Allan, *Community Life. An Introduction to Local Social Relations* (Harlow: Pearson Education, 1994), which interestingly refers to Winston Parva really only minimally: pp. 67, 70-72.

[32]Vered Amit, ed., *Realizing Community. Concepts, Social Relations and Sentiments* (London: Routledge, 2002), largely reassessing the influence of Tony Cohen and Benedict Anderson; cf. Ekman who follows Cohen closely; Ann-Kristin Ekman, *Community, Carnival and Campaign. Expressions of Belonging in a Swedish*

Region, Stockholm Studies in Anthropology vol. 2 (Stockholm, 1991). See chapter 12 for further references.

[33]Rosser, *Medieval Westminster 1200-1540* , 248. The same implication might lie behind his "Going to the Fraternity Feast: Commensality and Social Relations in Late Medieval England, "*Journal of British Studies* 33 (1994): 430-46.

[34]Susan Wright, "Image and Analysis: New Directions in Community Studies," in *The English Rural Community. Image and Analysis,* ed. Brian Short (Cambridge: Cambridge University Press, 1992), 195-217

[35]Elias and Scotson, *The Established and the Outsiders,* 147 (italics original).

12

"Community": Ins and Outs of the Medieval Village

One interpretation placed on personal pledging in medieval villages emphasizes *solidarity*, a concept reminiscent of sociological and anthropological investigations into twentieth-century rural communities, although notions about the commonality of the medieval village have an historiographical tradition that dates from the nineteenth century. In the case of medieval villagers, it has always been easy, if not necessarily accurate, to move from pragmatic communal organization, such as field systems and co-aration (joint plowing by villagers), to symbolic representations of community. The criterion that justified this interpretation in the case of personal pledging was its perceived personal commitment.[1]

Personal pledging, or suretyship, required peasants to stand as security for other villagers in a variety of circumstances at the manorial court, whether in cases of litigation between peasants, such as debt/detinue, trespass, and covenant, or vis-à-vis their lord in cases of trespass, admission to land, or guarantee of good behavior. Although some sureties were short-term obligations, others, such as for the maintenance of tenements, were of indeterminate length. Serving as a pledge was a common role within the English medieval rural community.

This chapter examines pledging at Kibworth Harcourt, a manor of Merton College in Leicestershire, using social-network-analysis software. One of the principal arguments throughout is that pledging was an institutional relationship, not necessarily a multiplex, affective, or ideological one, and that its use by the peasant elite reinforced social differentiation. Moreover, pledging was not based on such primary sociological elements as friendship, gender, or current peer group, but was socially imposed.[2]

DeWindt's study of Holywell-cum-Needingworth (a manor of Ramsey Abbey) cogently presented the case that personal pledging was partially responsible for villagers' solidarity before the plague. Although the village community was socio-economically stratified, personal pledging extended from the peasant elite to the margins of the community, thereby reflecting communal identity. Since most pledges were drawn predominantly from outside the family, neighborliness was significant.[3]

In contrast, Pimsler, considering another Ramsey Abbey manor (Elton), found that personal pledges were drawn largely from neighbors rather than kin, and pledging often involved asymmetrical relationships. He also suspected that pledges were paid. Smith also found that socioeconomic divisions remained significant in relationships of pledging, since smaller landholders were more likely to pledge within their own quartile of landholding, contrary to any notion of reciprocity.[4]

More recently, Razi's study of Halesowen suggested that pledging was a genuinely binding force: That pledges were fined between 2d. and 4d. if their pledgee lost implied a personal commitment (though the level of fine was no higher than the common scale). Razi also maintained that it was "very unlikely that pledges were normally paid for their service"; that the constant need for sureties was an incentive for reciprocity (between 1270 and 1349 men acted as pledges a mean of 16.3 times); and that, although pledging was dominated by the peasant elite, eighty percent of the male peasant population pledged for their neighbors or received pledges, "at least a few times." Olson's examination of pledging by two core families in Ellington (also Ramsey Abbey) tended toward a similar notion of solidarity.[5]

Any discussion of pledging should treat the following broad questions: Could pledging have had alternative symbolic meanings, how personal was the commitment, and how inclusive was pledging within the community? Pledging in unequal relationships may not necessarily demonstrate solidarity. Bourdieu, writing about North African societies, regards such relationships, whether of debt or other obligation, as "symbolic capital," extending influence over subordinates, that is, debtors.[6]

Material aspects of personal commitment may be assessed by crude cost-benefit analysis. It is well established, for example, that pledges were placed in mercy for non-suit by their principal, that pledges as well as principals were fined in lost cases, and that pledges could be liable for their principals' debts or, in trespass, damages. Pledges had something tangible to lose. Despite the difficulty of accumulating evidence, partly because of the peremptory nature of many court rolls, material loss was not always drastic. Referring to cases of debt at common law, as early as 1187-1189, the author of *Glanvill* acknowledged that pledges were responsible for debts, but described the principal plea of debt by which they could recover their losses against the pledgee's chattels, excluding fines.[7]

Similar recourse was available in numerous pleas of pledge at manorial courts, for example in *William Pert v. Agnes Holcombe* at Uplyme in

1366, in which Pert claimed 40s. lost as pledge for Thomas Skittish. Skittish was a member of the Holcomes kinship group. Agnes defended the issue that, since she had requested Pert to be Skittish's pledge, she should redeem Pert's losses.[8]

Unredeemed losses were normally restricted to fines incurred by non-suit or loss of the case, determined by Razi at Halesowen as 2d. to 4d., and in many other courts, a consistent 3d., perhaps equivalent to three days of labor. This cost, too, may have been liquidated, if, as Pimsler maintained, pledges were commonly paid. That peasants placed in mercy were exonerated from finding a pledge, for reasons of poverty, is evidence in Pimsler's favor. Although uncertainty remained, reasonable expectation prevailed that pledges would not be out of pocket.[9]

The potential costs might have been low, but the corresponding benefits to the peasant elite were considerable, foremost among them social control. It was in the interests of the peasant elite, as well as of lords, to preserve harmony in the community by controlling the margins of society. Pledging across socioeconomic transects may have been entirely self-interested. Recent research into population turnover and migration in late-medieval, agrarian society suggests a highly volatile fringe: "Extensive geographical mobility had already become an integral experience of county life in Essex well before the Black Death." Pledging might have been an agency through which core families controlled transients as well as women and adolescents.[10] The issues are whether pledging included all social elements, whether it could bind them all effectively, and whether it was voluntary. The extent of free choice might have been circumscribed because of seigniorial interest, the concerns of the peasant elite, and the formal procedures of manorial courts. Wider interests were represented when original pledges failed to deliver their bailee in court, the bailee was attached (secured) by better pledges (*per meliores plegios*) and the former pledges were summoned to hear judgment. In such cases, better pledges may have been imposed on, rather than selected by, pledgees.[11]

The matter of inclusiveness involves those excused from finding pledges and thus exempt from the system as well as those unable to find personal pledges and thus pledged by their chattels (technically, gages). One group sometimes exonerated from finding pledges in the late thirteenth century were the unfree, that is *nativi* (*native*) or *rustici*. At Halesowen, between 1293 and 1300, twelve *nativi* or *native* were not required to find pledges because of their status. At Barkby, in 1289, Richard *prepositus* was placed in mercy for poor performance of his office "plegius se ipse quia rusticus" that is, as his own pledge, because of his unfree status, as was Sampson in a case of covenant.

These peasants were outside the institution of pledging reserved to *probi homines*, the "law-worthy" men. This exclusivity may have been a residual element from earlier times, but earlier, more widespread, incidence occurred at Alrewas, where, in 1259-1261, parties frequently found *plegium hus et hom*, a gage, rather than a personal pledge. Gages may have lapsed because they contravened lords' interests; since the chattels of villeins legally belonged to lords, gages were prejudicial. Such exceptions suggest that pledging did not bind the whole community.[12]

Examples of people who could not find pledges are, admittedly, rare, but a significant case occurred at Yarcombe in 1287, when John Mautrauers, unable to find pledges in a case of debt, was distrained (that is, his chattels were seized) until his creditors were satisfied. At Shalston (Buckinghamshire) in 1316, William Golowe, defendant in two cases of debt and unable to find a pledge, was distrained from day to day until the debts were liquidated. Although he had to redeem the debts, William's fine (*misericordia*) was condoned because he was poor; this fact, as well as his inability to buy a pledge, indicates his marginal status.[13]

There were also cases in which personal pledges were not received, so no personal commitments were involved, as in pledging by officials, in evidence from the late thirteenth century, well before the plague. A beadle or bailiff pledged constantly at Halesowen from ca. 1300, as did a reeve and bailiff at Ingoldmells after 1291, when there was no shortage of male personal pledges. The possibility remains, as Olson suggested, that such pledging represented less the office than personal status.

Yet, it is equally plausible that pledging by officials was an extension of community or seigniorial control over people through the official. This explanation seems particularly pertinent when the whole homage (the entire body of the court) pledged, most frequently when villagers without social standing, often widows, were admitted to land. For example, at Burbage (Wiltshire), Walter Hugon was admitted in 1323 to a tenement lately held by John Pope in villeinage, his pledge comprising the whole homage. His need for such an extensive pledge is revealed by the fact that his entry fine of 3s. 4d. was condoned because he was poor (*quia pauper*). These instances of impersonal pledging before 1348 show that this phenomenon existed before the predicated decline of personal pledging after that date.[14]

Moreover, as Beckerman has indicated, institutional factors may have caused pledging's decline: for example, the use of the jury of presentment (originally a seigniorial device) to initiate litigation between peasants. Another pragmatic cause of change was the demographic decline after the plague, which severely reduced the number of male pledges, especially since one case, prosecuted to its conclusion, required at least four pledges for each party.[15]

Qualitative evidence suggests that, although pledging was an extremely common relationship, it did not create binding ties throughout the
community. It seems more exclusive than inclusive and more obligatory
than voluntary. It is difficult to relate pledging precisely to primary social,
multifaceted or multiplex, groupings (kin, neighbors, and friends); pledging, because of its institutional nature, was often uniplex (single-faceted).
By its very nature, it ignored affective social ties, to the peer group or age
cohort (life-course), and, to a large extent, gender. Pledging was largely an
artificial, institutional relationship grafted onto more natural ties.

Kibworth Harcourt is located ten miles southeast of Leicester, adjacent to Kibworth Beauchamp. From a tithing list of ca.1280, Howell proposed a population of 140 males over twelve, but cancellations reduce the
figure to 120, in accord with a contemporary memorandum about the four
tithings, which record 112 or 115 males *in toto*. The inconsistency resulted
from contemporary confusion whether thirty-one or twenty-eight males
comprised one of the tithing groups.[16]

The demographic trend can be estimated from the payment of *capitales denarii* (tithing pennies), at the rate of 1d. per male aged over twelve,
through the late thirteenth and early fourteenth century. Before 1348, the
mean population was 84.56 males over the age of twelve (standard deviation 14.62) and the median of eighty (inter-quartile range seventy-five to
eighty-eight). Disparity between the payments and the lists is explained
by administrative changes.

Merton College held the view of frankpledge (supervision of all males
over twelve) for the entire village, but its collection of pence from other
lordships in the vill varied. In some years the pence were collected, in others exonerated, and permanently condoned after 1315. In 1304/5, the court
roll omitted the earl's men (*sine hominibus domini Comitis*) and in 1306-7,
the pence were relaxed (*et relaxantur de hominibus domini Comitis*) leaving
7s. 4d. to be paid by the College's own males. In other years, pence from
different manors were collected, as indicated by the sums of 8s. 10d., 9s.
8d., 10s. 6d., and 9s. 7d. (bis) in 1281/2, 1287/9, and 1312-15. It is necessary to distinguish between the population of the village, which attained a
maximum of 126 males, and that of the College's manor, which was fairly
stable at eighty to eighty-five. These figures are important for determining
the number of males involved in pledging.

The marginal sector of Harcourt's society also affected the nature of
pledging. The evidence is fragmentary, but qualitatively suggests considerable volatility at the edge of village society. Presentments and fines of
those who sheltered outsiders indicate much turnover and movement:
one fine each in 1277, 1281, 1283; six in 1291; four in 1294; three in 1296
and again in 1298; four in 1325; one in 1326 and 1327; four in 1330; nine

in 1331; and four more in 1333. Immigrants paid fines in recognition of lordship. Robert *Textor* gave 6d. in 1283 for license to remain in the vill; John de La3tone and Simon *Textor de Rouele* gave 12d. in 1289 and 6d. in 1291, respectively, to enter the lordship. Female immigration was just as extensive: Emma de Langton and Matilda Leche each paid the lord in hens for the privilege of staying in the village (*pro aduocacione domini dum manet in villa*), the former from 1296 to 1320 and the latter in 1309/10. However, because of the trouble that they often caused, female immigrants were widely proscribed after 1324.[17] Anonymous migrants (*extranei*) were also involved in innumerable cases of battery; this manner of their identification suggests fluidity at the margins.

Two of the variables understood to affect social networks are time and accessibility. The former has two stages in relation to society: development and duration. Both worked theoretically and, at least initially, against the strong involvement of outsiders in the life of the local society. Recent arrivals had not had the time to become involved in social networks.[18]

The usual requirement at Harcourt was two pledges at each stage of interpersonal litigation. Serious cases involving the lord's interest, however, required more. For his debts to the lord in 1287, Robert Sibilie, junior, needed seven pledges, and in the following year had to find three. A subsequent case also involved this core family, the Sibiles. Mr. John Sibile, abetted by Nicholas Polle, was convicted of a serious battery, compounded by his being harbored by his father, Robert Sibile. Although both men found four pledges, Robert Sibile was required to find twelve.[19]

The character, social position, and number of pledges, all drawn from the village elite in such cases, were determined by the social position of the miscreants, as well as the gravity of their offenses. Given these numbers, the frequency of pledging, and the size of the manor, personal pledging might have embraced the entire community, but did not. Analysis of pledging at Harcourt is based on two cohorts one for 1277-1298 and the other for 1320-1348, corresponding with the best, surviving court rolls. The analysis is gender-biased, since the objective is to assess reciprocity, or symmetrical relations, in pledging; women, by and large, were excluded from giving, though not receiving, pledges. At Harcourt, women pledged on five occasions, but in three simply as mothers, and in the other two apparently as kin.[20]

Between 1277 and 1298, 309 instances of pledging involved 194 different male principals and/or pledges. This figure compares with a maximum of 126 males over the age of twelve who had been residents in the community for more than one year, that is, in a tithing group and not recent migrants. Part of the discrepancy in the numbers is explained by fluidity at the margin. Precision is confounded further, however, by the instability of bynames; hereditary surnames were just beginning to appear among core unfree peasant families in Leicestershire. Hence, the 194 men in the first cohort may be an over-enumeration. Such problems of identification, however, do not affect the second cohort, from 1320 to 1348, since surnames had stabilized by then. That cohort thus comprised 131 different people involved in 162 incidences of pledging, whether as recipients or givers.[21] (See Table 12.1, page 293, Summary of the Data)

Significant discoveries emerge from the raw data. In the first cohort, only 101 of the 194 actors gave a pledge; ninety-three or 47.9 percent were merely recipients of pledges, perhaps reflecting the asymmetrical nature of the relationships. This discrepancy is even greater in the second cohort, in which only fifty-six of the 131 actors gave a pledge. Univariate descriptive statistics of pledges actually given, that is, pledging per pledge, again reveal large differences. The mean number of pledging per pledge in the first and the second cohort was about six and three, respectively, with even lower medians at two and one. The inter-quartile range, dispersion around the median, is relatively high for 1277-1298, but narrow for 1320-1348. Nevertheless, in both cohorts, the maximum number of pledging per pledge is high.

In 1277-1298, thirty-five pledges each gave only one pledge and seventeen gave two; the total of fifty-two comprises 86.14 percent of all pledges but only 11.5 percent of pledging. At the other extreme, one pledge gave twenty-nine pledgings: 4.9 percent of all pledging (598). Out of the total of 101 pledges, those eight who pledged more than twenty times accounted for 42.3 percent of all pledging. A large concentration of pledging occurred within a small nucleus of men, but the full significance of the interrelationships can be assessed only through social network analysis.[22] (See Table 12.2, page 294, Descriptive Statistics of Pledging per Pledge)

Examined first is the output from graph theory, which defines the characteristics of the overall sociogram, or graph of the networks. The figure for network block density describes the general level of linkage within the sociogram, produced by comparing the observed or actual number of connections with the potential maximum number; 0 represents no density (sparseness) and 1, maximum density (completeness). In both cohorts, the density is insignificant: 0.02 and 0.01, indicating fragmentary and loose overall contacts. This observation would seem to imply that pledging was not an effective agency for binding together local society. (See Table 12.3, page 295, Statistics of Density and Overall Centralization)

The values for centrality comprise two different outputs: Local (degree) centrality measures how well each actor was connected and integrated in the network; centralization measures the extent to which the whole sociogram has a consolidated structure or core. The figures for local centrality of all actors (strictly a vertex) can be compared to assess their relative involvement. The data for local centrality are complementary to those for density, but, whereas density relates to the degree of cohesion *per se*, centralization signifies the convergence of cohesion around particular points. Both are measures of the graph's "compactness." The two measures for centrality are divided into in-degree and out-degree, representing, in this context, receiving and giving pledges, respectively.

The output for network centralization reveals a stronger in-degree core for the first cohort than for the second, but they are more or less similar in out-degree. Evidently, from 1277-1298, there was a group of actors engaged in mutual pledging, but by 1320, they had disappeared.

Local centrality defines the activity of each actor as a giver and a recipient of pledges, counted through the number of different connections (degrees) rather than the amount of pledging. The first output shows univariate descriptive statistics for every one; the second is a selective output for those who acted significantly above the mean, which has, in both cohorts, a value of ten, although it includes as exceptions two additional actors in the first cohort who approached that value. (See Table 12.4, page 296, Descriptive Statistics of Local Centrality of Actors). Judging from the output for 1277-1298, connections in thirteen cases resulted overwhelmingly from pledges given, whereas, in ten, the element of reciprocity seems clear, since in-degree and out-degree are similar. Moreover, the level of in-degree of the dominant twenty-three far exceeded that of the other 171, with one clear exception and a few other minor exceptions. Hugh Harcourt, whose in-degree value is twenty-three (normalized 11.92) and out-degree is eight (normalized 4.15), mainly received pledges but also gave some. The vast proportion has low in-degree and null out-degree values, meaning that most were predominantly recipients of pledges. The output for 1320-1348 reveals the dominance of two villagers. (See Table 12.5 Freeman's Degree Centrality for Significant Actors)

Matrix procedures elicit a more profound explanation of these patterns, through *k-core* and *k-plex* analysis. K-cores denote areas of relatively high cohesion within a sociogram; k-plexes detect any overlaps and so may have more value in this context. Ucinet IV v1.06 yields output for k-plexes until the value of *k* (the set size) is exhausted. In this case, the significant set size has been taken as the highest level found: a minimum set size of six in 1277-1298 and four in 1320-1348, which identified k-plexes of five actors in the first cohort and two in the second cohort. These k-plexes represent small groups involved in reciprocal and mutual pledging.

Some prosopographical flesh can be fitted to the pledging participants of 1277-1298, allowing further conclusions about the nature of pledging. Almost all of them held at least half a virgate and thus belonged to the principal tenantry, despite some differences in legal status. Nevertheless, they did not comprise all of the tenants of standard holdings; a number of such tenants did not serve consistently as pledges nor did they establish connections through pledging. At least seventeen tenants held half a virgate but did not pledge frequently. (See Table 12.6, page 298, Prosopography of Principal Pledges)

Comparison with several rentals suggests that at least half the tenants of standard holdings were not frequent pledges. Although the main pledges were drawn from the peasant elite, they constituted only a small segment of the upper stratum. Their pledging was mainly reciprocal, within their own social tranche; it tended to confirm solidarity among this privileged core.

Comparison of pledging by kin and by neighbors does not require network analysis, since the level of involvement of kin was small. The conclusion is not exact because of the instability of bynames in the earlier cohort and the lack of extensive prosopographical information about extended kinship ties among persons with differing bynames. Because the determination of the kinship tie is based solely on the pledgee and at least one pledge sharing the same byname, some margin of error is inevitable.

Nevertheless, some indication of the rarity of intra-kin pledging is possible. In twenty-five of the 309 instances of pledging in 1277-1298, at least one pledge had the same byname as the principal, whereas in four cases two pledges had the same byname as the principal. Moreover, in five of these cases father pledged for son and in another six, brother pledged for sibling. An extended household relationship, in which master pledged for servant, is clearly perceptible in only two cases. Four of the twenty-five kin relationships involved the Polle family, nine the Harcourts, and seven the Sibiles, all evidently from the peasant elite and core kinship groups, and these cases comprised 80 percent of intra-familial pledging. A large proportion of these incidences was reciprocal pledging by Hugh and Nicholas Harcourt. Both were principals on four occasions, and one pledged for the other seven times.

Intra-familial pledging was a minor part of the overall network of pledging, but was significant within a small nucleus of the core kinship groups. Intra-familial pledging was not characteristic of the lower echelons in Kibworth, as it was in Ellington and Redgrave, perhaps because the margins there were largely composed of singletons and transients, not small landholders.[23] Personal pledging at Harcourt segregated the core from the periphery in village society, its principal effect being to maintain cohesion among a coterie of core families and to "form norm enforcing groups."[24]

The existence of such norm-enforcing groups has been intimated by measures of local centrality and k-plex analysis, albeit with only one variable, pledging. In the local society at hand, there are grounds, admittedly somewhat speculative, for investing pledging with the significance of hegemony and social control. In this manner, the core validated its own norms and regulated deviance: in the broad cultural and sociological sense. Those on the margins were inhibited from developing network relationships because they had neither the time nor the opportunity to forge dense ties. In this context, the importance that Granovetter and others have attached to weak ties, the "strength" of weak ties, has no relevance, since the medieval village does not seem to be analogous to those "complex social systems" that these other sociologists address.[25]

Although pledging at Harcourt was predominantly and almost exclusively by neighbors rather than by kin, this pattern does not ineluctably lead to a notion of solidarity within the whole local society. Social network analysis has come under criticism by, for example, Bollen and Hoyle, who state that "Sociometric or social network definitions of cohesion that count the frequency and nature of interactions of group members are analytically distinct from perceived cohesion." Such arguments imply that a sense of belonging (the "cognitive elements") and of morale (the "affective elements") are independent of social networking. However, by assessing the effectiveness and extent of ties, social network analysis can help to evaluate concepts of belonging and community.[26]

Pledging formed only loose ties overall; it does not seem to have been capable of binding an entire local society. On the contrary, pledging helped to distinguish core from periphery and to confirm hegemony; it was a non-affective institutional arrangement designed for control. To the extent that the experience at Kibworth was different from perceived attitudes on the manors of Ramsey Abbey or at Halesowen, however, these findings do not represent the end of the discussion.

	1277–1298	1320–1348
Incidences of Pledging	309	162
Different Actors (Pledgers and Pledgees)	194	131
N of Different Pledgers	101	56
Intrafamilial Incidences[a]	25	14

[a] Excluding fathers (*pater eius/suus*) without a byname; all the data exclude officials as pledgers (for example, *plegius prepositus*).

Table 12.1   Summary of the Kibworth Data

	N	MEAN	STANDARD DEVIATION	MEDIAN	Q1	Q3	MIN	MAX
1277–1298	101	5.921	6.934	2	1	8	1	29
1320–1348	56	3.214	5.211	1	1	3.75	1	32

Table 12.2   Descriptive Statistics of Pledging per Pledge

NETWORK BLOCK DENSITY[a]

	MEAN VALUE WITHIN BLOCKS	STANDARD DEVIATION WITHIN BLOCKS
1277–1298	0.02	0.15
1320–1348	0.01	0.12

NETWORK CENTRALIZATION (%)

	IN-DEGREE	OUT-DEGREE
1277–1298	19.695	17.651
1320–1348	5.176	23.924

[a] Range = 0–1, where 1 = absolute density. Modeling has shown, however, that in large networks, density is unlikely to exceed 0.5; even so, the levels found here are totally insignificant. The values given are from valued matrices. To allow for simple connections— rather than frequency of connections—a control binary matrix was produced for 1277–98 (by dichotomizing the valued matrix), but it resulted in similar values. Ucinet calculates density by block-modeling the matrix.

Table 12.3   Statistics of Density and Overall Centralization

VARIABLE	OUT-DEGREE	IN-DEGREE	NORMALIZED OUT-DEGREE	NORMALIZED IN-DEGREE
1277–1298				
Mean	3.09	3.09	1.60	1.60
Standard Deviation	5.79	4.40	3.00	2.28
Sum	599.00	559.00	310.36	310.36
Variance	33.50	19.37	8.99	5.20
Euclidean Norm	91.37	74.88	47.34	38.80
Minimum	0.00	0.00	0.00	0.00
Maximum	29.00	32.00	15.03	16.58
1320–1348				
Mean	1.37	1.37	1.06	1.06
Standard Deviation	3.73	1.33	2.87	1.02
Sum	180.00	180.00	138.46	138.46
Variance	13.93	1.76	8.24	1.04
Euclidean Norm	45.52	21.86	35.01	16.82
Minimum	0.00	0.00	0.00	0.00
Maximum	32.00	8.00	24.62	6.15

Table 12.4   Descriptive Statistics of Local Centrality

ACTOR	OUT-DEGREE	IN-DEGREE	NORMALIZED OUT-DEGREE	NORMALIZED IN-DEGREE
1277–1298				
William Brun	16.00	2.00	8.29	1.04
Nicholas Polle	18.00	11.00	9.33	5.70
Nicholas Harcurt	22.00	23.00	11.40	11.92
Hugh *filius Alexandri*	22.00	3.00	11.40	1.55
Robert Sibile	15.00	20.00	7.77	10.36
William de Reyns	29.00	32.00	15.03	16.58
Robert Arun	14.00	10.00	7.25	5.18
William *ad fontem*	10.00	2.00	5.18	1.04
Robert (le) Cuper	13.00	2.00	6.74	1.04
Robert *Paruus*	24.00	15.00	12.44	7.77
Nicholas *faber*	14.00	15.00	7.25	7.77
Ivo Sibile	12.00	4.00	6.22	2.07
Hugh Seluestre	26.00	2.00	13.47	1.04
Ralph *carectarius*	23.00	4.00	11.92	2.07
Hugh Godwyne	12.00	4.00	6.22	2.07
Robert Bonde	17.00	11.00	8.81	5.70
Robert *ad fontem*	16.00	21.00	8.29	10.88
Roger Wade	10.00	3.00	5.18	1.55
John Polle	13.00	2.00	6.74	1.04
William *filius Reginaldi*	23.00	14.00	11.92	7.25
Nicholas Thort	12.00	3.00	6.22	1.55
Richard *filius Rogeri prepositi*	20.00	7.00	10.36	3.63
William Peek	16.00	2.00	8.29	1.04
1320–1348				
Robert Heyne	32.00	1.00	24.62	0.00
[William Heyne	9.00	0.00	6.92	0.00]
Robert Broun	23.00	3.00	17.69	2.31
[Thomas Harcourt	8.00	5.00	6.15	3.85]

NOTES   *Significant* means significantly above the mean in Table 3—10 in the out-degree—but two actors, within brackets, with values close to 10 have been included for 1320–1348.

Table 12.5   Freeman's Degree Centrality for Significant Actors

NAME	STATUS	HOLDING
William Brun	Free tenant	messuage
Nicholas Polle	Free tenant	0.5v
Hugh Harcurt	Custumarius	0.5v
Nicholas Harcurt		
Hugh *filius Alexandri*	Free tenant	1v
Robert Sibile	Custumarius	1v
William de Reyns	Free tenant	0.5v
Robert Arun	Free tenant	1v
William *ad fontem*	Custumarius	0.5v
Robert Cuper	Custumarius	0.5v
Robert *Paruus*	Custumarius	0.5v
Nicholas *faber*	Free tenant	1v
Ivo Sibile	Custumarius	0.5v
Hugh Seluestre	Custumarius	0.5v
Ralph *carectarius*	Custumarius	0.5v
Hugh Godwyn	Custumarius	0.5v*
Robert Bonde	Custumarius	0.5v
Robert *ad fontem*	Custumarius	1v
Roger Wade	Custumarius	0.5v
John Polle	Custumarius	0.5v
William *filius Reginaldi*		
Nicholas Thort	Custumarius	1v
Richard *filius Rogeri*		
prepositi	Free tenant	1v
William Peek		3v

NOTE   *v* means virgate; *custumarius* means customary, or unfree, tenant.
SOURCE   Merton College, Oxford, MM 6367 and 6369 (rentals).

Table 12.6 Prosopography of Principal Actors

Notes

[1]Raftis, *Tenure and Mobility*, 101-104; DeWindt, *Land and People at Holywell-cum-Needingworth*, 242-50; Cohen, *Belonging*; idem, *The Symbolic Construction of Community* (London: Routledge, 1985); Susan Wright, "Image and Analysis: New Directions in Community Studies"; Crow and Allan, *Community Life*. For the persistence of the use of "community" in this context, Phillip R. Schofield, *Peasant and Community in Medieval England, 1200-1500* (Basingstoke: Palgrave, 2002). See also Chapter 11 above.

[2]For background about Kibworth Harcourt, Howell, *Land, Family and Inheritance in Transition*; Litwak and Szelengi, "Primary Group Structures and Their Function: Kin, Neighbors, and Friends."; D. R. Hoyt and Nicholas Babchuk, "Adult Kinship Networks: The Selective Formation of Intimate Ties with Kin," *Social Forces* 62 (1983): 84-101; L. Verbrugge, "Multiplexity in Adult Friendships," *Social Forces* 57 (1978): 1286-1309.

[3]DeWindt, *Land and People*, 242-250.

[4]Martin Pimsler, "Solidarity in the Medieval Village? Personal Pledging at Elton, Huntingdonshire," *Journal of British Studies* 17 (1977): 1-11; Raftis noted payment, too: *Tenure and Mobility*, 102, 102, n.27. Smith, "Kin and Neighbors in a Thirteenth Century Suffolk Community"; Smith, "'Modernisation' and the Corporate Medieval Village Community: Some Sceptical Reflections," in *Explorations in Historical Geography: Interpretive Essays* ed. Alan R. H. Baker and Derek Gregory (Cambridge: Cambridge University Press, 1984), 140-245.

[5] Zvi Razi, "Family, Land and the Village Community in Later Medieval England," in *Landlords, Peasants and Politics in Medieval England* ed. Trevor H. Aston (Cambridge: Cambridge University Press, 1987), 360-93; Sherri Olson, "Jurors of the Village Court: Local Leadership Before and After the Plague in Ellington, Huntingdonshire,"*Journal of British Studies* 30 (1991): 237-256; Olson, "Family Linkages and the Structure of the Local Elite in the Medieval and Early Modern Village," *Medieval Prosopography* 13 (1992): 53-82. .

[6]Pierre Bourdieu, *The Logic of Practice* trans. Richard Nice (London, 1992), 123.

[7]G. Derek G. Hall, ed., *Tractatus de Legibus et Consuetudinibus Regni Anglie qui Glanvilla Vocatur* (London: Nelson for the Selden Society, 1965), 118-119, Bk. X, c3-5.

[8]Longleat MS. 11181, m. 20d: "que quedam Agnes venit et dicit quod eum rogauit deuenire plegium ipsius Thome . . . et de amerciamentis ea occasione super ipsum assessis tempore predicto dicta Agnes eundem Willelmum versus dominum acquietat et sic est ad legem . . ."; see also 10771, m. 52.

[9]Miri Rubin, *Charity and Community in Medieval Cambridge* (Cambridge: Cambridge University Press, 1987), 40; Christopher Dyer, *Standards of Living in the Later Middle Ages* (Cambridge: Cambridge University Press, 1989), 211-33; David L. Farmer, "Prices and Wages," in *The Agrarian History of England and Wales, 1042-*

1350 ed. Herbert E. Hallam (Cambridge: Cambridge University Press, 1988), vol. 2, 760-72.

[10]Poos, "Population Turnover in Medieval Essex."

[11]Leslie J. Downer, ed.. *Leges Henrici Primi* (Oxford: Oxford University Press, 1972), 170-1 (c.53, 1c and 3) has an interesting understanding of the phrase "to find pledges."

[12]Amphlett. Hamilton. and Wilson, *Court Rolls of the Manor of Hales* (hereafter *Halesowen*), vol. 1, 240, 254, 259, 265, 283, 308-10, 324; vol. 2, 383, 407; Merton College, MM 6565; W. N. Lander, "Alrewas Court Rolls, 1259-61," in *Collections for a History of Staffordshire* vol. 10 (1907), 262, 269, 281-3.

[13]Devon Record Office CR 1429; Gerald R. Elvey, ed., *Luffield Priory Charters Part I,* Northamptonshire Record Society vol. 26 (Oxford, 1975 for 1973), 210.

[14]The National Archives, London, SC2/183/57; see also Longleat MSS. 10770, m. 28; 10774, m.2; *Halesowen,* vol. 1, 135-6; William O. Massingberd, ed. , *Court Rolls of the Manor of Ingoldmells in the County of Lincoln* (London: Spottiswoode, 1902), 1-2, 12, 19, 53, 118.

[15]John S. Beckerman, "Procedural Innovation and Institutional Change in Medieval English Courts," *Law and History Review* 10 (1992): 197-252.

[16]I have examined all the court rolls and the account rolls: MM 6196-6244 and 6367-6392; MM 6213-6214.

[17]MM 6206-6222.

[18]Karen E. Campbell and B. A. Lee, "Personal Neighbor Networks: Social Integration, Need or Time?" *Social Forces* 70 (1992), 1081; T. Cubitt, "Network Density among Urban Families," in *Network Analysis: Studies in Human Interaction* ed. Jeremy Boissevain and J. Clyde Mitchell (The Hague: Mouton, 1973), 67-82.

[19]MM 6379.

[20]Judith M. Bennett, *Women in the Medieval English Countryside: Gender and Household at Brigstock before the Plague* (Oxford: Oxford University Press, 1987), 24-25, 37-88, 154-5, 193-5. For a sociological comment, see Hoyt and Babchuk, "Adult Kinship Networks," 188.

[21]Judith Bennett, "Spouses, Siblings and Surnames: Reconstructing Families from Medieval Village Court Rolls," *Journal of British Studies* 23 (1983): 26-46.

[22]Steve P. Borgatti, Martin G. Everett, and Simon C. Freeman, *Ucinet IV version 1.06* (Columbia, S.C., 1992), is the software used. For an introduction to social network analysis, see Scott, *Social Network Analysis*; Berkowitz, *An Introduction to Structural Analysis*; Hage and Harary, *Structural Models in Anthropology.*

[23]Olson, "Jurors"; Smith, "Kin and Neighbors."

[24]R. Niemeijer, "Some Applications of the Notion of Density to Network Analysis," in *Network Analysis* ed. Boissevain and Mitchell, 81.

[25]Mark. S. Granovetter, "The Strength of Weak Ties," *American Journal of Sociology* 78 (1973): 1360-80, is the classic statement on weak ties.

[26]K. A. Vollen and R. H. Hoyle, "Perceived Cohesion: A Conceptual and Empirical Examination," *Social Forces* 79 (1990), 483; Karen E. Campbell, "Networks Past: A 1939 Bloomington Neighborhood," *Social Forces* 69 (1990): 139-55.

13
What Was Core about "Core" Families?

The concept of the persistence of "core" or "focal" families in parishes, and even in kinship networks across groups of contiguous parishes, has attracted considerable attention in some quarters.[1] The implication behind the notion is that the continuity provided by these kinship groups allowed the perpetuation of local custom and notions of "community", although "community" is a problematic concept with its dark as well as nostalgic sides.[2] For some historians, social relationships in the parish in the late sixteenth century were contested and negotiated, informed by dispersed "power" with a small p which was contingent and characterized by resistance.[3] "Community" is thus not always a consensual or imagined construct.[4] This permanence was not incompatible with the high levels of mobility into and out of such settlements, for the intensely localized nature of migration itself confirmed local norms within the confines of a "country".[5] Even the migrational patterns of the most mobile of life-course migrants, servants in husbandry, was tightly circumscribed, helping to define "countries" and, indeed, in some of the remoter parts of England the employment of servants was an exchange between households within the parish.[6] The localization of surnames within parishes or groups of parishes has been used as a surrogate instead of reconstitution to illustrate long-term persistence of families.[7]

Two recent studies in particular seem to represent this school of thought which associates the local persistence of longevous families with the continuity of local norms and traditions. One suggests that a "neighborhood" area was delineated by the kinship network of "dynastic families" in a group of adjacent parishes in south-west Nottinghamshire between ca.1580 and 1700.[8] These persistent families were drawn from the middling sort, from the yeomanry or better husbandry, usually wealthier than their neighbors, and frequently held parochial offices, so that they comprised "a group able to exert some influence in the community"; "the dynastic families helped to create the character of the neighborhood area", their stability promoting "enduring traditions and characteristics."[9] The other study adopts a wider approach than the single settlement, assessing the social space around the urban center of St Ives, again characterized by the activities of core families. Accounting for some sixty surnames *in grosso*, this nucleus of families comprised four percent of urban society, but, through their longevity in the area, encouraged "continuity of communal feelings", so that "we would expect that this core of families would be the repository of the traditional values of the community."[10]

In this chapter, we combine two approaches, reconstitution of families and isonymy, in a detailed local study of a single parish, Barkby, the demographic data collected and interpreted by Suella Postles and the medieval nominal data by Dave Postles.[11] First, however, we wish to make some obvious points. The persistence of surnames is a minimal and not a maximal measure of the persistence of local people, since familial continuity may have occurred through females who are not transmitters, in normal circumstances, of surnames. The extent to which continuity proceeded through females depends very much on demographic circumstances: sex ratios and male replacement rates. The major question about using surnames is that it reflects only "male-stream" in another sense, since it ignores the contribution made by women, less overtly and formally than males, to the confirmation and regulation of "community" norms and to local cultural and social developments which are only now being explored.[12] We are very conscious of this considerable failing of our nominal evidence.[13]

Returning to demographic criteria, we are equally conscious that the experience of Barkby, our selected example, will not be representative of many other places. Even within Leicestershire, the experiences of Barkby and, for example, some settlements with greater opportunities for by-employment, are likely to be quite different. In these terms, perhaps Barkby was closer to Bottesford than to Shepshed, two other places in the county subjected to detailed demographic scrutiny, although the influence of lordship there was a contrast.[14] Located at the junction of river valley and Wold, Barkby was an agrarian parish with local resident lordship and limited economic opportunities for outsiders, approximating to a "closed" character.[15] The conditions thus encouraged stability and continuity. Greater social and demographic volatility was occurring in parishes in north-west Leicestershire which was more conducive to industries in the countryside and even industrialization.

The comparison was, indeed, even closer to home. Until the early nineteenth century, Thurmaston was divided between two parishes, north Thurmaston attached to the parish of Barkby. The fortunes of Thurmaston and Barkby diverged dramatically from the late eighteenth century as Thurmaston developed into a framework-knitting settlement of considerable size, whilst Barkby, just a few miles along the road, remained essentially an agrarian settlement, affording economic opportunity only to its own established families. There seems no point in suggesting that core families persisted or facilitated the continuity of notions of "community", belonging and "community norms" in all settlements. Certain types of parish were more favorable to the phenomenon which was not universal.

One final point of circumspection, which we wish to elaborate further below, is that the persistence of "core" families was possibly *not* a timeless prospect. Rather we should prefer to conceive of the restoration of "core" families and continuity in the sixteenth century in some areas, advisedly in some areas, since the Kentish Wealden experience was different, for example.[16] At this point, we encounter one debate about familial continuity in the late middle ages and another about the invention of customs and traditions in the late middle ages.[17] There is no doubt that within individual parishes there was immense discontinuity of family names during the later middle ages.

From the early sixteenth century, and even after enclosure in 1780, Barkby was dominated by two lordships, the resident Pochins, inhabiting the hall adjacent to the parish church, and the absentee Merton College. Landholding was concentrated in the hands of the Pochins, their tenants, the copyholders of Merton College and sundry freeholders. No opportunities were offered for immigrants, squatters or cottagers, so that, despite divided lordship, the parish presented to all intents and purposes a "closed" aspect, although our use of the term "closed" is imprecise and only a term of convenience for what is a complex construct.[18]

Population and surnames in the late Middle Ages

For the later middle ages, we are principally forced to rely upon the records of the College's manor, supplemented by records of central government (taxation), some material from the rentals of Leicester Abbey, but little from the Pochin angle or indeed from Langley Priory.[19] The analysis is therefore not comprehensive. The *lacunae* are serious to the extent that we cannot categorically be certain that when a byname or surname disappeared from the records of the College, it equally vanished from the parish. Conversely nor can it be proven that the appearance of a byname or surname in the College's records marked its introduction into the village. The possibility remains that people and bynames or

surnames migrated between lordships in the parish, although the extent
was probably inconsiderable. John Fraunceys, for example, was presented
in the manor court of the College because he had settled in the lordship of
the abbot of Leicester in Barkby.[20]

The data presented in Figure 13.1 (p. 311) derive from lay subsidies
of central government, charters and the College's court and account rolls
and rentals, sporadically from 1202 but more consistently from ca.1270
through to 1544. Surnames introduced in the 1530s and 1540s thus have
an ostensibly short duration in this figure, which is misleading. At the
other chronological end, before the 1330s, the considerable instability of
cognomina is partly the attribute of the volatility of bynames which had not
developed into hereditary surnames in all kinship groups. The problem
is demonstrated simply by the total number of *cognomina* generated (291),
far too many for a manor of this size. What Figure 13.1 does illustrate is
a fairly high level of continuity of some bynames and surnames into the
1350s followed by a rapid transformation of the corpus thereafter.

These changes are confirmed by analysis of the *cognomina* of tenants
rather than all appearances in manorial and fiscal records, with some
problems, however. The rentals of ca.1300, 1311, 1312 and 1315 seem to
represent a wider structure of the tenantry, including small tenants and
perhaps some undersettles, since many fragmented holdings are listed.
The subsequent rentals of 1354-1355, 1450 and 1475, in contrast, contain
more consolidation. Thus, whilst sixty holdings were enumerated in that
of ca.1300, only twenty-eight were listed in 1354, twenty in 1450 and nineteen in 1475 (although the number of tenants is even smaller because of
multiple holdings in the late middle ages). Consolidation and engrossment in the later middle ages would not seem to account for all the difference in the tenemental structure.

From the rentals of ca.1300-1315, some fifty-four different bynames
can be accumulated. Although one tenant, Sampson, was listed without
a byname (but was once alluded to as *de Bark'*), his immediate descendants assumed the *cognomen* Sampson. Of the fifty-four bynames, ten or
eleven persisted into the rentals of 1354-1355, about twenty percent. Absolute numbers elude us, because *Faber* existed in 1300 and 1315 and both
Faber and Smyth in 1354-1355. About half of the twenty-three different
surnames in the rentals of 1354-1355 had existed on the manor in the earlier rentals, some of which are sufficiently distinctive to suggest that continuity resulted not simply from their commonplace nature but the survival
of kinship (which, indeed, has been established by reconstitution from the
court rolls): Arnold; Sampson; Playtour; Tante; and Styword.[21]

Although about half of the surnames of 1354-1355 existed some forty
years earlier, only one or two, however, persisted from 1354-1355 to 1450.

Of the sixteen different surnames in 1450, only Johnson (and possibly its variant Jakson) had occurred in the rentals of 1354-1355, in the Latin equivalent *filius Johannis*. Here again the actual transmission of the byname from Latin form to vernacular has been established by reconstitution from the court rolls. At least fourteen of the sixteen surnames of tenants in 1450 had been introduced into the manor during the previous century. By the next rental, in 1475, merely four of the surnames of 1450 had survived: Braunston; Beregh' (Beverage); Jakson; and Bo(w)cher. Thirteen of the seventeen surnames of 1475 had been introduced into the manor during the previous quarter of a century, perhaps a generation. This extreme discontinuity after 1350 is replicated in other places and may be one of the reasons for the invention of traditions during the late middle ages to exert some form of "social memory."[22]

Early modern demography and surnames

From the middle of the fifteenth century, dominant customary tenants became established in the manor through the consolidation and engrossment of multiple holdings, but their pre-eminence was individual, life-course and not dynastic. Towards the end of the century, stability of landholding was being re-established in kinship groups and a small nucleus of core families in terms of longevity and landholding resurfaced. Their position was consolidated during the early-modern period, which is more widely the time of the formation of "core" kinship groups represented in the persistence of surnames, their establishment associated with the demographic conditions of the period.

In 1563, the parish of Barkby comprised an estimated 288 souls in forty-four families in the township of Barkby, twelve in the hamlet of Barkby Thorpe and eight in North Thurmaston. In the census of 1801, the parochial population had attained 576, comprising 389 in the main township, seventy-two in Barkby Thorpe, four in Hamilton (an essentially deserted hamlet) and 111 in North Thurmaston. Whilst the population of Thurmaston had expanded enormously over the time, Barkby had experienced a much lower rate of increase, below the general level for the county as a whole.[23]

Nonconformity does not complicate the calculations unduly, since the Compton census of 1676 made a return of 256 communicants but only sixteen dissenters. Subsequently, the *Speculum* of the Diocese maintained that ninety-four of the total of ninety-seven families communicated, but we are conscious of the lack of consensus about the complications of some of these types of static listings and the different notions about acceptable multipliers.[24]

Considering vital events, burials ranged from sixteen to twenty-nine per 1000, but baptisms remained at a remarkably low level, between twenty and twenty-seven per 1000, with a mean of twenty-five. Marriages fluctuated closely around a mean of 7.5 per 1000. Net growth accumulated very much more highly before 1686 than after: a mean of 3.36 accretions *per annum* between 1586 and 1642 compared with 1.86 from 1691 to 1790. Over the whole time-scale, burials exceeded baptisms in forty-two years, thirty of which occurred after 1686. A deficit happened in at least three years in each decade between 1686 and 1780, with severe difficulties in 1715-1730 resulting from a total net deficit of fifty-seven. Accordingly, the level of population of 1715 was not restored until 1745. These years coincided with the heaviest levels of child mortality.

Global demographic change may also be calculated from estimates of population from the periodic listings (Table 13.3, p. 314), which presents an ostensible contrast with aggregative analysis. For example, the increase indicated by aggregative analysis between 1586 and 1642 was 202, whilst the estimated population in the Bishop's census of 1563 was 288. Combined, these two figures suggest a resident population in 1641-1642 of 500. In fact, the estimated population in 1641-1642 (Protestation Oath) was 370 inhabitants. The dissonance between these two methods was more apparent than real, since the difference is explicable by out-migration.

Continuity of some residence is reflected in the analysis of surnames in the township of Barkby, presented in Table 13.4 (p. 315); it should be emphasized that these data relate exclusively to the township of Barkby. Only forty-two different surnames can be extracted from probate records, court rolls of the Merton manor (which held the court leet or view of frankpledge and thus comprehended at intervals the entire township), and parish registers, between 1555 and 1565. A subsequent compilation of surnames in 1666 has been derived from the Hearth Tax and parish registers. Of the initial forty-two surnames of 1564, as many as twenty-two persisted a century later. A further listing of surnames has been constructed for 1772 from the lists of suitors to the court leet. Of the seventy-four surnames in 1772, twelve had existed in 1666 and seven in 1564. The continuous surnames over this bicentennial period were thus a very narrow and restricted corpus. In contrast, some thirty-four new surnames had been introduced between 1564 and 1666, whilst a further forty-two appeared after 1680. Quantitatively, therefore, the newly-introduced surnames were much more significant than the established and continuous core.

It has, nevertheless, been suggested that the importance of the nucleus of surnames resided in their representation of core families and consequently communal values. It is important therefore to consider the actual demographic continuity of these families, through replacement by comparison with out-migration. Summarized below are data about child-bearing by the families of the township, principally divided into "stayers" (core families) and immigrants.[25] The data, of course, relate to baptisms of children rather than births.[26] Newly-introduced surnames accounted at various times for twenty-five to sixty percent of families producing offspring. Although some of these surnames remained for more than a single generation, they were a minority of persistent surnames. For all periods, the new surnames existed in the township for only a few years. Families representing established surnames were responsible for twenty-five to fifty percent of child-births at various times, despite being in a significant minority quantitatively. In some decades, half of the new families remained to produce children in the subsequent decade, as in the 1710s, 1720s and 1770s, which compared with only thirty-two and twenty-four percent in the 1740s and 1760s.

Taking an illustrative decade, 1595-1605, forty-five couples were responsible for a mean of 2.06 children, but families with established surnames accounted for more than fifty percent of the total. Six transient families produced only eight baptisms, a mean of 1.3, their productive life-cycle in Barkby curtailed by repeated migration. In contrast, the mean of children baptized from marriages with established surnames was much higher: 2.71.

Core surnames were thus associated with a large proportion of baptisms within the township. Demographic stability was maintained through out-migration, even by offspring from core families. Between 1585 and 1595, 114 baptisms were performed in the township and the fortunes of 104 of these individuals can be perceived to 1642, before the *lacunae* in registration, the sample of 104 issuing from fifty-one families. By 1600, fifty-five, the issue of twenty-eight families, still remained in the parish, but this number was reduced to twenty by 1620 (at mean age of thirty-two years). Of the fifty-one original productive families, twenty-seven persisted in the township. Although the migration of individual offspring attained eighty percent, by contrast more than fifty percent of the productive families continued in the township. At least thirty children from continuous families left before 1620, about twenty-five percent of whom married in the parish before departure, but seventy-five percent left as singletons. Of at least twenty stayers from established and continuous families, five ostensibly did not marry and six (all male) were involved in exogamous marriages but returned to Barkby (thus uxorilocal marriages, it seems).[27]

Barkby thus illustrates one type of local parish society in which stability was restored in the sixteenth century by the continuity of core families, represented by the persistence of surnames. The relatively "closed" nature of the township, its agrarian character, the reservation of resources to continuous membership of the permanent members of this local society to the relative exclusion of outsiders, deterred substantial immigration. Although substantial out-migration was a feature, core kinship groups remained in the township and parish. The exodus, combined with a comparatively low reproductive rate and, after the 1680s, higher mortality, maintained a stable demographic regime.

Nevertheless, other local parish societies might undoubtedly have existed which did not share this experience and excessive generalization should be avoided. The transmission of localized norms, values and customs through core families is, moreover, a process which is not entirely clear and has yet to be elucidated. A relationship between the persistence of surnames, core families and local custom, is assumed rather than proven and is at best an association. If the core families were also dominant families and not just longevous, problems ensue, for the analysis to date has not taken into account the increasing evidence that local social relationships were brokered, fragmented, contested, negotiated, and that in local societies "relationships of power and authority, dominance and subordination are established, maintained, refused and modified."[28]

It is, indeed, possible that at some critical points dominant families exercised a form of "social control" and hegemony which may have been directed towards change rather than continuity and such families might not always have constituted simply the "godly".[29] It is possible too that this sort of social regulation of misbehavior had a longer history through the later middle ages.[30] At this level, the association of local elites and the impact of state formation might have induced change in local *mores* rather than continuity, perhaps from the sixteenth century and the impact of the Reformation (although again in a brokered and sometimes contested manner, but crucially through the parochial elite), at least from the late sixteenth century.[31] The further difficulty then is to whom is attributed the influence in the continuity of local customs: to the genealogically continuous families or to the dominant families? As has been suggested, the latter might, at times, have been equally concerned to change local custom. Other than agreement that persistent surnames are a useful surrogate indicator of the continuity of some continuous families, the further relationships, with continuous local societies and their persistent customs and ways, are suggestive, but not affirmed.[32]

Decade	Growth decadal	annual	Baptisms	Burials	Marriages
1586–95	29	2.9	114	85	26
1596–1605	21	2.1	93	72	28
1606–15	33	3.3	118	80	36
1616–25	53	5.3	120	67	34
1626–35	34	3.4	105	71	25
1636–46[ie]	38	3.8	96	58	20
1646–72[iie]	89	3.3			
1673–78	7	1.2	51	44	15
1679–90[iiie]	22	1.9			
1691–1700	26	2.6	89	63	21
1701–10	34	3.4	104	70	26
1711–20	7	0.7	87	80	27
1721–30	-57	-5.7	83	140	44
1731–40	41	4.1	113	72	39
1741–50	27	2.7	108	81	26
1751–60	23	2.3	122	99	36
1761–70	43	4.3	128	85	43
1771–80	31	3.1	118	87	39
1781–91	31	3.1	142	111	50

Table 13.1   Vital Events: by Ten-year Periods

Decade commencing	Child burials	Total Burials	Child burials as per cent of total	Child burials as per cent of baptisms
1606	17	80	21.25	15.00
1616	14	67	20.90	11.60
1626	7	71	10.00	7.00
1636[–42]	7	35	20.00	10.40
1673[–79]	13	44	29.70	25.40
1691	25	63	39.60	28.00
1701	32	70	45.70	30.70
1711	37	80	46.20	54.20
1721	45	140	32.00	54.00
1731	34	72	47.00	30.00
1741	33	81	40.70	30.00
1751	46	99	46.00	37.70
1761	22	85	25.00	17.20
1771	22	87	25.20	18.60
1781	37	111	33.30	36.00

* – During the period 1606–42, the proportion of child baptisms to burials was 25.70 per cent and 31.20 per cent between 1691 and 1790.

Table 13.2   Child Mortality by Ten-year Periods

Date	Raw data	Multiplier	Sub-total	Total
1563	B 44 families	4.5	198	
	BTh 12 families		54	
	NTh 8 families		36	288
1603	260 communicants	40 per cent added		364
1670	B55 houses	4.5	247	
	BTh 14 houses		63	
	NTh 15 houses		67	
	Ham 1 house		5	383
1676	274 communicants	40 per cent added		384
1717	97 families	4.5		437
1761	B 76 suit	4.5	342	
	BTh 12 suit		54	
	NTh 18 suit		81	
	Ham 1 suit		5	482
1772	B 89 suit	4.5	360	
	BTh 12 suit		54	
	NTh 18 suit		81	
	Ham 1 suit		5	500
1784	B 89 suit	4.5	405	
	BTh 13 suit		59	
	NTh 18 suit		81	
	Ham 1 suit		5	545
1801	B389			
	BTh 72			
	NTh 111			
	Ham 4			576

B – Barkby; BTh – Barkby Thorpe; NTh – North Thurmaston; Ham – Hamilton.

Table 13.3 Population Estimates from Listings

1564	1666	1680–1772: introductions	1772
42 Surnames	22 survived from 1564	7 introduced 1680–1720	7 survived from 1564
	34 new additions	7 introduced 1721–30	5 survived from 1666
		3 introduced 1731–40	62 introduced 1680–1772
		5 introduced 1741–50	
		10 introduced 1751–60	
		8 introduced 1761–70	
		2 introduced 1772	
Totals:			
42 surnames	56 surnames	42 surnames	74 surnames

Table 5 — Fertile families, 1596–1605

Fertile couples	Total	No. of children
Married in Barkby	7	14
New families 1596–1605	21	45
Sub-totals	28	59
Families established by 1596	17	34
New surnames (longer stay: three years or more)	7	19
New surnames (transient: two years or less)	6	8
Total: children with new surnames		25

Table 13.4 Persistence and Loss of Surnames

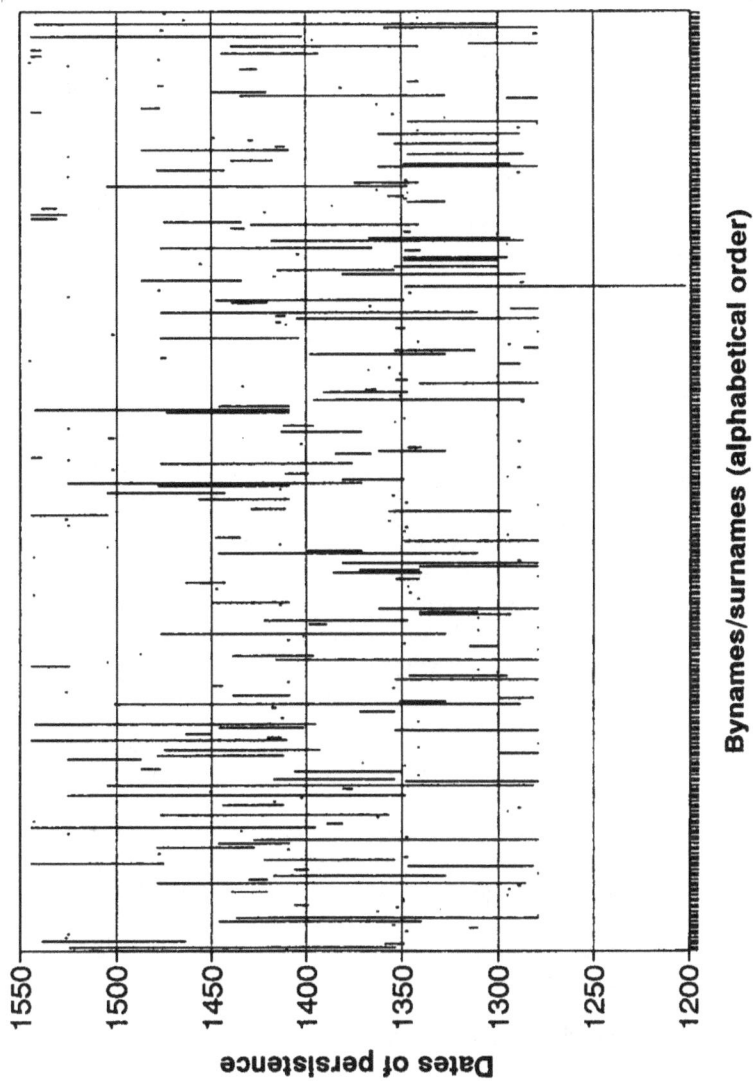

Fig. 13.1   The Longevity of Bynames and Surnames

Notes

[1]Strathem, *Kinship at the Core*; Mary P. Carter, "An Urban Society and its Hinterland: St Ives in the Seventeenth and Eighteenth Centuries," unpublished Ph.D. dissertation (University of Leicester, 1989) ("focal"); Phythian-Adams, ed., *Societies, Cultures and Kinship 1580-1850*; Mary Prior, *Fisher Row. Fishermen, Bargemen and Canal Boatmen in Oxford 1500-1900* (Oxford: Oxford University Press, 1982).

[2]Chapter 12 above.

[3]Keith Wrightson. "The Politics of the Parish in Early Modern England," in *The Experience of Authority in Early Modern England* ed. Paul Griffiths, Adam Fox and Steve Hindle (London: Macmillan, 1996), l0-46.

[4]For references, again, see Chapter 12.

[5]As well as Chapter 4 above, Everitt, "Country, County and Town."

[6]Kussmaul, "The Ambiguous Mobility of Farm Servants"; Mary R. Bouquet, *Family, Servants and Visitors:The Farm Household in Nineteenth and Twentieth Century Devon* (Norwich: Geo, 1985).

[7]E.g. Lasker, *Surnames and Genetic Structure*.

[8]Mitson, "The Significance of Kinship Networks in the Seventeenth Century: South-west Nottinghamshire."

[9]Mitson, "The Significance of Kinship Networks in the Seventeenth Century: South-west Nottinghamshire," 51-52, 71-72.

[10]Mary P. Carter, "Town or Urban Society? St Ives in Huntingdonshire, 1630-1740," in *Societies, Cultures and Kinship*, ed Phythian-Adams, 110-12.

[11] Suella Postles, "Barkby: The Anatomy of a 'Closed' Township," unpublished M.A. thesis (University of Leicester, 1979); Merton College, Oxford, MM; Pochin MSS. in ROLLR; Barkby parish registers deposited in ROLLR. We would like here to record our debts to Roger Highfield and John Burgass of Merton College and to all the staff of ROLLR.

[12]For our period, see Gowing, *Domestic Dangers*; for a later time, Melanie Tebbutt, *Women's Talk. A Social History of "Gossip'" in Working-class Neighbourhoods 1880-1960* (Aldershot: Ashgate, 1995).

[13]Peter Spufford. "The Comparative Mobility and Immobility of Lollard Descendants in Early Modern England," in *The World of Rural Dissenters 1520-1725* ed. Margaret Spufford (Cambridge: Cambridge University Press, 1995), 309-31, addresses some of the issues.

[14]David Levine, *Family Formation in an Age of Nascent Capitalism* (New York: Academic Press, 1977), for the demographic regimes at Bottesford and Shepshed, both in Leicestershire.

[15]Fox, "The People of the Wolds in English Settlement History."

[16]Michael Zell, *Industry in the Countryside. Wealden Society in the Sixteenth Century* (Cambridge: Cambridge University Press, 1994), 26.

[17]Zvi Razi, "The Erosion of the Land-family Bond in the Late Fourteenth and Fifteenth Centuries: A Methodological Note" and Christopher Dyer, "Changes in the Link Between Families and Land in the West Midlands in the Fourteenth and Fifteenth Centuries," in *Land, Kinship and Life-cycle*, ed. Richard M. Smith (Cambridge: Cambridge University Press, 1984): 295-312; Ronald Hutton, *The Rise and Fall of Merry England. The Ritual Year 1400-1700* (Oxford: Oxford University Press, 1994).

[18]See, for example, Banks, "Nineteenth-century Scandal or Twentieth-century Model?"

[19]The principal sources for the medieval account are: MM 6556-6629

[20]MM 6570.

[21]See generally Dave Postles, "Notions of the Family, Lordship and the Evolution of Naming Processes in Medieval English Rural Society: A Regional Example" *Continuity and Change* 10 (1995): 169-98, esp. 189-90.

[22]For this term, James Fentress and Christopher Wickham, *Social Memory* (Oxford: Blackwell, 1992); see also Paul Connerton, *How Societies Remember* (Cambridge: Cambridge University Press, 1989).

[23]*VCH Leicestershire 3,* 146, 166-7. For the background, E. A. (Tony) Wrigley and Roger S. Schofield. *The Population History of England 1541-1871. A Reconstruction* (Cambridge: Cambridge University Press, 1981), esp. 207-15.

[24]Anne Whiteman, "The Compton Census of 1676," in *Surveying the People. The Interpretation and Use of Document Sources for the Study of Population in the Later Seventeenth Century*, ed. Kevin Schürer and Tom Arkell (Oxford: Leopard's Head Press, 1992), 97-116.

[25]See David Souden, "Movers and Stayers in Family Reconstitution Populations," *Local Population Studies* 33 (1984): 11-28.

[26]For the comprehensive data, see Suella Postles, thesis, 109 (Table F), which provides details by decade.

[27]See David Souden, "'East, West - Home's Best?' Regional Patterns in Migration in Early Modern England' in *Migration and Society in Early Modern England* ed. Clark and Souden, 292-332.

[28]Wrightson, "Politics of the Parish," 18-22.

[29]Wrightson and Levine, *Poverty and Piety in an English Village;* Martin Ingram, "Puritans and the Church Courts, 1560-1640," in *The Culture of English Puritanism 1560-1700,* ed. Christopher Durston and Janet Eales (London: Macmillan, 1996), 43-50; Joan R. Kent, *The English Village Constable 1580-1642* (Oxford: Oxford University Press,, 1986); Wrightson, "'Sorts of People' in Tudor and Stuart England," in *The Middling Sort of People. Culture, Society and Politics in England, 1550-1800,* ed. Jonathan Barry and Christopher Brooks (London: Macmillan, 1994), 28-51, esp. 36-40; Wrightson, "Politics of the Parish," 25-31.

[30]Marjorie McIntosh, *Controlling Misbehavior.*

[31]Joan R. Kent, "The Centre and the Localities: State Formation and Parish Government in England, c.1640-1740," *Historical Journal* 38 (1995): 363-404.

[32]We are grateful to Professor Alan Everitt who supervised the M.A. thesis on which much of this paper was constructed and Paul Ell and Linda McKenna for many kindnesses in the past.

Conclusion

The Public Space of the Market Place in Early-Modern England

According to the deposition of Robert Littler of Northwich, saddler, in August 1705, himself aged about thirty, Samuel Phillips assaulted Catherine Basnett of Barnton and took her goods by force. Littler professed that, in his capacity as constable of Northwich, he approached Phillips and demanded why he maltreated anyone who came to the public market to the great injury of the market. No doubt Littler engaged in some rhetoric in his narrative to impress the Cheshire justices; none the less his words do inform us about the perceived status of the market place and what occurred in it. It was a place of negotiation, not only commercial, but social.[1] It was a place of conflict, in this case perhaps commercial, but also social conflict. Above all, it was a place representing civic honor.[2] To perpetrate an abuse in its space was to abuse the dignity of the town; to improve market facilities enhanced the dignity of the town.[3]

Since it had that attribute of civic dignity, so the market place conversely provided a place of resistance, defiance and subversion, whether collective or individual.[4] Objecting to the oligarchy which had selected the mayor of Stafford in 1614, the bailiff, John Lees, refused to surrender his staff but walked up and down the market place most of the day and there chastised one of the oath-takers of the mayor in open market.[5] Personal and private conflict were acted out in the market place and vengeance was exacted there. Perhaps as a measure of personal non-compliance it was also a space for loitering, which inevitably caused suspicion.[6] Although it was public, its crowded nature allowed a measure of private subversion of space. Through action obscured from authority, order and hierarchy could be overturned in this crowded urban space, despite or because of its public nature.[7]

While there were a multitude of social interactions, official and non-official, in the market place, the concentration here is on the use of the market space as a site of public punishment and humiliation and what that means for the interpretation of it as space. The understanding of space will be reserved to the second part of this chapter, which may be a relief for some.[8] To commence with some examples of the material investigated here may illustrate the contexts. In January of 1572/3, Richard Laurence and Elizabeth Syblye, both of Ely, were sentenced in the Ely consistory court:

> That they haue committed the abhomynable synne of Incest tog-ither she beinge his former wyves brothers daughter.

As a consequence, the penance imposed on them included:

> To stand at the market Crosse of Elye upon Saterdaye beinge the xxxjth [sic] of Januarye 1572 from x of the clocke before noone un-til ij of the clocke in the after noone clothed in whyte shetes hold-inge ij whyte wands in theyre hands haveinge eche of them ij pa-pers wrytten with great lettres with this poesye for abhomynable synne of Incest pynned one upon theyre backs and the other upon theyre brests &c.[9]

As we know, the market place was recognizably a public and open space, open in the sense that many (but certainly not all) social interactions there were visible. Thus another sentence in the Ely consistory court on a couple engaged in an illicit relationship prescribed:

> & the one not to frequent and use the cumpanye of another but openlye & publyquelye, as in market Fayre churche and open congregation.[10]

Correspondingly, all other spaces which were not open were represented as *loca suspecta*.[11]

In short, one principal source of the evidence used here is the ecclesi-astical court, particularly causes which involved sexual delinquency and incurred the sentence of penance to be performed visibly in the market place. Occasionally, another forum imposed the same punishment:

> And that the saide Alice Emerye shoulde be Whipped once at Great Woodford aforesaide & a seconde time at Sarum one some market daie but if shee shoulde be penitent for her offence & confesse

Willingly Whoe is the reputed father then the said punishment at
Sarum to be spared.

So pronounced the bench, the justices of the peace, for Wiltshire at the
Epiphany Sessions in 45 Elizabeth, the justices believing the father to
be Alice's employer (she was a servant), Christopher Whitehorne.[12] It is,
however, not only with the justices' response to sexual impropriety and
bastardy that this article is concerned; the context is also their judgments
relating to petty larceny, that is, for the theft of items valued at less than
12d.

To illustrate this latter aspect, at another meeting of the same county's
bench, the following two illustrative judgments were enacted. For respectively stealing shirts valued at 10d. and for theft of clothing appraised at
8d., one felon was to be whipped from the gaol near Salisbury (probably
Fisherton Anger gaol just outside the city) to the market place on the next
market day and then whipped back to the gaol until bloody; two other felons received the penalty of being whipped from the gaol (now specifically
at Fisherton Anger) to the public market in Salisbury and then back to the
gaol, also until bloody.[13] The consistent policy of the Wiltshire bench in the
late sixteenth and particularly the early seventeenth century was thus to
refer petty felons for a whipping in public in the public market place on
a market day, in other words, to inflict public, ritual humiliation through
spectacle in the public and open market space at the height of the market,
for the humiliation of the prisoner and the edification of the wider public
as an exemplary retribution.

Such offenses were not the only ones to provoke punishment in the
market place, but they were the characteristic derelictions in ecclesiastical
courts and in the quarter sessions in Wiltshire which demanded referral
to the market place. In other civil jurisdictions, a variety of other actions
and activities incurred humiliation in the market place. For example, the
justices of the North Riding of Yorkshire consigned the perpetrators of an
outbreak of hedge-breaking in 1614 to the market place to be whipped
there in the open market by the constable of Thirsk.[14] The North Riding
justices used the market place to humiliate other offenders such as those
guilty of cozening letters, errant apprenticeship and lack of kindness to
parents.[15]

The nature of the public space of the market place in early-modern
England can be explored through these referrals of delinquents to punishment in the market place by these two distinct fora: the courts spiritual;
and the criminal jurisdiction of quarter sessions. How were these punishments delivered and what was the nature of these jurisdictions?

Ecclesiastical courts and the market place

Now the direction of penitents by ecclesiastical courts to perform penance in the market place had been a consistent procedure in spiritual punishment from at least the middle of the thirteenth century into the late Middle Ages.[16] By the early sixteenth century its deployment had declined, although in some dioceses it persisted in sporadic and discretionary use to the 1540s.[17] From the 1560s, however, public humiliation in the market place was revived by ecclesiastical jurisdictions. Indeed, Bishop Hooper had anticipated this reintroduction of the market place for the punishment of moral offenses in the early 1550s in the diocese of Gloucester.[18] In short, the late medieval English church courts by and large abandoned the use of the market place in spiritual punishment, while the early restored Protestant *ecclesia anglicana* of the 1560s revived its use. Such transformations in the nature of the disciplinary activities of ecclesiastical courts in England raise questions about the nature of the *ecclesia anglicana* in the 1560s: the extent to which it was consensual and to which it was individualistic or communitarian as well as the origin of the disciplinary regimes imposed in the 1560s.[19] Notwithstanding those important issues, the questions to be explored here pertain only to the use of space.

Let us consider first the basis of the transformations. In the early sixteenth century a diversity of penitential spaces was involved: the parish church and particular stations within it; the churchyard; and imposed pilgrimage, often of a very localized nature. Occasionally, the market place was still invoked as a penitential space for moral derelicts, but only in isolated cases. Enforced pilgrimage extended back into the Middle Ages, but became something of a feature of spiritual punishment in the early sixteenth century. For carnal knowledge of his servant, Alice Hussey, for example, William Fletcher was sentenced to make a pilgrimage from his place of residence, Littleton in Hampshire, to the image of the Blessed Virgin Mary at Southwick (also in Hampshire) and to hear masses in the Lady Chapel there. There he was to offer an oblation to the image and make a benefaction of 5d. to five paupers. Thereafter, he should make a pilgrimage to the image of the Blessed Virgin of Grace in Southampton to hear mass in the chapel and proffer further oblations and alms.[20] Accused of carnal knowledge of Joan Clarke, Giles Mawyer of Chalfont St Giles received a penance of pilgrimage on five feast days of the Virgin to Missenden.[21] In sum, penitential spaces in the early sixteenth century remained: pilgrimage to specified *loca* and the parish church and its cemetery. Increasingly, the market place as a space for penance had been relinquished.

That variety of penance was superseded in some ecclesiastical jurisdictions in the 1560s by a reliance on penance in both market place and
parish church, reviving the consistent use of the market place for punishment by ecclesiastical courts. Usually, penitents were required to perform
penance in both spaces, but occasionally the market alone was designated.
In some jurisdictions, the imposition of the market place became a regularized procedure so that every sexual or moral infraction was uniformly
punished by penance in market place and parish church. In other jurisdictions, nevertheless, the market place was invoked only irregularly as a
discretionary measure. Without engaging in too much detail, the jurisdictions where punishment in the market place consistently obtained, were
those dominated by the "Godly". The archdeaconry of Colchester under
archdeacon George Withers was a principal example.[22] (See Fig. 1, page
330 Penance in Market Places, Archdeaconry of Colchester) Less unam-
biguously, the archdeaconry of Nottingham under archdeacon Lowth exhibited the same policy between 1566 and 1578.[23] The archdeaconries of
Essex and Leicester in these decades belonged in the same category.[24] (See
Figs. 2-4, pages 331-33).

By contrast, jurisdictions where punishment in the market place was
irregularly used, and deployed only as a salutary example, included the
new diocese of Peterborough, the consistory court of Winchester acting
for the archdeaconry, the consistory court of Lichfield acting for that archdeaconry, and the diocese of Ely.[25] When the market place was deployed in
the last (Ely), the punishment was indeed a spectacle, but the market place
was only used intermittently.

By the end of the 1570s, consistent referral of sexual and moral delinquents to the market place lapsed and thenceforth the market place featured only irregularly in all jurisdictions as a space for punishment by
the courts spiritual. From the 1580s penance was usually only imposed
in the parish church, culminating in Archbishop Laud's later designation
of the three stations in the parish church for penance on three successive
Sundays.

The magistracy and the market place

Turning now to civil punishment, that is, discipline administered
on the order of the justices of the peace, bodily discipline in the market
place was as its zenith at the very time when ecclesiastical imposition
of regulation of the body in public space was declining: after the 1580s.
That is one context, but others are equally important. In some sessions
jurisdictions, punishment on the body persisted into the eighteenth

century.[26] By that time, however, another transition was in progress: the gradual eclipse of public whipping by private whipping, that is, the change from whipping in a public place as a spectacle to whipping behind closed doors, withdrawn from the public gaze. Indeed, the prolonged nature of that transition is reflected in the institution of some private whipping in houses of correction in the early seventeenth century. In a small number of cases, very much a minority, the convicted felon was directed to the house of correction to be whipped there and then dismissed.[27]

Of particular interest is the policy of the justices of the Wiltshire bench in their direction of "criminals" to the market place for bodily punishment.[28] Their actions have this significance because, from the second decade of the seventeenth century, they did not simply direct each person guilty of petty larceny to his or her *nearest* market place. Instead, only the market places in the sessions towns were employed. Moreover, all those accused at one meeting of the sessions were directed to the same market place, usually the market place of the current sessions town. Those convicted of petty felony therefore had to traverse Wiltshire, not merely attend in the nearest market town. Moreover, to ensure their compliance, most were first committed to prison before punishment.

Intensifying the concentration, the principal market places for the spectacle were Salisbury and Devizes. Although Marlborough, the other sessions town, continued to be used, many fewer punishments were administered there. The midsummer session held at Warminster was relocated to Devizes from about 1618.[29] In the two years prior to the abandonment of Warminster as a sessions town, nine persons convicted of petty felony had been punished in Warminster market. Of the "criminals" punished in market places by the Wiltshire bench, consequently, 44 per cent experienced their penalty in Salisbury market place and forty-two per cent in Devizes market place.[30] (See Figs. 5-6, pages 334-35).

Although predominantly associated with the market place, some punishments might have been fulfilled in a wider geographical frame. For example, a small proportion of whippings were prescribed not in the market place of the sessions town, but "in", "through" or "in and through" the borough or town: "per opidum de Devizes", "per Burgum de Devizes", "per Burgum de Marlborough", "Et tunc instanter flagelletur in & per Marleborough", "in & per Burgum de Marlebrough", "per Civitatem de Noua Sar'". These directions to a wider processional space occurred interstitially and continuously alongside direction to the market place. On a few occasions, the wider space exceeded the market place in sentences: at Easter 18 James I, the justices directed only one convicted person to the market place, but five others "per Burgum"; similarly the session at Marlborough in 21 James I exploited the whole urban space in four cases compared with only once in the market place. It was not until ca.1620 that this addition of wider urban space was formulated.[31] In overall terms, thirty-three percent of punishments in Devizes were enacted in the wider urban space, while in Marlborough twice as many disciplinary actions were performed in the wider urban space than in the market place. In Salisbury, however, the wider urban space accounted for only a tenth of corporal discipline.

The theater of punishment of delinquents in adjacent Somerset was apparently quite different, although the evidence for discipline in the market place derives almost exclusively from moral delinquency: fornication and the production of bastard children.[32] In this county, the bench consigned unmarried or adulterous mothers to be whipped in the market place of the nearest market town, not restricted to sessions towns (See Fig. 7, p. 336). In numerous cases, the formula employed recites the words "the next market town", as in the case of the unmarried mother of a child born in the parish of Wedmore in 1634 when she was conveyed to the next market town to be publicly whipped.[33] In other cases, the precise market is specified: Elizabeth Stuckey of Muchelney, mother of a bastard child, Dorothy, received the judgment to be whipped at Langport up and down the market until her back be bloody on Saturday about noon in 1613.[34] Examining the distribution map of these punishments, three spatial aspects become evident: a wider range of markets was still employed by the Somerset justices, including small market towns; the sessions towns were used, but not exclusively, and only as the nearest market to the habitation of the offender; and distances traveled by offenders were small.[35]

Comment might be made here, too, on the different policies about bodily punishment between the two jurisdictions. In Wiltshire it became the norm after ca.1615 to inflict punishment on the bare arms until they were bloody.[36] A more severe punishment was exacted by the Somerset magistracy. Margaret Addames, because she was the mother of a bastard child, was sentenced in 1614 to be conveyed by the tithingman of Compton to Pensford on the next market day and be stripped from the shoulders to the waist and whipped about the market as an example to others.[37] Naked from the waist upwards and whipped until the back was bloody appears to have been the normative judgment of the Somerset justices. Another mother was directed to be stripped naked from the middle upwards by the officers of Cameley and whipped until her back be bloody once at Pensford on the next market day and once at Cameley on the following Monday.[38] More specifically, the exposure was occasionally described as stripped from the neck to the girdle.[39]

Although these differences in policy existed, the market place remained the forum for discipline in both civil jurisdictions. The more extreme humiliation of such whipping at the cart's tail through the market place was imposed only as exemplary punishment and thus infrequently. Several female delinquents experienced this retribution in 1636, imposed by the Hertfordshire justices.[40] Ann Benyson and Mary Carde, detained in the county gaol, were sentenced to be whipped through the open market in Hertford at the cart's tail and then returned to Yorkshire, while Mary Boxfield was ordered to remain in gaol until the next Saturday and then to be whipped through the full and open market at the cart's tail before her discharge after paying the court's fees. The Wiltshire justices occasionally resorted to the cart's tail for exemplary justice, although at the sessions of Christmas 18 James I they ordered all six convicted of petty larceny to undergo this treatment in Salisbury market place.[41]

Theorization of space

How, then, do we conceive of these different spaces, in particular the market place? Perhaps we might first review some of the theoretical conceptualizations of space by geographers and anthropologists. Following the symbolic structuralism of Mary Douglas, Stallybrass and White and latterly Sibley have represented space in terms of binary oppositions in structured relationships, so that any unstructured space is regarded as liminal and inappropriate actions in structured space as transgressive: or Douglas's impurity. In the context of early-modern England, Mullaney has adopted this conceptualization to suggest a structured spatiality, in which the theater occupied a liminal space in the Liberties outside the walls of the City: the theater was both licensed and licentious so that it was located in an area outside the normal socio-spatial structures.[42]

More recently, Dodgshon has extended the structural-functionalist argument to maintain that inertia is important in the organization of space (and time), producing an argument somewhat similar to the *structures* or *longue durée* of the Annales School.[43] That sort of homology did not obtain here, however, for the use of penitential spaces was transformational and changing.

Most recently, the structuration theory of Giddens and Bourdieu has attracted much attention, and Giddens has been imported into the geographical context by Allan Pred.[44] At its basis is an attempt to relate structures and agency through mimetic human processes (recursiveness) [Giddens] or Bourdieu's *habitus,* that restricted the repertoire of available actions. It might be argued that such mimesis might be construed in ritual processional routes and penitential processes, but what applies here is the general criticism of structuration theory: what is the precise role of agency? Again, it is necessary to account for transformation and change.[45]

To some extent, all the conceptualizations of space outlined above omit two formative elements: diachrony (transformation) and power: that is, politics with a small p. In all, the emphasis is on synchrony, but the chronology of change of penitential spaces and actions quite clearly introduces the problem of diachrony. While this theorization emphasizes the static characteristic of space, transformational and generative actions in the penitential data have a large influence on space. Both locations and the nature of space were transformed and altered over the sixteenth and seventeenth centuries.

Related to the problem of synchrony is power; at base, theorization emphasizing synchrony lacks an account of power, for power is both dramatic and dynamic. Changes in the locus of penance must have proceeded from local negotiation and contest. The reintroduction of the use of the market place for spiritual punishment through humiliation in a secular environment must have involved negotiation between local civic and ecclesiastical authorities.

To understand that transformation and change, perhaps we need to reinsert the micro-politics of power into spatial exegesis. Space is formed, used and represented through relationships of power: it is the product of social and political relationships of power at diverse levels. Space is thus negotiated, contested and ambiguous. In that sense, some agreement is possible with Lefebvre, for space is socially produced before it is represented; it cannot be represented without that prior social interaction.[46] The obvious points are, then, that space is not neutral; it is socially inhabited; and while there is validity in the notion of representation of space, it is secondary to the human processes and practices in the formation of space. Nevertheless, space retains a strong element of ambiguity and is not structured in a binary manner; it can be confused and compounded by human action.[47]

Let us therefore recapitulate some of the social actions which influenced the organization of space through penitential practices. It seems reasonably clear that space was not thus clearly differentiated as, say, sacred or profane space. Spiritual punishment was enacted in secular space, the market place; secular aspects of punishment (humiliation) were integral to penance in the spiritual space, the parish church. Moreover, in Nottingham, there was the (re-)introduction of a penitential route in the 1560s and 1570s, so that penitents consigned to the market place for punishment reported first to the parish church of St. Mary, processed through the streets of Nottingham to the market place, performed penance there, and then returned in procession to St. Mary's before being certified and absolved. It is possible to construe that geography as a removal from sacred space into secular space and then a reintegration of the spiritual space of the community of the parish and church, but it was equally a confusion of secular and spiritual space. (See Fig. 8, page 337, The Ritual Route of Penance in Nottingham)

Processional routes described by civil authority were more naturally largely restricted to civic space. In Wiltshire, one such processional route, mentioned above, was whipping from the gaol at Fisherton Anger into Salisbury, around the market place and back to the gaol. In 1694, the Shropshire justices prescribed a route for three males convicted of petty larceny who were to be whipped on Saturday in full market from the gaol to the market house in Shrewsbury, round the market house and back to the gaol.[48]

The ambiguous relationship between secular/profane and sacred space can, nevertheless, be detected in other contexts of punishment. Punishment imposed by the civil authority in cases of bastardy might be conducted in the parish church. In 1608, William Lycheat, miller of Wedmore, the reputed father of a child of Margery Chalcrofte, was ordered to pay 6d. weekly to the churchwardens and overseers every Sunday after morning prayer. In the same year, the maintenance of a bastard child born at West Buckland comprised 9d. to be paid weekly by the reputed father every Sunday after divine service to the churchwardens at or upon the communion table of the parish church.[49]

As interesting was the order to William Kenytye who, on Sunday next in 1601, was to stand and remain in the church of Oldham near the choir door during divine service and at noon naked from the waist up with papers on his head: "This person is punished for disobeying the justice of the peace and constable".[50] No rigid separation existed between sacred and secular/profane space, but rather they were rendered confused and ambiguous by social and political action. The spaces seem less separate, even if with pervious boundaries, than ambiguous in the social mind.[51]

One final aspect of spatial relationships thus remains: that between urban and rural, which has indeed recently been addressed in terms of Raymond Williams's separation of urban and rural, as part of the rediscovery of that essential work, *The Country and the City*. Carl Estabrook has proposed that the alleged urban renaissance of the late seventeenth century emphasized the cultural difference between urban and rural in the context of Bristol and its hinterland, although two issues confront us here: first, the discovery of an indigenous urban culture from the 1540s by Bob Tittler and second the distinctive nature of Bristol itself.[52] Focusing on the century before then, the contributors to a very recent collection of essays edited by MacLean, Landry and Ward about the urban and the rural in early modern England have evaluated further Williams's conceptualization.[53] To some extent what an analysis of penance reveals is that the market place as a site provided one (limited) element in a cultural conduit between urban and rural, but not the more certain "cultural cement" attributed by Alex Walsham to providentialism in early-modern England.[54] Alternatively, however, the relationship might be perceived as a (temporary) imposition of the cultural values of some urban places on their rural hinterlands (defined by ecclesiastical jurisdiction, nevertheless).

Whereas penance in the parish church restricted the performance of ritual expiation to the parochial inhabitants, penitential discipline in the urban market place imported offenders from the countryside into the town for a cultural episode. In this respect, localized but rural cultural hinterlands were perpetuated around the significant urban market centers, mitigating the development of cultural differences spatially constructed between urban and rural. Penance in the market place thus allowed a shared cultural resource between urban and rural, although it was contained within urban space. Of course, that shared cultural experience was dissolved when penance in the market place was renounced from the 1580s, so that ritual humiliation and expiation were restricted to the parish where rural no longer met urban. At about that time, referral of offenders to the market place by the justices compensated for that withdrawal by the spiritual courts. The spatial containers of penance in the market place were, furthermore, at least to some extent, ecclesiastical jurisdictions, deaneries and archdeaconries. In these cultural and spatial terms, the hinterlands of urban places were constituted to some degree from the context of ecclesiastical administration.

While the manifest nuances of penance imposed by ecclesiastical courts have not been addressed here, it is permissible to perceive spatial transformations in the deployment of public penance through the sixteenth century. While the space for penance resulting from confession was the self, that is, mainly interior contrition, the space associated with penance imposed by ecclesiastical courts for sexual and moral dereliction was external, informed by satisfaction as an element of penance. Public penance involved ritual humiliation and expiation in public space. While one forum for that ritual public shaming was continuously the parish church, an episode in the 1560s and 1570s which referred public humiliation also to the market place rendered space ambiguous. Penitential space in this episode was public, secular space. The use of that space in the market place was negotiated, informed by the micro-politics of place and confessional category. It was ambiguous space, secular, but also the *locus* of a spiritual punishment imposed by courts spiritual. It was space produced by social practice, and social practice was and remains unstructured, contingent and ambiguous.

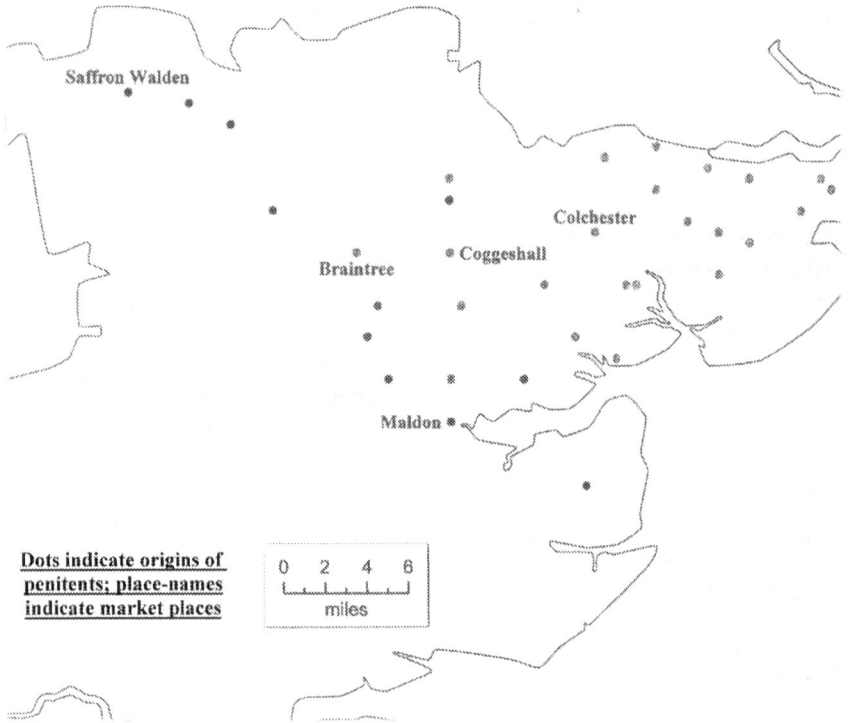

Figure Conc. 1   Penance in Market Places, Archdeaconry of Colchester

In all cases, dots represent
origins of penitents and
place-names market places.

Melton Mowbray

Loughborough

Mountsorrel

Leicester

Hinckley

Market Harborough

0   2   4   6
miles

Figure Conc. 2   Penance in Market Places, Archdeaconry of Leicester

In all cases dots represent
origins of penitents and
place-names market places.

• Blyth

East Retford

• Worksop

Warsop

• Mansfield

• Newark

Nottingham

0 1 2 3 4 5
miles

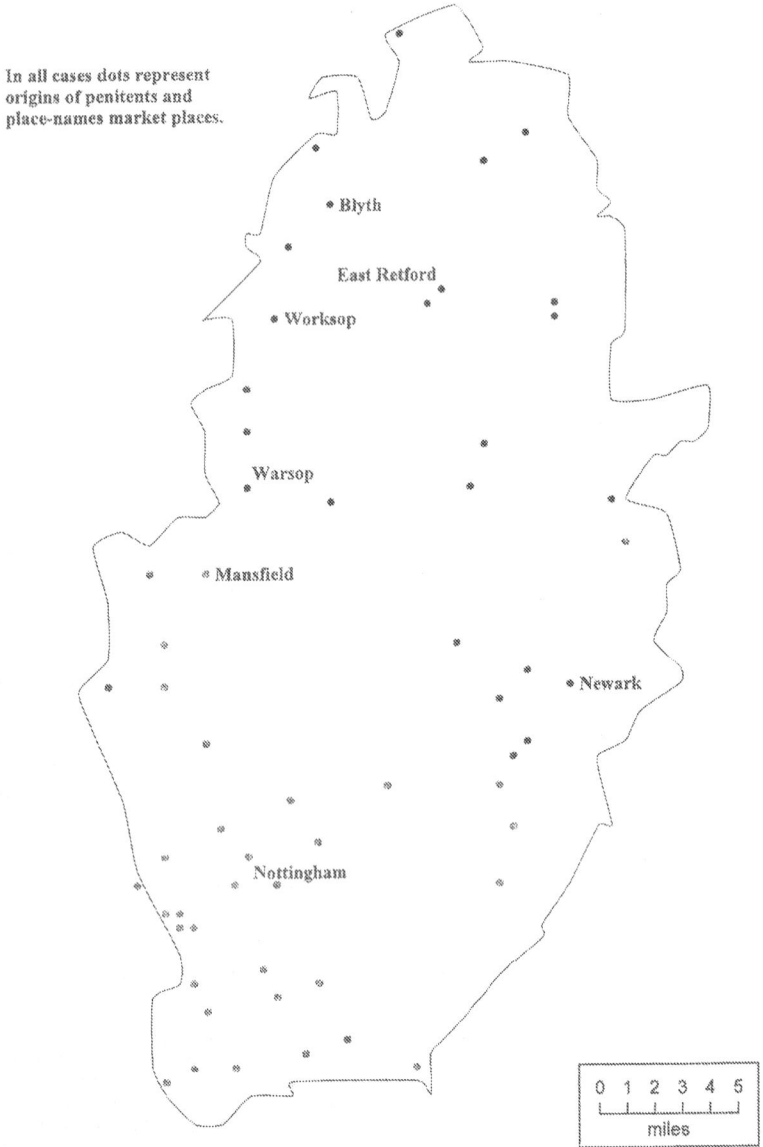

Figure Conc. 3   Penance in Market Places, Archdeaconry of Nottingham

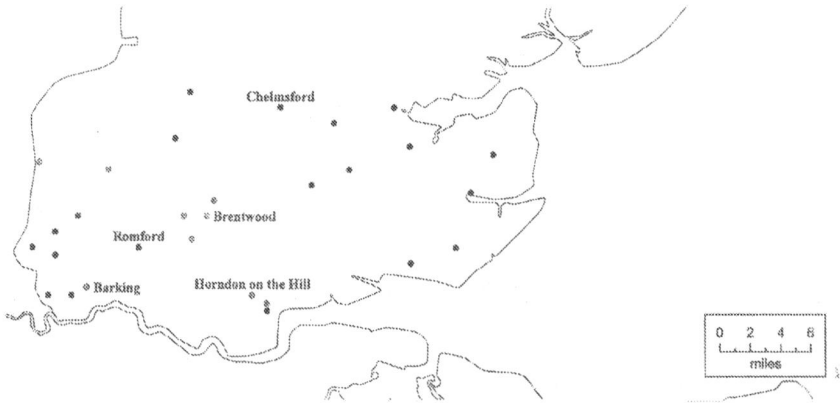

Figure Conc. 4   Penance in Market Places, Archdeaconry of Essex

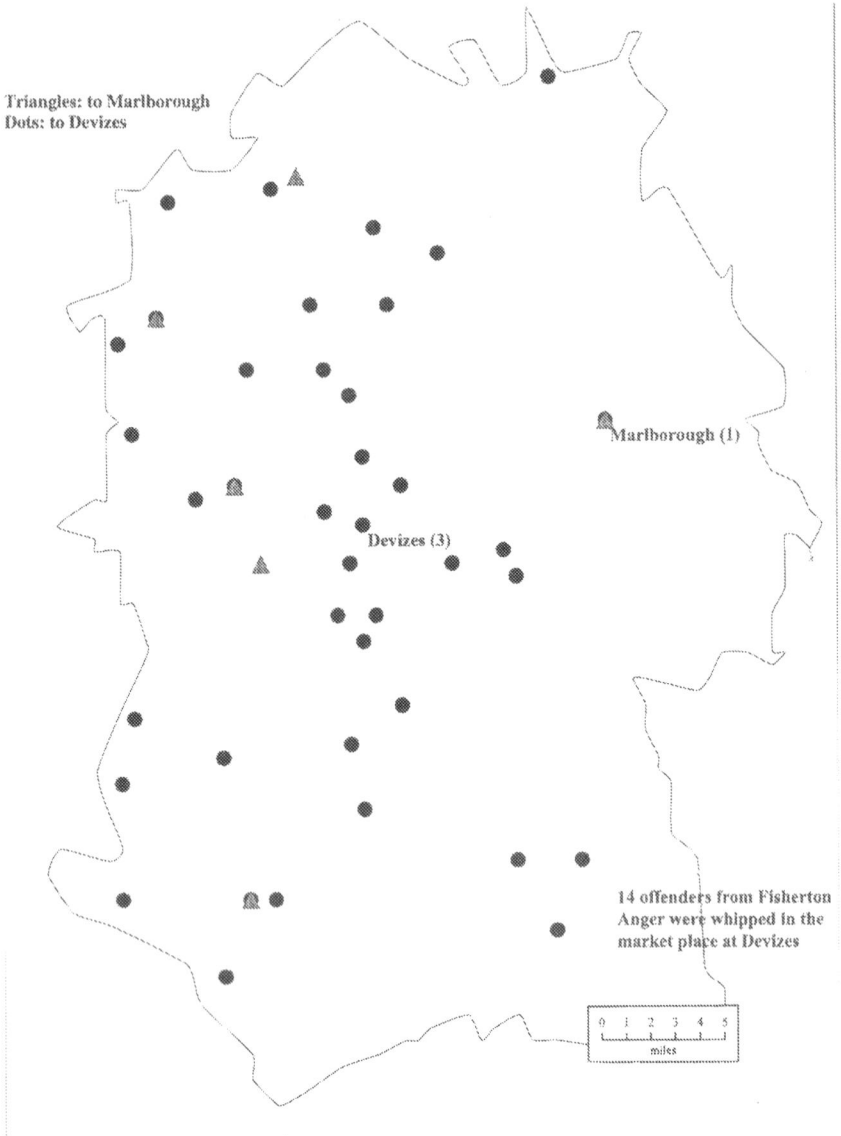

Triangles: to Marlborough
Dots: to Devizes

Marlborough (1)

Devizes (3)

14 offenders from Fisherton
Anger were whipped in the
market place at Devizes

0 1 2 3 4 5
miles

Figure Conc. 5   Punishment in Market Places, Devizes and Marlborough

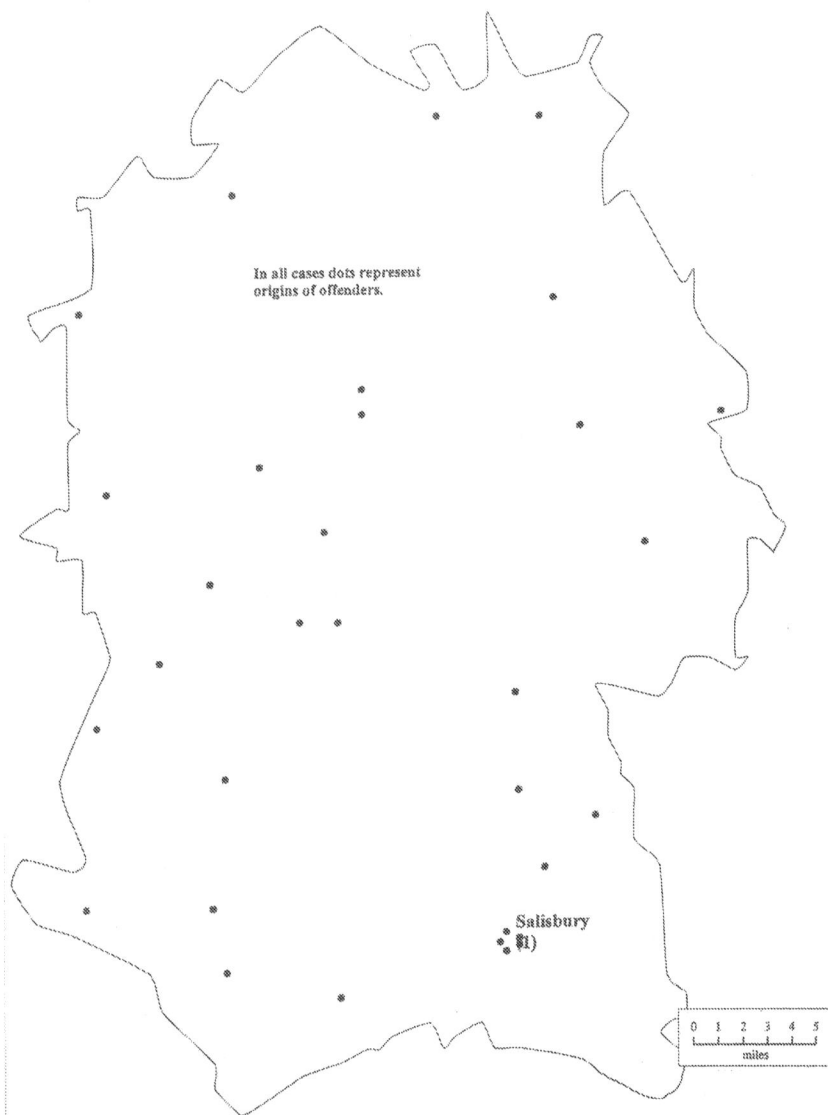

In all cases dots represent
origins of offenders.

Salisbury
(1)

0 1 2 3 4 5
miles

Figure Conc. 6   Punishment in Market Places, Salisbury

Figure Conc. 7   Punishment in Market Places, Somerset

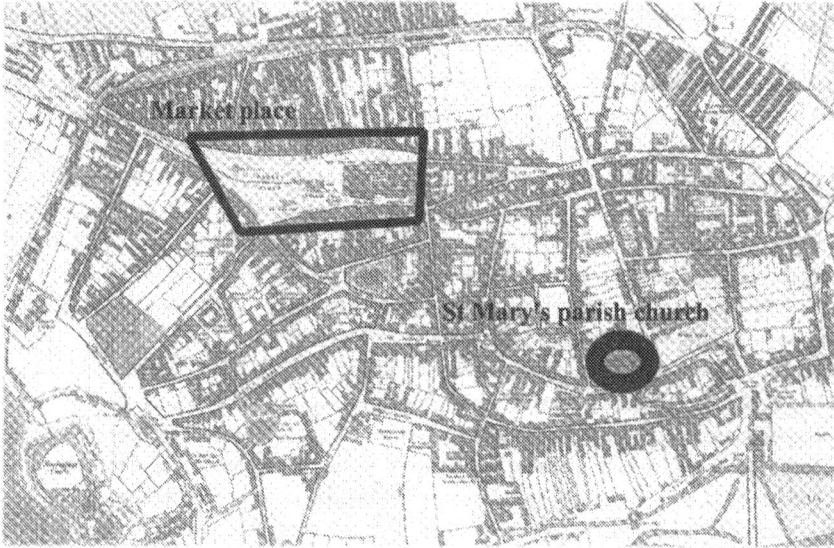

Figure Conc. 8   Ritual Route of Penance in Nottingham
[*Source:* based upon Mary D. Lobel, ed., *Historic Towns. Maps of Towns and Cities in the British Isles* (London: Scolar Press , 1969), with acknowledgments)

Notes

[1]Emma Griffin, "Sports and Celebrations in English Market Towns, 1660-1750," *Historical Research* 75 (2002): 188-208.

[2]John H. E. Bennett and John C. Dewhurst, eds., *Quarter Sessions Records ... County Palatinate of Chester 1559-1760*, Lancashire and Cheshire Record Society vol. 94 (1940), 201-2.

[3]WSRO 865/588: a letter from Mr Fitzharding in Bruton, 25 June 1654: "You may thinke me very confident to write to a person of your quality & we much a stranger in a business of this nature but the concerne of this place to see your servant & severall others who frequent this Market endure soe much severity as often they doe by rigeur of weather have set them on a very good worke the building a convenient Market house but it will be too hard for them with out great assistance" and then alluding to the office of Mr. John Stephens as one of the treasurers for the building.

[4]For its extreme civic dignity, Mary D. Harris, ed., The *Coventry Leet Book or Mayor's Register,* 4 vols., Early English Text Society (Oxford, 1908-9), vol. 1, 134-5, 138-9; II, 289; III, 662, 775. For a discussion of the culture of the market place, but focusing on the "moral economy", Andrew Randall and Andrew Charlesworth, eds., *Markets, Market Culture and Popular Protest in Eighteenth-century Britain and Ireland* (Liverpool: Liverpool University Press, 1996).

[5]Anne Kettle, "Matthew Craddock's Book of Remembrance, 1614-15," in *Collections for a History of Staffordshire,* 4th ser., vol. 16 (1994), 75.

[6]Derek Shorrocks, ed., *Bishop Still's Visitation 1594 and The 'Smale Book' of the Clerk of the Peace for Somerset 1593-5* (hereafter The *'Smale Book')*, Somerset Record Society vol. 84 (1998), 159: two men presented at North Curry for living suspiciously and idly haunting fairs and markets (1594).

[7]An interesting example of the insinuation of civic hierarchy into the market place concerns the use of the so-called "Penniless Bench" in Oxford market: O. Ogle, "The Oxford Market," in *Collectanea,* vol. II, Oxford Historical Society vol. 16 (Oxford, 1890), 32, 38 and 41.

[8]For ethnographic studies of the market place in its non-economic activities see Clifford Geertz, *Negara. The Theater State in Nineteenth-century Bali* (Princeton: Princeton University Press, 1980), where his comments on markets and the market place are essentially compressed at 99; E. P. Skinner, "Trade and Markets among the Lossi people," in *Markets in Africa* ed. Paul Bohannan and George Dalton (Northwestern University Press, 1962), specifically at 267-8; in the introduction, Bohannan and Dalton briefly indicate the "non-economic aspects of market places" (15-19); M. S. Romar, "Lakshmi in the Market Place: Traders and Farmers in a North Indian Market," unpublished Ph.D. (University of Edinburgh, 1992); G. C. Clark, "The Position of Ashante Women Traders in Kumasi Central Market, Ghana," unpublished Ph.D. (University of Cambridge, 1984).

[9]CUL EDR D2/9 fol. 31v.

[10]CUL EDR D2/9c fol. 151r.

[11]CUL EDR D2/1 fols. lxxxvj recto and lxxxxvij recto-verso.

[12]WSRO A1/150/2, p. 275 (paginated not foliated).

[13]WSRO A1/150/3, pp. 690-1 (paginated not foliated) .

[14]J. C. Atkinson, ed., *Quarter Sessions Records*, North Riding Record Society vol. 2 (1884), 44.

[15]Atkinson, *Quarter Sessions Records,* vol. 2, 201, 207; *Quarter Sessions Records,* North Riding Record Society vol. 3, (1885), 134, 260.

[16]For the public significance of the medieval market place, see Masschaele, "The Public Sphere of the Market Place."

[17]See above, Chapter 6.

[18]Price, "Gloucester Diocese under Bishop Hooper 1551-3," 90-93.

[19]For recent perspectives emphasizing genuine acceptance of the reformed *ecclesia anglicana,* Christopher Marsh, *Popular Religion in Sixteenth-century England. Holding their Peace* (Basingstoke: Palgrave, 1998); Judith Maltby, *Prayer Book and People in Elizabethan and Early Stuart England* (Cambridge: Cambridge University Press, 1998), 1-82.

[20]HRO 21M65/C1/1 fol. 57r (1522).

[21]Bowker, ed., *An Episcopal Court Book,* 109.

[22]Higgs, *Godliness and Governance in Tudor Colchester,* 216; Byford, "The Price of Protestantism," 319-400 and "The Birth of a Protestant town," 43. An example of processing the length of the market and then confessing at the Moot Hall door is provided by Pressey, "The Records of the Archdeaconries of Essex and Colchester," 17; for Withers, Burchill, "On the Consolation of a Christian Scholar," 573; Cameron, *The European Reformation,* 415.

[23]For the context of the archdeaconry and for Lowth, see Marchant, *The Church under the Law,* chap. 5 and Marchant, *The Puritans and the Church Courts,* 132-6.

[24]UoN Dept. of MSS. Archdeaconry Act Books A3; ERO D/AEA and D/ACA; ROLLR 1D41. For the background for Essex, Pressey, "The Records of the Archdeaconries of Essex and Colchester"; Anglin, "The Essex Puritan Movement and the 'Bawdy' Courts"; Hunt, *The Puritan Movement.*

[25]HRO 21M65; NRO Peterborough consistory court act books; LRO B/C/.

[26]R. L. Kenyon, ed., *Abstract of the Orders made by the Court of Quarter Sessions for Shropshire January, 1660-April, 1694,* Shropshire County Records (SCR) vol. 12 (1908); Rowland G. Venables, *Abstract of the Orders ... July 1741-January 1757,* SCR vol. 4 (n.d.); Venables, *Abstract of the Orders. . . April 1757-June 1772* (SCR 5, n.d.); Offley Wakeman, ed., *Abstract of the Orders ... July 1772-October 1782,* SCR vol. 7 (n.d.); all illustrate the mixture of private and public whippings in the eighteenth century and the persistence of public whippings, including specifically in the market place. WSRO A1/150/22 confirms this persistence of public whipping and its mixture with private whippings in the 1780s. For an example of private whipping,

see p. 330, "To be privately but severely Whipt at Devizes Bridewell ..." (bis).

[27]WSRO A1/150/7 (not foliated or paginated), Christmas 8 Chas I: an idle man, who left his wife and children to become chargeable, was directed to the house of correction at Fisherton Anger (one of the three new houses of correction) and whipped, then to be set on work. As noted above, the gaol had been located at Fisherton Anger, but an additional house of correction was also constructed there at the order of the justices.

[28]The following is based on WSRO A1/150/2-7: sessions "entry books", ca.1615-36.

[29]WSRO A1/150/4 (not foliated or paginated), 15 James I.

[30]There are some complications: (a) in a few cases the market place is not specifically stated; these incidences are excluded from the calculations; (b) there are numerous entries where the whipping is ordered to be performed "in" or "through" or "in and through" the borough or town, for which, see below for more detail; and (c) idiosyncratically, the justices used the market place of Westbury in one year only, in the mid-1630s, to punish four felons from Westbury and one each from two other adjacent villages, a total of six criminals: WSRO A1/150//7, pp. (sic, not foliated) 750-1. Occasionally, the pillory was substituted, but it too was often located in the market place: thus two convicted persons were confined to the pillory in the market place of Devizes for a period of two hours each: WSRO A1/150/4.

[31]This paragraph is based on WSRO, A1/150/4-7 (all unfoliated and unpaginated).

[32]Edward H. Bates, ed., *Quarter Sessions Records for the County of Somerset*, vol. 1, Somerset Record Society vol. 23 (1907); Edward H. B. Harbin, ed., *Quarter Sessions Records for the County of Somerset*, vol. 2, Somerset Record Society vol. 24 (1908) (hereafter *Somerset Quarter Sessions)*, vol. 1, 11. For whipping for petty larceny in Somerset, however, see *The 'Smale Book'*, 163-4, 167 (1595).

[33]*Somerset Quarter Session*, vol. 2, 219.

[34]*Somerset Quarter Sessions*, vol. 1, 108.

[35]The evidence is at: *Somerset Quarter Sessions*, vol. 1, 2, 18-19, 51-3, 112-13, 119, 131-2, 148, 156, 169, 176-7, 187, 202-3, 207, 211, 213, 219, 226, 233-4, 243, 252, 276-7, 285, 290-1, 298, 305, 319, 322, 326, 329, 333, 338, 348; vol. 2, 68, 91, 123, 198, 300-1.

[36]WSRO A1/150/3, p. 722 is the first reference: "super suos nudos humeros" in Devizes market.

[37]*Somerset Quarter Sessions*, vol. 1, 131.

[38]*Somerset Quarter Sessions*, vol. 1, 176.

[39]*Somerset Quarter Sessions*, vol. 1, 234, 290. See also Lister, *West Riding Sessions Records*, vol. 2, 16-17 (stripped naked from the middle up and whipped for bastardy, 1614).

[40]William Le Hardy, ed., *Hertfordshire County Records*, vol. 5 (Hertford: Hertfordshire County Council, 1928), 209, 221.

[41]WSRO A1/150/4 (not foliated or paginated).

⁴²   Douglas, *Purity and Danger.* Peter Stallybrass and Allon White, *The Politics and Poetics of Transgression* (Ithaca, N.Y.: Cornell University Press, 1986), not least in the first chapter on the market place and fair; Sibley, *Geographies of Exclusion*; Mullaney, *The Place of the Stage.* The genealogy extends back perhaps to Victor Turner, who might have derived his structural explanation of pilgrimage and sacred space from Mircea Eliade; ultimately the genealogy of ideas might be traced back to van Gennep, but more in the structuring of time than space. Victor and Edith Turner, *Image and Pilgrimage in Christian Culture*, critically evaluated by John Eade and Michael J. Sellow, "Introduction" in *Contesting the Sacred*, who demonstrate that the "sacred" site of the destination of pilgrimage is/was compromised by secular activity in its immediate vicinity. Jonathon Sumption has indicated that pilgrimage might equate with banishment, in which case it negates the "voluntarism" of the Turners' pilgrimage: Sumption, *Pilgrimage*, 105.

⁴³Dodgshon, *Society in Time and Space.*

⁴⁴Pred, *Making Histories and Constructing Human Geographies..*

⁴⁵Compare, however, in this context perhaps, Michel de Certeau's notion of the subversion of structured space by the powerless: because structured space has been discursively formed, it can be inadvertently as well as meaningfully compromised by the wanderings and meandering of the powerless, so the structured aspect remains a subjective representation. For the difference of strategies and tactics in relation to space and in relation to power, see de Certeau, *The Practice of Everyday Life*, 29-30; see also, for a suggestion about entitlement to the use of public space, Goheen, "The Ritual of the Streets in Mid-nineteenth-century Toronto."

⁴⁶Lefebvre, *The Production of Space, pace* the criticisms of Tim Unwin: "A Waste of Space? "

⁴⁷Kay Anderson and Fay Gale, *Cultural Geographies* (London: Routledge, 1992) and Michael Keith and Steve Pile, *Place and the Politics of Identity* (London: Routledge, 1993); Soja, *Postmodern Geographies.* In an historical context, Penny Roberts, "Contesting Sacred Space: Burial Disputes in Sixteenth-century France," and Peter Marshall, "'The Map of God's Word': Geographies of the Afterlife in Tudor and Early Stuart England," both in *The Place of the Dead. Death and Remembrance in Late Medieval and Early Modern Europe* ed. Bruce Gordon and Marshall (Cambridge: Cambridge University Press, 2000), 110-48.

⁴⁸Kenyon, *Abstract of the Orders ... January 1660-April1694*, 152. See also the male convicted of petty larceny publicly whipped at the cart's tail from Castle Gates through High Street to Stone Bridge in 1770: Venables, *Abstract of the Orders ... 1757-1772*, 219; Sarah Ford who was to be led from the house of correction in Shrewsbury to the market house, round the market house, with a label on her back ("Sarah Ford, a notorious Cheat") on a Saturday between noon and 1 p.m. and there to be severely whipped until her back was bloody (1782): Wakeman, *Abstract of the Orders ... July 1772-October 1782.* In the eighteenth century, a public whipping stock had been established in Shrewsbury's market place: Kenyon, *Abstract of the*

Orders. . ., 157, 161, 165.

[49]*Somerset Quarter Session,* vol. 1, 18-19.

[50]Tait, *Lancashire Quarter Sessions,* vol. I, *1590-1606,* 97.

[51]Zerubavel, *Social Mindscapes.*

[52]Estabrook, *Urbane and Rustic England;* Tittler, *The Reformation and the Towns in England.*

[53]MacLean, Landry and Ward, *The Country and the City Revisited,* especially "Introduction" at 1-23.

[54]The phrase "cultural cement" is from Alex Walsham, *Providence in Early Modern England* (Oxford: Oxford University Press, 1999).

Works Cited

Primary Sources

Manuscripts cited

Bodleian Library, Oxford
Queen's College Roll 99
MS. Laud Misc. 625
Rawl. MS. 350
MS. Wood empt. 7
MS Charters Oxon d1, no. 41
Bristol Record Office [BRO]
JQS/M/2
British Library, London
 Cotton MS. Tib. BII
Cambridgeshire Record Office (CRO)
Q/SO1
City Archives Common Day Book 1610-1646
Cambridge University Library (CUL)
Ely Diocesan Records (EDR) D/2/1-10
Chicago University Library
Bacon MS. 114
Devon Record Office, Exeter
CR 1429
CR 1435
Essex Record Office (ERO)
D/ACA 1-27
D/AEA 1-27
Q/SR 106/28
Q/SR 109/19
Hampshire Record Office (HRO)
21M65/C1/1
21M65/C1/12
Lichfield Record Office (LRO)
B/C/1/A

B/C/2/2
B/C/2/3
B/C/3/1
B/C/3/10
B/C/11 (probate)
Longleat House
(microfilm: Chivers)
Longleat MS 10770
Longleat MS 10774
Longleat MS. 11181
Massachusetts State Archives
Microfilms of Quarterly Courts
Merton College, Oxford
MM 6196-6244
MM 6367-6406
MM 6556-6629
(The) National Archives, London
C260/86
SC2/183/57
Northamptonshire Record Office (NRO)
Peterborough Diocesan Records (PDR) X610/24
PDR X610/27
PDR Episcopal Correction Book X611/28
PDR X611/29
PDR X614/27
PDR archdeaconry correction book, 1610-1618
PDR Archdeaconry Correction Book 41
PDR consistory court office act book 14
PDR consistory court office act book 18
50P/1
NBR 3/1
Norwich and Norfolk Record Office (NNRO)
NNRO NCR Case 12a/1a
NCR case 16 shelf c no. 5
NCR Case 12a/1c
NCR case 12a/1d
Y/C19/4
ANF/9/1
Archdeaconry of Norwich Register Cook
Archdeaconry of Norwich register of wills (microfilm 503)
Nottinghamshire Archives Office (NARO)
CA1 series

(The) Queen's College, Oxford
MS. 366
Record Office for Leicestershire, Leicester and Rutland (ROLLR)
1D41/13/1-38
BRII/12/7/5
Pochin MSS.
Barkby parish registers
Probate records
Sheffield Archives Office
CB
Staffordshire Record office
D1721/1/4
University of Nottingham (UoN) Dept. of MSS.
Archdeaconry A1
Archdeaconry A3 series
AN/LB 216/5/1/7
AN/LB 218/2/7/4
AN/LB 220/4/2/1
AN/LB 222/5/2/1-2
AN/LB 222/5/12/1-2
AN/LB 223/2/1/1/1-2
AN/LB 223/2/15/2
AN LB 223/2/15/3/1-5
AN/LB 224/1/6/1
AN/LB 224/1/8
AN/LB 224/1/35/2
AN/LB 224/1/50/1-6
Wiltshire and Swindon Record Office (WSRO)
Quarter Sessions A1/150/6
G23/1/3
D3/4/1
A1/150/2-7
A1/150/22
865/588
Worcestershire Record Office (WRO)
794.011 BA 2513 1 (i) (act book, 1530-1537)
794.011 BA 2513 2 (i) (act book, 1557-1563)
794.011 BA 2513 1(ii) (act book, 1540-50)
716.093 BA 2922.
794.011 BA 2513
716.093 BA 2922
Wills to 1530 (microfilm in University of Leicester Library)
BA 9360/A14 496.5,

Secondary works

Abate, Corinne S., ed. *Privacy, Domesticity, and Women in Early Modern England.* Aldershot: Ashgate, 2003.

Abrams, Philip. "Towns and Economic Growth: Some Theories and Problems." In *Towns in Societies: Essays in Economic History and Historical Sociology,* edited by Abrams and E. A. (Tony) Wrigley, 9-33. Cambridge: Cambridge University Press, 1978.

Adair, Richard. *Courtship, Illegitimacy and Marriage in Early Modern England.* Manchester: Manchester University Press, 1996.

Ahearne, Jeremy. *Michel de Certeau: Interpretation and its Other.* Stanford: Stanford University Press, 1995.

Amit, Vered, ed. *Realizing Community: Concepts, Social Relations and Sentiments.* London: Routledge, 2002.

Anderson, Kay, and Fay Gale. *Cultural Geographies.* London: Routledge, 1992.

Andrew Pettegree. *Reformation and the Culture of Persuasion.* Cambridge: Cambridge University Press, 2005.

Arkell, Tom, Nesta Evans and Nigel Goose, eds. *When Death Do Us Part: Understanding and Interpreting the Probate Records of Early Modern England.* Oxford: Leopard's Head Press, 2000.

Armitage, David, Michael J. Braddick, eds. *The British Atlantic World, 1500-1800.* Basingstoke: Palgrave, 2002.

Arnold, John H. *Belief and Unbelief in Medieval Europe.* London: Hodder Arnold, 2005.

Asad, Talal. "Remarks on the Anthropology of the Body." In *Religion and the Body,* edited by Sarah Coakley, 42-52. Cambridge: Cambridge University Press, 1997.

Baines, Dudley. *Migration in a Mature Economy: Emigration and Internal Migration in England and Wales 1861-1900.* Cambridge: Cambridge University Press, 1985.

Banks, Sarah, "Nineteenth-century Scandal or Twentieth-century Model? A New Look at 'Open' and 'Closed' Parishes." *Economic History Review* 2nd ser. 41 (1988): 51-73.

Barbalet, Jack, ed. *Emotions and Sociology.* Oxford: Blackwell Publishing for The Sociological Review Monographs, 2002.

Barnes, Barry. *Understanding Agency: Social Theory and Responsible Action.* London, Routledge, 2000.

Barry, Jonathan. "Provincial Town Culture, 1640-1680: Urbane or Civic?" In *Interpretation and Cultural History,* edited by Joan Pittock & Andrew Wear, 198-234. Basingstoke: Palgrave, 1991.

Becker, Howard. *Outsiders: Studies in the Sociology of Deviance.* New York: Free Press, 1963.

Beckerman, John S. "Procedural Innovation and Institutional Change in Medieval

English Courts." *Law and History Review,* 10 (1992): 197-252.

Beier, A. Lee. *Masterless Men: The Vagrancy Problem in England 1560-1640.* London: Methuen, 1985.

Beier, A. Lee. "The Social Problems of an Elizabethan Country Town: Warwick, 1580-90." In *Country Towns in Pre-Industrial England,* edited by Peter Clark, 45-85. Leicester: Leicester University Press, 1981.

Bell, Catherine. *Ritual Theory, Ritual Practice.* Oxford: Oxford University Press, 1992.

Bell, Catherine. *Ritual: Perspectives and Dimensions.* Oxford: Oxford University Press, 1997.

Bell, Colin, and Howard Newby, eds. *Community Studies: An Introduction to the Sociology of the Local Community.* New York, Praeger Publishers, 1972.

Bell, Michael. *Childerley: Nature and Morality in a Country Village.* Chicago: University of Chicago Press, 1994.

Bennett, Judith M. *Women in the Medieval English Countryside: Gender and Household at Brigstock before the Plague.* Oxford: Oxford University Press, 1987.

Bennett, Judith M. "Feminism and History." *Gender and History 1* (1989): 251-72.

Bennett, Judith, and Amy Froide, eds. *Singlewomen in the European Past 1200-1800.* Chicago: University of Chicago Press, 1999.

Bennett, Judith. "Spouses, Siblings and Surnames: Reconstructing Families from Medieval Village Court Rolls." *Journal of British Studies* 23 (1983): 26-46.

Berkowitz, Steven D. *An Introduction to Structural Analysis: The Network Approach to Social Research.* Toronto: Butterworths, 1982.

Bernard, George W. "Vitality and Vulnerability in the Late Medieval Church: Pilgrimage on the Eve of the Break with Rome." In *The End of the Middle Ages: England in the Fifteenth and Sixteenth Centuries,* edited by John L. Watts, 199-237. Stroud: Sutton, 1998.

Bettey, Joseph. *Church and Parish.* London: Batsford, 1987,

Birch, D. J., "Selling the Saints: Competition Among Pilgrimage Centres in the Twelfth Century." *Medieval History 2* (1992): 20-34.

Bloch, Maurice. "Symbols, Song, Dance and Features of Articulation: Is Religion an Extreme Form of Traditional Authority?' In Bloch, *Ritual, History and Power: Selected Papers in Anthropology,* 19-45. London: Athlone, 1989.

Blu, Karen I. "'Where Do You Stay At?'" In *Senses of Place,* edited by Feld and Basso, 197-227.

Boissevain, Jeremy. *Friends of Friends: Networks, Manipulators and Coalitions.* Oxford: Blackwell, 1974.

Boissevain, Jeremy, and J. Clyde Mitchell, eds. *Network Analysis: Studies in Human Interaction.* The Hague: Mouton, 1973.

Borgatti, Steve P. Martin G. Everett, and Simon C. Freeman, *Ucinet IV Version 1.06.* Columbia, S.C.: Analytic Technologies, 1992.

Borsay, Peter. *The English Urban Renaissance: Culture and Society in the Provincial Town, 1660-1770.* Oxford: Oxford University Press, 1989.

Bossy, John. "Moral Arithmetic: Seven Sins into Ten Commandments." In *Conscience and Casuistry in Early Modern Europe*, edited by Edmund Leites, 214-34. Cambridge: Cambridge University Press, 1988.

Bossy, John. "Prayers." *Transactions of the Royal Historical Society* 6ᵗʰ ser. 1 (1991): 137-50.

Bossy, John. "The Mass as a Social Institution, 1200-1700." *Past and Present* 100 (1983): 29-61.

Bossy, John. "The Social History of Confession in the Age of the Reformation." *Transactions of the Royal Historical Society* 5ᵗʰ ser. 25 (1975): 21-38.

Boulton, Jeremy. "Residential Mobility in Seventeenth-century Southwark." *Urban History Yearbook* (1986): 1-14

Bouquet, Mary R. *Family, Servants and Visitors: The Farm Household in Nineteenth and Twentieth Century Devon*. Norwich: Geo, 1985.

Bourdieu, Pierre. *The Logic of Practice*. Trans. Richard Nice. Cambridge: Polity, 1992.

Bowker, Margaret. *The Secular Clergy in the Diocese of Lincoln 1495-1520*. Cambridge: Cambridge University Press, 1968.

Braddick, Michael. *State Formation in Early Modern England c.1500-1700*. Cambridge: Cambridge University Press, 2000.

Braun, Willi. "Religion." In *Guide to the Study of Religion*, edited by Braun and Russell T. McCutcheon, 3-18. London and New York: Cassell, 2000.

Brett, Martin. *The English Church Under Henry I* . Oxford: Oxford University Press, 1975.

Britnell, Richard H. *The Commercialisation of English Society 1000-1500*. Cambridge: Cambridge University Press, 1993.

Brown, Andrew. *Popular Piety in Late Medieval England: The Diocese of Salisbury 1250-1550*. Oxford: Oxford University Press, 1995.

Buchanan, Ian. *Michel de Certeau: Cultural Theorist*. London: Sage, 2000.

Burchill, Christopher J. "On the Consolation of a Christian scholar: Zacharias Ursinus (1534-83) and the Reformation in Heidelberg." *Journal of Ecclesiastical History* 37 (1986): 565-83.

Byford, Mark S. "The Birth of a Protestant Town: The Process of Reformation in Tudor Colchester." In *The Reformation in English Towns 1500-1640*, edited by Patrick Collinson and John Craig, 23-47. Basingstoke: Palgrave, 1998.

Byford, Mark S. "The Price of Protestantism: Assessing the Impact of Religious Change in Elizabethan Essex." Unpublished D.Phil diss. (University of Oxford, 1988).

Cameron, Euan. *The European Reformation*. Oxford: Blackwell, 1991.

Campbell, Karen E. "Networks Past: A 1939 Bloomington Neighborhood." *Social Forces* 69 (1990): 139-155.

Capp, Bernard. *When Gossips Meet: Women, Family, and Neighbourhood in Early Modern England*. Oxford: Oxford University Press, 2003.

Carlson, Eric. *Marriage and the English Reformation*. Oxford: Blackwell, 1994.

Carter, Mary P. "An Urban Society and its Hinterland: St Ives in the Seventeenth and Eighteenth Centuries." Unpublished Ph.D. diss. (University of Leicester, 1989).

Carter, Mary P. "Town or Urban Society? St Ives in Huntingdonshire, 1630-1740." In *Societies, Cultures and Kinship*, edited by Phythian-Adams, 77-130.

Carus-Wilson, Eleanor M. "The First Half-century of the Borough of Stratford-upon-Avon." Repr. in *The Medieval Town: A Reader in English Urban History 1200-1540*, edited by Richard Holt and Gervase Rosser, 49-70. London: Longman, 1990.

Casey, Edward S."How to Get from Space to Place in a Fairly Short Stretch of Time. Phenomenological Prolegomena." In *Senses of Place*, edited by Field and Basso, 13-52.

Chambers, Douglas. *The Reinvention of the World: English Writing 1650-1750*. London: Arnold, 1996.

Charlesworth, Simon. *A Phenomenology of Working Class Experience*. Cambridge: Cambridge University Press, 2000.

Clark, G. C. "The Position of Ashante Women Traders in Kumasi Central Market, Ghana." Unpublished Ph.D. University of Cambridge, 1984.

Clark, Peter and David Souden, eds. *Migration and Society in Early Modern England*. London: Hutchinson, 1987.

Clark, Peter. "The Migrant in Kentish Towns, 1580-1640." In *Crisis and Order in English Towns 1500-1700*, edited by Clark and Paul Slack, 117-63. London,: Routledge and Kegan Paul, 1972.

Clarke, C. A. "Peasant Society and Land Transactions in Chesterton, Cambridgeshire, 1277-1325." Unpublished D.Phil. University of Oxford, 1985.

Claval, Paul. *An Introduction to Regional Geography*. Trans. Ian Thompson. Oxford: Blackwell, 1998.

Cohen, Anthony P., ed. *Belonging: Identity and Social Organisation in British Rural Cultures*. Manchester: Manchester University Press, 1982.

Cohen, Anthony P. *The Symbolic Construction of Community*. London: Routledge, 1985.

Cohen, Esther. *The Crossroads of Justice: Law and Culture in Late Medieval France*. Leiden, 1993.

Cohen, Esther. "The Animated Pain of the Body." *American Historical Review* 105 (2000): 36-68.

Coldewey, John. "Carnival's End: Puritan Ideology and the Decline of English Provincial Theatre." In *Festive Drama*, edited by Meg Twycross, 279-86. Cambridge: D. S. Brewer, 1996.

Collinge, Chris. "The *Différence* Between Society and Space: Nested Scales and the Return of Spatial Fetishism." *Society and Space* 23 (2005): 189-206.

Collinson, Patrick. *The Birthpangs of Protestant England: Religious and Cultural Change in the Sixteenth and Seventeenth Centuries*. London: Macmillan, 1988.

Collinson, Patrick. "The Protestant Cathedral, 1541-1660." In *A History of Canterbury Cathedral,* edited by Collinson, Nigel Ramsay, and Margaret Sparks. Oxford: Oxford University Press, 1995.

Conklin Hays, Rosalind, and C. E. McGee, eds. *Records of Early English Drama: Dorset.* Toronto: University of Toronto Press, 1999.

Connell, R. W. *Masculinities.* Cambridge: Polity Press, 1995.

Connerton, Paul. *How Societies Remember.* Cambridge: Cambridge University Press, 1989.

Cosgrove, Denis, and Steven Daniels, eds. *The Iconography of Landscape: Essays on the Symbolic Representation, Design and Use of Past Environments.* Cambridge: Cambridge University Press, 1988.

Cosgrove, Denis *Mappings.* London: Reaktion Books Ltd., 1999.

Coster, Will, and Andrew Spicer, eds. *Sacred Space in Early Modern Europe.* Cambridge: Cambridge University Press, 2005.

Coster, Will. "Purity, Profanity and Puritanism: The Churching of Women 1500-1700." In *Women in the Church,* edited by William J. Sheils and Diana Wood, 377-387. *Studies in Church History* vol. 27. Oxford: Blackwell, 1990.

Craig, John. "Co-operation and Initiatives: Elizabethan Churchwardens and the Parish Accounts of Mildenhall." *Social History* 18 (1993): 357-80.

Craig, John. "Psalms, Groans and Dogwhippers: The Soundscape of Worship in the English Parish Church, 1547-1642." In *Sacred Space in Early Modern Europe,* edited by Coster and Spicer, 104-23.

Crang, Mike. *Cultural Geography.* London: Routledge, 1998.

Cranston, Maurice W. *Philosophy and Language.* Toronto: Canadian Broadcasting Corporation, 1969.

Cressy, David. "Purification, Thanksgiving and the Churching of Women in Post-Reformation England." *Past and Present* 141 (1993): 106-46.

Cressy, David. *Birth, Marriage and Death: Ritual, Religion, and the Life-cycle in Tudor and Stuart England.* Oxford: Oxford University Press, 1997.

Crow, Graham, and Graham Allan. *Community Life: An Introduction to Local Social Relations.* Harlow: Pearson Education, 1994.

Cubitt, T. "Network Density among Urban Families." In *Network Analysis: Studies in Human Interaction,* edited by Jeremy Boissevain and J. Clyde Mitchell, 67-82. The Hague: Mouton, 1973.

Davenport, Frances. "The Decay of Villeinage in East Anglia." In *Essays in Economic History* vol. 2, edited by Eleanor M. Carus-Wilson, 112-24. Reprinted London, 1966.

De Certeau, Michel. *The Practice of Everyday Life.* Trans. Steven Rendall. Berkeley: University of California Press, 1988.

De Certeau, Michel. *The Writing of History.* Trans. T. Conley. New York: Columbia University Press, 1988.

Dennis, Richard. *English Industrial Cities of the Nineteenth Century: A Social*

Geography. Cambridge: Cambridge University Press, 1984.

DeWindt, Anne. "Redefining the Peasant Community in Medieval England: The Regional Perspective." *Journal of British Studies* 26 (1987): 163-20.

DeWindt, Edwin B. *Land and People in Holywell-cum-Needingworth: Structures of Tenure and Patterns of Social Organization in an East Midlands Village 1252-1457.* Toronto: Toronto University Press, 1972.

Diamond, Arthur S. *Primitive Law: Past and Present.* London: Methuen, 1971.

Dillow, Kevin. "The Social and Ecclesiastical Significance of Church Seating Arrangements and Pew Disputes, 1500-1740." Unpublished D.Phil. diss. University of Oxford, 1990.

Dodgshon, Robert A. *Society in Time and Space: A Geographical Perspective on Change.* Cambridge: Cambridge University Press, 1998.

Douglas, Audrey, and Peter Greenfield, eds. *Records of Early English Drama: Cumberland. Westmorland. Gloucestershire.* Toronto: University of Toronto, 1986.

Douglas, Mary. *Purity and Danger: An Analysis of the Concept of Pollution and Taboo.* London: Routledge and Kegan Paul, 1966.

Duff, Robin A., and David Garland, eds. *A Reader on Punishment.* Oxford: Oxford University Press, 1994

Duffy, Eamon. *The Stripping of the Altars: Traditional Religion in England 1400-1580.* New Haven: Yale University Press, 1992.

Duffy, Eamon. "The Dynamics of English Pilgrimage." In *Pilgrimage,* edited by Morris and Roberts, 164-77.

Dunning, R. W. "The Wells Consistory Court in the Fifteenth Century." *Proceedings of the Somerset Archaeological and Natural History Society* 106 (1962): 46-61.

Dyer, Alan. *The City of Worcester in the Sixteenth Century.* Leicester: Leicester University Press, 1973.

Dyer, Christopher C. *Lords and Peasants in a Changing Society: The Estates of the Bishopric of Worcester 680-1540.* Cambridge: Cambridge University Press, 1980.

Dyer, Christopher C. *Standards of Living in the Later Middle Ages.* Cambridge: Cambridge University Press, 1989.

Dyer, Christopher C. "Changes in the Link Between Families and Land in the West Midlands in the Fourteenth and Fifteenth Centuries." In *Land, Kinship and Life-cycle,* edited by Richard M. Smith, 277-94. Cambridge: Cambridge University Press, 1984.

Dyer, Christopher C. "Towns and Cottages in Eleventh-century England." In Dyer, *Everyday Life in Medieval England,* 241-56. London: Hambledon. 1994.

Eade, John, and Sallnow, Michael J. "Introducton." In *Contesting the Sacred: The Anthropology of Christian Pilgrimage,* edited by Eade and Sallnow. Urbana, IL: University of Illinois Press, 1991.

Ekman, Ann-Kristin. "Community, Carnival and Campaign: Expressions of Belonging in a Swedish Region." *Stockholm Studies in Anthropology* vol. 2 (Stockholm, 1991).

Ekwall, Eilert. *Studies on the Population of Medieval London*. Stockholm: Vitterhets Historie och Antikvitets Handlingar. Filologisk-filosofiska Serien 2, 1956.

Elias, Norbert, and John Scotson. *The Established and the Outsiders: A Sociological Enquiry into Community Problems*. New edn., London: Sage, 1994.

Estabrook, Carl B. *Urbane and Rustic England: Cultural Ties and Social Spheres in the Provinces, 1660-1780*. Stanford: Stanford University Press, 1998.

Everitt, Alan. "Country, County and Town: Patterns of Regional Evolution in England." *Transactions of the Royal Historical Society*, 5th ser. 29 (1979): 79-108.

Farmer, David L. "Prices and Wages." In *The Agrarian History of England and Wales, 1042-1350*, edited by Herbert E. Hallam. Cambridge: Cambridge University Press, 1988.

Farnhill, Ken. *Guilds and the Parish Community in Late Medieval East Anglia c.1470-1550*. Woodbridge: Boydell, 2001.

Fenster, Thelma, and Daniel Lord Smail, eds. *Fama: The Politics of Talk and Reputation in Medieval Europe*. Ithaca, NY: Cornell University Press, 2003.

Fentress, James, and Christopher Wickham. *Social Memory*. Oxford: Blackwell, 1992.

Field, R. K. "Migration in the Later Middle Ages: The Case of the Hampton Lovett Villeins." *Midland History* 8 (1983): 29-48.

Field, Steven, and Keith H. Basso, eds. *Senses of Place*. Santa Fe: School of American Research Press, 1996.

Fines, J. "Heresy Trials in the Diocese of Coventry and Lichfield, 1511-12." *Journal of Ecclesiastical History* 14 (1963): 160-74.

Finucane, Ronald C. *Miracles and Pilgrims: Popular Beliefs in Medieval England*. Repr. London, 1995.

Flather, Amanda. *Gender and Space in Early Modern England*. Woodbridge: Boydell for the Royal Historical Society, 2007.

Fleming, Robin. *Kings and Lords in Conquest England*. Cambridge: Cambridge University Press, 1991.

Fletcher, Anthony. *Gender, Sex and Subordination in England 1500-1800*. New Haven and London: Yale University Press, 1995.

Flynn, M., "The Spectacle of Suffering in Spanish Streets." In *City and Spectacle in Medieval Europe*, edited by Barbara Hanawalt and Katherine L. Reyerson, 153-68. London, 1994.

Foucault, Michel. *Discipline and Punish: The Birth of the Prison*. Harmondsworth: Penguin, 1977.

Fox, Harold S. A. "Exploitation of the Landless by Lords and Tenants in Early Medieval England." In *Medieval Society and the Manor Court*, edited by Zvi Razi and Richard Smith, 518-68. Oxford: Oxford University Press, 1996..

Fox, Harold S. A. "The People of the Wolds in English Settlement History." In *The Rural Settlement of Medieval England*, edited by Michael Aston, David Austin and Christopher Dyer, 77-101. Oxford: Blackwell, 1989.

Frankenberg, Ronald. *Communities in Britain: Social Life in Town and Country*. Harmondsworth: Penguin, 1969.

Frankenberg, Ronald. *Village on the Border: A Social Study of Religion, Politics and Football in a North Wales Community*. London: Cohen and West, 1957.

French, Henry. "Social Status, Localism and the Middling Sort of People in England, 1630-1750." *Past and Present* 166 (2000): 66-99.

French, Katherine, Gibbs Gary and Beat Kümin, eds. *The Parish in English Life, 1400-1600*. Manchester: Manchester University Press, 1997

French, Katherine. *The People of the Parish: Community Life in a Late Medieval English Diocese*. Pennsyvlania: University of Pennsylvania Press, 2001.

Froide, Amy. *Never Married: Singlewomen in Early Modern England*. Oxford: Oxford University Press, 2005.

Fujita, Masahisa, Paul Krugman, and Anthony J. Venables. *The Spatial Economy: Cities, Regions, and International Trade*. Cambridge, MA: MIT Press, 1999.

Fumerton, Patricia. *Unsettled: The Culture of Mobility and the Working Poor in Early Modern England*. Chicago: Chicago University Press, 2006.

Gabel, Leona. "Benefit of Clergy in England in the Later Middle Ages". *Smith College Studies in History* 14, 1928-1929.

Galley, Chris. *The Demography of Early Modern Towns: York in the Sixteenth and Seventeenth Centuries*. Liverpool: Liverpool University Press, 1998.

Garland, David. *Punishment and Modern Society: A Study in Social Theory*. Chicago: University of Chicago Press, 1990.

Geertz, Clifford. *Negara. The Theater State in Nineteenth-century Bali*. Princeton: Princeton University Press, 1980.

Gibson, Gail. "Blessing from Sun and Moon: Churching as Women's Theater." In *Bodies and Disciplines: Intersections of Literature and History in Fifteenth-century England*, edited by Barbara A. Hanawalt and David Wallace, 139-54. Minneapolis: University of Minnesota Press, 1996.

Gillis, John. *For Better, For Worse: British Marriages, 1600 to the Present*. Oxford: Oxford University Press, 1985.

Goffman, Erving. *Stigma: Notes on the Management of Spoiled Identity*. Englewood Cliffs, NJ: 1963.

Goheen, P. G. "The Ritual of the Streets in Mid-19th-century Toronto." *Society and Space* 11 (1993): 127-45.

Goldberg, P. Jeremy P. *Women, Work, and Life Cycle in a Medieval Economy: Women in York and Yorkshire c.1300-1520*. Oxford: Oxford University Press, 1992.

Goldberg, P. Jeremy P. "Female Labour, Service and Marriage in the Late Medieval Urban North." *Northern History* 22 (1986): 18-38

Goldberg, P. Jeremy P. "Marriage, Migration, and Servanthood: The York Cause

Paper Evidence." In *Women in Medieval English Society*, edited by Goldberg, 1-15. Gloucester: Sutton, 1997.

Goldberg, P. Jeremy P. "Marriage, Migration, Servanthood and Life-cycle in Yorkshire Towns in the Later Middle Ages." *Continuity and Change* 1 (1986): 141-69.

Goldberg, P. Jeremy P. "The Public and the Private: Women in the Pre-Plague Economy." In *Thirteenth Century England III*, edited by Peter R. Coss and Simon D. Lloyd, 75-89. Woodbridge: Boydell, 1991.

Goldberg, P. Jeremy P. "Urban Identity and the Poll Taxes of 1377, 1379, and 1380-1." *Economic History Review* 2nd ser. 43 (1990): 194-216.

Goose, Nigel "Household Size and Structure in Early Stuart Cambridge." *Social History* 5 (1980): 347-85.

Gould, Peter, and Rodney White. *Mental Maps*. Harmondsworth: Penguin, 1974.

Gowing, Laura, "The Freedom of the Streets: Women and Social Space, 1560-1640." In *Londinopolis*, edited by Paul Griffiths and Mark Jenner, 130-51.

Gowing, Laura. *Common Bodies: Women, Touch and Power in Seventeenth-century England*. New Haven: Yale University Press, 2003.

Gowing, Laura. *Domestic Dangers: Women, Words, and Sex in Early Modern London*. Oxford: Oxford University Press, 1996.

Granovetter, Mark. "The Strength of Weak Ties." *American Sociological Journal* 78 (1973): 1360-80.

Gransden, Antonia. "Some Late Thirteenth-century Records of an Ecclesiastical Court in the Archdeaconry of Sudbury." *Bulletin of the Institute of Historical Research* 32 (1959): 62-69.

Grantley, Darryll, and Nina Taunton, eds. *The Body in Late Medieval and Early Modern Culture*. Aldershot: Ashgate, 2001.

Graves, C. P. "Social Space in the English Medieval Parish Church." *Economy and Society* 18 (1989): 297-322.

Green, Thomas. *Verdict According to Conscience: Perspectives on the English Criminal Trial Jury, 1200-1800*. Chicago: University of Chicago Press, 1985.

Greenwood, Walter. *Love on the Dole*. London: Verso, 1993, originally London, 1933.

Gregory, David, and John Urry, eds. *Social Relations and Spatial Structures*. London: Macmillan, 1985.

Griffin, Emma. "Sports and Celebrations in English Market Towns, 1660-1750." *Historical Research* 75 (2002): 188-208

Griffiths, Paul, John Landers, Margaret Pelling, and R. Tyson, "Population and Disease, Estrangement and Belonging." In *The Cambridge Urban History of Britain Volume II 1540-1840*, edited by Peter Clark, 195-233. Cambridge: Cambridge University Press, 2000.

Griffiths, Paul. "Politics Made Visible: Order, Residence and Uniformity in Cheapside, 1600-45." In *Londinopolis*, edited by Griffiths and Jenner, 176-96.

Griffths, Paul, and Mark Jenner. *Londinopolis: Essays in the Cultural and Social History of Early Modern London*. Manchester: Manchester University Press, 2000.

Grigg, D. B. "E. G. Ravenstein and the 'Laws of Migration'." In *Time, Family and Community: Perspectives on Family and Community History*, edited by Michael Drake, 147-64. Oxford: Open University Press, 1994.

Grosse, Christian. "Places of Sanctification: The Liturgical Sacrality of Genevan Reformed Churches, 1535-1566." In *Sacred Space in Early-modern Europe*, edited by Coster and Spicer, 60-80.

Hage, Per, and Frank Harary. *Structural Models in Anthropology*. Cambridge: Cambridge University Press, 1983.

Haigh, Christopher. *Reformation and Resistance in Tudor Lancashire*. Cambridge: Cambridge University Press, 1975.

Hallam, Herbert E. "Some Thirteenth-century Censuses." *Economic History Review* 2nd ser. 10 (1957-8): 340-61

Hamilton, Sarah. *The Practice of Penance, 900-1050*. Woodbridge: Boydell, 2001.

Hanawalt, Barbara A., and Michael Kobialka, eds. *Medieval Practices of Space: Medieval Cultures* vol. 23, Minneapolis: University of Minnesota Press, 2000.

Hanawalt, Barbara A., and David Wallace, eds. *Bodies and Disciplines: Intersections of Literature and History in Fifteenth-century England*. Minnesota: University of Minnesota Press, 1996.

Hanawalt, Barbara A. *Crime and Conflict in English Communities 1300-1348*. Cambridge, MA: Harvard University Press, 1979.

Haren, Michael. *Sin and Society in Fourteenth-century England: A Study of the Memoriale Presbitorum*. Oxford: Oxford University Press, 2000.

Harper-Bill, Christopher. "A Late Medieval Visitation: The Diocese of Norwich in 1499." *Proceedings of the Suffolk Institute of Archaeology* 34 (1980): 35-47.

Harris, Tim, ed. *Popular Culture in England, c.1500-1850*. Basingstoke: Palgrave, 1995.

Harrison, Paul "Making Sense: Embodiment and Sensibilities of the Everyday." *Society and Space* 18 (2000): 497-517.

Harvey, Barbara F. *Living and Dying in England 1100-1540: The Monastic Experience*. Oxford: Oxford University Press, 1993.

Harvey, Barbara F. *Westminster Abbey and its Estates in the Middle Ages*. Oxford: Oxford University Press, 1977.

Harvey, Barbara F. "The Population Trend in England Between 1300 and 1348." *Transactions of the Royal Historical Society* 5th ser. 16 (1966): 23-42.

Harvey, David. *Consciousness and the Urban Experience*. Oxford: Blackwell, 1985.

Harvey, David. *Social Justice and the City*. London: Edward Arnold, 1973.

Haselmayer, L. A. "The Apparitor and Chaucer's Summoner." *Speculum* 12 (1937): 43-57.

Heal, Felicity. *Hospitality in Early-modern England*. Oxford: Oxford University Press, 1990.

Hebbert, Michael. "The Street as a Locus of Collective Memory." *Society and Space* 23 (2005): 581-96.

Helmholz, Richard H. *Marriage Litigation in Medieval England*. Cambridge:

Cambridge University Press, 1974.

Helmholz, Richard H. *Roman Canon Law in Reformation England*. Cambridge: Cambridge University Press, 1990.

Helmholz, Richard H. "Harboring Sexual Offenders: Ecclesiastical Courts and Controlling Misbehavior." *Journal of British Studies* 37 (1998): 258-68

Herrup, Cynthia. *The Common Peace: Participation and the Criminal Law in Seventeenth-century England*. Cambridge: Cambridge University Press, 1987.

Higgs, Laquita M. *Godliness and Governance in Tudor Colchester*. Ann Arbor, MI: University of Michigan Press, 1998.

Hill, Rosalind M. T. "Public Penance: Some Problems of a Thirteenth-century Bishop." *History* 36 (1951): 213-26

Hilton, Rodney H. *The Economic Development of Some Leicestershire Estates in the XIVth and XVth Centuries*. Oxford: Oxford University Press, 1947.

Hilton, Rodney H. "Lords, Burgesses and Hucksters." in Hilton, *Class Conflict and the Crisis of Feudalism*. London: Hambledon. 1985.

Hinde, Andrew. *England's Population: A History Since the Domesday Survey*. London: Arnold, 2003.

Hindle, Steve. *On the Parish? The Micro-politics of Poor Relief in Rural England, c.1550-1750*. Oxford: Oxford University Press, 2004.

Hindle, Steve. "A Sense of Place? Becoming and Belonging in the Rural Parish, 1550-1650." In *Communities in Early Modern England*, edited by Alexandra Shepard and Philip Withington, 96-114. Manchester: Manchester University Press, 2000.

Hindle, Steve. "Dependency, Shame and Belonging: Badging the Deserving Poor, c.1550-1750." *Cultural and Social History. The Journal of the Social History Society*, 1 (2004): 6-35.

Hjertstedt, Ingrid. *Middle English Nicknames in the Lay Subsidy Rolls for Warwickshire*. Acta Universitatis Upsaliensis, Studia Anglistica Upsaliensia vol. 63, Uppsala, 1987.

Holly, D. "Leicestershire." In *The Domesday Geography of Midland England*, edited by Henry C. Darby and L. B. Terrett, 315-53. Cambridge: Cambridge University Press, 1954.

Holt, James C. *What's in a Name? Family Nomenclature and the Norman Conquest*. University of Reading, Stenton Lecture, 1981.

Holt, Richard, and Gervase Rosser, eds. *The Medieval Town: A Reader in English Urban History 1200-1540*. London: Longman, 1990.

Homans, George C. *English Villagers of the Thirteenth Century*. Cambridge, MA: Harvard University Press, 1941.

Howell, Cecily (Sally.) *Land, Kinship and Inheritance in Transition: Kibworth Harcourt 1280-1700*. Cambridge: Cambridge University Press, 1983.

Hoyt, D. R., and N. Babchuk. "Adult Kinship Networks: The Selective Formation of Intimate Ties with Kin." *Social Forces* 62 (1983): 84-101.

Humphrey, Caroline, and James Laidlaw. The Archetypal Actions of *Ritual: A*

Theory of Ritual Illustrated by the Jain Rite of Worship. Oxford: Oxford University Press, 1994.

Hutton, Ronald. *The Rise and Fall of Merry England: The Ritual Year 1400-1700.* Oxford: Oxford University Press, 1994.

Hyams, Paul R. *King, Lords and Peasants in Medieval England: The Common Law of Villeinage in the Twelfth and Thirteenth Centuries.* Oxford: Oxford University Press, 1980.

Ingram, Martin. *Church Courts, Sex and Marriage in England, 1570-1640.* Cambridge: Cambridge University Press, 1987.

Ingram, Martin. "Juridical Folklore in England Illustrated by Rough Music." In *Communities and Courts in Britain 1150-1900,* edited by Christopher Brooks and Michael Lobban, 61-82. London: Hambledon, 1997.

Ingram, Martin. "Puritans and the Church Courts, 1560-1640." In *The Culture of English Puritanism 1560-1700,* edited by Christopher Durston and Janet Eales, 43-50. London: Macmillan, 1996.

Ingram, Martin. "Ridings, Rough Music and Mocking Rhymes in Early Modern England." In *Popular Culture in Seventeenth-century England,* edited by Barry Reay, 166-95. London: Croom Helm, 1985.

Jenner, Mark. "From Conduit Community to Commercial Network? Water in London, 1500-1725." In *Londinopolis,* edited by Griffiths and Jenner, 250-72

John Eade. "Order and Power at Lourdes: Lay Helpers and the Organization of a Pilgrimage Shrine." In *Contesting the Sacred,* edited by Eade and Sallnow, 51-76.

Jones, Ernie. "Villein Mobility in the Later Middle Ages: The Case of Spalding Priory." *Nottingham Medieval Studies* 36 (1992): 151-66

Jones, Hugh. *Population Geography.* London: Chapman, 1990.

Keene, Derek J. "Suburban Growth." In *The Medieval Town,* edited by Holt and Rosser, 97-119.

Keene, Derek. *Survey of Medieval Winchester. Winchester Studies* vol. 2, Oxford: Oxford University Press, 1985.

Keith, Michael, and Steve Pile. *Place and the Politics of Identity.* London: Routledge, 1993.

Kent, Joan R. *The English Village Constable 1580-1642.* Oxford: Oxford University Press, 1986.

Kent, Joan R. "The Centre and the Localities: State Formation and Parish Government in England, c.1640-1740." *Historical Journal* 38 (1995): 363-404.

Kermode, Jenny. *Medieval Merchants. York, Beverley and Hull in the Later Middle Ages.* Cambridge: Cambridge University Press, 1998.

Konig, David T. *Law and Society in Puritan Massachusetts: Essex County, 1629-1692.* Chapel Hill, NC: University of North Carolina Press, 1979.

Kowaleski, Maryanne. *Local Markets and Regional Trade in Medieval Exeter.* Cambridge: Cambridge University Press, 1995.

Kowaleski, Maryanne. "Introduction." *Journal of British Studies* 33 (1994): 337-9.

Kristensson, Gillis. *A Survey of Middle English Dialects 1290-1350: The West Midland Counties*. Lund: Publications of the New Society of Letters at Lund, vol. 78, 1987.

Kristensson, Gillis. *Studies on the Early Fourteenth Century Population of Lindsey*. (Lund: Lund University, 1976-7).

Kümin, Beat. *The Shaping of a Community: The Rise and Reformation of the English Parish, c.1400-1560*. Aldershot: Ashgate, 1996.

Kussmaul, Ann. "The Ambiguous Mobility of Farm Servants." *Economic History Review* 2nd ser. 34 (1981): 222-35.

Labande, E. R. "De Saint Edouard à Saint Thomas Becket: Pèlerinages Anglais au XIIe Siècle." In *Medievalia Christiana XIe-XIIe siècles. Hommage à Raymond Foreville*, edited by C. E. Viola, 307-19. Tournai, 1989.

Langton, John (Jack). "Residential Patterns in Pre-industrial Cities: Some Case Studies from Seventeenth-century Britain." Repr. in *The Tudor and Stuart Town: A Reader in English Urban History 1530-1688*, edited by Jonathan Barry, 166-205. Harlow: Longman, 1990.

Lasker, Gabriel. *Surnames and Genetic Structure*. Cambridge: Cambridge University Press, 1985.

Laughton, Jane, and Christopher Dyer. "Small Towns in the East and West Midlands in the Later Middle Ages: A Comparison." *Midland History* 24 (1999): 24-52.

Lefebvre, Henri. *The Production of Space*. Trans. D. Nicholson-Smith. Oxford: Blackwell, 1998.

Lerer, Seth. "'Represented now in yower syght'. The Culture of Spectatorship in Fifteenth-century England." In *Bodies and Disciplines,* edited by Hanawalt and Wallace, 29-62.

Leslie, Esther. *Walter Benjamin. Overpowering Conformism*. London: Pluto Press, 2000.

Levett, A. Elizabeth. *Studies in Manorial History*. Edited by Helen M. Cam, M. Coate and Lucy S. Sutherland. Oxford: Clarendon Press, 1938.

Levine, David. *Family Formation in an Age of Nascent Capitalism*. New York: Academic Press, 1977.

Lilley, Keith D. "Mapping Cosmopolis: Moral Topographies of the Medieval City." *Society and Space* 22 (2004): 681-98.

Litwak, E., and N. Babchuk. "Primary Group Structures and their Function: Kin, Neighbors and Friends." *American Sociological Review* 34 (1969): 465-81.

Lobel, Mary D., ed. *Historic Towns. Maps of Towns and Cities in the British Isles*. London: Scolar Press , 1969.

Lomas, Tim. "South-east Durham: Late Fourteenth and Fifteenth Centuries." In *The Peasant Land Market in Medieval England*, edited by Paul D. A. Harvey. Oxford: Oxford University Press, 1984.

Lyotard, Jean-François. *The Postmodern Condition*. Manchester: Manchester University Press, 1984.

MacLean, Gerald, Donna Landry, and Joseph P. Ward, eds. *The Country and the City*

Revisited: England and the Politics of Culture 1550-1850. Cambridge: Cambridge University Press, 1999.

Maddicott, John R. "The English Peasantry and the Demands of the Crown 1294-1341." Oxford: *Past and Present* Supplement 1, 1975.

Maltby, Judith. *Prayer Book and People in Elizabethan and Early Stuart England.* Cambridge: Cambridge University Press, 1998.

Mander, R. P. "Pilgrimages to East Anglian Shrines." *East Anglian Magazine* 7 (1948): 223-8.

Mansfield, Mary. *The Humiliation of Sinners: Public Penance in Thirteenth-century France.* Ithaca, NY: Cornell University Press, 1995.

Marchant, Robin A. *The Church Under the Law: Justice, Administration and Discipline in the Diocese of York 1560-1640.* Cambridge, Cambridge University Press, 1969.

Marchant, Robin A. *The Puritans and the Church Courts in the Diocese of York 1560-1642.* London: Longman, 1960.

Marris, Peter. *The Politics of Uncertainty: Attachment in Private and Public Life.* London: Routledge, 1996.

Marsh, Christopher. *Popular Religion in Sixteenth-century England: Holding Their Peace.* London: Macmillan, 1998.

Marsh, Christopher. "Order and Place in England, 1580-1640: The View from the Pew." *Journal of British Studies* 44 (2005): 3-26.

Marsh, Christopher. "Sacred Space in England, 1560-1640: The View from the Pew." *Journal of Ecclesiastical History* 53 (2002): 286-311.

Marshall, Peter. "'The Map of God's Word': Geographies of the Afterlife in Tudor and Early Stuart England." In *The Place of the Dead. Death and Remembrance in Late Medieval and Early Modern Europe,* edited by Bruce Gordon and Marshall, 110-48. Cambridge: Cambridge University Press, 2000.

Marshall, Peter. *Beliefs and the Dead in Reformation England.* Oxford: Oxford University Press, 2002.

Masschaele, James. *Peasants, Merchants and Markets. Inland Trade in Medieval England, 1150-1350.* London: Macmillan,1997.

Masschaele, James. "The Multiplicity of Medieval Markets Reconsidered." *Journal of Historical Geography* 20 (1994): 255-71.

Masschaele, James. "The Public Space of the Market Place." *Speculum* 77 (2002):383-421.

McClure, Peter. "Patterns of Migration in the Late Middle Ages: The Evidence of English Place-name Surnames." *Economic History Review* 2nd series 32 (1979): 167-82

McIntosh, Angus, M. L. Samuels, and Michael Benskin. *A Linguistic Atlas of Late Mediaeval English.* 4 vols.. Aberdeen: Aberdeen University Press, 1986.

McIntosh, Marjorie K. *Controlling Misbehavior in England, 1370-1600.* Cambridge: Cambridge University Press, 1998.

McIntosh, Marjorie K. *Working Women in English Society 1300-1620.* Cambridge:

Cambridge University Press, 2005

McIntosh, Marjorie K. "Local Responses to the Poor in Late Medieval and Tudor England." *Continuity and Change* 3 (1988): 209-45.

McKinley, Richard A. *The Surnames of Lancashire*. English Surnames Series (hereafter ESS) vol. 4, London: Leopard's Head Press, 1981.

McKinley, Richard A. *The Surnames of Oxfordshire*. ESS vol. 3, London: Leopard's Head Press, 1977.

McSheffrey, Shannon. *Marriage, Sex, and Civic Culture in Late Medieval London*. Philadelphia: University of Pennsylvania Press, 2006.

McSheffrey, Shannon. "Place, Space, and Situation: Public and Private in the Making of Marriage in Late-Medieval London." *Speculum* 79 (2004): 960-90.

Medcalf, S. "Motives for Pilgrimage: *The Tale of Beryn*." In *England in the Fourteenth Century*, edited by Nicholas Rogers, 97-108. Harlaxton Medieval Studies vol. 3, Stamford: Paul Watkins, 1993.

Mendelson, Sarah, and Patricia Crawford. *Women in Early Modern England*. Oxford: Oxford University Press, 1998.

Mentzer, Raymond A. "Notions of Sin and Penitence Within the French Reformed Community." In *Penitence in the Age of Reformations*, edited by Katharine Jackson Lualdi and Anne T. Thayer, 84-100. Aldershot: Ashgate, 2000.

Miller, Edward, ed. *The Agrarian History of England and Wales vol. III 1348-1500*. Cambridge: Cambridge University Press, 1991.

Miller, Edward. *The Abbey and Bishopric of Ely*. Cambridge: Cambridge University Press, 1951.

Miller, William I. *Faking It*. Cambridge: Cambridge University Press, 2003.

Miller, William I. *The Anatomy of Disgust*. Cambridge, MA: Harvard University Press, 1997.

Mitson, Anne. "The Significance of Kinship Networks in the Seventeenth Century: Southwest Nottinghamshire." In *Societies, Cultures and Kinship*, edited by Phythian-Adams, 24-76.

Morris, Colin. "Pilgrimage to Jerusalem in the Late Middle Ages." In *Pilgrimage*, edited by Morris and Roberts, 141-63.

Morris, Colin, and Peter Roberts, eds. *Pilgrimage: The English Medieval Experience from Becket to Bunyan*. Cambridge: Cambridge University Press, 2002.

Morrison, Susan. *Women Pilgrims in Late Medieval England. Private Piety as Public Performance*. London: Routledge, 2000.

Muir, Edward. *Ritual in Early Modern Europe*. Cambridge: Cambridge University Press, 1997.

Mullaney, Steven. *The Place of the Stage: License, Play, and Power in Renaissance England*. Chicago: Chicago University Press, 1988.

Newby, Howard. *The Deferential Worker: A Study of Farm Workers in East Anglia*. London: Allen Lane 1977.

Newcombe, D. G. "John Hooper's Visitation and Examination of the Clergy in the Diocese of Gloucester, 1551." In *Reformations Old and New: Essays on the Socio-*

economic Impact of Religious Change, edited by Beat A. Kümin, 57-70. Aldershot: Ashgate, 1996.

Newman, Karen. "Walking Capitals. Donne's First Satyre." In *The Culture of Capital. Property, Cities, and Knowledge in Early Modern England,* edited by Henry S. Turner, 203-221. London: Routledge, 2002.

Nilson, Ben. *Cathedral Shrines of Medieval England.* Woodbridge: Boydell, 1998.

O'Hara, Diana. *Courtship and Constraint. Rethinking the Making of Marriage in Tudor England.* Manchester: Manchester University Press, 2000.

Offutt, William M. "The Atlantic Rules. The Legalistic Turn in Colonial British America." In *The Creation of the British Atlantic World,* edited by Elizabeth Mancke and Carole Shammas, 160-81. Baltimore and London: Johns Hopkins University, 2005.

Olson, Sherri. "Family Linkages and the Structure of the Local Elite in the Medieval and Early Modern Village." *Medieval Prosopography* 13 (1992): 53-82.

Olson, Sherri. "Jurors of the Village Court: Local Leadership before and after the Plague in Ellington, Huntingdonshire." *Journal of British Studies* 30 (1991): 237-256.

Otto, Rudolf. *The Idea of the Holy: An Inquiry into the Non-rational Factor in the Idea of the Divine and its Relation to the Rational.* Trans. John W. Harvey. London: Oxford University Press, 1969.

Padel, Oliver. "Cornish Surnames in 1327." *Nomina* 9 (1985): 81-8.

Palmer, Robert. *English Law in the Age of the Black Death 1348-1381: A Transformation of Government and Law.* Chapel Hill, NC: University of North Carolina Press, 1993.

Parker, Charles H. "The Rituals of Reconciliation: Admonition, Confession and Community in the Dutch Reformed Church." In *Penitence in the Age of Reformations,* edited by Katharine Jackson Lualdi and Anne T. Thayer, 101-15. Aldershot: Ashgate, 2000.

Parker, John. *Structuration.* Buckingham: Open University Press, 2000.

Parker, S. L., and Laurence R. Poos. "A Consistory Court from the Diocese of Rochester, 1363-4." *English Historical Review* 106 (1991): 652-65.

Pedersen, Frederick. "Demography in the Archives: Social and Geographical Factors in the Fourteenth-century Cause Paper Marriage Litigation." *Continuity and Change* 10 (1995): 405-36.

Peet, Richard. *Modern Geographical Thought.* Oxford: Blackwell, 1998.

Pelling, Margaret. *The Common Lot. Sickness, Medical Occupations and the Urban Poor in Early Modern England.* London: Longman, 1998.

Penn, Simon. "The Origins of Bristol Migrants in the Early Fourteenth Century: The Surname Evidence." *Transactions of the Bristol and Gloucestershire Archaeological Society* 101 (1983): 123-30.

Peters, Christine. "Gender, Sacrament and Ritual: The Making and Meaning of Marriage in Late Medieval and Early Modern England." *Past and Present* 169 (2000): 63-96.

Pettegree, Andrew. *Reformation and the Culture of Persuasion.* Cambridge: Cambridge University Press, 2005.

Pevsner, Nicklaus. *The Buildings of England. Suffolk*. Second edn, rev. by E. Radcliffe. Harmondsworth: Penguin, 1996.

Phythian-Adams, Charles. *Re-thinking English Local History*. University of Leicester, Occasional Papers in English Local History 4th ser., 1, Leicester, 1987.

Phythian-Adams, Charles. "Introduction: An Agenda for English Local History.' In *Societies, Cultures and Kinship*, edited by Phythian-Adams, 1-23.

Phythian-Adams, Charles, ed. *Societies, Cultures and Kinship, 1580-1850: Cultural Provinces and English Local History*. Leicester and London: Leicester University Press, 1993.

Pickering, Michael. *Stereotyping: The Politics of Representation*. Basingstoke: Palgrave, 2001.

Pimsler, Martin. "Solidarity in the Medieval Village? Personal Pledging at Elton, Huntingdonshire." *Journal of British Studies* 17 (1977): 1-11.

Platts, Graham. *Land and People in Medieval Lincolnshire. History of Lincolnshire* vol. 4, Lincoln 1985.

Pooley, Colin, and Jean Turnbull. *Migration and Mobility in Britain since the 18th Century*. London: UCL Press, 1999.

Poos, Laurence R. "Population Turnover in Medieval Essex: The Evidence of Some Early-fourteenth Century Tithing Lists." In *The World We Have Gained. Histories of Population and Social Structure*, edited by Lloyd Bonfield, Richard Smith and Keith Wrightson, 1-22. Oxford: Blackwell, 1986.

Postles, Dave. *The Surnames of Devon*. ESS vol. 7, Oxford: Leopard's Head Press, 1995.

Postles, Dave. "Notions of the Family, Lordship and the Evolution of Naming Processes in Medieval English Rural Society: A Regional Example." *Continuity and Change* 10 (1995): 169-98.

Postles, Dave. "Surnames and the Composition of Local Populations: Rutland, 13th to 17th Centuries." *East Midland Geographer* 16 (1993): 27-38.

Postles, Suella. "Barkby: The Anatomy of a 'Closed' Township." Unpublished M.A. thesis (University of Leicester, 1979).

Pred, Allan. *Making Histories and Constructing Human Geographies: The Local Transformation of Practice, Power Relations and Consciousness*. Boulder, CO: Westview Press, 1990.

Prelli, Lawrence J., ed. *Rhetorics of Display*. Columbia SC: University of South Carolina Press, 2006.

Price, F. Douglas. "Gloucester Diocese under Bishop Hooper 1551-3." *Transactions of the Bristol and Gloucestershire Archaeological Society* 60 (1938): 51-151.

Prior, Mary. *Fisher Row: Fishermen, Bargemen and Canal Boatmen in Oxford 1500-1900*. Oxford: Oxford University Press, 1982.

Pritchard, Richard M. *Housing and the Spatial Structure of the City*. Cambridge: Cambridge University Press, 1976.

Raber, Karen. "Recent Ecocritical Studies of English Renaissance Literature." *English Literary Renaissance* 37 (2007): 151-71.

Raftis, J. Ambrose. *Tenure and Mobility: Studies in the Social History of the Mediaeval English Village.* Toronto: University of Toronto Press, 1964.

Raftis, J. Ambrose. "Geographical Mobility in Lay Subsidy Rolls." *Mediaeval Studies* 38 (1976):385-403.

Randall, Andrew, and Andrew Charlesworth, eds. *Markets, Market Culture and Popular Protest in Eighteenth-century Britain and Ireland.* Liverpool: Liverpool University Press, 1996.

Rappaport, Roy. *Ritual and Religion in the Making of Humanity.* Cambridge: Cambridge University Press, 1999.

Razi, Zvi. "Family, Land and the Village Community in Later Medieval England." In *Landlords, Peasants and Politics in Medieval England,* edited by Trevor H. Aston, 360-393. Cambridge: Cambridge University Press, 1987.

Razi, Zvi. "The Erosion of the Land-family Bond in the Late Fourteenth and Fifteenth Centuries: A Methodological Note." In *Land, Kinship and Life-cycle,* edited by Richard M. Smith, 295-312. Cambridge: Cambridge University Press, 1984.

Reaney, Percy H. *The Origin of English Surnames.* London, 1967, repr. 1987.

Rees, Alwyn D. *Life in a Welsh Countryside. A Social Study of Llanfihangel yng Ngwynfa.* Cardiff: University of Wales Press, 1951.

Reynolds, Susan. "Social Mentalities and the Case of Medieval Scepticism." *Transactions of the Royal Historical Society* 6th ser. 1 (1991): 21-41.

Rigby, Steven H. *Medieval Grimsby: Growth and Decline.* Hull: Hull University Press, 1993.

Roberts, Michael. "Women and Work in Sixteenth-century English Towns." In *Work in Towns 850-1850,* edited by Penelope Corfield and Derek Keene. Leicester: Leicester University Press, 1990.

Roberts, Penny. "Contesting Sacred Space: Burial Disputes in Sixteenth-century France." In *The Place of the Dead: Death and Remembrance in Late Medieval and Early Modern Europe,* edited by Bruce Gordon and Marshall, 110-48. Cambridge: Cambridge University Press, 2000.

Rollison, David. *The Local Origins of Modern Society.* Gloucestershire 1500-1800. London: Routledge, 1992.

Romar, M. S. "Lakshmi in the Market Place: Traders and Farmers in a North Indian Market." Unpublished Ph.D. diss. (University of Edinburgh, 1992)

Rosenwein, Barbara H., ed. *Anger's Past. The Social Uses of an Emotion in the Middle Ages.* Ithaca, NY: Cornell University Press, 1998.

Rosenwein, Barbara. *Negotiating Space: Power, Restraint, and Privileges of Immunity in Early Medieval Europe.* Chicago: University of Chicago Press, 1999.

Rosenwein, Barbara. "Worrying About Emotions in History." *American Historical Review* 107 (2002): 821-45.

Rosser, Gervase. *Medieval Westminster 1200-1540.* Oxford: Oxford University Press, 1989.

Rosser, Gervase. "Sanctuary and Social Negotiation in Medieval England." In *The Cloister and the World: Essays in Medieval History in Honour of Barbara Harvey,* edited by John Blair and Brian Golding, 57-79. Oxford: Oxford University Press, 1996.

Rubin, Miri. *Charity and Community in Medieval Cambridge*. Cambridge: Cambridge University Press, 1987.

Ruggles, S. "Migration, Marriage and Mortality: Correcting Sources of Bias in English Reconstitutions." *Population Studies* 46 (1992): 507-22.

Salinger, Sharon V. *Taverns and Drinking in Early America*. Baltimore and London: Johns Hopkins University Press, 2004.

Sanford, Rhonda L. *Maps and Memory in Modern England: A Sense of Place*. Basingstoke: Palgrave, 2002.

Schein, Sylvia. "Bridget of Sweden, Margery Kempe and Women's Jerusalem Pilgrimages in the Middle Ages." *Mediterranean Historical Review* 14 (1999): 44-58.

Scott, James C. *Domination and the Arts of Resistance: Hidden Transcripts*. New Haven: Yale University Press, 1990.

Scott, John. *Social Network Analysis: A Handbook*. London: Sage, 1991.

Shaw, David G. *The Creation of a Community: The City of Wells in the Middle Ages*. Oxford: Oxford University Press, 1993.

Shepard, Alexandra, and Philip Withington, eds. *Community in Early Modern England*. Manchester: Manchester University Press, 2000.

Shields, Rob. *Places on the Margin: Alternative Geographies of Modernity*. London: Routledge, 1991..

Short, Brian, ed. *The English Rural Community: Image and Analysis*. Cambridge: Cambridge University Press, 1992.

Sibley, David. *Geographies of Exclusion: Society and Difference in the West*. London: Routledge, 1995.

Skinner, E. P. "Trade and Markets among the Lossi People." In *Markets in Africa*, edited by Paul Bohannan and George Dalton. Northwestern University Press, 1962.

Slack, Paul. *From Reformation to Improvement: Public Welfare in Early Modern England*. Oxford: Oxford University Press, 1999.

Slack, Paul. *Poverty and Policy in Tudor and Stuart England*. London: Longman, 1988.

Smith, Richard M. "Some Issues Concerning Families and Their Property in Rural England, 1250-1800." In *Land, Kinship and Life-cycle*, edited by Smith, 1-86. Cambridge: Cambridge University Press, 1984.

Smith, Richard M. "'Modernisation' and the Corporate Medieval Village Community: Some Sceptical Reflections." In *Explorations in Historical Geography: Interpretive Essays*, edited by Alan R. H. Baker and Derek Gregory, 140-245. Cambridge: Cambridge University Press, 1984.

Smith, Richard M. "Hypothèses sur la nuptialité en Angleterre au XIIIe-XIVe siècles." *Annales: Economies, Sociétés, Civilisations* 38 (1983): 107-36.

Smith, Richard M. "Kin and Neighbors in a Thirteenth-century Suffolk Community." *Journal of Social History* 4 (1979): 139-55.

Smith, Richard M. "Marriage Processes in the English Past: Some Continuities." In *The World We Have Gained: Histories of Population and Social Structure*, edited by Lloyd Bonfield, Smith, and Keith Wrightson, 43-99. Oxford: Blackwell, 1986.

Soja, Edward W. *Postmodern Geographies: The Reassertion of Space in Critical Social Theory*. London: Verso, 1989.

Sommerville, C. John. *The Secularization of Early Modern England: From Religious Culture to Religious Faith*. Oxford: Oxford University Press, 1992.

Souden, David. "'East, West - Home's Best?' Regional Patterns in Migration in Early Modern England." In *Migration and Society in Early Modern England*, edited by Clark and Souden, 292-332.

Souden, David. "Movers and Stayers in Family Reconstitution Populations." *Local Population Studies* 33 (1984): 11-28.

Spierenburg, Pieter. *The Spectacle of Suffering: Executions and the Evolution of Repression*. Cambridge: Cambridge University Press, 1984.

Spufford, Peter. "The Comparative Mobility and Immobility of Lollard Descendants in Early Modern England." In *The World of Rural Dissenters 1520-1725*, edited by Margaret Spufford, 309-31. Cambridge: Cambridge University Press, 1995.

Stacy, Margaret. *Tradition and Change: A Study of Banbury*. Oxford: Oxford University Press, 1969.

Stacy, Margaret. "The Myth of Community Studies." *British Journal of Sociology* 20 (1969): 134-47.

Stallybrass, Peter, and Allon White. *The Politics and Poetics of Transgression*. Ithaca, NY: Cornell University Press, 1986.

Stouffer, Samuel. "Intervening Opportunities and Competing Migrants." *Journal of Regional Science* 2 (1960): 1-26.

Stouffer, Samuel. "Intervening Opportunities: A Theory Relating Mobility and Distance." *American Sociological Review* 5 (1940): 845-67

Strathern, Marilyn. *Kinship at the Core: An Anthropology of Elmdon, a Village in North-West Essex in the Nineteen-sixties*. Cambridge: Cambridge University Press, 1981.

Sumption, Jonathan. *Pilgrimage: An Image of Medieval Religion*. London: Faber, 1975.

Swanson, Heather. *Medieval British Towns*. Basingstoke: Palgrave, 1999.

Swanson, Robert N. "Indulgences for Prayers for the Dead in the Diocese of Lincoln in the Early Fourteenth Century." *Journal of Ecclesiastical History* 52 (2001): 197-217

Swanson, Robert N. "Fund-raising for a Medieval Monastery: Indulgences and Great Bricett Priory." *Proceedings of the Suffolk Institute of Archaeology & History* 40 (2001): 1-7

Tate, R. B. *Pilgrimage to St James of Compostella from the British Isles During the Middle Ages*. E. Allison Peers Lectures 4, Liverpool, 1990.

Tebbutt, Melanie. *"Women's Talk: A Social History of 'Gossip'"* in *Working-class Neighbourhoods 1880-1960*. Aldershot: Ashgate, 1995.

Tentler, Thomas. *Sin and Confession on the Eve of the Reformation*. Princeton, NJ: Princeton University Press, 1977.

Thompson, F. M. L. (Michael). *The Rise of Respectable Society: A Social History of Victorian Britain, 1830-1900*. Harmondsworth: Penguin, 1988.

Thompson, Flora. *Lark Rise to Candleford*. Harmondsworth: Penguin, 1973; originally Oxford 1939.

Thomson, John A. F. *The Later Lollards 1414-1520*. Oxford: Oxford University Press, 1965.

Titow, Jan Z. "Some Differences Between Manors and Their Effects on the Condition of the Peasantry in the Thirteenth Century." *Agricultural History Review* 10 (1962): 113-28

Tittler, Robert. *The Reformation and the Towns. Politics and Political Culture c.1540-1640*. Oxford: Oxford University Press, 1998.

Tittler, Robert "'For the "re-edification of townes': The Rebuilding Statutes of Henry VIII." *Albion* 22 (1990): 591-605.

Tittler, Robert. "Seats of Honor, Seats of Power: The Symbolism of Public Seating in the English Urban Community, c.1560-1620." *Albion* 24 (1992): 205-23.

Todd, Margo. *The Culture of Protestantism in Early Modern Scotland*. New Haven: Yale University Press, 2002.

Tringham, Nigel. "A Visitation of Tarvin Prebend, Cheshire, in 1317." *Journal of the Chester Archaeological Society* 73 (1994-5), 88.

Turner, Bryan S. *The Body and Society: Explorations in Social Theory*. Oxford: Blackwell, 1984.

Turner, Victor & Edith. *Image and Pilgrimage in Christian Culture: Anthropological Perspectives*. New York: Columbia University Press, 1978.

Turner, Victor. *The Ritual Process: Structure and Anti-Structure*. Ithaca, NY: Cornell University Press, 1969.

Unwin, Tim. "A Waste of Space? Towards a Critique of the Social Production of Space ." *Transactions of the Institute of British Geographers* n.s. 25 (2000): 11-29.

Verbrugge, L. "Multiplexity in Adult Friendships." *Social Forces* 57 (1978): 1286-1309.

Wakelin, Martyn, *English Dialects*. London: Athlone, 1972.

Walker, J. "The Burges [sic] Courts, Wakefield." in *Miscellanea 2*, Yorkshire Archaeological Society Record Series vol. 74, Leeds, 1929.

Walsham, Alexandra. *Providence in Early Modern England*. Oxford: Oxford University Press, 1999.

Wasserman, Stanley, and Katherine Faust. *Social Network Analysis: Methods and Applications*. Cambridge: Cambridge University Press, 1994.

Webb, Diana. *Medieval European Pilgrimage c.700-c.1500*. Basingstoke: Palgrave,

2002.

White, Paul W. "Drama in the Church': Church-playing in Tudor England." *Medieval and Renaissance Drama in England* 6 (1993): 15-35.

Whiteman, Anne. "The Compton Census of 1676." In *Surveying the People: The Interpretation and Use of Document Sources for the Study of Population in the Later Seventeenth Century*, edited by Kevin Schürer and Tom Arkell, 97-116. Oxford: Leopard's Head Press, 1992.

Whyte, Ian D. *Migration and Society in Britain 1550-1830*. London: Macmillan, 2000.

Willard, James F. *Parliamentary Taxes on Personal Property 1290-1334: A Study in Medieval English Financial Administration*. Cambridge, MA: Medieval Academy of America, 1934.

Williams, Raymond. *The Country and the City*. London: Chatto & Windus Ltd., 1973.

Williams, William M. *The Sociology of an English Village. Gosforth*. London: Routledge and Kegan Paul, 1956.

Williams, William M. *A West Country Village: Ashworthy*. London: Routledge and Kegan Paul, 1963.

Woodcock, Brian L. *Medieval Ecclesiastical Courts in the Diocese of Canterbury*. Oxford: Oxford University Press, 1952.

Wright, Susan J. "Sojourners and Lodgers in a Provincial Town: The Evidence from Eighteenth-century Ludlow." *Urban History Yearbook* 17 (1990): 14-35.

Wright, Susan. "Image and Analysis: New Directions in Community Studies." In *The English Rural Community: Image and Analysis*, edited by Brian Short, 195-217. Cambridge: Cambridge University Press, 1992.

Wrightson, Keith, and David Levine. *Poverty and Piety in an English Village: Terling, 1525-1700*. Second edn., Oxford: Oxford University Press, 1995.

Wrightson, Keith. *Earthly Necessities: Economic Lives in Early Modern Britain*. New Haven and London: Yale University Press, 2000.

Wrightson, Keith. "The Politics of the Parish in Early Modern England." In *The Experience of Authority in Early Modern England*, edited by Paul Griffiths, Adam Fox and Steve Hindle, 10-46. London: Macmillan, 1996.

Wrightson, "'Sorts of People' in Tudor and Stuart England." In *The Middling Sort of People. Culture, Society and Politics in England, 1550-1800*, edited by Jonathan Barry and Christopher Brooks, 28-51. London: Macmillan, 1994.

Wrigley, E. A. (Tony), and Roger S. Schofield. *The Population History of England 1541-1871: A Reconstruction*. Revised edn., Cambridge: Cambridge University Press, 1981.

Wrigley, E. A. (Tony). "The Effect of Migration on the Estimation of Marriage Age in Family Reconstitution." *Population Studies* 48 (1994): 81-97.

Wunderli, Richard. *London Church Courts on the Eve of the Reformation*. Cambridge, MA: Medieval Academy of America, 1981.

Young, Lorraine. "The 'Place' of Street Children in Kampala, Uganda: Marginalisation, Resistance, and Acceptance of the Urban Environment." *Society and Space* 21 (2003): 607-27.

Young, Michael, and Peter Willmott. *Family and Kinship in East London.* London: Routledge and Kegan Paul, 1957.

Zell, Michael. *Industry in the Countryside: Wealden Society in the Sixteenth Century.* Cambridge: Cambridge University Press, 1994.

Zerubavel, Eviatar. *Social Mindscapes: An Invitation to Cognitive Sociology.* Cambridge, MA: Harvard University Press, 1997.

Zutshi, Patrick. "Collective Indulgences from Rome and Avignon in English Collections." In *Medieval Ecclesiastical Studies in Honour of Dorothy M. Owen*, edited by Michael J. Franklin and Christopher Harper-Bill. Woodbridge: Boydell, 1995.

Index

agency 3

Barkby (Leicestershire) 40-1, 43, 57-8, 63-5, 285, 303-17
Bedfordshire 113
belonging 97-102
benefit of clergy 86-7, 90
Beverley (Yorks. E.R.), sanctuary 85-6, 89
Bristol, city of 230-1
Buckinghamshire 113, 149, 151
burial, in the church porch 210-14
bynames, see names

Cambridge, borough of 237
Cambridgeshire 36, 38-9, 156-9, 162, 185-7
Chesterton (Cambridgeshire) 36
church, see sacred space
churching 203-4
Colchester, borough of (Essex) 156, 165
community 97-8, 271-301, 303
"core" families, see kinship
"country" 16-17, 37, 44, 60-3, 70, 73, 98-9
courtship 123-41

de Certeau, Michel (1925-86) 4, 216, 218, 341
demography, Barkby 304-15
    child mortality 313
    Kibworth Harcourt 287-8

marriage formation 123-41
population estimates 307-8, 314
vital events 308, 312
Derby, borough of 108
Devizes, borough of (Wiltshire) 324, 334, 340
Douglas, Mary (1921-2007) 3, 12, 326
Durham, sanctuary 85-6, 88

Eliade, Mircea (1907-86) 12
Elias, Norbert (1897-1990) 271-82
Elmdon (Essex) 276-8
Ely, estates of the bishop of 38-9
    cathedral 186-7
    consistory court 81, 156-9, 162, 204-5, 245, 320, 323
    diocese of 81, 156-9, 162
emotions, and space 12-13, 177-9, 191
Essex 155-6, 159, 164-5, 185-6, 192, 205, 210, 247-9, 252-61, 263-4, 276-8, 323, 330, 333

family, see kinship

harboring women 258, 262
Hethe, Hamo, bishop of Rochester (1319-62) 82-3, 147

Kibworth Harcourt (Leicestershire) 41, 57-8, 65-6, 283, 287-92
kinship 250-2, 276-7, 291, 303-17

"lawless" churches 129
Leicester, borough of 231
  abbey 38, 57, 67
Leicestershire 38, 40-1, 43, 55-76, 102-
  4, 106, 116, 125, 129, 133, 137, 149,
  150, 152-3, 205, 277-8, 283, 285, 287-
  91, 303-17, 323, 331
liminality 13-14, 326
Lincoln, city of 128
Lincolnshire 105-6, 108, 114, 129, 137-
  9, 178
locality, and "localism" 16-17, 33-141
lordship 37-43, 46, 67

market place 8, 78, 92, 145-73, 209,
  319-42
market towns 129
Marlborough, borough of (Wiltshire)
  324, 334
marriage, formation of 123-41, 203
masculinity, male attitudes 245-70
Melton Mowbray (Leicestershire) 57,
  68-9, 131, 153
Merton College, Oxford 40-1, 43, 57-8,
  63-6, 283, 287, 303-17
migration 14-16, 33-96, 225-43, 245-70,
  288, 309
mobility, of people, see movement
movement, of people 14-16, 33-96,
  123-41, 245-70

names, bynames and migration 34-6,
  38-9, 55-73
  instability of bynames 289-90
  persistence of surnames 307-11, 315
Norfolk 112, 175, 179, 182, 210, 264
North America, British colonial 6-9
Northampton, borough of 235
Northamptonshire 123-4, 131-2, 156,
  214, 248-51, 255-6
Norwich, cathedral 188
  city of 188, 207, 210, 226-7, 232, 234, 236
Nottingham, borough of 128, 215,
  227-9, 327, 337
Nottinghamshire 11, 14-15, 17, 129,
  131, 137-8, 153-4, 159, 160, 180, 200-2,
  207, 245, 303, 323, 332

Otto, Rudolf (1869-1937) 12

patriarchy 246
pays, see "country"
penance 7, 77, 81-5, 92, 145-73, 180,
  204-5, 248-9, 255-7, 322-3, 327, 329,
  337
Pentecostal processions 46, 78-81
Peterborough, diocese of, see
  Northamptonshire
pews, see seats
pilgrimage 46, 77, 81-5, 322
plays 187, 192
pledging, personal 283-301
population, see demography
porches, church 200-22
poverty 225-43
private space 10-11
public space 10-11, 319-42
punishment 6-9, 81-5, 92, 145-73, 204-
  5, 248-9, 255-7, 319-42

representation of space 3, 5-11, 13, 18-
  19, 21-2, 45-6, 179, 202-6, 215
Rochester, diocese of 82-3, 147
Rothley, soke of (Leicestershire) 57, 63

sacred space 5-9, 13, 45-6, 145-222, 328
Salisbury, city of (Wiltshire) 230, 321,
  324-5, 328, 335
sanctuaries (greater) 45-6, 85-6
seats, in church 189-90
Shropshire 107
social network analysis 273-4, 288-97
Somerset 115, 184, 210, 325, 336
South Wigston (Leicestershire) 271-82
space 3-5, 319-29
  and emotions 12-13, 177-9, 191
  consciousness of 200-2
  gender and 9
  public/private 10-11, 319-42
  representation of 3, 5-11, 13, 18-19,
    21-2, 45-6, 179, 202-6, 215
  sacred 5-9, 13, 45-6, 145-222, 328
  urban 17-21, 225-43
structuralism 3, 179, 191, 326
structuration 179, 191, 218, 326

Suffolk   104-5, 112, 206-10, 217, 264
surnames, see names
Swaffham (Norfolk)   179

Thame (Oxfordshire)   178
tithing pennies   287-8

urban space   17-21, 225-43

Wakefield (Yorkshire W.R.)   42, 178, 232
Warwickshire   106-7

West Ham (Essex)   187-8, 192, 258-9, 263-5
wills, testamentary bequests   97-121, 206-9, 217
Wiltshire   183, 262, 321, 324-5, 328
"Winston Parva", see South Wigston
women, and space   9, 203-4
   churching of   203-4
   single mothers   245-70
   singlewomen   41
Worcester, city of   233-4, 236
Worcester, diocese of   86-7, 90, 92

www.ingramcontent.com/pod-product-compliance
Lightning Source LLC
Chambersburg PA
CBHW020654270326
41928CB00005B/107